D0883932

TORCH of LIBERTY

Louise Pettibone Smith

הגרים.... והיו לכם

כאזרח

TORCH of LIBERTY

Twenty-Five Years in the Life of the Foreign Born in the U.S.A.

by Louise Pettibone Smith

Professor of Biblical History, Emeritus
Wellesley College, Wellesley, Massachusetts

DWIGHT - KING PUBLISHERS, INC.
NEW YORK

Published by Dwight-King Publishers, Inc.
Suite 405, 49 East 21 St., New York 10, N. Y.
Manufactured in the United States of America

412

To the

MEMORY

of

Defenders of Foreign Born

IRVIN GOODMAN
CAROL KING
DWIGHT C. MORGAN
IRVING SCHWAB

Fighters for the Foreign Born

EDITH ABBOTT
BASIL N. BASS
JOSEPH BRODSKY
ANTON CARLSON
TOM DOMBROWSKI
FRANK GRODSKI
JOHN A. KINGSBURY
ROBERT MORSS LOVETT
HUGH E. McBETH, Sr.
THOMAS MANN
VITO MARCANTONIO
MORRIS B. MILLER
SAMUEL NIKOLAUK
HUGO PAASIKIVI
BEN PROBE
MICHAEL RAKOCHI
VIDA SCUDDER
WILLIAM SENTNER
MORRIS SHAFRITZ
BERNHARD J. STERN

Victims of Foreign Born Persecution

JAMES BARKER
CONSTANCIO CARGADO
HERBERT BLACHE
MATT BLASCOVICH
KOSMOS CHIFICOS
LOUIS COREY
CARLOS SOLE ECHEVERRIA
RUTH FABIAN
MIKE GATES
NICK KARMAN
JACK KOZLAK
CHARLES KRATOCHVIL
MARIE KRATOCHVIL
JACOB LEVINSON
SAM MANEWITZ
JOSEPH MANKIN
REFUGIO ROMAN MARTINEZ
CARL PAIVIO
THEMISTOKLES PARASHIADES
HARRY ROAST
IDA ROTHSTEIN
FRITZ RUST
JOE SEDANOFF
MORRIS SEDER
ALEX SHINKEVITCH
JOHN STENSON
NORMAN TALLENTIRE
MORRIS TAFT
JOHN URBAN
FRED WAGENER
WILLIAM WEINER
PAUL ZANRICA
THEODORE ZDELARICH

Weep ye not for the dead
Neither bemoan him:
But weep sore for him that goeth away
Which went forth out of this place.

CONTENTS

Foreword 9

I. Immigrants All . . .

1. The Modern Migration 13
2. Strains and Stresses 30

II. The Great Depression

3. Mass Arrests 35
4. The Defense Organizes 43

III. The Ante-Bellum Years

5. The Right of Asylum 55
6. Legislative Action and Counter-Action 69
7. "No Crumbs for the Alien" 87
8. What Price Citizenship? 96
9. Dwight C. Morgan 104
10. Vigilant Against Injustice 113

IV. The War Years

11. Patriotism at Cost Plus 131
12. Rallying the Foreign Born 140
13. Even-Handed Justice? 152

14. The Fruits of Unity 164
15. "Man's Intolerance of Man" 183

V. The Cold War

16. Turning the Clock Back 201
17. Tension Tightens 206
18. The Fight for Public Opinion 222

VI. The Attempt to Silence America

19. The Free and the Brave 245
20. McCarran Un-Americanism 256
21. Direct Attack 269
22. A Year of Defeats 284
23. Carol King 299

VII. The Fight-Back

24. The Opposition Mounts 311
25. Mitigating Interpretations 327
26. A People's Movement at Work 343
27. Punitive Measures 357

VIII. . . . Americans All

28. The Atmosphere Improves 381
29. The Bitter-Enders 404
30. "Step-Children of a Nation" 417
31. Issues and Policy 425
32. One Country—One Freedom 435

Index of Topics 443
Index of Persons 446

Foreword

On January 12, 1954, advocating the repeal of the Walter-McCarran Immigration and Nationality Act, Herbert Lehman, then Senator from New York, declared:

> Our crusade . . . is not an isolated or parochial struggle. . . . It is part of the whole, the immemorial, the never won, the never ending fight for decency and tolerance, and for humanitarianism and brotherhood. It is part of the same fight which men have been waging for centuries to establish the truth that the end does not and cannot justify the means.

In one sense, of course, the whole history of the United States of America is part of the history of that struggle towards "liberty and justice for all"—words which now, as always, state an aim to be fought for rather than a secure possession to be enjoyed.

In that struggle, the recognition of the rights of minorities has always been the surest gauge of the progress of the fight. Suppression of the rights of individuals naturally begins at the weakest point in the social structure. In America, as elsewhere, the rights of unpopular minorities, religious, political, national or racial, are the first curtailed. The foreign born often belong to all these categories, and also often lack sufficient voting power to make their favor important to office seekers. As Will Maslow wrote in 1956 in the *Columbia Law Review*:

> A unique insight into a country is provided by a scrutiny of its laws excluding and expelling aliens. Unrestrained for all practical purposes by the prohibitions of a Constitution and undeterred by the fear that the voteless objects of its antipathies will resort to political reprisals, a legislative body is free to embody into law its fears, hostilities and suspicion of the alien.

The work of the American Committee for Protection of Foreign Born* is a part of the "immemorial struggle" of which Senator Lehman spoke. It is as the account of a particularly significant part of the struggle for justice and liberty for the individual in America in the 20th Century that this history of the work of the ACPFB for the 25 years from 1933 to 1958 is published. These twenty-five years have included perhaps the most concerted attempts at repression in the United States since a rhymer of Revolutionary days wrote proudly

> 'Tis heaven-born freedom fires us all
> And strengthens each brave son
> From him who humbly guides the plow
> To god-like Washington.

The content of this book is based chiefly on the publications and the office files of the ACPFB. It is therefore largely "first hand material." No one can regret more than the author that it was impossible to include also material from the records of the independent defense committees (which were organized in defense of individuals; of members of specific national groups; or by areas). To give even a brief survey of their sacrifices and their sometimes almost incredible successes would require a second volume; yet their work is an essential part of the struggle to defend the rights of the foreign born. In this book, reference to the work of the independent committees is made only to clarify the national situation or a specific action of the ACPFB.

---

* The American Committee for Protection of Foreign Born will hereafter be referred to as ACPFB or the Committee.

When the ACPFB was first organized in 1933 to defend the rights of those foreign-born Americans who were being literally railroaded on the "Deportation Specials" from the West Coast to Ellis Island, it understood its task from the beginning as a part of the defense of American democracy as a whole. But the Committee has always limited its work to the attempt to preserve the rights guaranteed by the Constitution to foreign-born Americans, leaving activity in other areas where civil rights are infringed to other groups.

Partly as a by-product of this consistent limitation, but more as a matter of deliberate conviction, the ACPFB has made a conspicuous contribution to the struggle not only in its direct defense work, but also by demonstrating that men and women of widely divergent views (even at the height of the McCarthy aberration) can work together for the attainment of a common, clearly defined purpose. The Sponsor lists of the Committee at all periods bring together names honored among extreme radicals and among conservatives. The support of the Committee has come from those who desired to save fellow communists or "communist sympathizers" from "fascist persecution" and from those who desired to demonstrate the superiority of "American democratic justice" over that of "communist totalitarian" states. The Committee has consistently asserted that its work is the defense of the right of foreign-born Americans to hold opinions; never has it been defense of the various opinions they hold. Sponsors and supporters have left the ACPFB because they thought it too far to the left or not far enough to the left. Resolutions against totalitarian communism and against fascism in general, have been ruled "out of order." At the beginning of the second World War, members of the German Bund and refugees from Nazism came to the Committee office for advice and protection against persecution. Naturally the Committee and the conferences held under its auspices have not always been immune to prevailing prejudices, but on the whole the record is clear.

This book makes no claim to impartiality. The author agrees

wholly with Justice Murphy of the Supreme Court of the United States:

> Once an alien lawfully enters and resides in this country, he becomes invested with the rights guaranteed by the Constitution to all people within our borders.

But the book does claim to present a factual and reasonably objective record of events as they occurred.

Such a record of what actually happens when an attempt is made to oppose by legal means discriminatory actions against a minority group, undertaken by the government and by powerful forces outside the government, should be important not only to those immediately concerned but to all who are interested in the history and the government of the United States.

For the choice of material from the Committee's files and for the opinions expressed in the book, the author is responsible. For much of the general background material and for the final form credit belongs to a friend of the ACPFB, without whose skilled and sympathetic editorial handling of the whole the book could never have been printed.

I. IMMIGRANTS ALL ...

1. The Modern Migration

THE United States is the only nation in the world whose historic development has included almost no contributions from the original indigenous stock, either as constituting a significant proportion of its population or as influencing the character of its culture. The foreign born and their first generation offspring constituted a majority of the settled population until the turn of the last century.

In no other area of this earth were immigrants so eagerly sought after. While the early settlers were still coming voluntarily for political, economic, social and religious reasons, vigorous efforts were continually made to get others to follow them. Pardons were dangled before imprisoned criminals who would go to the New World. Indebtedness could be wiped out by migration to the colonies. Unwary tipplers in taverns were kidnapped and shipped across the sea where their labor was in demand. In Africa, Negroes were hunted and carried into slavery in America.

During much of the nineteenth century agents roamed the lands of Europe enticing people with their vague promises and with descriptions of an impossible Utopia to leave their homes and start for America. In 1886 the plea to "ancient lands" to send "your tired, your poor, your huddled masses yearning to be free" (from the poem by Emma Lazarus) was placed on the pedestal of the Statue of Liberty in New York Harbor. And today we self-consciously celebrate "I Am An American Day" as an expression of our diverse origins and our relatively recent fusion into "One Nation." No other people of the world could even imagine the celebration of a national equivalent.

Dwight Morgan, a founder and the first Executive Secretary of the American Committee for Protection of Foreign Born, could say of the American tradition in his pamphlet *The Foreign Born in America* (published in 1936):

> For more than one hundred years after the Revolution this country maintained the policy of the open gate and the tradition of right of asylum which distinguished her among nations. . . . In his inaugural address in 1801, Jefferson said, "Are we to refuse the unhappy fugitive from distress that hospitality which the savages of the wilderness extended to our forefathers arriving in this land? Is oppressed humanity to find no asylum on this globe?"
>
> When America was young and vigorous it did not inquire into the race or nationality of its workers but felt their muscles and hired them as long as money could be made from them. American employers made the most of their opportunities for profit.

The two motives continued to keep the doors open, but Dwight Morgan's statement tells only part of the story as the content of his pamphlet shows.

The United States has never been immune to the virus of racial and national prejudice. The treatment of the American Indians, the American Negroes, the Filipinos, the Mexicans, the Puerto Ricans, Chinese, Japanese and other minority groups has not only brought dire consequences to the groups themselves and to the American economy as a whole, it has distorted that image of democracy with freedom and justice for all, of which we are so proud. However, a consideration of the total effect of such prejudice in America is beyond the scope of a book which is concerned with the expression of racial intolerance only as it affected the treatment of the foreign born in America, primarily in the last quarter century.

Jefferson's statement quoted by Dwight Morgan was directed against the Alien and Sedition Acts of 1798. Even while white natives were still a small minority on the North American continent, Americans showed that they could be "anti-foreign." While the memory of Puritan, Huguenot and Quaker experiences in the Old World was still fresh in men's minds, intolerance made its voice heard in the land. Even the first settlers in the colonies had succumbed to the human desire to force conformity upon later comers. A tabulation of all the regulatory measures passed by the various colonies and a listing of all the expulsions of religious non-conformists (to Puritanism in New England, to the Church of England in Virginia) can give an impression of extreme rigidity and intolerance.

However, it is only fair to note that in general the colonics granted far more freedom of opinion and practice than did contemporary Europe; partly from conviction, partly because they recognized the need of more settlers too clearly to set up stiff barriers against them. One of the specific complaints against England was that immigration to the colonies was discouraged and often prevented. Furthermore the early colonists at least understood the difference between non-conforming thought and overt act as a letter from Massachusetts shows:

> As for those who dwell peaceably among us, the law has never been invoked against any of them.

In due time the colonies became the United States and wrote into their Constitution and the Bill of Rights their hatred of tyranny and injustice.

The new nation, according to M. L. Hansen in *The Atlantic Migration*, began with "no encouragement to immigration except that offered by its opportunities and with no barriers except those confronting native and foreigner alike." As Benjamin Franklin wrote to a friend in Europe,

> Our country offers to strangers nothing but a good

climate, fertile soil, wholesome air, free government, wise laws, liberty, good people to live among and a hearty welcome.

President Washington put it more strongly in 1783:

> The bosom of America is open to receive not only the opulent and respectable stranger but the oppressed and persecuted of all nations and religions, whom we shall welcome to a participation of all our rights and privileges, if by decency and propriety of conduct they appear to merit the enjoyment.

That these were not empty phrases seems clear from a description of America published in London in 1782:

> . . . whence came all these people? They are a mixture of English, Scotch, Irish, French, Dutch, Germans and Swedes. From this promiscuous breed, that race now called Americans have arisen. . . .
>
> In this great American asylum, the poor of Europe have by some means met together. . . . Urged by a variety of motives here they came . . . here they have become men; here they rank as citizens. The indulgent laws protect them as they arrive, stamping on them the symbol of adoption.
>
> What then is the American? . . . I could point out to you a family whose grandfather was an Englishman, whose wife was Dutch, whose son married a French woman, and whose present four sons have now four wives of different nations.
>
> *He* is an American, who leaving behind him all his ancient prejudices and manners, receives new ones from the new mode of life he has embraced, the new government he obeys, and the new rank he holds.
>
> [J. Hector St. John de Crevecoeur, see Edith Abbott, *Historical Aspects of the Immigration Problem,* pp. 416ff.]

On the whole, as Morgan wrote, this remained the American way for more than a century in spite of sporadic outbreaks of hostility to newcomers.

One of the earliest of these outbreaks, and the only one before 1882 to produce federal legislation, came in 1798, when the Federalists succeeded in passing the Alien and Sedition Laws. Their success rested on a complexity of causes: horror at the excesses of the French Revolution and its avowed atheism; the fear, which now seems ludicrous, that revolutionary France was about to extend her power to the New World; an equally unrealistic fear of domination by the Pope to be established through the increasing numbers of Irish immigrants. Some groups even managed to combine these fears, and William Cobbett wrote in his *Porcupine's Gazette* that the Irish were conspiring with the French to overthrow the government of the United States! Apart from these terrors, and profiting by them, was the quite rational self-interest of the Federalist "aristocracy" who sought to consolidate their position and establish what they considered a sound financial policy. The vote was close (46-40 on the Alien Act). Jefferson called it "detestable" and James Madison "a monster that will disgrace its parents." The election of Jefferson to the Presidency in 1800 and the triumph of the Democrats ended prosecution under the laws.

But, although the Alien and Sedition laws lasted only two years, hostility to newcomers remained as a recurrent phenomenon. The "wild Irish" coming in increasing numbers after the Irish revolt of 1790 did not fit easily into the pattern of settled communities; the German religious groups fleeing from persecution at home tended to keep themselves separate, holding to their own ways and to their own language. Protests against the admission of both groups were sometimes vociferous. The numbers who came were not very large; an estimate for 1817 gives 20,000 from the British Isles, 8,000 Germans and 2,000 French.

A characteristic attitude toward immigration in the early 1800's is expressed by Timothy Dwight who, in 1822, wrote of the population of New York as made up of the descendants of the original Dutch and early English inhabitants together with "immigrants from New England, Long Island and New Jersey," from Ireland, Scotland, England, Germany, France and Holland; Jews; "and a few Swedes, Danes, Italians, Portuguese, Spaniards and West Indians."

> Some [of the inhabitants] are well informed, read, converse and investigate. Others scarcely do either and a small number are unable to read at all. Most of these are Europeans. The language spoken is very various.

He went on to characterize the more important of the groups which had changed the wilderness from the Hudson to Lake Erie into a "well inhabited and well cultivated-country." The Southern Irish are "absolutely uneducated" and were prone to transfer their original hostility to the government of Ireland to any government under which they lived.

> In many instances it will follow that they must be bad managers, poor and vicious. These evils, however, are not derived from the native character of these people. . . . Give them the same advantages . . . and they will stand upon a level with any of their neighbors.

He closed his account with a prediction which, fortunately for America, time has proved false.

> Of all these classes of colonists it is to be observed generally that they will soon be so entirely amalgamated with those from New England as to be indistinguishable.
>
> [Abbott, op. cit., pp. 426-429]

Obviously this early conception of the "melting pot" has not been exemplified by the spreading of New England over the whole continent.

From 1830 to 1850 the number of immigrants arriving annually increased enormously. The famines in Ireland (especially the potato famine of 1846) and in parts of Germany; unsuccessful revolutions in Germany, Poland, Ireland; and religious persecutions and discrimination in Germany, Switzerland, Norway and Wales sent thousands across the Atlantic. Shipowners found immigrants a very profitable one-way cargo and began sending out agents to attract full loads by promises of immediate release from poverty and hard work. From the coastal cities of the United States where these human cargoes were dumped came increasing efforts to limit or regulate immigration. Those arriving "with visions of wealth unattended by labor," as one writer put it, "must feel the sharp encounter of many a prejudice. . . . Wide as the country may be, and urgent as is everywhere the demand for mechanical industry, the access of foreign population may yet be too rapid for easy and healthful absorption into the community." (A. H. Everett 1835, see Abbott, op. cit., pp. 440f.)

Various attempts to organize the opposition were made locally and nationally under varying names: American-Republican, Native-American, the Order of United Americans, finally the American Party (the name adopted officially by the "Know-Nothings" in 1854). An example of their propaganda is given by Edith Abbott (pp. 478-482):

> Emigrants have been induced to prefer such arrogant claims, they have nurtured their foreign feelings and their foreign nationality to such a degree . . . that the American people can endure it no longer. . . . The name and character of the foreigner has . . . become odious. . . . We have now to resist the *momentous* evil that threatens us from *Foreign Conspiracy*. A subtle attack is making upon us by foreign powers. . . . The arbitrary governments of Europe . . . with Austria at their head have combined to attack us. . . . Will you despise the cry of danger? Invite, nay allure your enemies? Enlarge your almshouses and prisons; complain not of the outrages in your streets, nor of the burden of your taxes. . . .
>
> *Now* immigration is the accession of weakness, from

> the ignorant and the vicious, or the priest-ridden slaves of Ireland and Germany, or the outcast tenants of the poorhouses and prisons of Europe.

In 1835 a "Native American" candidate for Congress appeared in New York City. The Native American Association was formed in 1837 and the Native American National Convention was held in Philadelphia on July 4, 1845, to plan "concerted political action in defense of American institutions against the encroachments of foreign influence." The movement was not confined to the cities. The "Know-Nothings," who at first acted as a secret society (hence their name, since the members when questioned answered "I know nothing"), were scattered over the country. They gave their support at first to such candidates of the regular parties as seemed ready to further their various "anti" purposes. In 1854 they organized as a political party and took the name "American Party." In that year they carried the elections in Massachusetts and Delaware. In 1855 they elected governors and the majority of the legislature in New York and in four New England states. They had some success also in nine southern states. In 1856 they nominated Millard Fillmore for the Presidency. Eight states had "Native American" governors; and Congress in 1857 included five Senators and fourteen Representatives from the Party. However in the next Congress there were only two Senators and all their Representatives (23) were from the South.

Obviously opposition to the "Native Americans" had not been lacking. And it appealed to many motives. Edward Everett Hale's plea for the immigrant in 1852 presents a curious mixture of genuine humanitarianism and the New England sense of deserved privilege.

> By every spade blow which foreign hands have driven, by every child which foreign mothers in their own homes have reared to this country, is the country the richer. By the worth of every spade blow, by the worth of every child would the country be the poorer if it debarred them

> from this privilege, of doing its meanest work, and of taking its hardest fare. . . . [Without their work] the whole organization of our society must descend . . . you would press into service those fit for better things . . . you will chain down to the service of the spade and the barrow [those] who might triumph among your own sons. . . . Nation, State or man should feel that the Emigration is the greatest instead of the least element of our national prosperity.
>
> The State should stop its effort to sweep them back. . . . It should welcome them; send them at once to the labor-needing regions; care for them if sick; and end all that mass of unsystematic statute which handles them as outcasts or Pariahs.
>
> [Abbott, op. cit., pp. 460-66]

The "Native Americans" publicized local difficulties. The Irish working for the Baltimore and Ohio Railroad, in retaliation against a contractor who absconded with their wages, destroyed company property with "pickaxes and hammers and sledges" and even resisted the county sheriff. The Germans in Cincinnati were attacked by a mob. Throughout the South, the Germans were suspect as radicals. State immigration laws were passed, aimed chiefly at excluding criminals and paupers or at collecting revenue from the immigrants or from the owners of the ships which carried them. But in spite of all the outbursts of varying bitterness, Congress steadily refused to legislate *against* the immigrant.

The first federal law, passed in 1819, was in the nature of a traffic regulation (Constantine Panunzio, *Immigration Cross Roads,* p. 27), requiring a full report and the keeping of records of the number admitted at the different ports. In 1847 a law to restrict overcrowding on the immigrant ships was passed and amended in 1848. In 1853 a Congressional Committee was appointed to investigate immigration and the result was the law of 1855, which required ships to provide a minimum of floor space for each immigrant (instead of the limitation by ship tonnage which had proved of little value) and making also certain requirements for ventilation, cooking facilities, etc. In 1860, a law for the protection of women passengers was added.

America still felt the obligation of hospitality to the stranger. President Tyler's message to Congress in 1841 included:

> We hold out to the people of other countries an invitation to come and settle among us as members of our rapidly growing family, and for the blessings which we offer them we require of them to look upon our country as their country and to unite with us in the great task of preserving our institutions and thereby perpetuating our liberties.

And an anonymous writer some ten years later wrote:

> America preeminently owes its growth and prosperity to the amalgamation of foreign blood. To cut off therefore or to discourage its influx will be to check the current from which our very life is drawn. The better course is evidently to welcome and provide for this tide of immigration, rather than to oppose and turn it away; to cherish the good influence it brings and to regulate the bad, rather than to trample them both under foot.
>
> [Panunzio, op. cit.]

The Democratic Party Platform of 1856 still called America the "Asylum of the oppressed of every nation."

The Civil War obviously stopped most immigration for its duration, although the so-called "second stage" of nineteenth century immigration is usually dated from 1860. In 1864 Congress enacted a law to "encourage immigration," and authorized the President to appoint a Commissioner of Immigration. The need for labor, especially in the Northern factories and on the Western railroads, was so obvious that no national opposition to immigration was possible. There were still local outbreaks against the most recent arrivals, where the earlier comers joined forces with "native Americans" against the "foreigners" who threatened their jobs by accepting lower wages. In 1862 and 1869, Congress acted against the admission of contract labor.

Professor Panunzio generalizes:

> [For] a round century . . . America not only permitted [immigrants] to enter freely, but *encouraged* them to come. Americans protected the migrants during the voyage, welcomed them on arrival, took care of those who needed it after reaching this country, gave most of those who came a chance to work.

There were all too many exceptions to the policy he describes; but they were *exceptions,* not the approved practice. Bayard Taylor's *Centennial Ode* (1876) runs:

> [America] gathers the chosen of her seed
> from the hunted of every crown and creed
> . . . .
> Fused in her candid light
> To one strong race all races here unite.
>
> [See John Higham, *Strangers in the Land,* p. 12]

But by 1880 voices demanding restriction or limitation, some even advocating the total suspension of immigration, were making themselves heard from many quarters. Increase in unemployment; the approaching end of available land in the West; vague fears of socialism added to the ever present anti-Romanism; even Darwinism with its survival of the fittest; and anxiety over the debasing of the English language contributed supporters to the demand. In 1888 the American Economic Association offered a prize for the best essay on "The Evil Effects of Unrestricted Immigration" (Higham, p. 41). In 1882, in response to the West Coast demand, Congress passed the first Exclusion Act, barring Chinese laborers. (The act had so many loopholes that it was relatively ineffective until it was amended two years later.) Congress also passed in 1882 the first general immigration law, levying a fifty cent tax on each immigrant, establishing examination at entry, and excluding convicts (except political offenders), lunatics, idiots and those "liable to become a public charge." The steamships were required to take back those who were excluded.

New forces of hostility to the immigrants were building up as the century drew to a close. The American Protective Association was formed in 1887, and numerous pseudo-patriotic fraternal orders were enrolling members. The days of "Know Nothing" success seemed about to repeat themselves, but there were significant differences. In New England, New York and the cities of the West, Darwin rather than orthodoxy was invoked in favor of exclusion. "The hereditary character of pauperism and crime" was taken for granted. Humanitarian groups, horrified at the city slums described by Jacob Riis in *How the Other Half Lives* and in similar reports, hoped to eliminate slums by stopping the coming of those who were forced to inhabit them. The earlier hostility to the Irish and the Germans was transferred to the Italians and the East Europeans; the descendants of the Irish and Germans joined in expressing it. The use of newly-arrived immigrants as strike-breakers roused the anger of organized labor, although very few unions advocated more than a tightening of the law against contract labor. The Haymarket riots of 1886 gave color to the fear of foreign radicals. We were being invaded by "longhaired, wild-eyed, atheistic, reckless foreign wretches who never did an honest hour's work in their lives." The large numbers of immigrants (more than 560,000 in 1890) prompted a cry for more effective regulation.

In 1888 Congress responded to the pressures by authorizing the Secretary of the Treasury to deport within one year of entry those who had entered contrary to law; and in 1891 passed a general law adding to the reasons for exclusion. But the law was on the whole moderate. The exclusion section expressly exempted political offenders, ministers of any religious denomination and college professors. The publishing in any foreign country of advertisements or promise of employment in the United States was forbidden. However, for the first time the law included a specific provision for deportation of non-citizens within one year of entry for causes other than illegal entry.

The economic prosperity of the nineties turned Congress' attention in other directions; and although Senator Henry Cabot Lodge brought in the "literacy bill" favored by the Immigration Restriction League and it was passed by the Republican Senate, the House did not concur. The successful war with Spain induced such national confidence that no changes in our ways seemed desirable.

The anti-foreign agitation might well have followed the earlier pattern and subsided without achieving restrictive legislation; but in 1901 the assassination of President McKinley by an anarchist who, although American born was obviously from his name, Czolgosz, of foreign descent, gave what seemed spectacular justification to those who had urged that America dam the flood from "reservoirs of European anarchy." (See Higham, op. cit., p. 111) Theodore Roosevelt declared:

> We should aim to exclude absolutely not only all persons who are known to be believers in anarchistic principles or members of anarchistic societies, but also persons who are of a low moral tendency or of unsavory reputation . . . to secure by a careful and not merely perfunctory test some intelligent capacity to appreciate American institutions and act sanely as American Citizens. . . . All persons should be excluded who are below a certain standard of economic fitness to enter our industrial field. . . . This would stop the influx of cheap labor . . . and it would dry up the springs of the pestilential social conditions in our great cities where anarchistic organizations have the greatest possibilities of growth. Both the educational and economic tests should be designed to protect and elevate the general body political and social.
>
> [See Roy L. Garis, *Immigration Restriction,* p. 102f.]

As a result the Immigration Law of 1903 was passed. For the

first time since 1798, the law "penalized new-comers for their opinions." Anarchists were excluded and they could be deported. (The law also extended from one year to three the time of possible deportation for any reason.) Anarchists could not be naturalized. The authority of the Commissioner of Immigration was more clearly defined. That same year the Immigration and Naturalization Service was included in the newly created Department of Labor.

On the whole, even after the assassination of President McKinley, the influence of the restrictionists was surprisingly slow at producing legislation, as the history of the "literacy test" in Congress shows. A literacy test for immigrants was advocated by Senator Lodge in 1891. It was the chief objective of the Immigration Restriction League and was supported by various "patriotic" groups and by labor organizations, including the American Federation of Labor (AFL). Much of the general support was given in the belief that it would operate selectively against the "new immigration" from Italy and Eastern Europe. Between 1886 and 1916, the bill came sixteen times before the Senate or House, and one or the other or both gave it a majority. It was vetoed by three Presidents: Cleveland, Taft and Wilson. The last named stated in his veto:

> This bill embodies a radical departure from the tradition and long established policy of this country. . . . It seeks to all but close entirely the gates of asylum which have always been open to those who could find nowhere else the right and opportunity of constitutional agitation for what they conceived to be the natural and inalienable rights of men; and it excludes those to whom the opportunities of elementary education have been denied without regard to their character, their purpose or their natural capacity.
>
> [See Panunzio, op. cit., p. 68]

The law was finally passed over President Wilson's veto in 1917.

There had been abuses and denial of due process of law

in deportation cases under the law of 1903. Morgan's pamphlet tells of a Japanese woman deported as liable to become a public charge, whose case the Supreme Court of the United States refused to review although she did not know the English language, did not understand the questions asked, and did not even know that the investigation concerned her deportation. John Turner, an English laborer, was deported in 1904 as an "anarchist" in spite of the arguments of Clarence Darrow and the poet, Edgar Lee Masters, before the Supreme Court. The Law of 1917 gave the legal basis for concerted action against the foreign born which marked the years following World War I.

In the years following 1918, the old anti-foreign groupings were re-inforced by new theories and new prejudices. The favorite motto was AMERICA FOR AMERICANS! The slogan surviving from the war was DOWN WITH THE HYPHEN! The 1917 Immigration Act had included not only the literacy test but general provisions against radicals, not only against members of anarchist societies but against members of the Industrial Workers of the World. All who belonged to revolutionary organizations advocating or teaching anarchy or the overthrow of the government by force and violence were to be deported and for such deportation there was no time limit. An Asian "barred zone" defined by latitude and longitude was established; it included India, Siam, Indo-China, Afghanistan, parts of Turkestan and Arabia and the West Indies. The stage was set for the Palmer raids of 1920 and the Quota Law of 1924—and a new period in the history of American immigration began.

Although general indignation halted the mass arrests of the Palmer Raids, the assumption was still widely accepted that immigrants, especially "the people of Central, Southern and Eastern Europe [were] not only people extremely difficult of assimilation, but also importers of 'anarchistic' and 'radical' doctrines. If permitted to come in large numbers, they might possibly overthrow the government and the capitalistic system." (See Panunzio, op. cit., p. 92)

A total of 805,228 immigrants entered the United States in 1921; and in future years anywhere from one to two million could be expected. Some limitation in the number seemed desirable even to many of those who did not share the absurd fear that America would be "hopelessly bogged down in the mire of mongrelization." (See Higham, op. cit., p. 313)

There were certainly still some defenders of the American tradition of welcome. Newell Dwight Hillis wrote a pamphlet entitled *The Boon of Immigration* in which he declared:

> Those who read some pessimist's statement about the diseased and criminal classes that are coming to this country will feel troubled by the thought of a million immigrants. But the man who goes to Ellis Island, who will study the people leaving not one steamer but twenty steamers will conclude his personal investigation with enthusiasm for the newcomers and with high hopes for his country! . . .
>
> Immigrants make the slums, [they say]. Why the three greatest slum centers in the world are where the population is absolutely pure—East London, Glasgow, South Ireland. . . .
>
> So far from one million immigrants overstocking the country, the Republic needs five million workmen.
>
> Criminal classes! Carl Schurz broke the law of his country because that law represented despotism. Garibaldi was a criminal, judged by the laws of despotic Italy. Today Tolstoi is a criminal.

But the protests were relatively few, and Congress reacted to the pressures against foreigners by enacting, in May, 1921, the first quantitative limitation of immigration. And they chose a method of limitation which accorded with the prejudice against the "New Immigration" from Eastern and Southern Europe. The Law of 1921 provided (with some minor qualifications) that the number admitted from any country in one year be limited to 3% of the persons of that nationality resident in the United States according to the census of 1910. The total admitted could be 357,803. Only 20% of the quota from one country could be admitted in any one month.

This monthly limitation resulted in the absurd and, for the

losers, tragic races of the ocean liners across the Atlantic to be the first to arrive on the first of the month. The original goal was Ellis Island but since ocean liners racing in New York Harbor were an obvious danger to shipping, the Government agreed to reckon the arrival at Ambrose Lightship. The great ships halted therefore on the last day of the month just ouside the three mile limit and waited under full steam to cross the line at the last stroke of midnight. The ship which lost the race had to return its passengers to Europe. The justice of the protest made by Senator Reed of Pennsylvania (1924) is obvious:

> This racing in the first five months of the year . . . is entirely unfair to the immigrant who is excluded. It is not at all his fault that his boat loses in the race; and yet as a result of it, he is apt to be deported and barred from return for nearly a year. [See Panunzio, op. cit., p. 101]

The Law of 1924 at least eliminated the boat races.

In 1923 President Coolidge's first message to Congress urged further restrictive legislation:

> New arrivals should be limited to our capacity to absorb them into the ranks of good citizenship. America must be kept American. . . . It would be well to make such immigration of a selective nature . . . based either on prior census or upon the record of naturalization. . . . We should find additional safety in a law requiring the immediate registration of all aliens.
>
> [See Garis, op. cit., p. 170]

The Act of 1924 followed the President's advice. The new quota was reduced to 2% (a total of 164,667) and was based on the census of 1890 which discriminated still more against Southern and Eastern Europe. The burden of proof of admissability was put upon the immigrant; the government did not have to *prove* that he should be excluded. All those ineligible for citizenship were excluded. Five years later the total was further reduced to 153,000. (President Coolidge's recommendation of registrations had to wait until 1940.)

2. Strains and Stresses

There is hardly any people on the face of the earth which is not represented in the population of this country. And there is hardly any nationality group in our population which has not at one time or another, some of them almost consistently, felt the sting of subtle or overt persecution and been subject to vulgar caricature. The reasons for the periodic waves of hostility to the foreign born on a national scale, and especially for the upsurge in the twentieth century which has so altered government policy, are many and complex. All such periods have been closely associated with political and economic crises.

The tendency of newcomers to crowd together in specific areas where they can continue to use their old language and practice their old customs often has been cited as proof of the unassimilability of the immigrants. It is easy for such hostile critics to forget that they (or their ancestors) are merely immigrants who have been assimilated. The social consequences of this isolation are also cited as reasons for considering "foreigners" undesirable. Obviously psychological factors play a part in the existence of such segregated groups; but the natural tendency would be towards increased intercourse with fellow Americans and the final end of the segregated community.

However, other causes have often prolonged the isolation; the predominant factors are political and economic. A group in isolation is especially vulnerable to political and economic exploitation, and those who profit from such exploitation have deliberately fostered divisions among the foreign born by keeping alive "imported" national animosities and by artifically creating new prejudices. A distinct pattern is discernable in the employment of specific national groups as laborers in specific industries; and not only in specific industries but in specific departments in one plant. Here, again, the purpose was to utilize the same antagonisms to perpetuate economic and political exploitation of the labor force. At a conference of the ACPFB in 1943, George F. Addes, then secretary-treasurer of the United Automobile Workers, CIO, described the pattern:

> In the River Rouge plants of Mr. Henry Ford there are now workers representing at least fifty-five known nationalities of Europe and Asia. In the old days, before the union, Mr. Ford's personnel department hired very carefully according to strict rations of national representations. . . . By the shrewd placement of workers throughout the plant Mr. Ford hoped to perpetuate in his shop the same national rivalries which had written many a bloody page in the history of Europe and Asia. The schemes . . . to Balkanize [the] labor force did work out for a while.

Thus "ghettos" are kept alive for economic and political motives not only in large metropolitan centers such as New York or Chicago, but in major industrial centers throughout the country and particularly in one-industry communities. Whatever tendencies work toward ending isolation are in fact thwarted by the designs of those who see political and economic "advantages" in segregation. This creates an immediate evil, and is a source of many contingent evils which only await periods of crisis to appear in full strength in our midst.

At the Annual Conference of the ACPFB in 1940, Rep. Rudolph G. Tenerowicz, of Michigan, whose state is a center of East European immigration, placed the cause emphatically:

> These recurring waves of anti-alienism, in a doctor's jargon, are highly symptomatic of a state of national re-

> lapse. They come with historical precision and thus far have always followed pretty much the same pattern. First it is anti-alienism. Then it is anti-unionism. Next it is the minority religious beliefs that become the scapegoat. . . . The cause is always the same—a surfeit of misery abroad in the land.

And Dwight Morgan, in the pamphlet already cited, spelled out the problem in some detail.

> They [American employers] forced the foreigner to accept low wages only to condemn them [later] for their "low standard of living." In this way they deflected attacks on the profit system into agitation for the exclusion of workers. . . . The employers have shifted the responsibility for each depression to the victims of the system of exploitation which produced these crises. . . .
>
> While the bars are up to prevent millions from becoming citizens, the attacks upon them for their non-citizenship are being intensified.
>
> In the attempt to rid themselves of the foreign-born workers most active in trade unions and working class political organizations, the employers fostered the system of laws to expel the most militant from the country. Thus while some workers were excluded because it was said that they lowered the standard of living, others who fought to raise it were deported. . . .
>
> Almost every struggle for higher wages and better working conditions has been classed by reactionaries as the attempt of "foreign agitators" to "undermine" American institutions.

It is clear that Morgan did not express opinions exclusively his own at that time. A newspaper like *The New York Post* called his pamphlet "interesting and informing reading." The American Civil Liberties Union (ACLU), an organization prominent in American life for its defense of constitutional liberties, said of it that it "for the first time completely covers governmental and political history and the law in the light of pending cases and legislation," and included it in its sales list of literature.

Again, at the same 1940 Annual Conference, Rep. Lee E. Geyer, of California, a state whose population includes immigrants from Mexico, Japan, China and the Phillipine Islands among others, threw the spotlight on certain aspects of this national problem, revealing the inter-connection between the plight of the foreign born and that of the Negro people and democratic liberties generally.

> The existence of the poll-tax as a requirement for voting in eight states is a national, and not a regional, evil. . . . Representatives of the poll-tax states who come to Congress year after year are responsible only to the financial oligarchy which elects them to office. So long as they carry out the will of these political and economic overlords they enjoy an almost uncontested lien on their seats. . . .
>
> Length of service is a key to power in the Congress of the United States. Ranking place on the Committees which do the main work of the Congress goes by seniority right. . . . Thus, in a Congress supposedly representative of all 48 states, we have a great concentration of power in the hands of the eight poll-tax states. These representatives do not even represent the majority of adult citizens within their own states, as do Senators and Congressmen from the 40 "free" states. In all the 40 "free" states a majority of eligible voters go to the polls. But only a minority—the minority which can afford the price of admission—votes in a poll-tax state.
>
> You can easily see then that the poll-tax system in eight states subverts the democracy of our entire nation. And therefore it adds its part to the growing danger of anti-democratic oppression and persecution which the foreign born and their friends face today.
>
> But there is an even more direct and specific relation between the problems before this Conference and the question of the poll-tax. Of the many anti-alien bills you have been discussing, the most vicious, the most anti-democratic, and the ones most likely to pass because of powerful support are nearly all sponsored by Congressmen and Senators from poll-tax states. . . .

> Have you ever stopped to wonder why the warning against the "alien menace" comes precisely from those districts where the alien is practically unknown and the foreign born population negligible? You would think that if the alien and the foreign born presented any real danger to democracy, or competed seriously with native Americans seeking employment, or engaged in industrial sabotage—you would think that if these things were happening the alarm would be raised from representatives of the big industrial areas where the foreign born are concentrated. What we have here is a very convenient division of labor among reactionaries. Senator [Arthur] Vandenberg is Mr. Henry Ford's able representative in the Senate, and Mr. Henry Ford could make good use of the Stewart Bill, or the Smith Bill, or the Hobbs Bill [anti-foreign born measures] in his efforts to keep the trade unions out of his plants. But, hundreds of thousands of foreign born workers in the State of Michigan, still vote. Mr. Vandenberg takes on more congenial, and less hazardous tasks—and leaves the "alien menace" to his Democratic friends from the poll-tax states.

Representative Geyer gave emphasis to his observations by citing some arithmetical facts that explain the geometrical political consequences. The four southern sponsors of anti-foreign born legislation—Representatives Joe Starnes, Sam Hobbs, Martin Dies and Howard Smith—were chosen in elections in which a total of 49,132 ballots were cast. But a single opponent of anti-foreign born legislation, Representative Warren G. Magnuson, of Washington, was chosen in an election in which 147,061 ballots were cast. Thus while Magnuson represented three times the number of franchises represented by the four southerners together, he could be outvoted four to one. The continuation of the poll-tax system in the eight states is itself a reflection of a political and economic situation of long-standing. Mr. Geyer's speech well illustrates how the difficulties of the foreign born are related to other chronic dislocations in the country as well as to the tensions caused by particular crises.

II. THE GREAT DEPRESSION

3. Mass Arrests

THE Palmer raids of January 2, 1920, in which 10,000 people were arrested simultaneously in night raids in seventy different cities, marked the culmination of the post World War I attacks on the foreign born. Within a year that attack had moderated. But in the 1930's, the multiple arrests and deportations, based on the same 1918 Law with the amendments of 1920, were effected less spectacularly by the Federal agents. Caution had been learned. (J. Edgar Hoover had been second in command in the Palmer raids.) In the 1930's, however, the period of terror was prolonged, the numbers involved were greater, and the consequent suffering among the people involved, both native and foreign born, went much deeper. And the political and moral results were more serious

The crisis responsible for the 1930 attack was primarily economic; although as the economic situation improved the increased tensions in Europe were felt as a threat to American security. There had been three years of precipitous crash and subsequent business stagnation under President Herbert Hoover. It was a time of bread lines, of apple selling, of evictions, of Hoovervilles, of hunger marches, of angry workers walking the streets in bitterness at their inability to find work to feed, house, and clothe their families. It was a time of foreclosures, of bankruptcies, of stock market suicides, of closing banks, of big business men keeping a sullen silence in their fear of the consequences of the debacle. It was the time of "that man" Roosevelt's inundation of the country with a confusing torrent of emergency measures in the hope that their currents might sweep away the worst of the mess.

It was a dangerous time, economically and politically. On the one hand, President Franklin Delano Roosevelt and his "brain trust" labored to halt the collapse, to climb out of the economic debris and start the arduous climb back to prosperity. On the other hand, conservative forces, aided by J. Edgar Hoover and his like, sought to silence, disorganize, and demoralize both organized and individual efforts to make the welfare, the needs, the dignity and security of all the people the decisive factor in determining government policy. And as usual, in a period of stress, the foreign born were among the first to bear the brunt of frustration, fear, anger and skullduggery.

Victims from among them were snatched up for deportation with as little publicity as possible, removed quickly from their home towns, taken to Ellis Island, to Boston or to other ports of exit, and shipped to their "country of origin" with a speed anything but deliberate. Under William L. Doak, as Secretary of Labor, 18,142 people were deported and 11,719 "left voluntarily" in 1931. In 1932 the totals were 19,426 and 10,775. A "Deportation Special" started from the West Coast where arrests were especially numerous, stopped at towns and cities across the country to pick up those held for deportation, and brought them to New York to be held on Ellis Island until they could be shipped to Europe. *The New York Times* for January 5, 1933, reported 98 put on board the S.S. *President Roosevelt*. Christmas was celebrated by the deportation of 38 from San Francisco.

The report of the Commissioner of Immigration, Daniel W. MacCormack, transmitted to Congress in 1936, described Mr. Doak's policy in these words:

> A record number of deportations was the chief objective. . . . Arrests without warrant were the rule. Illegal raids were of frequent occurrence. Aliens were held in jail for many months. . . . Bonds were set in unjustifiable amounts.

But while deportation was the most brutal form of oppression, it was not the only danger facing the foreign born. Pressures to limit relief funds to citizens and to bar non-citizens from government and municipal jobs increased. A serious discriminatory movement against all aliens occurred in private industry, jeopardizing their means of livelihood. For example, in 1935, the Waldorf-Astoria in New York announced the dismissal of all non-citizens from its employment. By the end of 1933, twenty-three states had either forbidden the employment of non-citizens in public service or had achieved the same end by requiring that preference be given to American citizens. In 1935, a similar law passed the New York State Senate. New York City hospitals fired 1,400 non-citizen workers with the intention of replacing them by 600 citizens at lower pay. Even holders of student visas, foreign nationals here to gain knowledge of American culture and American democracy in American institutions of learning, suddenly found themselves among the victims of the anti-foreign born hostility. Abruptly forbidden to cut lawns or do other odd jobs for pay, how were they to get money for the incidental expenses, which are unavoidable even for students on scholarships?

The process of naturalization by which some of the disabilities might be avoided was full of pitfalls. The development of restrictive legislation on naturalization in the 1920's is briefly summarized in Dwight Morgan's pamphlet, with a few instances of some of the resulting absurdities and abuses. Thus while "white persons" were supposedly eligible for naturalization, the law did not define a "white person." A decision of 1922 declared the term meant a person of Caucasian race. But in 1923 a high caste Hindu was declared non-white, because he would not be considered white by "the man in the street." Mexicans, originally classed as white, were listed as non-white in the census of 1930. They were usually considered white in naturalization cases but a Buffalo court denied them citizenship in the 1930's on the ground that they have Indian blood.

Also, naturalization was expensive, difficult to obtain and

sometimes dangerous. The required information was hard to find. Applications which were filed were sometimes lost. Witnesses who were required often were expensive since they had to be transported to court or compensated for loss of time. Nor was naturalization always secure when acquired. Jacob Kershner's citizenship was revoked *after his death* so that his wife would lose her derivative citizenship and be deportable. In the 1930's citizenship was often refused to those on relief. A New Orleans Judge ruled that the privilege of citizenship required "obligations . . . and service and financial support to the body politic by way of taxation." Applications for citizenship were often followed by perjury charges or by arrests for deportation.

The rights of the foreign born were in no less jeopardy in the legislative halls of Washington. The Dies Bill before Congress in 1934 would deport non-citizens for advocating the overthrow of Mussolini or for any kind of strike activity which the bill labeled "sabotage." Between January and the end of March 1935, no less than 107 bills were introduced into Congress for the deportation of, or for discrimination against, the foreign born. One of them, the Kerr Bill, although it contained certain ameliorating provisions which would prevent the break up of families, made deportation easier by including minor offenses under "moral turpitude," and furthermore specifically authorized arrest without warrant. The AFL was among the organizations protesting this last provision.

And who were the people chosen to be victimized by such harsh treatment? Some were active workers in the movement to establish the principle of unemployment insurance. Some were participants in the Unemployed Councils that sought to alleviate the suffering of destitute families. Others were active union leaders and members who fought to throw the weight of their organized groups on the side of the workers' demands, and worked to prevent their trade unions from disintegrating as a result of mass unemployment. Others were men and women who had become frankly critical of the *status quo* for labor and society. Still others were innocent bystanders caught up in the spreading net. Some were politically knowledgeable. Others were politically apathetic. Still others were political innocents and illiterates. The dragnet was not especially selective.

There was Stella Petrosky of Wilkes-Barre, Pa., the mother of eight children. She was fifteen when she came to America in 1914. In the war years which followed she lost all trace of her family in Poland. After three years she married a coal miner, who until 1925 supported his family (including a set of triplets). Then came strikes, picket lines, idleness. Stella went with her husband to union meetings, joined him on picket lines. In 1930, her husband deserted her, and she supported the family by taking in washing and doing outside housework, and she kept a cow.

By 1932, forty-five percent of the workers in the county were on relief. No one could pay for housework help or for clothes washing. The cow had to be sold to pay debts. Government relief was $4.00 a week. It would not feed nine people but the Poor Board would not raise the amount. Mrs. Petrosky appealed to the Unemployed Council. With its aid, she got a ton of coal a month and $7.00 a week instead of $4.00. The Council leader helped her with planning a budget. The $7.00 was raised to $10.00. Mrs. Petrosky joined the Council herself, and began to help her neighbors. A group joined together to demand more relief and to resist evictions. In 1933, the high school students "struck" in order to join a miners' picket line. Stella led a group of mothers to the Mayor to warn him against police brutality to the children.

On April 25, 1935, Stella Petrosky was arrested at her home for deportation and taken to the county jail. Opportunity to send word to her children or neighbors was denied her. She was "a dangerous woman," charged with using force and violence to overthrow the government, and specifically with instigating the high school strike.

There is a letter from a staff member of the ACPFB describing his first meeting with Stella:

> The houses are little two-story boxes, 16 feet wide and

three between. Stella's has the most rakish slant. A brown shepherd dog and the baby Frank with corn-colored hair pasted down and face shined for school greet me on the porch. Frank with true Polish politeness takes me into the house, and I am surprised to find no picture of the be-whiskered Karl Marx who, the city detective said, was hanging on the wall as Stella's God. Instead were pictures of Claudette Colbert and James Cagney and a few more of the usual American idols from Moviedom. . . .

I have loaned my money to various comrades for leaflets and stamps, but Stella feeds me good. She feeds everybody good. The firm foundation of the strong and powerful [defense] movement is in her five gallon stew pot that always sits on her coal stove simmering. It is filled up in the morning and is empty again at night. Today it is big red beans, sauerkraut and spareribs. All day long comrades will be dropping in for a big bowl and a pound or so of Stella's homemade bread.

It seemed fairly clear that the arrest was not so much action against Stella individually as against the Unemployed Councils and the labor organizations. The Council headquarters were visited almost simultaneously by two immigration inspectors, two building inspectors and two State Troopers. The immigration inspectors asked questions of all and sundry; the building inspectors condemned the building and ordered the Council out of it; the State Troopers made arrests.

Meet Oscar Mannisto. He had come to the United States from Finland in 1912. For eighteen years he worked as a printer in Astoria, Oregon. In February 1931, he was arrested for deportation on the charge of "criminal syndicalism." He had been a member of the Workers Party before it went out of existence in 1925, and he was not a citizen because he had been one day late in filing his second papers. After a long legal battle on the West Coast he was brought to Ellis Island on the Deportation Special in October 1934.

The last item in Mannisto's file in the office of the ACPFB is a letter written from Finland after his deportation, leaving his wife and three children in Oregon. "I have travelled in several cities looking for a job, but no luck so far." He had a three-hour examination by Finnish police. "They could not find anything against me only that I had been deported from the U.S.A. which they knew very well." Wages in Finland were low, families needed relief even if the father was working. The letter concludes: "Well, I feel I belong more to America than here. I have been too long time away from this country. . . . I lived nearly half my life and the best part of it in the U.S.A."

Then there was Paul Kettunen. He was fifteen years old when he came to this country with his mother in 1925. He was arrested in 1934, charged with being a member of or affiliated with a group teaching the overthrow of the government by force and violence. He had once made out an application for membership in the Communist Party but changed his mind before it was acted upon. He had sold copies of the *Daily Worker,* the communist paper, along with other newspapers, at a newsstand in the Labor Temple, in New York; and he was charged with having sold some copies at a Finnish picnic in Duluth.

Many arrests were aimed or timed to interfere with strikes or with union activity. The head of the United Mine Workers local and 100 Mexican-American members were seized at one time in Gallup, New Mexico. The Greek-American organizer for the Railroad Brotherhood Unity Movement was arrested in Spokane after he had established lodges in the Union Pacific and Great Northern railroad yards. Among the many others were a Romanian-American organizer of the automobile workers in Detroit, a Russian-American leader of a picket line in the general strike of shoeworkers in Massachusetts.

Now take the case of Mrs. Henrietta Vendemmia, as reported in the *Congressional Record,* 75th Congress, 3rd Session, March 30, 1938. Mrs. Vendemmia, 61 years of age at the time of the report, arrived in this country in 1930. She was the wife of an American citizen and the mother of three American citizens. In 1932, she was committed to the State hospital, and was confined there until 1933, when she was ordered deported as being a public charge, despite the fact that she and her husband were supported by their three children, though they could not meet the $2,000 hospital bill. In 1936, examining physicians of the Marine Hospital and of the U.S. Public Health Service declared that she was not insane, found no abnormality at the time, and seriously doubted whether she had ever been of unsound mind. At the time of the report she was physically ill, weighing only 92 pounds, and liable to die at almost any time. Here, indeed, was the epitome of the menace to our national security!

Mme. Frances Perkins, Labor Secretary in the Roosevelt cabinet, had promised the "humanizing" of the administration of the deportation laws and had appointed the Ellis Island Commission of 48 to make recommendations. A copy of a letter to Madam Perkins from Morris Miller who had been arrested when he applied for relief and was held on Ellis Island suggests that recommendations were, indeed, in order. "You railroaded me to Ellis Island without a warrant and kept me there four days without a hearing. . . . During the four days, I found that you are keeping American citizens there. I mean the cockroaches and mice which I counted in the room where you kept me four days without a warrant."

In spite of her "humanizing" promises, when Governor Merriam of California asked for the aid of immigration officials in the San Francisco General strike of 1934, Madam Perkins responded by promising full cooperation of the Immigration Department and listing the legal grounds for deportation. In a report to Congress, a year later, the Commissioner of Immigration, Daniel W. MacCormack, stated that in the deportation drive which ensued 373 "alien radicals" were arrested according to the newspaper headlines. Of these, 272 were proved to be United States citizens, and only eighteen were legally deportable. The same Commissioner, in an address at Yale University on November 2, 1935, compared the deportation laws and their administration to the measures of the Czar of Russia.

Banishment was a favorite medieval penalty; it was supposedly discarded by modern civilized nations.

4. The Defense Organizes

THE 1920 attack on the foreign born was relatively short-lived because of the outcry of protest that roared through the United States. There was the statement, *To the American People, Report upon the Illegal Practices of the United States Department of Justice*, published and distributed by the National Popular Government League, and signed by twelve outstanding American lawyers including Felix Frankfurter, now Associate Justice of the U. S. Supreme Court; Roscoe Pound, dean of Harvard Law School; Zechariah Chafee, Jr.; Francis Fisher Kane and David Wallerstein of Philadelphia; Alfred S. Niles of Baltimore; Ernst Freund of Chicago; Jackson H. Ralston of Washington, D. C.; Swinburne Hale and Frank P. Walsh of New York; Tyrrell Williams of St. Louis; and R. C. Brown of Memphis, Tennessee. Francis Fisher Kane, then U.S. Attorney in Philadelphia, resigned his office in protest.

One of the first to condemn the action of the Justice Department was Federal Judge George W. Anderson of Boston. Objection also came from labor. The Chicago Federation of Labor was among the first to raise its voice. Jackson H. Ralston, general counsel of the AFL, faced a congressional committee to denounce the raids. Groups of business and religious leaders spoke up against the outrage, one such from Detroit included S. S. Kresge and Bishop Charles D. Williams of the Protestant Episcopal Church. Jane Addams of Hull House, Chicago, came to the defense of victims. And finally both the Secretary of Labor,

William B. Wilson and the Assistant Secretary, Louis F. Post, declared against the action of the Justice Department.

The attack of the 1930's met with no such general and effective condemnation. Labor was still disorganized by the experience of the depression. Management was chiefly intent on maintaining its control for the future, and fostered whatever antagonism—racial, religious or political—would be effective in preventing labor unity. The increasingly explosive European situation, the growing influence in America of reactionary groups more or less in sympathy with the "master race" theory of Nazism or the fascist belief in the efficiency of a dictatorship, contributed to the general acquiescense in the policy of government. So also did the alteration in the procedures of the Immigration and Naturalization Service. The government carefully avoided in the thirties the spectacular, Hollywoodish and Gestapo-like simultaneous night arrests of January 1920. Nor would it be amiss to note that many who should have been expected to speak up were themselves silenced, intimidated and frightened by the serious character of the economic and political crisis that had hit our country.

In any case, the foreign born found themselves floundering rather ineffectually in their efforts to defend themselves. The International Labor Defense (ILD) and its various sections throughout the country, set up several years earlier for the specific purpose of aiding through legal and mass action the radical and labor elements who came under police and government persecution, fought the arrests and deportations locally as best they could. But the victims were too often transferred from the area in which they were known, before the defense work could get under way. Appeals were made again and again to the ACLU for aid in defending rights guaranteed the foreign born by the Constitution.

But both organizations were actively engaged in opposing encroachments of many kinds on the civil liberties of citizens, and they had neither sufficient experience nor sufficient funds nor personnel to meet the special demands of the kind of infringement of justice created by the policy of the Immigration and Naturalization Service. It seemed clear that successful action required an organization which could devote its full time and energy to the protection of the rights of the foreign born, and acquire in the process the particular experience necessary to deal with the specialized problems of the foreign born.

The American Committee for Protection of Foreign Born (ACPFB) was formed in 1933 in New York City to answer an immediate and pressing need.

Roger Baldwin of the ACLU took the initiative, writing to various men and women interested in liberal causes, asking them whether they would join him in forming such a group. When a few affirmative answers had been received the letters were changed to read, "Will you join us?" Union leaders and individual victims under deportation orders made similar appeals. A conference was held in November, 1933, at the Manhattan Lyceum in New York City, and the American Committee for Protection of Foreign Born came into existence. Dwight C. Morgan was chosen as its first secretary.

It is now, twenty-five years later, almost impossible to present an orderly picture of the early work and problems of the Committee. The pressing and recurring necessity of preventing an immiment deportation or getting the breadwinner of a family out on bail; the answering of letters of appeal arriving daily from all parts of the country, their numbers steadily growing as the Committee became better known; the ever increasing need of money both for legal expenses and for publicity and general education—these left no time for precise formulations of purpose and policy. no time even for the keeping of records of committee actions. What documents have survived from those first years are in the main letters and records of decisions in individual cases, together with printed appeals for funds, posters for meetings, and an occasional leaflet intended to arouse the general public.

Coordinating the work of defense with the ILD and with the actions of separate labor unions was not easy, as some of the letters exchanged concerning individuals show. Important information was sometimes sent too late to be of use. Names, addresses of relatives, dates and other pertinent matter were often wrongly given. The ACLU forwarded appeals, made suggestions, agreed to cooperate in a joint meeting if other organizations also agreed, and carried on the usual inter-organizational relations. A letter to a newspaper protests that credit for a successful defense was wrongly given to the ILD for a case carried on *wholly* by the ACPFB.

Even the name of the Committee turned out to be something of a difficulty and a cause for friction. Some of the supporting groups had had difficulties with "America First" organizations such as the Ku Klux Klan or the followers of Gerald L. K. Smith and Father Charles Coughlin, and they objected to the inclusion of *American* in the name. Some of the earlier publicity material was signed simply Committee for Protection of Foreign Born. The choice of name, however, had been made deliberately. The Committee was and would be American in the true sense of the word. Dwight Morgan's insistence on "keeping the movement from being sectarian or extremist" never weakened. By the end of 1935 the full name was invariably used.

But the overriding purpose of the Committee's existence was the protection of the rights of the foreign born; and whatever its early troubles, disputes and confusions, the purpose never altered. The ACPFB gained momentum as it went along, growing in experience and prestige. There was no lack of cases, unfortunately. But fortunately, neither was there a lack of determination, of drive and of practical wisdom.

How frequent and varied were the demands made upon the Committee once its existence became known can be seen not only from the representative cases described in the previous chapter, but from some of the letters that have survived from the early days. They are reproduced exactly as written:

Dear Frend and Secretary

Wil you ples try to locaite my sister's adress, plase

> let me know if you are going to help me to find where my sister leaves now.

A postscript to another letter written from the correction hospital on Welfare Island ran: "I am here on domestic trouble charged by father-in-law." One from Auburn Prison read:

> Being destituted and unable to secure the helps of Counsel, I'm so anxious at least of your legal advice. With my advanced thanks I'm Respectfully yours . . .

From the New York City Penitentiary:

> An immigration officer came to see me and read out a deportation warrant to me. I did not understand what it was all about so I am writing you for advice. I came to this country legally, have many years been in this country.

He hoped the Committee would send him someone who spoke Greek. The same helplessness appeared in many others.

> I have no money with wich to retain a lawyer. . . . I have been in this country for so many years that if I was to be deported to Italy I would be utterly lost. To the best of my knowledge I have no relatives there wich makes matters worse.

And again, this one addressed to "Community for Foreign Born Protections":

> As I'm Foreign decent, was borned in Russia and come to the United States in the year 1913. I'm underleased for deportation to Soviet Russia.

He had written to the Russian Embassy in Washington and had been refused a passport because he was not a Soviet citizen. His second letter asked that the Committee communicate with his wife and added that even if he were not likely to be sent to Russia, "while they have me behind the bar they likely would do anything."

There was no doubt that the foreign born needed protection. The fight against deportations was continuous. *Who's Who in Deportations,* a twelve-page mimeographed bulletin published September, 1935, gave forty-three brief biographies of current cases in which the Committee was active or interested. A similar bulletin with the title *Case History* in July, 1936, included more than sixty. Many, though not all, of those listed were the so-called "political cases," ordered deported under the law of 1918 by which freedom of association was denied to the non-citizen. Opposing a deportation order involved all kinds of difficulties and required at times stupendous efforts.

An obvious first imperative was delaying the summary deportation of those brought to Ellis Island until legal action in their behalf could be instituted. Almost equally immediate was the necessity to gain the right to bail for those held under deportation orders. Sometimes this could be accomplished directly by personal interview with the Commissioner of Immigration in Washington. A letter from him has survived, thanking Dwight Morgan for "a sensible dispassionate discussion," and stating that bail of $500 had been ordered for three of those held for deportation, and promising further consideration of certain other cases. The letter, however, ended with a reference to "mandatory" deportation and a defense of high bail in some instances.

Most often the battle had to be fought with the local immigration officials and in the Federal courts of New York. Paul Kettunen and Oscar Mannisto, already mentioned, were taken off the S.S. *President Harding* by a writ of habeas corpus fifteen minutes before the boat sailed. Sometimes word of a deportation arrest on the West Coast reached the Committee after the deportee had already sailed.

But once a victim was saved temporarily from deportation, or was freed on bail, the real fight for the non-citizen's rights began. And a many-sided, exhausting and costly fight it had to be, indeed!

After rescuing Mannisto from the S.S. *President Harding,*

the Committee carried his case to the Federal courts. At the hearing he was asked who of his friends were communists. He replied that he did not know; that it was none of his business. Asked what he thought of the Soviet form of government, he said it was a good one for the workers. "Lenin is all right for Russia." He himself had left the Communist Party in 1928 because he "didn't care about it much." The court upheld the deportation order and the U.S. Supreme Court refused to review the case. The refusal of the Supreme Court to act ended the case and Mannisto was deported in January, 1936, after living in the United States for twenty-five years. But this simple description of the defeat gives little idea of what it had cost the Committee in time, effort and money.

His companion on the *President Harding*, Paul Kettunen, was more fortunate. The charges against him were sustained by the Immigration Board of Review and habeas corpus was denied him in Minnesota. He petitioned for it again from Ellis Island and the New York Federal court granted it. The case was carried to the U.S. Circuit Court of Appeals from which he won a favorable decision. When examined, he had refused to answer questions about his political beliefs. Certain sentences from the Federal court decision as given by Judge Chase expressed the same understanding of justice for which the Committee was fighting. "We have not yet reached the point where proof of one's belief can rest solely upon his refusal to answer questions." A definition of affiliation as used in the statute was "very likely as impossible as it is now unnecessary." But the word meant more than "merely being in sympathy with its aims or even willing to aid it in a casual, intermittent way. Affiliation includes an element of dependability."

In the case of Stella Petrosky, the method of fighting was entirely different. Immediately upon her arrest the local ILD and the local representative of the ACLU managed to secure bail for her and sent her to New York to confer with the ACPFB. The Committee at once began to organize protest meetings, especially of Polish-Americans. (There were three such meetings in the New York area in one week!) The Committee printed petitions with text in Polish and English, illustrated with a picture of the family, to be signed and sent to President Roosevelt and Secretary of Labor Perkins. (Since the establishment of the Department of Labor in 1913, the Immigration and Naturalization Service had been included in that Department.) Press releases were issued to newspapers throughout the country.

In the course of the campaign, a pamphlet on the case was printed with the title *A Dangerous Woman*. This pamphlet so bothered Mr. Byron Uhl of the Immigration Service on Ellis Island that he sent a copy to the Commissioner in Washington warning him that it "constitutes an attack upon the Service and the Secretary (of Labor), and I thought you might be interested in it, particularly the general instructions . . . which if disseminated generally will unquestionably interfere with the functioning of this Service and perhaps even interfere with the interests of the individuals involved. . . . The Committee has become rather active in immigration matters during the past eight months." The "instructions" in the pamphlet advised keeping passports, birth certificates, etc., where they could not be seized by "raiders," i.e., men who searched a house without a warrant; avoiding "idle conversation" with immigration inspectors; and getting the advice of a lawyer or of an organization familiar with the law before a hearing.

Mrs. Petrosky's first hearing was so manifestly unfair that the attorney demanded a postponement on the ground that he had to take up certain points with Washington. One state policeman had testified that he saw Stella at a meeting where "she stood up several times, raised her hands and shouted, 'Communism must prevail.'" Stella had not been at the meeting and the word "prevail" sounded most unlikely from her. A witness, who could not recognize her at the hearing, testified that she was a communist. During the delay, Stella and her family made a trip to Washington where they had an interview with Madam Perkins. Finally on October 31, 1935, the Immigration Department dropped the case on the ground that there was no evidence either of Communist Party membership or of responsibility for the school strike. The *New York World-Telegram* published Stella's picture with the headline, "Mrs. Petrosky to stay in the U.S."

The victory was important and not only for the family immediately involved. There grew out of it a renewed faith in American justice, a realization that false testimony was not always accepted. The Committee learned methods of procedure useful in many later cases. More important, the foreign born learned of the work of the Committee and realized that an organization could at times accomplish what would be impossible for an individual. It was not the Immigration and Naturalization Service alone which learned that the ACPFB was "rather active in immigration matters."

There is a postscript to the case of Stella Petrosky which should not be omitted. Under the sweeping provisions of the Walter-McCarran Law of 1952, the Justice Department presented new warrants for the deportation of Stella Petrosky on August 12, 1953. (By then she had sixteen grandchildren.) Protection against "double jeopardy," standing trial for the same crime more than once, like so much else supposed to be fundamental in American legal procedure, so important in fact, that it was written into Article V of the Bill of Rights as the Fifth Amendment to the U.S. Constitution—this protection has no meaning in deportation proceedings.

But on June 22, 1956, Judge Francis L. Van Dusen of Philadelphia ordered the government to produce within thirty days the secret statements of the government witnesses against Mrs. Petrosky, declaring that "a long-time resident of the United States, having a large family here, would seem entitled to have in her trial at least those safeguards given to an accused in a felony case, if not those granted to an accused in a capital case." The government did not produce the statements and, on July 23, Judge Van Dusen set aside the deportation order as unlawful. Stella Petrosky is still in the Untied States.

In the case of the 61-year-old Mrs. Vendemmia, the Committee pursued different methods. After interesting itself in the case, the ACPFB defrayed the court expenses while fighting to cancel the deportation order, as well as the expenses for the various medical examinations. Failing in the courts, the Committee interested Rep. James Lanzetta of New York in the case. At the request of the Committee, the Congressman introduced a bill authorizing the Secretary of Labor to cancel the warrant of arrest and order of deportation. The bill was referred to the House Committee on Immigration and Naturalization. It held hearings at which a representative of the ACPFB appeared and pressed for relief of the ailing Mrs. Vendemmia. After due consideration, the legislative committee reported back to the House, recommending passage of the bill without amendment and Mrs. Vendemmia remained with her family.

While concentrating its main efforts on the fight against deportation, the Committee was busy on other fronts as well. Help was continually needed by individuals—and was freely given by the Committee—in meeting the difficulties of naturalization. Discrimination against the foreign born in employment could be fought only by publicity and public condemnation. A mass meeting was organized to protest such discrimination in New York City. The speakers were Dwight Morgan, Eli Maurer of the American League Against War and Fascism, and Abraham Unger of the ILD. Nor was vigilance in the defense of the rights of the foreign born neglected in Washington. A Committee press release for April, 1935, reported Dwight Morgan's appearance at congressional hearings on the Kerr Bill, already mentioned.

The effectiveness of one method used by the ACPFB against anti-alien legislation was illustrated in the Kerr hearings, when Rep. Samuel Dickstein of New York exhibited a large pack of postcards. There followed this exchange:

> Dickstein: "Did you send all these cards to us?"
> Morgan: "No."

> Dickstein: "Well, you had something to do with putting them out, didn't you?"
> Morgan: "Yes, our Committee circulated them."

The card pictured four people labelled Dickstein, Hearst, Dies and Perkins pulling the Statue of Liberty from her pedestal. The press bulletin added that the protest on the back of the card was read into the hearing record and urged that the members of the House Committee on Immigration and Naturalization be flooded with copies at once. It should be noted that neither the Dies nor the Kerr bills were passed by the 74th Congress.

Throughout all this indispensable activity, there was the inevitable problem of finances. To raise the necessary funds for legal expenses, collection sheets were circulated by hundreds of "little people," including friends and relatives of victims. On one such sheet which has survived, and which urged the raising of a thousand dollars for legal expenses, the names of Mannisto and Kettunen appeared with three others: Karlsen, Poppov and Ujick. Mass meetings were held. Press releases were issued. Knowledge of the work of the Committee spread widely.

Perhaps the clearest picture of the imperative need for the existence of the ACPFB and of the character of its early work is to be gained by reading the 70 page, 1936 pamphlet, *The Foreign Born in the United States,* written by Dwight Morgan, and already quoted. It is much more than a listing of cases. The relation of the procedures of the Immigration Department to other forces and to other issues is stated clearly and usually illustrated by concrete examples. The pamphlet ends with a brief account of the work of the ACPFB, the cases defended, the victories already won and the Committee's program for the future.

> While the chief pressure in remedying these injustices should be directed at congressmen and senators for repeal of the present laws . . . much can be done toward saving

the lives of political refugees and gaining civil liberties for the foreign born by bringing public pressure upon the Labor Department to outweigh the reactionaries who attack the Administration for being too liberal.

In conclusion the author appeals for cooperation in words which embody the reason for the Committee's existence.

> If we accept as "mandatory" the arbitrary rulings intended to deny all democraitc rights to non-citizens we accept as inevitable the growth of tyranny in America. . . .
>
> Every defense of a worker held for deportation, every struggle against discrimination, every part of the fight for equal rights for the foreign born will help to maintain and extend the democratic rights of the native born workers. Every protest against injustice, every voice raised against oppression, aids in the age-old struggle of the masses to be free.
>
> Every individual who believes in the principles upon which this Republic was established should take part in the fight against deportation and persecution of the foreign born.

III. THE ANTE-BELLUM YEARS

5. The Right of Asylum

When the Rev. Herman F. Reissig, as Chairman of the ACPFB, opened the Annual Conference in February 1939, he declared that the histories of the future might well call the 1930's the "Age of Refugees." Most of those refugees were fugitives from the fascism of Europe.

Fascism may be said to have begun in Italy in 1920. The success of *Il Duce* Mussolini led to attempts, more or less effective, to establish similar fascist dictatorships in other countries. At first, the terror of fascism showed itself primarily on the national scene: in the destruction of political parties; the imprisonment of political opponents and their physical torture (sometimes their death) before or after a formal arrest; the control of trade unions by putting them under government officials who were trusted members of the Fascist Party; the stimulation of hatred against national minorities, particularly the encouragement of anti-Semitism; the elimination of the free press; the creation of a horde of secret police, informers, youth drill-masters; and the establishment of a military elite. Not all of these procedures appeared immediately in all fascist countries, but the character of the movement and its aims were unmistakable.

However, it was not until 1933, when Nazism consolidated its power by the sudden investment of Hitler with the chancellorship of Germany, that fascism emerged as a world power with its rigid alliances and disciplined adherents. Then self-imposed exile, flight in the night, secret plans for escape became the all absorbing activity of vast numbers of people. By 1938, some 220,000 applications for entry to the United States, the traditional refuge of the persecuted, had been filed in Germany alone, against a maximum quota of 27,370 to be admitted. The right of asylum was a matter of life and death to hundreds of thousands outside the boundaries of the United States, and it became a vital matter to countries other than our own. It became, indeed, a world wide problem. An International Conference on the Right of Asylum was held in June, 1936, in Paris, and was attended by a representative of the ACPFB. In March, 1937, Belgium granted asylum to all who could prove themselves refugees. On February 25, 1938, the League of Nations convention on asylum was signed by thirteen European countries. In April of the same year, an international conference was held in Evian, France.

The tragic situation of the refugees forced the ACPFB to reconsider the limits of its work. Its increasing reputation and the wider basis of its support had led to a manifold increase in the demands upon its resources. The foreign born were still being faced with arrest and deportation; cases still had to be carried to the Federal courts to win some limitation upon the arbitrary acts of officials of the Immigration and Naturalization Service. Public interest still had to be aroused and kept alive.

But the specific problem of admission of refugees from Nazi and fascist Europe was growing more and more pressing. To deny such admission was to deny the validity of a cherished American tradition as well as to inflict suffering on countless individuals. Would the original American "Right of Asylum" endure? As the situation in Europe worsened, the numbers of political and religious refugees grew larger and larger. In this world emergency and with knowledge of the penalties for dissent in Germany, Italy and elsewhere, the Committee felt it necessary to include in its program an active fight for the right of asylum and for the defense of refugees.

The desperate need of the right of asylum was only too clear.

A group of stowaways fleeing Hitler and Mussolini, to whom the government had refused entry, was being held on Ellis Island. Among them were Rudi Miller and George Piermont, both 23, from Italy; and Hans Goepel who joined an anti-Nazi organization in 1928 and fled from Germany in 1935 when some of his friends were arrested. Norman Thomas interceded for him and delay was granted. Sixteen-year-old Werner Krieger had provided himself with a knife and three apples for the voyage before he slipped on board a ship. For some of these, the Committee succeeded in winning permission to go to a country where they would be granted asylum. France offered refuge to Alfred Gallinat of Danzig, and Mexico accepted several (nine in 1937).

But the Committee press bulletin sadly reported that Friederich Beyerbach and Heinrich Reining had been put on board ship from Ellis Island to be returned to Germany, without notice to the Committee or to their attorneys, after assurance had been given that a hearing would be granted. Reining was only twenty-one. He had fled to Holland when his underground anti-Nazi activity had been discovered, and to escape being returned to Germany he had stowed away on a Dutch ship bound for New York.

The Committee press bulletin for May, 1937, devoted five and a half out of six pages to emphasizing the necessity to fight for the right of asylum in the United States. It reproduced a letter from twelve members of the Committee's Advisory Board, including Roger Baldwin, John Dewey, the publisher, Donald Friede, and Rabbi Edward L. Israel of Baltimore asking for a hearing on a bill introduced by Congressman Emanuel Celler in that year, seeking to establish the right of asylum in American law. "We sincerely feel," these signers wrote, "that the traditional right of asylum which this country long cherished should be re-established by law. . . . Right of asylum is a foundation stone of democracy."

A similar letter had been signed and sent by thirty-one authors, educators and lawyers, among them Marie Allen

(*Northern Frontier News Service*), Sherwood Anderson, Dan Brummitt (*Christian Advocate*), Dorothy Bromley (columnist, *New York World-Telegram*) H. W. L. Dana, Jerome Davis (Yale), Guido Ferrando (Vassar), Granville Hicks, Quincy Howe, Rockwell Kent, Ruth Norden (*Living Age*), Upton Sinclair, Oswald Garrison Villard.

The bulletin also presented a full page statement of the position of the Committee, declaring that the denial of asylum was a threat to democratic institutions. Its readers were urged to send letters and telegrams to the House Committee on Immigration in support of the bill introduced by Rep. Celler, and selections from Celler's radio address were reproduced. Some of the most pertinent and pointed remarks follow:

> America was discovered by one who was endeavoring to find a new passage to the East. Columbus never realized that he had failed to reach the Orient. . . . [He] and the explorers who followed him, however, opened up to the mass populations of Europe avenues of escape from oppression—economic, religious and political—for many years to come. Many have been the brave who came here from Germany, England, France, Russia, Italy, all actuated by the same motives as our immigrants today. All were determined to escape religious and political torture and to improve their economic and living conditions. To me it seems anomolous when the descendants of the first settlers "turn up their noses" at recently arrived immigrants. . . .
>
> Many of the great names of Revolutionary history are those of early settlers who likewise came here to evade torture and persecution—Schuyler from Holland, Herkimer from Germany, John Jay from Wales, Baron Steuben from Prussia, Hoffman from Sweden, Haym Solomon from Poland. . . .
>
> Political and religious refugees still seek to escape from the leash of oppression. . . . Catholics fleeing the scourge of Hitler; the Jews avoiding the cruel despotism of Rumania; and Italians seeking surcease from Fascisti evils.
>
> We have always gloried in the fact that our country has been a haven for the oppressed. . . .

> I believe it is a blot on our escutcheon that the principle of asylum, which has so long been a cornerstone of our democratic institutions is being daily weakened and, in fact, is being well nigh destroyed. . . .
>
> I cannot remind my listeners too strongly of the historic policy of our country of affording asylum to political and religious refugees—and emphatically draw their attention to the fact that many of these "tempest tossed" contributed much to the wealth and welfare of our land. . . .
>
> It is well to remember George Washington's Thanksgiving proclamation of January 1, 1795, when he said: ". . . humbly and fervently to beseech the kind Author of these blessings to render this country more and more a safe and propitious asylum for the unfortunate of other countries. . . ."
>
> Unfortunately, the administration has refused to distinguish between the cases of political and religious refugees from the general deportation cases. There are some very distressing cases where our own Government has caused the arrest of aliens because of their political opinions and pronouncements and where our Government seeks to deport them to the country of their origin, where, in most cases, long prison terms, or even death, awaits them. In other words, political dissenters are being included among the deportees. This is decidedly wrong, if not tragic.

Two years later on March 6, 1939, Rep. Celler offered as his own resolutions in Congress and had printed in the *Congressional Record* the resolutions adopted by the Annual Conference of the ACPFB in February of that year.

The 1937 Celler Bill provided that, "No alien shall be excluded from admission to or deported from the United States if such alien is a refugee for political, racial or religious reasons from the country of his origin." (A similar bill introduced by Rep. Vito Marcantonio of New York, the preceding year had died in committee.) But the House Committee on Immigration found its schedule "too crowded" in 1937 to allow the hearing and it was not until April of the following year that hearings on a similar bill were scheduled. And those hearings were indefinitely postponed because of the Evian Conference. The ACPFB's program for 1939 again included the establishment by law of the right of asylum and urged the passage of Rep Celler's Bill, as well as one introduced by Sen. Robert F. Wagner of New York, for admitting 10,000 German children.

Congress did not establish by law the right of asylum, but the publicity accompanying the attempt to get hearings on the bill did prevent the return of individual refugees. Also it aroused public interest in what was, after all, the Committee's major concern: protection for refugees who were already in the country. Here there was need for immediate action. Could non-citizen residents of the United States liable to deportation claim the right of asylum against deportation to Italy and Germany? The Wickersham Commission Report had recommended in 1931 that aliens should not be deported to any country in which their lives would be in danger because of their political opinions. But there was no law to implement the recommendation.

The acuteness of the danger to those liable to deportation to Germany and Italy was obvious. On April 10, 1936, it was graphically portrayed in *Haven of Refuge*, a "deportation play" written by Mariquita Villard and Dwight Morgan, which was presented by the Theatrecraft Players. The play was based on actual incidents in deportation cases, and the scenes were laid in the home of a deportee, a jail, Ellis Island and the office of the Assistant Secretary of Labor. In addition to the play itself, the ACPFB presented Congressman Marcantonio as guest speaker on "The Right of Asylum." Needless to say, play and speaker won full sympathy and enthusiastic support from the audience.

On the back cover of the program there were the photographs of eleven anti-Nazis ordered deported to Germany. One of them was Alfred Miller who had come to the United States from Germany in 1929. He had gone to Eastern Pennsylvania where he found the farmers engaged in a desperate struggle to get more money for their milk and to halt the sheriff's sales, in which all that a man possessed was sold at auction to satisfy creditors, mostly sellers of farm machinery, who had already received substantial parts of the agreed installments. In time Miller became executive secretary of the United Farmers' Protective Association. Their slogan, "Our wives and children hold the first mortgage," was widely publicized by the "$3.18 sheriff's sales" (maximum bid) in Bucks County, and the worst abuses were ended.

In 1934 Miller went to Montana where, after four years of drought, the farm situation was worse than it had been in Pennsylvania. There he became editor of a cooperative farm newspaper, *The Producers' News*. His arrest on March 21, 1935, was said to be the result of his editorial criticism of local relief work. The actual charges against him were membership in the Communist Party and advocating the violent overthrow of the United States government. When the examining inspector told him angrily "You would be put against a wall and shot if you were facing Hitler now," Miller gave the obvious retort, "Yes, and aren't you trying to send me back for that purpose?"

The Immigration Service demanded his deportation to Germany, from which his wife and child had already fled to Switzerland to escape the concentration camp. The deportation was fought on the issues of right of asylum and freedom of the press, as well as on questions of fact. Nothing could be found in any issue of the newspaper which advocated violence.

Meantime, Alfred Miller was held in isolation on Ellis Island with a few others classed as "politicals." There he was interviewed by Abner Green for a magazine article. The report of the interview has a double interest—both for the picture it gives of government procedure and for the concluding sentences which perhaps explain why Abner Green has devoted more than twenty years to the work of the ACPFB. (He has been its executive secretary since 1941.) Abner Green wrote in part:

> He was short. He wore rimless eyeglasses. . . . His shirt was torn at the collar. He was wearing a pair of corduroy

pants and a lumber-jacket. A former editor, I thought, the news item had said so. I told him how I had come to see him.

"It is good to see somebody," he said. "Most of the time I'm in a room with five others, all politicals."

"What do you mean, all 'politicals'?"

"We are anti-fascists, political agitators, reds and dangerous criminals. Ask Hearst, he'll tell you! . . . We're not allowed to speak to other prisoners. . . . They feed us in a special room. . . . We are political prisoners of the United States government. . . ."

"But they can't send you to Germany," I said.

"They can't? That's just what they are doing."

"Won't they let you go any place else?"

"Sure, any place. If I have the money and can get a passport, that is. But where is the money going to come from? This way, Uncle Sam pays the passage and I get my passport because I was born in Germany. . . ."

It was the law and I realized that I was quite a part of that law . . . sending him to his death—as long as I kept quiet.

It was nothing in Miller that made me feel I wanted to do something to gain his freedom. . . . It was just I felt that way because of the thing which was there and which I should be able to help but wasn't helping. . . .

"There are eleven anti-nazis in all," he said, "that they are trying to send back to Germany. But it isn't only Germany. It's Italy, Hungary, Poland, Cuba."

It was time to leave. The air felt good. Across the water I could see the Statute of Liberty. . . . She stood there apparently guarding freedom, promising security. But . . . from Ellis Island I could only see her back.

In 1937 Alfred Miller was granted asylum in Mexico. But the seriousness of the danger to others remained. It is dramatically seen in the *Review* of 1936, published by the Committee in January, 1937. The cover is a montage of newspaper clippings with the headlines: "Richter, Anti-Nazi, Must Go to Germany," "Richter Protest Is Asked," "Richter Begins Hunger Strike," "Anti-

Nazi Wins Haven in Mexico to Save His Life." Otto Richter was a twenty-year old German who fled in 1933 after the Reichstag fire which was made the excuse for launching the Brown Terror. He had jumped ship at Seattle, had been arrested the following year in the San Francisco general strike, and was ordered deported.

There were, of course, many non-citizen residents of this country who had been arrested for deportation for various reasons and whose "country of origin" was Italy or Germany. There was Thomas Scarpone, forty-six years old, who entered in 1906. His wife was an American citizen and they had six American-born children. In 1916 he had gone to Italy to serve in the Italian army and returned to the United States as a reservist in 1920. In 1937 he was arrested for deportation because of two crimes committed before his 1920 entry, one in 1908 and one in 1911. A presidential pardon for the federal offense was granted but Governor Wilbur Cross of Connecticut made difficulties. In response to cases like Scarpone's, the Italian Committee was established in 1936, with Edward Corsi, Dr. Carlo Fama, James Mangano (sheriff of Kings County, New York) and Congressman Marcantonio on its Advisory Board. In 1938, co-operating with the ACPFB, the Italian Committee defended more than forty cases. The Italian Committee page in the ACPFB Souvenir Journal for 1939 shows Mrs. Scarpone with the six children. Scarpone was released on $500 bail and in 1941 a Connecticut pardon was finally secured.

Many non-citizens were in danger of being sent to their former homelands to prison, concentration camps or death, solely on the charge of illegal entry into the United States. One German seaman had jumped his ship because its destination had been changed to Nazi Germany. A former Nazi, forced to leave Germany within twenty-four hours because he had criticized Hitler, had entered on a visitor's visa which had expired.

Others had been too active in labor disputes or in anti-Nazi demonstrations in America, or had incurred local hostility. In a publicity release issued by the ACPFB, the pictures of eight

Germans surround a printed letter to President Roosevelt in their behalf. Among them were Carl Ohm, who had demonstrated in behalf of Negroes in New York City; Erich Becker, with two brothers in German concentration camps, who was arrested at a protest demonstration at the German Consulate in Chicago; Walter Baer, who had antagonized certain interests in Portland, Oregon, by urging the establisment of a municipal sewage disposal plant to end pollution of the Columbia River.

Some were charged with Communist Party membership or with affiliation with communists or some other "radical" group. Vincent Ferrero and Domenick Sallitto ran a small restaurant in Oakland, California. They sublet space in it to the editor of the anarchist magazine *Man*, and were arrested for deportation on the charge of affiliation with anarchism. A special committee was organized to provide for their defense and to cooperate with the ACPFB. George Alexander, twenty years old, was ordered deported for student activities in connection with the Young Communist League in Pennsylvania.

The question of Communist Party membership as a ground for deportation was carried to the courts in the appeal of Joseph Strecker, of Arkansas. The Federal Circuit Court at New Orleans ruled in Strecker's favor. Judge Hutcheson who delivered the decision commented:

> It seems a kind of Pecksniffian righteousness, savoring of hypocrisy and party bigotry to assume (merely because he belonged to the Communist Party) that he advocated the overthrow of the Government of the United States by force and violence.
>
> It seems to me too that the cause of liberalism is more retarded than advanced by forays for deportation on evidence like this.

The Department of Labor appealed the decision but it was affirmed by the U.S. Supreme Court on the technical ground that the law, as written, did not provide for deportation for past membership in proscribed organizations. Not until Congress passed a new law in 1940 was past membership in the Communist Party a ground for deportation. On January 7, 1941, Joseph Strecker was re-arrested for deportation under the new law; but this time he could not be sent back to Austria on account of the war in Europe, and he was released on his own recognizance.

A special group among those whose deportation was opposed by the ACPFB was composed of returning fighters against Franco in Spain, members of the International Brigade, the Abraham Lincoln Brigade, the Garibaldi Battalion, and Spaniards from the Loyalist Army. All through 1938-40 they came. In May, 1938, four stowaways on the *Normandie,* then three on the *President Harding.* By October, seventeen were held for deportation; by the end of the year, twenty-five. In January, 1939, the Committee asked permission for a doctor to see six on Ellis Island. In May, fourteen had visas for Chile and money was needed to get them there.

Working with the ACPFB was a special "Committee to Aid Excluded Loyalist Veterans" which was composed, in part, of the officers of various interested organizations. "The League for the Protection of Greek Immigrants," founded in 1935, helped in the defense of Steve Tsermegas and Costa Halepsis of the International Brigade. The "Spanish Societies Confederated to Aid Spain" was also active.

Many of these veterans had come to America in the 1920's or earlier. Some had married here and had American-born children. But they had been too eager to get into the fight against fascist tyranny to consider legal difficulties, and many could not have gone "legally." At the end of the Spanish Civil War they had no money. Of the seventeen listed in October 1938, eleven had come back as stowaways.

In an article entitled "America Is Their Home," written for use by the various organizations cooperating, George Seldes compared the welcome these fighters for democracy received with that given to the veterans of World War I.

> Twenty years ago soldiers returning . . . were treated as heroes; the American press, the public, the government joined in welcoming them. . . . Today . . . soldiers are returning again. But instead of government officials, the press and public greeting them as heroes, there is not a word in the newspapers, and officials in Washington threaten many of them with deportation.

He goes on to tell of individuals with whom he had talked on Ellis Island:

> One is a veteran of the [first] World War on the German side. He was a conscript, a machine-gunner. He fought through three years and when the war was over he came to the United States. But in 1937, exactly twenty years after his entry into the German army, he volunteered as a machine-gunner against the Fascist Internationale in Spain. He fought Nazi machine-gunners. On more than one occasion when the Loyalists were overwhelmed by cannon fire . . . by material advantage sometimes fifty times as great as their own, and it became necessary to evacuate a position, it was up to the machine-gunners to hold up the Fascists. This German-born American hero was always last, holding the position and insuring the safety of the infantry.
>
> Another hero is Esthonian born. He figured in Herbert Matthews' dispatches in the [New York] *Times* months ago when he and two companions, caught on Franco's side of the Ebro, swam the river naked. Another is Greek-born. And there are the Italian anti-fascists who distinguished themselves in that great battle of Guadalajara when Mussolini's blackshirt division, 20,000 strong, turned in flight.

Seldes' title was used by the Committee for its "collection sheets." One, in German, had pictures of four returned German Americans, two Greeks, an Esthonian and a Serbian. The collection of funds was an urgent necessity. Lawyers had to be paid. The Immigration Department, under the pressure of publicity, allowed to those whom it refused to admit "voluntary departure" to other countries. Such departures required money for transportation and money to make admission possible. Mexico demanded that each refugee have $150.

The experiences of the men on Ellis Island are grim reading. Some had unhealed wounds. Frank Bonetti's leg had been amputated and it was impossible for him to use the showers. "You didn't get a bath in Spain, so it will not make much difference," the doctor said. Paul List, who had the chance of legal re-entry since his wife was American born, was held without bail on the Island although the papers he needed were at Niagara Falls, and in Rochester his three year old daughter was ill with polio. Rudolf Mills was ordered excluded on two grounds: "liable to become a public charge," and "immoral purpose of entry." Judge Leibell of the Federal District Court set aside the exclusion order. The reasons for the decision are enlightening. The evidence showed that Mills' brother-in-law had promised him a $30 a week job, and that the Friends of the Abraham Lincoln Brigade was ready with a guarantee and a bond of $1,000. His "immoral purpose" was his intention to return to his common-law wife with whom he had lived from 1934-37.

Frank Navarro's story also had a happy ending. He had come to the United States legally in 1925 and married. His wife was a Puerto Rican. In 1932 he went to Spain with his family to find work. When Franco began his revolt, Navarro joined the government army. In 1937 his wife and three American-born children were repatriated by the United States consul in Spain. His wife's efforts to have her husband admitted were unsuccessful because the family was on relief. In March, 1940, Navarro took a crewman's job and when the boat docked in Port Richmond he tried to get to New York to see his family. He was arrested in Philadelphia and ordered sent back to Spain. But the Committee's bulletin *These United States* for May 3, 1940, carried the news that he had been given three weeks to leave and re-enter legally on the basis of his wife's citizenship. The two attorneys who represented him were retained by the ACPFB.

The "victories" over which the Committee rejoiced in its

publications meant not merely the rescue of this or that individual from persecution or death. A favorable court decision on one case was a protection for countless others in a similar situation. Furthermore, aroused public opinion was in itself a defense for the refugees. A general report issued in May, 1938, lists nine refugee deportations in 1935; six in 1936; three in 1937 and only one in the first five months of 1938. For the time being, the right of asylum had been at least partially won in the court of public opinion.

6. Legislative Action and Counter-Action

But the European conflicts had other effects on the foreign born in the United States, more widespread than the acute problem of the deportation of refugees. The fascist war for world domination started with the Japanese invasion of Manchura in 1931 and then leap-frogged across the face of the earth to Ethiopia, to Spain, to Austria, to Czechoslovakia. Its rapid and dismaying progress necessarily increased tensions and antagonisms in America. By the time Poland was invaded and world war had really begun, the political situation in the United States had become critical. The admirers of Hitler and Mussolini on the one side and the admirers of Soviet Russia on the other sought to advance their own cause and to influence government policies. Adherents of both the Axis and Russia equally condemned as disloyal to true Americanism the conservatives and the liberals, the moderates and the extremists, the conspicuous leaders and the ordinary citizens who disagreed with them at any point or who advocated delay in action.

To accusations of "un-Americanism" the foreign born were especially vulnerable. They could be called dangerous to the United States either as alleged members of the German-American Bund and as fascist supporters of Mussolini, or as crypto-communists planning to "sabotage" American industry and "subvert" the American way of life. Furthermore, in localities where unemployment was still a problem and the WPA still a necessity, the foreign born were already objects of dislike, held responsible for taking jobs or relief from the native born. In all parts of the country, attacks on the foreign born offered a safe outlet for the prevalent anxieties and hostilities.

The situation was further aggravated by those who felt their own economic or personal interests especially menaced and yearned for a quick and definitive solution. Homecoming Americans reported increased economic stability in Italy and Germany. Mussolini's trains ran on time; the streets of Naples were free of beggars. Hitler was building moderate priced housing, initiating the cheap *Kraft durch Freude* excursions; business, especially big business, was prospering; unemployment was decreasing. Fascism apparently brought results, and too many Americans succumbed to the attractions of the fascist ideology.

Support for something approaching a dictatorship in the United States came from unexpected sources. Not only the American Legion, the U.S. Chamber of Commerce and Owen D. Young of General Electric urged at least "a mild form of dictatorship" but even men like Alfred E. Smith felt the need to "resort at least in part to the processes of autocratic government." John Nance Garner, then Speaker of the House, proposed that Congress give the President almost dictatorial powers.

There was a mushrooming of individuals and organizations dedicated to furthering this anti-democratic ideology. It is enough to recall the names of Father Charles Coughlin, Gerald L. K. Smith, William Pelley, Huey Long, Martin Dies; of the Liberty League, the revived Ku Kux Klan, the Black Legion, the Gold Shirts, the Silver Shirts. There was an epidemic of pestilential news-sheets and journals preaching race superiority and race hatred. City, state and national legislative bodies were infected.

The foreign born were, of course, the first targets of the attack. Congress reacted to the pressures with dozens of bills dealing with the status of the foreign born, especially of the non-citizen who could be penalized without danger of offending voters. As we have already noted, a surprisingly large proportion of these bills were introduced by men from sections of the southern states where almost no foreign born were to be found.

Of thirteen bills listed by the ACPFB for opposition in March, 1939, eleven were of Southern origin, as were two-thirds of the thirty so listed at the beginning of 1940. In the first three months of 1941, half of the fifty-one "anti-alien" bills introduced came from the South.

Rep. Stephen Pace of Georgia sought to stop all immigration after December 31, 1939, and deport all non-citizens after that date. Other bills would stop all immigration for ten years or five. One 1940 bill would reduce all immigration quotas by 90%. In 1941, Rep. Pace re-introduced his bill with the date shifted to December 31, 1941. Other bills dealt with establishing grounds for the deportation of non-citizens: for example, being on relief for six months within three years of arrival; for the possession of concealed weapons; for "believing in any form of government contrary to that now existing in the United States"; for anyone "whose presence is inimical to the public interest"; for anyone who "engages in any way in domestic political agitation"; for anyone who failed to apply for citizenship; for anyone who "interferes with the good order and happiness of any local community."

There were bills excluding aliens from various kinds of work. It would be "unlawful for non-citizens to bear, own, lease, conceal, buy or sell any implement of war," to fish in certain waters, to own a printing press, or to print anything. The Dempsey Bill, which was passed by the House and in amended form was approved by the Senate Judiciary Committee, provided for the deportation of all non-citizens who belonged to any organization advocating *any change* in the American form of government.

Of this bill, Senator Lewis B. Schwellenbach of Washington said in the Senate on May 30, 1941:

> Looking at it upon its face, [the bill] appears to be a very desirable measure . . . to deport aliens who may either openly or secretly favor a change in our form of government. It is pretty difficult to oppose a bill of that sort on the basis of the present frantic attitude of the American

> people, and yet we should appreciate the fact that when we stop a man from discussing a question we stop ourselves from discussing it, and we do not have any democracy left. After all, the ultimate purpose of any action we take at the present time is the protection and preservation of democracy.

The ACPFB pointed out in its material on this legislation that if the bill became a law, trade unions, churches, fraternal orders, in fact any group which accepted non-citizens as members, would be unable to support needed reform measures, "even health programs."

Active opposition to this wholesale attack on the foreign born was certainly needed. As the Hon. Stanley Nowak, Michigan State Senator, put it at the 1940 Annual Conference of the ACPFB:

> There have been several waves of anti-alien legislation at different times in the history of this country, but never were there as many and as vicious bills introduced at one time [as were then in Congress].

Such opposition was not lacking. *These United States*, an ACPFB bulletin, reflects the broad reaction in combatting "so-called anti-alien legislation." In successive issues, under the heading "America Speaks," protests from organizations and individuals are listed. The issue of May 3, 1940, records the sixteenth Biennial Convention of the Young Women's Christian Association (YWCA), John L. Lewis's special report to the Congress of Industrial Organizations (CIO), a Westchester Conference at Sarah Lawrence College, the New England Regional Conference of the American Jewish Congress. Issue number 7, 1940, lists some thirty organizations which had protested by letter or by resolutions. Among them were labor union locals, the Committee of Catholics for Human Rights, the Boston YWCA, the National Lawyers Guild, the ACLU.

But those organizations were concerned with many different problems affecting human welfare. Only the ACPFB was primarily concerned with infringement of the rights of the foreign born. And the Committee could, by combining all protests against such injustice, give cumulative effect to the opposition. Thus the Committee found itself faced with the need of more and more specific legislative activity.

It became one of its chief tasks to rouse popular opposition against oppressive bills, to have legislation introduced which would safeguard the rights of the foreign born and to muster support for such legislation. As Rev. Herman Reissig, the Committee's Chairman at that time, put it in the annual report to the 1940 Conference:

> From its original and simple function of defending persons threatened with deportation and giving assistance in the naturalization of aliens, the Committee has gone on to interest itself in all the problems affecting the foreign born in the United States.
>
> Our main attention in the past year has been focussed on legislation introduced in Congress. Through bulletins, printed folders and press releases, the attention of the public has been called to proposed legislation which would imperil the rights of the foreign born and inevitably threaten the liberties of all our people.

The publications of the Committee to which the Chairman referred, varied in name and form to suit the changing situation: in 1939, *The Foreign Born,* a series of mimeographed pamphlets on various topics and reproductions of public addresses; in 1940-41, *These United States,* published twice a month as a survey of activities relating to the foreign born; in 1941, *This Month.* The report of the 1940 Conference was printed, and certain of the addresses at the Committee's Annual Conferences were printed and distributed separately. For example, *Science Discusses Race* by the Rt. Rev. John Montgomery Cooper, chairman of the Department of Anthropology at the Catholic University of America; and *Poll Taxes and Anti-Alien*

Bills by Rep. Lee E. Geyer of California, already referred to, were issued. Printed folders and leaflets were innumerable.

Typical is a large single sheet headed NO ROOM FOR INTOLERANCE. Under the heading is a quotation from the Hon. Frank Murphy, then United States Attorney General: "There is no room for intolerance in the America which our fathers planned." On the front of the sheet, Liberty holds her torch high. The text gives a general summary of the legislation before Congress with quotations from Sen. James E. Murray of Montana and Rep. Caroline O'Day of New York. On the back are listed thirty anti-alien bills whose defeat was urged upon the public. During the year 1939, the Committee secured 50,000 signatures to petitions against such legislation. In 1941, the ACPFB sent out 40,000 postcards against the Dempsey Bill alone, and distributed widely the statement made by Senator Schwellenbach, already cited. The bill was never passed.

The resolutions passed at the 1940 Annual Conference of the Committee and those of a year later in March, 1941, had the same emphasis. The Conference resolutions early in 1939 had mentioned specifically for opposition only the five outrageous Starnes-Reynolds bills (one of them would deport all non-citizens on relief) and had asked in general for better laws on immigration and naturalization, and for the passage of the Right of Asylum Bill. In 1941, the first resolution was against "almost 100 so-called anti-alien bills" then pending in Congress which "contradict the American principles of equality of opportunity for all regardless of place of birth, regardless of political, economic or social viewpoint." In 1941, the third resolution dealt with almost forty such bills, singling out the Hobbs Bill for special mention. So important had the legislative field become in the judgment of the ACPFB that the 1941 Conference recommended and the Board of Directors of the Committee established a Washington office to which it assigned Abner Green with the title of "Educational and Legislative Director."

Some of the bills before Congress were undoubtedly unconstitutional, and many had little chance of being passed against an aroused opposition. But two stood out as especially menacing to the rights and security of the foreign born—the Hobbs Bill and the Smith Omnibus Bill.

"THE CONCENTRATION CAMP BILL"

The Hobbs Bill, "the Concentration Camp Bill," was first introduced in the House on April 4, 1939. It contained a provision for "acreage of farming" upon which aliens would be "detained" before or instead of deportation, an idea perhaps adapted from southern chain gang labor. Six days later, Mr. Hobbs offered a substitute bill with different wording but with the same content. This was passed in the House on May 5 by a vote of 288 to 61, was favorably reported by the Senate Judiciary Committee and came up for a vote in the Senate at the end of the session. Because Sen. Lewis Schwellenbach and others objected, it failed to become law.

Before the end of May the American Committee issued *Concentration Camps in America,* a mimeographed bulletin which listed the sixty-one representatives who voted against the Hobbs Bill (together with the three who paired against it) and included six pages of excerpts from speeches against it in the House and the Senate. The points made by the speakers have obviously more than a specific relevance. Rep. Celler declared:

> The anomaly of providing prison terms which in some cases might amount to life imprisonment for persons who, through no fault of their own, are unable to obtain travel documents to foreign countries [is obvious] . . . [The bill] contemplates the creation of detention camps in this country, release from which becomes dependent entirely upon the whim of an administrative officer, since the bill provides no legislative standards for administration. It sets up a procedure for the arrest and in some cases permanent detention of persons in a way which contravenes well-established principles of the United States Constitution.

Rep. Jerry Voorhis of California is quoted:

I am not against the bill because of what it is going to do to these alien people primarily. I am against it because I am afraid of what it is going to do to the United States.

Rep. Thomas F. Ford of California said:

I rise in opposition to H.R. 5643, because I am convinced that this democracy of ours should not stultify itself by employing the methods of dictator nations. Among these methods is the "detention" of suspected or feared or "undesirable" persons, not as a punishment of crime but because the government fears or hates them. Such detention is without due process of law and is therefore inimical to all.

Rep. Louis Ludlow of Indiana expressed sharp fears:

Mr. Chairman, I love democracy and I hate everything that strikes it down. I am against this bill because I am afraid of its ultimate implications. I fear that it would imperil the individual freedom which is so zealously sought and guarded in the Bill of Rights. I believe that it sets up an instrumentality which might be used to destroy personal liberty in America and so great are the potentialities for evil in this bill I shudder to see it go on the statute books.

Sen. William Lemke of North Dakota was unequivocal:

I am opposed to this bill because I am against concentration camps. I do not care whether they are constitutional or unconstitutional, they are Un-American.

Rep. Abe Murdock of New Mexico stated:

Imprisonment without due process of law is one of the oldest and certainly the most cruel instruments of tyranny. I do not think the time has arrived when we should begin to assault the foundations of our freedom. I do not believe

> that any excuse whatever would justify an act of Congress which, directly or indirectly, denied equal justice to any man under the protection of the American flag. . . . Once we begin to tear down the temple of equal justice we have destroyed its symmetry. It can only exist as a whole. If one part is torn away, the rest will surely fall.

These quotations were obviously chosen because they made particularly clear that the struggle for the rights of the foreign born in which the Committee was engaged was not an isolated skirmish but a part of the common effort to preserve what Rep. Murdock called "the temple of equal justice."

In August, the Committee issued a special number of the *The Foreign Born* in which the votes cast in Congress on both the Hobbs Bill and the Smith Bill were listed. Local and individual action of various sorts was urged.

Rep. Hobbs again introduced his bill in January, 1941. It was amended slightly in Committee and favorably reported on March 19, 1941. On May 8, the ACPFB called an "Emergency Conference to Defeat the Hobbs Bill" in New York City. Among the 138 delegates were the representatives from fraternal and nationality organizations, organized labor and groups interested in civil liberties.

At the conference, the close relation between the legislative and the defense work of the Committee was made clear in the report of the secretary, Curt Swinburn. He pointed out that the recent arrest of some 200 alien seamen had apparently been timed to gain support for the Hobbs Bill. As a matter of fact, seamen who had overstayed their sixty day leaves had done so only because no ships were leaving on which they could get jobs. Many of the men were long time residents of this country, had married American citizens, and had American-born children.

In a May press release, the Committee gave a more specific analysis of this group of seamen which had grown to more than five hundred. Newspaper headlines had called them "Axis Seamen," but the group included Greeks, Dutch, East Indians, English, Cubans and others, as well as Germans and Italians.

Furthermore, many from Germany and Italy had come here to avoid tyranny at home. The men fell into two classes: (1) Those already known to the Immigration Service as unable to leave the country. These were arrested on warrants, but were not allowed counsel or permitted to communicate with friends or to give bail. (2) Those collected wholesale and at random from places of employment, taverns and poolrooms. These were lined up for questioning by an immigration official, a policeman and an agent of the FBI. All who admitted that they were not legally in the country were arrested without proper warrants and crowded together in inadequate accommodations. A hundred and fifty were put into one room at Ellis Island which had a capacity of sixty.

Just previously the Commissioner of Immigration, Watson Miller, had testified to the House Judiciary Committee that the Hobbs Bill was necessary to take care of those arrested by the immigration officials. A planned connection between the timing of the mass arrests and the Commissioner's testimony urging the passage of the bill seems more than probable.

In August, the National Lawyers Guild joined the opposition to the bill with an article in the *Guild Review* called "A Long Step in the Wrong Direction." The article declared that the bill's provisions "added to the perils of every non-citizen; they accomplish no fundamental reforms; they continue methods that are unjust and unfair while creating whole new categories of injustices."

The bill provided that the Immigration Service might require "any alien to be subject to supervision and detention" by ordering the non-citizen (1) to appear from time to time for examination; (2) to submit to medical and psychiatric treatment; (3) to give information under oath as to his circumstances, habits and associations; (4) to conform to restrictions imposed by the Immigration Service. Any alien could be detained for fifteen months and for various reasons he might be confined for an unrestricted period. He could be held without trial "in the name of public safety and public interest." It is clear that although the bill did not use the words "concentration camp," it merited the label which was immediately applied to it. It was called the "Concentration Camp Bill" by Rep. Beam of Illinois and by the Chairman of the House Judiciary Committee as well as by the newspapers.

The label undoubtedly gave help to the opposition in preventing passage by the Senate in 1941. But the defeat of the Hobbs Bill afforded clear evidence that the work of an organization like the ACPFB was indispensible if the rights of the foreign born are to be successfully defended. This truth was illustrated equally—although in reverse—by the course of events preceding the passage of the Smith Act.

ALIEN REGISTRATION

It may have been because attention in 1940 was so concentrated on the necessity of preventing concentration camps in America that the supporters of the Smith Bill were successful. In 1939, eight different bills requiring the registration of aliens had been introduced in Congress. Such bills were no novelty. They had been opposed early in the 1920's by Samuel Gompers in behalf of the AFL, and in the years which followed by such men as Sidney Hillman, Alfred E. Smith and Herbert H. Lehman. In a *Memorandum* on alien registration put out in 1939, the Committee quotes from this opposition.

Said Sidney Hillman:

> The real effect of a measure of this character will be felt not only by the individual workers but by all of organized labor in its attempts to organize. A law of this kind will merely provide the anti-labor forces with a new weapon to be used in terrorizing workers and preventing them from joining organizations which protect their economic and social rights.

And Alfred E. Smith declared:

> I am opposed to the registration of aliens because, under our American conception of government, the state exists for the welfare and protection of the individual, when the enjoyment of that freedom does not conflict with the rights and freedom of others. . . . This proposal . . . would create abuses and problems more fundamental and more destructive of American freedom than any evil it might aim to cure.

In 1939 state bills requiring registration were also introduced in California, New Jersey and Pennsylvania. The Pennsylvania law was passed but was declared unconstitutional by a Federal court in November. The December issue of *The Foreign Born* was devoted exclusively to this Federal court decision which was given in detail, because in the judgment of the Committee it made "a distinct contribution to the welfare of the American people." It may also have contributed to the unwarranted expectation that a similar bill in Congress would fail to pass.

The decision of unconstitutionality was based on two counts of which the first, that the Act encroached on a field reserved for federal action, was technical. The second declared that the Act denied equal protection of the law to the alien and that the section referring to those who did not apply for citizenship or who failed to become citizens was "unreasonable and capricious." An appeal was taken to the U.S. Supreme Court for which the Committee filed an *amicus* (friend of the court) brief. The appeal was withdrawn after the Smith Act made state laws unnecessary.

Of the eight bills before Congress in 1939, the Smith Bill received House approval in August, and the next year was before the Senate. In the legislative panel of the ACPFB Annual Conference in March, 1940, various uncomplimentary references to it were made. Rep. Thomas Ford (California) said of it:

> The most Un-American activity that I can possibly conceive is in some of these measures for the so-called

> preservation of Americanism. They want to regulate and fingerprint aliens and have every alien carry an identification card. . . . The American citizen, not having a card, would presumably have to produce a birth certificate or his citizenship papers.

Rep. Tenerowicz was equally emphatic:

> Particularly repugnant are the Smith and Hobbs Bills. . . . The sponsors of both these insidious measures. . . . I feel, could profit by a re-reading of the Constitution of the United States.

These United States in April quoted the headline "A Tricky Bill" used by Raymond Clapper, the Washington correspondent for Scripps-Howard, and his statement:

> To pass such legislation as the Smith Bill would be to put a weapon in the hands of any official inclined toward political intolerance, and one that is not needed for peace time purposes since we already have adequate protective laws.

The opinion of Rep. Bruce Barton of New York, follows:

> Any law that picks out any particular element in our population for special restrictions and penalties is likely to be dangerous; and all the more so when the group thus legislated against is a minority and relatively defenseless. Any nation that begins attacking minorities is beginning to destroy democracy. For minorities are the outposts of democracy's ramparts.

The Committee fought the bill—but the fight began too late, and apparently lacked the intensity and concentration necessary to gain widespread support and achieve success in Congress.

On May 3, 1940, the bill was before the Judiciary Committee of the Senate. On May 23, Attorney General Robert Jackson publicly advocated the registration of all non-citizens as a necessary safety measure; and on May 29, the Judiciary Committee reported favorably with some amendments the "Smith Alien and Sedition Bill." As amended, it combined the requirements of registration and fingerprinting of aliens with a "deportation for previous membership" in the Communist Party clause and various provisions affecting American citizens. The bill was passed by the Senate and was signed by President Roosevelt on June 28.

Obviously, the passage of such a measure would have been impossible except under the exaggerated fears and tensions preceding the United States entry into World War II. According to Vito Marcantonio, it was "blitzkrieged through Congress as part of the so-called 'National Defense Program.'" The only argument for it was that it "was necessary to fight Trojan horses and Fifth Columnists, spies and saboteurs." He wondered whether "a real Trojan Horse" would actually go to the Post Office and "disclose the nature of his activities."

The speed with which the Senate acted had prevented effective opposition, but after the passage of the Act, disapproval was loud and vehement. On July 29, 1940, Rep. Marcantonio delivered a radio address on the Columbia Broadcasting System on the registration of aliens which the ACPFB printed at once, with an introduction by Carey McWilliams, California State Commissioner of Immigration and Housing and Chairman of the American Committee. (An Italian translation was issued at the same time by the Italian Committee for the Defense of Immigrants.) Part of the radio address is included in *I Vote My Conscience*, a collection of the Congressman's speeches and writings. But a few paragraphs from the introduction and from the address are given below as a vigorous expression of views which the Committee shared.

From the introduction:

> We weaken our claim to our democratic rights when we deny these rights to one section of the population. The

> Constitution must apply to all of us equally and impartially, or it can apply to none. In order to defend our own rights as Americans and help preserve our democracy in this period of crisis, we must maintain the economic, social and political rights of the non-citizen and the foreign born.
>
> The registration and fingerprinting of non-citizens has been enacted into law. The American Committee for Protection of Foreign Born, in cooperation with other organizations, will work tirelessly to remove this blot upon the record of our democracy, to repeal this law because it contradicts and endangers the basic principles of American democracy, or to have it declared unconstitutional in the Courts.

From the address:

> Thus, in free America, we will witness the Hitler-imitating spectacle of 3,500,000 men, women and children, composed of loyal and hardworking people in all walks of life—priests, nuns, rabbis, ministers, bricklayers, carpenters, clerks, all of whom have been making a contribution to the greatness of America—being subjected to the criminal-like treatment of registration and fingerprinting.
>
> It has also been said that this amputation of our freedom was necessary in order to protect our American democracy. I believe this is the most incongruous proposition I have ever heard. On the one hand it is said that they want to preserve American liberties and then they set out to destroy them! They strangle American freedom under the demagogic excuse of seeking to protect it! My friends, if we carry out this course we will end with no freedom and no democracy.

The criticism may at first thought seem over-vehement. The native born do not yet, as Thomas Ford predicted, carry their birth certificates around with them. But the passage of the Alien Registration Act marked a definite turn toward imposing conformity of speech and action which is still with us and which in the opinion of many has seriously altered the character of America. Prof. Arthur S. Link, summarizing in *American Epoch* (pp. 464-468) the movement which began in 1940, writes of "the approval by leaders and judges of programs and measures that were, to say the least, contrary to the nation's traditions of civil liberties."

The passage of the Alien Registration Act in contrast to the defeat of the Hobbs Bill furnishes an excellent indication of the importance of vigorous, well-publicized opposition. The Committee and many other organizations and individuals opposed both bills. But efforts were so far absorbed in defeating the Concentration Camp Bill that no equally effective action was taken against the Smith Bill. Neither mass meetings, nor protest postcards, nor appeals for letters to congressmen were prepared in time to delay passage.

However forcibly the ACPFB denounced the Smith Act, it emphasized no less the necessity of compliance by non-citizens with its provisions after its passage. The sections of the law applying to them were reproduced in *These United States,* and the fifteen questions (later seventeen) to be answered in registering were given in full. During the year, the Committee distributed 100,000 copies of a four page folder, *Your Rights,* which included both the questions and the kind of answers required.

A "Discussion Outline" published in September, 1940, illustrates the two-fold aim of the Committee. The pamphlet begins with a statement made by Madam Frances Perkins in January, 1940:

> Any system of registration involves a radical departure from the American system and a return to the European system of government and police control of the individual. Once applied to aliens, it is only a matter of time when some similar measure is applied to citizens.

It goes on to declare that the Act is the result of unfounded concern over alien fifth columnists and continues with a statement of the rights of non-citizens, claiming for them "all of the constitutional guarantees" to life, liberty and property, and the equal protection of the law. It promises that the American Committee will work for the repeal of the law or to have it declared unconstitutional. But the pamphlet concludes with a statement of the requirements for proper registration and the penalties incurred by failure to register, and lastly offers the help of the Committee in filling out the registration form. The seventeen questions appear on the last page.

While noting that the Law must be obeyed, the December issue of *These United States* also reported the sending to the President and the Attorney General of a letter with 100 signatures:

> On December 26th, the compulsory fingerprinting and registration of non-citizens as ordered by Congress will be concluded. . . . We urge the Attorney General to administer the laws [affecting the foreign born] in a manner that will avoid creating unnecessary hardship or prejudice for either individuals or families in this country.
>
> In the spirit of the Christmas season, we call upon every American to exercise and display understanding for the problems of his fellow Americans who are not citizens. . . .
>
> We who are devoted wholeheartedly to the principles of freedom must not permit hysteria and prejudice to undermine our democracy by making a scapegoat of the non-citizens. This danger is aggravated by those who seek to take advantage of the public tension . . . created as a result of the war, by spreading false charges against the foreign born.
>
> We appeal on this day to the responsible officers of our government to use their office to help insure perpetuation of our democracy by taking the necessary steps to safeguard the rights and welfare of the foreign born.

Among the signers were the following: Dean Edith Abbott, Prof. Roland Bainton, Prof. Franz Boas, Rev. Dwight Bradley, Louis Bromfield, Van Wyck Brooks, Henry Seidel Canby, Dr. Everett Clinchy, Rev. Henry Hitt Crane, Waldo Frank, Rabbi

Henry S. Goldstein, Prof. Ralph Harlow, Rev. Ladislaus Harsanyi, Rev. Sidney Lovett, Helen Merrill Lynd, Clifford T. McAvoy, Jack McMichael, Edgar K. Morrow, George B. Murphy, Jr., Harry Overstreet, Rabbi David de Sola Pool, Kenneth C. M. Sills, Dr. T. A. Starzynski, Oswald Garrison Villard, J. Raymond Walsh, William Carlos Williams.

These names bear witness that the defense of the rights of the foreign born was widely recognized as an integral part of the defense of the constitutional rights of all Americans.

7. "No Crumbs for the Alien"

But quite apart from any failure to achieve timely, united and energetic opposition to the Smith Act, it was the hostility and prejudice against the foreign born, augmented by the pre-war tensions, which made its passage possible. The same prejudice and hostility were manifested also in the increasing discrimination against the foreign born in both government and private employment.

Such discrimination is of course a hardy perennial. It was even reflected in such nineteenth century ballads as "No Irish Need Apply," revived by folk-singers during more recent experiences of "anti-foreign" bias. Discrimination against non-citizens in the New York hospitals in 1932 was one factor in the original decision to form the ACPFB. But not since the fear of the French Revolution brought the Alien and Sedition Laws of 1798 into a brief existence, had panic and prejudice been so widespread in this country as in the period from 1936-1940. *The Review of* 1936, published by the ACPFB in January, 1937, summarized the situation:

> In addition to the numerous discriminatory laws . . . there is an endless chain of extra-legal forms of prejudice and discrimination against the foreign born. These prejudices, petty in detail and execution, are a daily occurrence in the life of the American immigrant. . . . Suffering hardships created by the economic depression to as great

> an extent as the average American, the immigrant underwent additional difficulties as a result of being the target of such epithets as "alien" and "foreigner."
>
> During 1936, each day brought a new crop of appeals . . . requesting aid in individual cases of discrimination because of foreign birth or non-citizenship. In each case the American Committee rendered aid . . . to the best of its ability. . . . These cases . . . comprise more than 50% of the Committee's activities.
>
> Through its general campaign of education, the American Committee hopes [to show] the injustice of this attitude toward the foreign born.

Press releases, bulletins and other publications of the Committee from 1937 on are filled with reports of congressional and state bills limiting or forbidding the employment of aliens on relief work, in government jobs and in private industry, and with descriptions of the effect of such discrimination on individuals and communities. As the slow recovery of business began, the ailing economy acquired all the irascibility of the convalescent. From unwilling and sullen acquiescence in the efforts of President Roosevelt to set the economy in motion, the representatives of conservative Big Business turned to violent denunciation of the New Deal and to a variety of measures to undermine it.

A particular target of their criticism was the program of the Work Projects Administration (WPA). Employers who objected to government relief because of its tendency to keep wages up in a period of unemployment could hope that employment of non-citizens on WPA projects provided an appeal which would arouse opposition to the New Deal as a whole among taxpayers anxious to reduce government spending, and among native-born workmen anxious to safeguard their own share of relief.

In spite of pressure, Congress did not pass the Lanham Bill which directly barred all non-citizens from relief work. It accomplished the same end, however, by passing the Hamilton Fish amendment to the Relief Appropriation Act. This amendment gave preference in all relief employment to veterans and citizens. Such preference in practice would, of course, exclude non-citizens. The amended Appropriation Bill was signed by the President on June 30. And in the concerted campaign of the conservative forces to "take the government out of relief work," more than a million people were dropped from the WPA rolls between September, 1936, and September, 1937. Obviously, the foreign born were among the first to be discharged.

From all directions came calls for help. On the West Coast all groups ineligible for citizenship (Chinese, Japanese, etc.) were automatically excluded from relief work. In Harlem, New York, a special conference (at which Dwight Morgan was one of the speakers) was called to see what could be done for Negroes from the West Indies who had been dropped from the WPA. New York City, after the Fish amendment was passed, at once dismissed seventy-six non-citizens from the Emergency Relief Bureau. In New York State, 17,000, many of whom had filed their first citizenship papers, were discharged from relief projects.

The issue of *The Foreign Born* for November, 1937, devoted half of its ten pages to "The Foreign Born and Relief." At the top of the first page was the story of Mrs. Rose Hurkin. She was less than a year old when she was brought to the United States in 1902. In 1926 she married a naturalized American citizen and assumed that this made her a citizen. She took a WPA job in "Pre-School Recreation Project #6097" after her husband deserted her, in order to support her two children, an eleven-year-old invalid and a seven-year-old. When she learned that she was not a citizen and was liable to be dropped from the WPA, she immediately filed her application for citizenship. A week later she was discharged—just one of 17,000.

Some of the results of the Fish amendment were quite unexpected. They might be ludicrous as an illustration of the boomerang effect of prejudice, were the direct effects not so tragic. In Fall River, Massachusetts, Chief Black Hawk of the Mohawk Indians was dropped from the WPA rolls! In New

Mexico, Spanish-speaking American-born farmers found themselves facing starvation when they could not show records of their American birth. Other restrictive bills also had unforeseen repercussions. Alaska tried to restrict certain of its fisheries to residents of Alaska and some thousands of American citizens found their livelihood endangered. Secretary of War, Harry Woodring, asked for a bill excluding non-citizens in the Canal Zone from "skilled, technical, clerical, administrative and supervisory" jobs. But the Republic of Panama protested that this was contrary to their "Good Neighbor" treaty, and the Canal officials said that they would be unable to keep the Canal open since trained American citizens were not available. The appropriation for the Bureau of Narcotics could not, by vote of Congress, be used to employ foreigners; and the effectiveness of the Bureau was threatened until a ruling was made that informers were not "employed"; the Bureau merely purchased information from them. Such items were systematically publicized by the ACPFB as a part of its campaign of education.

A bulletin entitled *Restrictions on the Economic Rights of Non-Citizens,* which displayed on the cover the words of Chief Justice Charles Evans Hughes: "They cannot live where they cannot work," listed by states the occupations forbidden to non-citizens. Illinois had the longest list (seventeen) including plumbers, life insurance agents, bank directors, pilots, certified shorthand reporters and undertakers. Almost all states barred non-citizens from becoming doctors and dentists, at a time when the country was admittedly ill-attended medically, and from holding liquor licenses. Other forms of discrimination were briefly mentioned in the pamphlet's introduction. In some sections of the country non-citizens were denied the right to acquire or inherit land; they were refused old-age benefits, blind assistance, etc.; they were charged higher fees than citizens for state hunting and fishing licenses; they were excluded from government low-rent housing projects and from work in certain so-called defense industries. There was widespread firing of non-citizens in many industries unconnected with defense, and many employers consistently refused to hire non-citizens at all.

In 1940-41 the fear of a war which seemed more and more inevitable heightened the emotional motive for discrimination. The government and even private industries very remotely, if at all, connected with armaments began to fire non-citizens. One plant fired all who were heard talking on the premises in any language other than English. In April, 1940, the ACPFB press service reported that various automobile plants in Detroit had dismissed non-citizens; in June, the Chrysler plant followed suit. In Chicago, in June, the Eitel Restaurant chain fired non-citizens; in July, the New Haven Clock Company and the Winchester Repeating Arms Company of Connecticut; in August, the Remington-Rand Company.

Italian-Americans were especially suspect and a particular target. *These United States* carried on July 12, 1940, a paragraph headed "Hysteria Against Italians in America," and devoted its final page to a "Warning to the American People" against unfounded prejudice:

> From all sides are to be heard unfounded and prejudice-inciting charges against Italians in America. Collaborating in this un-American campaign to stimulate hysteria have been the press, radio and certain war-minded individuals in public life. . . .
>
> We feel that it is imperative at this time to point out that those who will suffer most from these public incitations to hysteria will be American citizens, the children of immigrants, born in this country.
>
> Americans of Italian birth have displayed a devotion to the democratic ideals of our American government which cannot be questioned, except by those who are intent upon creating a war hysteria which would destroy the rights of all the American people. The Italian immigrant in America is today as much a part of the American people as any other group, ranging from the descendants of the first immigrants who came here on the Mayflower to the most recent newcomers to our shores.
>
> Any attempt to stimulate or spread discrimination

against Americans of foreign birth or of foreign parentage is un-American and endangers the democratic foundations of our society. The Italians, and all other immigrant groups in America, have time and again shown their devotion to our democracy and their readiness to defend their adopted country. Unless complete economic and democratic rights are maintained for the foreign born, no American can feel secure in his rights. The United States Constitution and our American traditions must apply to every one within this country or it can apply to no one.

We feel that any aspersions upon the character or loyalty of those of immigrant stock, whether by any so-called leader of foreign birth or any American hiding behind the flag of war patriotism, contradicts our American tradition of equality, tolerance and understanding.

As in every other aspect of the defense of the rights of the foreign born, condemnation of discrimination in employment came from many sources. Even in 1937-40, it was not the exclusive prerogative of the ACPFB. But the Committee, working specifically with the foreign born and co-ordinating the opinions and activities of other groups and of individuals, had a special function.

In its Press Service, as a part of the "general campaign of education" pledged in 1937, the Committee gave national publicity to the words of Governor Davey of Ohio, "The idea that aliens who are hungry cannot be given a crust of bread is repulsive" and to the comment on those words of the *St. Louis Post Dispatch* of February 16, 1938:

Governor Davey has taken a logical and humane attitude. The foreign born have contributed a great deal to this country. Those now in need are banned only by the national situation from continuing as workers and consumers. A country that has generously contributed to the needy in Belgium, China, India and elsewhere will not let its own inhabitants starve. To discriminate against resident aliens in the necessities of life is unthinkable.

Another Press Release quoted, from the *Congressional Record* of June 6 in the same year, an excerpt from an address by Congressman Celler:

> I am thinking particularly of the 4,000,000 elderly people who came here years ago, when this country was glad to have foreigners for hard manual labor at low wages. Many of them came; they worked hard and many of them put off naturalization. Now they find they are discriminated against at every turn they attempt. It is almost impossible for them to get jobs in private industry or with the government because they are not legally citizens. They are almost completely barred from WPA employment; they face steadily augmented threats to bar them from relief; they are denied old-age pensions in many states. In California, courts recently denied citizenship to aged applicants on the ground that their only purpose was to become eligible for old-age pensions. Most of these persons have done valuable work in helping to build this country. They have supported and educated families of good citizens; they have paid taxes; many of them even served their country in war—but that did not make them citizens.

In this educational publicity campaign, the Committee took care to emphasize especially facts of a kind not generally stressed. Again and again bulletins called attention to the small proportion of foreign born on the relief rolls and the relation of this proportion to the percentage of foreign born in the total population; or emphasized the number of native-born dependents whom the foreign born supported. The statement of Harry Hopkins, aide of President Roosevelt and an authority on social welfare, that more than 160,000 American citizens, mostly children, would be affected if certain non-citizen groups were denied relief, was prominently displayed.

By the end of 1940, the country's need for increased production strongly re-inforced the protest against anti-foreign prejudice. In September, 1940, the Committee bulletin could quote

Attorney General Jackson, who had written to Gen. Robert Wood, of Sears, Roebuck, to warn against the discharging of non-citizens:

> It would create a grave national problem if the employers of this country, in any great number, were to decide to discriminate against the aliens who happen to be working for them. . . . Aliens are ineligible for many, if not all, forms of public relief. To deprive them of their employment, therefore, is often to deprive them and their dependents of their sole means of livelihood and to leave them helpless. It is important for all American citizens to remember that probably a numerical majority of the aliens in this country are related by blood or marriage to American citizens and in large numbers of cases constitute their sole means of support. A blanket discrimination against aliens not only violates the American sense of fairness but frequently constitutes in its practical effect discrimination against American citizens.

In February, 1941, Philip Murray, president of the CIO, specifically reminded all affiliated bodies that there was no law which required the firing of non-citizens. If a special job in any plant were restricted, the union should insist that the non-citizens be transferred to other work in the same plant. The ACPFB promptly wrote to Mr. Murray expressing approval and support of his stand. As a matter of fact, high officials in the United States government and in labor unions were saying in 1941 what the ACPFB had been saying for years:

> Whereas . . . The unity of native and foreign born is essential in winning economic security for the American people.
>
> Resolved: That we, representatives of 110 organizations . . . are unalterably opposed to all discriminatory measures and practices. . . . That we support the program of the American Committee for Protection of Foreign Born for full economic, social and political equality for the foreign born

> in the United States. (Resolution passed at the 1939 Annual Conference.)

When the 1941 Annual Conference of the ACPFB was held in March, the letter of greeting sent by the Chairman, Carey McWilliams, who was unable to be present, still called for "courage, energy and clear thinking" to oppose "every manifestation of prejudice, bigotry and intolerance." The Summary Resolution passed by the Conference declared:

> We call to the attention of the American people the grave dangers to our democratic rights created by the existence of widespread discrimination against the foreign born. One of the factors contributing to aggravate the general situation has been during the past year a fundamental reversal of the policy of the Roosevelt Administration in dealing with the problem of the foreign born in the United States.
>
> Non-citizens are being dismissed from their jobs in both defense and non-defense industries in all sections of the country as part of the campaign to weaken and destroy trade unions and labor organizations. In many industries, naturalized citizens are denied jobs, and even native-born Americans cannot secure employment unless their parents were born in this country.

Discrimination against the foreign born in industry still existed and had to be vigorously opposed. But the Conference Proceedings viewed as a whole showed plainly that such discrimination was no longer one of the major problems facing the Committee. At the beginning of 1941 Curt Swinburn, the secretary of the ACPFB at that time, announced a tour to include Pennsylvania, Ohio, Michigan, Illinois and Wisconsin with the special purpose of investigating discrimination in employment in various parts of the country. But already the situation was changing and the tour was never made.

8. What Price Citizenship?

As discrimination against non-citizens increased, applications for citizenship increased proportionately. But the foreign born, facing the complicated procedures they had to undergo, could only draw the reasonable implication that they were unwanted. The process of initiation into citizenship seemed calculated to arouse fear rather than enthusiasm.

The fee for naturalization had been reduced in 1934 from $20 to $10 with a minimum of $7.50 in special cases. But even $7.50 for many non-citizens meant a dangerous hole in the family food budget. Also, according to statistics in an article by Harold Field in the *Quarterly Journal of Economics* of May, 1939, additional expenses incurred for necessary documents or for bringing the witnesses needed, etc., made the average cost from $20 to $40; and in some cases expenses were as high as $100. The general concern with the cost of naturalization was reflected in the inquiries sent to the ACPFB, one of which was included in a series of question and answer sheets issued by the Committee in 1937-38, in an effort to help immigrants overcome the obstacles to citizenship:

> Q. Will you please tell me if the bill to reduce the naturalization fees, introduced by Congressman Emanuel Celler in the last session of Congress has become a law?
>
> A. Unfortunately this bill did not pass Congress and therefore did not become law. This bill and similar ones

> will have to be introduced again when the next Congress meets.

The Committee advocated a uniform fee of $2.00, and Representative Celler repeatedly introduced a bill for the $2.00 fee.

Two bulletins by the Committee in May and December, 1936, deal with other barriers to citizenship. The literacy test was especially difficult for the older people (about 50% of the non-citizens were over 45) who had entered the country before a literacy test was required. Another question and answer indicate this:

> Q. My mother is unable to read or write any language. Is there any way whereby she can become a citizen?
>
> A. Under the present requirements, she cannot become a citizen unless she knows how to read or write. There is a bill in Congress, introduced by Representative James J. Lanzetta, which, if passed, will do away with the literacy test requirement for those over 50 years of age and who entered the United States when more than 30 years old.

The 1936 bulletin reminds its readers that, in 1906, Congressman Cochran of New York had argued:

> The men who can pass the [literacy] test are not men who will work at manual labor for $1.50 a day. . . . Do we need additional competition in these fields [where "intellectual attainments" are profitable]? On the other hand we cannot have enough men to wield the pick and shovel.

It was not fair to penalize in 1936 the kind of immigrant which the country had explictly preferred thirty years before. The requisite mastery of spoken English worked hardship for some whose occupations gave them little opportunity to hear and use it. As a spokesman for a group of Greek fishermen in Florida put it, "Unfortunately the fish do not talk English to us."

Lack of money for the fee or lack of sufficient knowledge of

English were not the only barriers. However carefully the applicant mastered the information in the Committee's pamphlet on citizenship, there was always a chance of a trick question: "How many stars are there on a quarter?" "How many legs has the Constitution?"

There were also ideas and actions which brought rejection. Christ Popoff of Syracuse is referred to in several Committee publications as "the man who knew too much." The first time he applied for citizenship the judge refused his application because of his lack of information and his poor English. He went home, continued to support his family and studied English and the history of the United States. He was also one of the leaders in a local strike. He came back to the judge a year later, speaking English easily, quoting the Declaration of Independence, Thomas Jefferson and Abraham Lincoln. "Didn't you lead a strike?" asked the judge. The answer was "Yes." "Now you know too much. Application denied," was the decision.

Judge Wayne Borah of Louisiana in 1936 denied citizenship to four men on relief on the ground that "the high privilege [of citizenship] requires . . . of the applicant obligations of allegiance and service and *financial* support to the body politic by way of taxation." One of the four men had entered the country in 1899 and had never had any form of relief until September, 1934, when he fell ill. The other three were married and had American-born children. The ACPFB promptly published in its bulletin a vigorous protest by Ernest L. Meyer, columnist for the *New York Post,* against Judge Borah's ruling:

> Judge Borah has said, "Admission to citizenship under these circumstances in my judgment would do violence to the immigrant laws."
>
> In my opinion the only violence that has been done is to the conscience of America, if it still has a conscience. To deny citizenship to an alien on relief is a greater crime than to kick out of one's own home a grandfather who after a century of hard work is unable to contribute to the family stewpot. . . .

> They [the aliens] manned our steel mills. They dug our ditches. They sweated in slaughter houses and fertilizer plants. They laid rails, hewed the forests and delved in the deserts. They worked ungodly hours for little pay. They contributed far more to the westward expansion of America than Wall Street did with its bullion.
>
> The decision of Judge Borah of New Orleans means that we place human flesh on a lower level than horse flesh. When a farmer's spring and summer planting and plowing and cultivation are over, and when the long winter sets in, the farmer does not turn his horses into the blizzard because they can no longer contribute to the upkeep of his farm. He feeds the horses, knowing that as good servants they are worthy of their oats during the lean months.

Mr. Meyer's metaphor may not "run on all fours," but he makes his objection to the decision clear.

The Committee also initiated practical and immediate action. With the cooperation of the ACLU and the Foreign Language Information Service, a New Orleans local committee was formed to secure a reversal of the decision. A re-hearing was granted and all four men became American citizens. The reversal in New Orleans of course affected decisions on similar applications throughout the country.

To help the foreign born to a somewhat clearer understanding of the intricacies of the naturalization laws, the Committee in 1937-38 published bi-monthly with its press service a sheet of questions on various problems chosen from the thousands of inquiries received by the Committee, together with answers and suggestions for proper action, such as those already quoted. Many of the foreign language newspapers translated these sheets regularly and printed them for the use of their readers.

A few more samples from the questions and answers service will show how complex and harassing had become the problems posed for the immigrant. In many instances it was not the spirit, the love of country, devotion to liberty and democracy, or even the sanctity of the family unit, but an arbitrary date that made the whole difference between citizenship and non-citizenship.

> Q. I entered the United States as a seaman in 1920. I served in the National Guard for two years. Do I automatically become an American citizen?
>
> A. Your service in the National Guard does not make you a citizen automatically. It appears that your entry was an illegal one. However, since you entered prior to June 3, 1921, and you resided in the United States continuously ever since, you may apply for a certificate of registry with a money order of $10 made out to the Commissioner of Immigration and Naturalization, Washington, D.C., and also two photographs, size 2 by 2 inches.
>
> Q. I am entitled to citizenship on my father's papers since I came to this country at the age of eight years and my father was then a citizen. However, they refuse to issue my papers until I produce my birth certificate. I come from a small town in Russia where all records were destroyed during the war, making it impossible for me to secure a birth certificate. What shall I do?
>
> A. If you show proof that a birth certificate cannot be secured, it may be substituted by two affidavits from individuals who were present at the birth or who know exactly when and where you were born. Notarized affidavits from abroad are acceptable, but affidavits from American citizens are preferred.
>
> Q. I came to the United States illegally in 1920, but I never left the United States since that date. In 1921 I married an American citizen and in 1926 my husband died. Will you please tell me if I am considered an American citizen?
>
> A. Regardless of your illegal entry, you are an American citizen because you married an American citizen before September 22, 1922.

As these questions show, if aliens were to be encouraged to become citizens, the process needed to be made simpler and less expensive. Vito Marcantonio put it much more bluntly: "It is not fair play to make it almost impossible for the immigrant to become naturalized and then starve him because he is not naturalized. This is not patriotism; it is just plain rotten." (*I Vote My Conscience,* p. 95)

From the beginning of its existence the ACPFB had given help to those who had difficulties in becoming naturalized. The Committee's own proposals for amendment of the naturalization laws were stated in the bulletin for December, 1936:

> The maximum fee to be $2.00.
>
> Every man or woman who has resided continuously in the United States for two years and has reached the age of twenty-one to be eligible for citizenship.
>
> The petition to include [only] full name, place of residence, occupation and date and place of birth.
>
> No person to be denied naturalization because of membership in any organization, trade union or otherwise; or because of his social or political beliefs or activities; or because of his race or national origin.

These are the most sweeping naturalization reforms the Committee ever advocated. Later proposals show more regard for the limits of possibility.

The call to the 1938 Conference phrased it: "Amend the naturalization laws by reducing the fees, by moderating the educational requirements and by abolishing discrimination on the ground of race and economic opinion." The 1940 Conference passed a specific resolution against denying citizenship to those who hold views which "a citizen is permitted to hold and profess," and approval was voted for several bills already before Congress: Celler's $2 Naturalization Fee Bill, Marcantonio's bill for naturalization of Filipinos living in the United States, bills eliminating the educational requirements for certain groups, and a bill forbidding the denial of citizenship to those on relief.

Also in May, 1937, in response to the increased demand for assistance, a special Naturalization Aid Service was established which continued to function until 1952. This Service filled out and filed documents, answered questions by letter or in personal interview, helped in getting the necessary evidence for derivative citizenship, etc. A report made at the 1941 Conference states that from May to December 1937, the Naturalization Aid Service of the Committee aided 680 foreign born to become citizens; in 1938, the number was 1,234. In 1940 more than 8,000 personal interviews were given, and 1,000 more people were given help by mail. The Service that year filled out and filed 2,000 applications.

An office folder from this period testifies to various activites of the ACPFB Naturalization Aid Service. It contains requests for copies of application forms: "One hundred copies of Form A2214 and fifty amendment sheets," "Fifty copies of A2213 and A2214." There are letters to Mr. Muller of the Immigration and Naturalization Service in New York City asking for information about the status of individual applications. A letter of April, 1938, and another of the next February report that claims were being made to the foreign born by unscrupulous individuals of their ability to get quick action on naturalization applications through personal connections with immigration officials. (One photographer asked $35 for such service.) A sheet giving information on repatriation was sent to Mr. Muller for his comment. And three copies of the pamphlet, *How to Become an American Citizen,* were sent to him immediately after its publication in December, 1938.

One of the greatest services rendered the non-citizen by the ACPFB was this pamphlet. It was necessary to reprint it with slight changes in 1939 and 1940. Approving letters and orders for copies came from all parts of the country. "All [the men and women] in our citizenship class want copies" (Iowa); an "excellent service to ourselves and our readers" (Ohio); "a great help to our club and a great benefit to us" (New Jersey). In 1941 the pamphlet was re-issued as revised by Attorney Irving Schwab with the help of Irving Novick, and it was revised again in 1944 and in 1946 by Attorney Carol King.

The purpose of the pamphlet as stated on the inside cover of the first edition was "to encourage and aid non-citizens in this country eligible for citizenship to become citizens." It stated (in the early editions in very simple language) the necessary procedures in making application for citizenship and summarized the pertinent legislation. The last six pages gave, under the heading "Educational Requirements," the questions and answers which had been prepared by the WPA Naturalization Service as likely to be asked in the examination. They begin with "What is our form of government?" and end with "What is the meaning of E Pluribus Unum?"

Congress made few changes in the law to ease the problem of naturalization but the Immigration and Naturalization Service did simplify the naturalization procedures, and aliens in increasing numbers became citizens, thanks in part to the activity of the ACPFB.

9. Dwight C. Morgan

THROUGH all the pressures and difficulties and discouragements with which attempts to defend the rights of the foreign born were beset from 1933 to 1938, Dwight C. Morgan, the executive secretary of the ACPFB, had directed the work of the Committee. He had brought the ACPFB to a position of widely recognized influence and effectiveness. He had kept it true to its original purpose. He had neither slackened work after defeat nor rested after victory. But there is a limit to a man's endurance of such intense and unremitting effort. On January 12, 1939, Dwight Morgan died.

The 1939 Annual Conference of the ACPFB was held in February, according to the program which Dwight Morgan had prepared. On its first page, the Souvenir Journal of the Conference carried Dwight Morgan's picture with a hurriedly prepared and all too brief account of his life and work. "Dwight C. Morgan came from the heart of the American people to serve patiently and well the cause of democracy and equality, to fight with all his strength against discrimination and oppression." Perhaps this first sentence really tells the whole story.

His father, James Fletcher Morgan, was born in Raymond, Illinois, and later went to Colorado, where he worked as a hard-rock miner and contractor. He met and married Sarah Bertha Case of Ottawa, Kansas, towards the end of the last century. Dwight Morgan was born on February 10, 1900, in Cripple Creek, Colorado. He was educated in the Colorado public schools. At the age of twenty-one he went to work with his father in the mines. Two years later he was off to Kansas to work on a farm, and from there to Pennsylvania where he worked in the coal mines. For a while he toured the country with a group of actors, presenting Shakespeare to small town audiences, an experience which must have added to "the rich acquaintance with the life of the American people" of which the Committee account spoke. Further information is lacking since Dwight Morgan was too little concerned with himself to leave a record of autobiographical details.

One of his contemporaries on the Committee remembers that his special interest in the treatment of the foreign born developed after the firing in 1932 of the non-citizen workers in New York City hospitals, and the attempt to replace them with citizens at lower pay. The Hospital Workers League had demanded re-instatement of those discharged, the abolition of the last wage cut and the establishment of the eight-hour day. Dwight Morgan was struck by the close connection between discrimination against the foreign born and the intolerable working conditions for the native born—apart from the welfare of the hospital patients.

Dwight Morgan continued to be deeply concerned with the plight of the foreign born and, by the time the ACPFB was organized in 1933, his experience in the field and his well-known ability made him an obvious choice as the Committee's first executive secretary. For the ensuing six years he "devoted himself diligently and tirelessly to building and strengthening the organized movement for the defense of the rights and the welfare of the foreign born in the United States," as the Committee biography stated. He planned the work of the Committee. He led the campaign against the deportation of the foreign born. He strove to establish the right of asylum especially for refugees from Hitler and Mussolini. He fought against the denial of relief to non-citizens and for lower naturalization costs and fairer naturalization procedures. He defended or attacked before committees of the House and Senate legislation which would affect the rights of the foreign born. He spoke whenever opportunity was offered to spread knowledge of the unfair treatment accorded to foreign-born Americans. He wrote articles for periodicals and letters to individuals. He prepared leaflets and pamphlets to aid the foreign born in meeting their difficulties and to inform the general public of the treatment accorded to the foreign born. At the time of his death, he was preparing material for a book which would cover the history and contributions to American culture of the different immigrant groups in the United States.

With all that, he carried the burden of the administrative work of the ACPFB and kept the Committee consistently on the course originally set, as "an independent non-partisan body" whose purpose was always and only "to secure equal rights for the foreign born in the United States." Somehow, the executive secretary managed to project, plan and carry out the activities of the Committee on an organizational budget so low it never merited that label. The secret of how an organization can function without funds is known only to the dedicated and seems to be based on the general principle of "Act first, and worry about financing later." For the dedicated it often works but at great cost in time, energy and human toll. And somehow, Dwight Morgan also managed to exist personally on the pittance he received irregularly from the barely existent funds of the Committee.

Words of personal sorrow and appreciation came from many outside the Committee who had known of his work. From Roger Baldwin, director of the ACLU:

> I have rarely seen in public life a man as devoted and as selfless in his chosen work as Dwight C. Morgan. . . . [He] had our entire confidence through his tactfulness, his scrupulous attention to detail, and his conscientious devotion to every case he handled. Such men are rare in any public cause.

From Anna Damon, secretary of the ILD:

His quiet, modest but tireless devotion to the cause of justice was truly an inspiration to all those who worked with him.

From Harold E. Fey, executive secretary of the Fellowship of Reconciliation:

We unite with all those who are determined that this life so sacrificially given, will live on in new courage and determination, that those rights for which he died shall live.

From Vito Marcantonio:

[Morgan was] outstanding in the many battles for the protection of the foreign born.

From Rosika Schwimmer:

I am deeply grieved by the loss of this fine and spirited worker for those who can ill afford to lose such a disinterested, indefatigable champion of their cause.

From David Clendenin, secretary-treasurer of the Workers Defense League:

The news of Dwight C. Morgan's untimely death came as a great shock to all of us who for years have known his untiring and single-minded devotion to the task of making America a haven of refuge. . . . His passing leaves a sorry gap, and one that we must do our best to fill.

From the National Executive Committee of the Russian Section of the International Workers Order:

[He] was one who devoted his life to the great principles of American democracy. We, as foreign born, particularly feel the loss of this man who devoted his life to

> protecting and advancing the interests of all the foreign born in America.

From Julius Loeb, vice-chairman of the American Friends of the Chinese People:

> His fight for the rights of the Chinese, as well as other foreign born people in this country, will always be remembered with deep reverence by members of the American Friends of the Chinese People and by all Chinese friends.

From Lewis Alan Berne, International president of the Federation of Architects, Engineers, Chemists and Technicians:

> We wish to testify to the high esteem in which we held [his] work and the work of your Committee. We have followed this work for several years and have been gratified by the excellent contributions made by Mr. Morgan. We feel that his death removes from the American scene an outstanding champion of the principles which we all hold dear.

From Bertel J. McCarty, International Secretary of the International Woodworkers of America:

> The International Woodworkers of America are deeply grieved at the untimely death of Dwight C. Morgan. The laboring men and women of our organization are grateful for an opportunity to pay tribute to this man and the important work for which he gave his life.

The ACPFB fully recognized the greatness of its loss when Dwight Morgan died and gave public expression to that recognition, both at the 1939 Annual Conference of the Committee and in its Souvenir Journal already quoted. The Conference was opened by the chairman, Rev. Herman Reissig, with these words:

> This Conference meets today in both a shadow and a

> light. It meets in the shadow cast by the death of our dear friend, Secretary of the Committee, Dwight C. Morgan. . . . All of us who are concerned with the welfare and problems of the foreign born and therefore because of that concern with the problems of American democracy—will deeply miss Dwight Morgan. Most of you who are here this afternoon knew him and knew well his selfless devotion as well as his ability, and those of us who did not know him personally will nevertheless miss his guiding spirit. But we meet also in a light because devotion and ability such as Dwight Morgan's always cast a light upon the road.

Marquita Villard who had worked closely with Dwight Morgan also spoke briefly:

> Every foreign-born person, and every friend of Dwight C. Morgan, has suffered a tragic loss in his untimely death, for his life was richly fruitful, and it is by his work that he did in behalf of the foreign born that he would be remembered. His was a self-sacrificing nature; to save some person from deportation and persecution, to fight for the rights of the foreign born, was to him its own reward. He gave not only his time and energy, but a personal devotion, inspiring hope and confidence—qualities that count in human terms. His welcome and hospitality made the Committee a real haven of refuge to the oppressed of other lands on American soil. And so Dwight Morgan leaves a challenge to all who work for the protection of the foreign born, to all believers in democracy, to the foreign born themselves, to carry on in the same spirit of selflessness and courage as much as every individual is able.

To each division into which work fell, Morgan devoted the same steady ardor. On the educational side, he made his most successful contribution with a pamphlet, *The Foreign Born in the United States,* followed two years later by *How to Become an American Citizen.*

When Rev. Herman Reissig thanked and paid tribute to

Irving Novick, the assistant secretary, "who very suddenly and without any warning at all was left with the direction of the office of the ACPFB" at the death of Morgan, and had become acting secretary, "carrying on that work splendidly in the interim," Mr. Novick replied by prefacing his summary speech at the end of the Conference with these remarks:

> Friends, much to my sorrow, I have to act as Acting Secretary because I can be assistant to none. I have been associated with Morgan, as you know, from the beginning when this organization was formed. I have not yet gotten over the shock and I am in no position to speak about Morgan. But the work must be carried on. There's no use crying. We have to carry on. So in tribute to Morgan we will do much better if instead of crying—a thing which he never believed in—we carry on the work that he started to organize, founded, a job the surface of which has not yet been scratched. . . .
>
> Morgan did more than his share towards the formation of [this] organization and [gave more] than his fair contribution. To replace him we'll need more than one. We are meeting now day and night to find an individual who can take his place. With all the recommendations, we couldn't find anyone as yet. So I say it will need more than one to replace him, and to support this organization.

The statement of the Committee itself, appearing in the Souvenir Journal, gave expression to the greatness of the loss for all: foreign born citizens and non-citizens, victims and their defense attorneys, leadership and active workers, sponsors and well-wishers.

> The foreign born lost a true and devoted friend and democracy a staunch defender in the untimely death of Dwight C. Morgan. . . . He wanted to see discrimination and oppression wiped out of the American scene. He extended a helping hand to those facing deportation and persecution in their homeland. He fought the denial of

relief to non-citizens. He appeared before many meetings of the House and Senate Committee on Immigration to voice support or disapproval of legislation affecting the foreign born.

A father facing separation from his family or being in this country illegally, a non-citizen worker arrested on the picket line or threatened with the loss of his job, an immigrant finding it difficult to understand all of the many ramifications of the naturalization laws—all of these people found in Dwight C. Morgan a ready listener, a friend and an adviser.

One could go on almost endlessly speaking of the many humanitarian activities into which Dwight C. Morgan entered. It would indeed be difficult to portray the spirit that was Dwight C. Morgan. It will be practically impossible to replace that spirit in this vitally important field of work, the defense of the rights of the foreign born. With a singleness of purpose, Mr. Morgan devoted himself tirelessly to the exercise of his duties as Secretary of the ACPFB, giving of his time and energies without stint or personal consideration.

Dwight C. Morgan's greatest contribution, perhaps, to the general movement for the defense of the foreign born was his keeping the movement from being sectarian or extremist, and helping it win the widest possible support among both native born and foreign born. At the same time, with a clear vision and understanding, in all his writings and his work, he showed plainly that he was fighting not only for the rights of the non-citizen and the naturalized citizen but for the native-born American as well. As an example, in *The Foreign Born in the United States* he said:

"Every defense of a worker held for deportation, every struggle against discrimination, every part of the fight for equal rights for the foreign born will help to maintain and extend the democratic rights of the native born."

Dwight C. Morgan is dead. It depends upon us who remain to see to it that the spirit that actuated his life and his work does not die, that the cause to which he gave his life continues to grow and become strong until such time

> as discrimination and persecution is wiped out of our country and our laws. To this goal, given to us by the unselfishness and devotion of the man, Dwight C. Morgan, we who remain dedicate ourselves. We shall continue to fight, we shall continue to organize the American people for the defense and advancement of the rights and welfare of the foreign born, to insure the continuation and the flowering of American democracy for both, the native and the foreign born.

This pledge has been kept. The ACPFB has continued to fight for the rights and welfare of the foreign born. The national situation and the international situation have altered, and the Committee's methods of work have altered correspondingly. But its fundamental purpose has not altered. And although the Committee has moved its offices four times since 1939, the photograph of Dwight C. Morgan still hangs on its office wall.

10. Vigilant Against Injustice

THE loss of the individual, serious as it may be, cannot halt a movement that is genuinely concerned with the pressing needs of masses of people and has a program to meet those needs. The determination reiterated by those who paid tribute to Dwight Morgan to carry on the work to which he had devoted himself was in itself a recognition of the necessity of that work. The determination has persisted and remains a most eloquent testimony to the character of the man and of the work he did.

While Dwight Morgan was still secretary, the work of the Committee had become widely known and had gained enough general support to make a more formal organization necessary. In the Call for the General Conference of October 1937, which effected such an organization, only "acting officers" are listed: Dwight Morgan, acting secretary, and with him, Irving Novick Wallace Spradling, Ann Lord and Lillian Apotheker.

At the Conference, held at the Irving Plaza in New York City and attended by 339 delegates from 221 organizations, the Rev. Herman F. Reissig was elected chairman. After a report on the work hitherto done by the Committee had been given by Dwight Morgan, the Conference elected fifteen members to the Executive Committee. A publication of July, 1936, listed six officers: Rev. Reissig, chairman; Miss Marquita Villard, vice-chairman; Morgan, secretary; Spradling, assistant secretary; Novick, treasurer; Abner Green, publicity. It also listed an Advisory Board of twenty-three, including: Louis Adamic, Roger N.

Baldwin, Dr. Harry Elmer Barnes, Rabbi Philip Bernstein, Heywood Broun, Winifred L. Chappell, Prof. George S. Counts, Anna Damon, Prof. John Dewey, Donald S. Friede, Rev. John Haynes Holmes, Sidney Howard, Inez Haynes Irwin, Rabbi Edward L. Israel, Walter Lowenfels, Carol King, Prof. Robert Morss Lovett, Hon. Vito Marcantonio, Bishop Francis J. McConnell, Prof. Bernhard J. Stern, Irving Schwab, Isaac Shorr and L. Hollingsworth Wood.

By 1938 a rather complicated "Structure of Organization" had been elaborated, providing for an Executive Committee, an Advisory Board and a Delegated Body. The Executive Committee would have the power to elect the six officers and to determine policy, subject to the approval of the Delegated Body and the Advisory Board. Any organization interested in the work of the Committee could become affiliated and entitled to send delegates on payment of a fee (the minimum was set at $3, for larger organizations it would be calculated at three cents per member). Individuals could become supporting members for a $1 a year or sustaining members for $10. Such members would be invited to attend the meetings of the Delegated Body and might speak but not vote.

This scheme was never actually put into effect. Various parts of it were tried, and simplifying modifications were offered from time to time. A much simpler Constitution was presented to the 1940 Annual Conference and was adopted. It was amended in 1941, and a few minor changes have been made more recently. But the declared purpose of the organization remained unchanged. Dwight Morgan had given it one of the briefest and clearest formulations ever made: "To win the fight for equal rights for the foreign born in the United States."

At the 1940 Annual Conference "Affiliated Organizations" were eliminated—the plan had never worked satisfactorily. Independent local groups in various parts of the country had cooperated with the Committee and used its material; but such groups were not interested in "affiliation." Labor unions had established their own committees on naturalization and immigration, which also made use of the material published by the Committee; but they saw no reason to "affiliate." Chairman Reissig in his report of the year's work stressed the fact that all the cooperating groups had full autonomy.

In the new Constitution and adopted unanimously by the Conference, the ultimate authority rested in the Annual Conference. Between Conferences, the Board of Directors (not less than fifteen nor more than thirty) elected by the Conference exercised that authority. They filled vacancies in their own membership, employed the office staff, raised and spent money. They chose the Sponsors. They had power to organize sub-committees. The Board of Directors, meeting after the 1940 Conference, elected Carey McWilliams as chairman of the ACPFB; Attorney Pearl Hart, of Chicago, and Dr. Max Yergan, of the College of the City of New York and director of the International Committee on African Affairs, as vice-chairmen; and continued Curt Swinburn as secretary, Irving Novick as Naturalization Director, and Abner Green in charge of publicity.

The proceedings of the 1940 Conference of the American Committee for Protection of Foreign Born, held in Washington, D. C. on March 2 and 3, are of importance not only for the history of the Committee, but as representative of the best liberal thought of the period just before America's entry into the Second World War. The difference between the effective protests of liberal leaders against the Palmer Raids of 1920 and the disheartening lack of such protest against deportations of the 1930's has already been noted. Defense of the rights of minorities in the 1930's was left largely to those who were directly concerned. By 1940, however, the silence had been broken; outstanding individuals were making their voices heard in defense of America's traditional freedoms and the rights of all residents in the United States.

The work of the ACPFB, of other similar organizations in the various areas of conflict, of many of the labor unions, had contributed to the change. But the chief factor was certainly the changed world situation.

The war in Europe and an increased understanding of the character and aims of "Das Dritte Reich" had inevitable reactions in America. The United States was officially neutral, but in the very proclamation of that neutrality President Roosevelt had declared "even a neutral cannot be asked to close his mind or his conscience" (Link, op. cit. p. 476). Increasingly large numbers of Americans in all parts of the country, faced with Hitler's totalitarianism, were awakened to a realization that democracy and freedom were threatened in America by the same forces which had ended both in Germany.

The success of the 1940 National Conference of the American Committee was one manifestation of this widespread concern. The distinguished speakers at the Conference reflected a responsible public opinion and in the national interest they were eager to give expression to that opinion. The plans for the Conference had been announced the preceding December and had been given prominent and favorable notice by the press. *The New York Times* said editorially of the Committee on December 7, "The American Committee for Protection of Foreign Born deserves non-partisan support." And the *New York World-Telegram* declared in an editorial the same day, "A farsighted and useful movement [is] now getting under way under the name of the American Committee for Protection of Foreign Born. . . . The movement for sanity and decency toward aliens is true Americanism." A sheet displaying clippings from the December 6 and 7 issues of these newspapers was used by the Committee to publicize the Conference. The Conference was attended by 310 delegates from 183 organizations, sixty observers from forty-three other organizations and 163 visitors.

The listing of names does not afford the most exciting reading. But nothing can so well mirror the proud cross-section of American life that responded to the needs of American democracy. The Sponsors included:

Louis Adamic, Dr. Janet Rankin Aiken, Sherwood Anderson, Roger Baldwin, Dr. Harry Elmer Barnes, George

Gordon Battle, Lewis Alan Berne, Prof. Charles A. Beard, Rabbi Philip Bernstein, Mary McLeod Bethune, Alice Stone Blackwell, Dr. Franz Boas, Van Wyck Brooks, Prof. Edwin Berry Burgum, Prof. Walter B. Cannon, Prof. Hadley Cantril, Prof. Edward P. Cheyney, Sarah Cleghorn, Edward Corsi, Howard Costigan, Prof. George S. Counts, Dr. Leonard Covello, Jerome Davis, Prof. John Dewey, John Dos Passos, Prof. Dorothy Douglas, Dr. Harl R. Douglass, Prof. Mildred Fairchild, Dr. Ernst Feise, Waldo Frank, Donald S. Friede, Miguel Garriga, Dr. Frank P. Graham, Sidney Hillman, Rev. John Haynes Holmes, Fannie Hurst, Rev. William Lloyd Imes, Inez Haynes Irwin, Hon. Stanley Isaacs, Rabbi Edward L. Israel, Prof. Charles S. Johnson, Rockwell Kent, Prof. William H. Kilpatrick, Dr. Frank Kingdon, Prof. Otto Klineberg, Prof. Oliver W. Larkin, Dr. William Ellery Leonard, Prof. Max Lerner, Dr. Eduard C. Lindeman, Robert Morss Lovett, Bishop Francis J. McConnell, Dr. Henry N. MacCracken, Dr. Malcolm S. MacLean, Paul Manship, Dr. Alexander Meiklejohn, Dr. Paul Monroe, Dr. Reinhold Niebuhr, Hon. Caroline O'Day, Hon. Culbert L. Olson, O. M. Orton, William Pickens, Ernest B. Price, Prof. Max Radin, A. Philip Randolph, Dr. Walter Rautenstrauch, Reid Robinson, Charles Edward Russell, Monsignor John A. Ryan, Rose Schneiderman, Adelaide Schulkind, Prof. Frederick L. Schuman, Prof. Vida D. Scudder, George Seldes, Dr. Guy Emery Shipler, Vilhjalmur Stefansson, Prof. Bernhard J. Stern, Donald Ogden Stewart, Maxwell S. Stewart, Prof. Harold C. Urey, Carl Van Doren, Oswald Garrison Villard, Dr. J. Raymond Walsh, L. Hollingsworth Wood, Dr. Mary E. Wooley, Charles S. Zimmerman.

The Endorsers included:

Prof. Josephine Truslow Adams, Prof. Thomas Addis, Brooks Atkinson, Emily G. Balch, Tallulah Bankhead, Fortunatus A. Bogacius, Prof. Edwin Borchard, Ohio State Senator William M. Boyd, Dean Ralph J. Bridgeman, Prof. Francis J. Brown, Frank Capra, Prof. Haakon M. Chevalier, Dr. Henry Sloane Coffin, Dr. Ada L. Comstock, Prof. Herbert Davis, Hon. Anthony DiGiovanna, Will Durant, Prof. Horace A. Eaton, Edgar J. Fisher, Osmond K. Fraenkel, Rabbi Solomon B. Freehof, Lewis Bennett, Prof. Christian Gauss, Dr. Roswell G. Ham, Prof. Frank N. Hankins, Prof. Ralph S. Harlow, Prof. Benjamin Harrow, Prof. Melville J. Herskovitz, Dr. Frank Ernest Hill, Prof. Norman E. Hines, Leo Huberman, Prof. Ellsworth Huntington, Dr. Oscar Jaszi, Dr. Charles S. Johnson, Matthew Josephson, Dorothy Kenyon, Alfred Kreymborg, Dr. John Howland Lathrop, Dr. Henry Smith Leiper, Dr. Emil Lengyel, Johanna M. Lindlof, Max Lowenthal, Dr. J. A. MacCallum, Dr. Gerald Machacek, J. Warren Madden, Albert Maltz, Thomas Mann, Prof. H. R. Manuel, Mrs. E. K. Marrow, Hon. P. S. Marthakis, Prof. Kirtley F. Mather, Prof. F. O. Mathiessen, Prof. D. H. Mowrer, Prof. Gardner Murphy, Prof. Alonzo F. Myers, Clifford Odets, Prof. Bernhard Ostrolenk, Prof. Ernest Minor Patterson, Clarence E. Pickett, Hon. Charles Poletti, Prof. Francis A. Preveden, Frederick L. Redefer, Prof. Joseph Slavey Roucek, Prof. Harold Rugg, Prof. Harlow Shapley, Irwin Shaw, Prof. George E. Simpson, Upton Sinclair, Prof. Robert K. Speer, Prof. Hans Otto Storm, Prof. C. Fayette Taylor, Mary Heaton Vorse, Dr. Harry F. Ward, Prof. Colston E. Warne, Max Weber, Prof. Louis Weisnir, Prof. Philip Wheelwright, Rev. Wayne White, Thornton Wilder, Prof. Carl Wittke.

Participants in the various sessions and panel discussions included:

Most Reverend Archbishop Athenagoras, Greek Archdiocese of North and South America.

Dr. L. R. Alderman, United States Office of Education; Harold Fields, New York City Board of Education; Younghill Kang, Metropolitan Museum of Art; Archibald MacLeish, Librarian of Congress; Rev. John Montgomery Cooper, Department of Anthropology of the Catholic University of America, president of the American Anthropological Association; Prof. Bernhard Ostrolink, College of the City of New York.

James B. Carey, Secretary of the CIO; Donald Henderson, president of the United Cannery, Agricultural, Packing and Allied Workers of America; E. S. Oliver, vice-president, Labor's Non-Partisan League.

Attorney Carol King, Secretary of the International Juridical Association; Judge Patrick H. O'Brien, Probate Court, Wayne County, Michigan; Attorney Franklin S. Pollak; Attorney Irving Schwab.

Rep. Emanuel Celler of New York, Rep. John M. Coffee of Washington, Rep. Thomas F. Ford of California, Rep. Lee E. Geyer of California, Rep. Kent E. Keller of Illinois, Rep. John Lesinski of Michigan, Rep. Vito Marcantonio of New York, Rep. Abe Murdock of Utah, Senator James E. Murray of Montana, State Senator Stanley Nowak of Michigan; Senator Claude Pepper of Florida; Rep. Rudolph G. Tenerowicz of Michigan.

Carey McWilliams, California State Commissioner of Immigration and Housing; Hon. Ralph T. Seward, Chairman of the Board of Immigration Review of the Department of Labor.

Edith Terry Bremer, National Institute of Immigration Welfare; Evelyn M. Hershey, executive director of the American Committee for Christian Refugees; John F. Rich, co-director Refugee Section, American Friends Service Committee.

Kenneth G. Crawford, president of the American Newspaper Guild; Erwin Klaus, editor of *The German American.*

Luisa Moreno, Spanish Speaking Peoples Congress; Dr. Charles Petioni, president of the Caribbean Union; Dr. Max Yergan director of the International Committee on African Affairs.

Joseph Cadden, Secretary of the American Youth Congress; Bertha Josselyn Foss, secretary of the National Emergency Conference for Democratic Rights; Max Geline, Wisconsin State Conference on Social Legislation; Dr. John A. Lapp, Chairman of the Chicago Civil Liberties Committee; Ira Latimer, executive secretary of the same; James

Waterman Wise, Research Consultant, Council Against Intolerance in America.

Greetings in the Souvenir Journal came from, among others:

Maritime Federation of the Pacific; United Wholesale and Warehouse Employees of New York; Thomas Durian, president of the International Glove Workers Union of America; General Executive Board of the International Fur and Leather Workers Union; Filipino American Citizenship Council; Cloak and Skirt Makers Union, Local 21; Chilean Workers Club; Alaska Cannery Workers Union, Local 5, CIO; Industrial Union of Marine and Ship Building Workers, CIO; Cafeteria Employees Union, Local 302, AFL; Pocketbook Workers Union; Detroit Fur Workers Union, Local 38; United Locomotive Workers Union; Washable Clothing, Sportswear and Novelty Workers, Local 169; Amalgamated Clothing Workers of America, Local 263; United Electrical Radio and Machine Workers of America, Local 1225; United Shoe Workers, Local 29; Journeymen Tailors Union, Local 1; Bakery and Confectionery Workers International Union, Local 79; Excavators and Building Laborers Union, Local 731; United Shoe Workers, Joint Council 13; Chefs, Cooks, Pastry Cooks and Assistants Union, Local 89; International Ladies Garment Workers of America, Local 144; Playthings and Novelty Workers of America, Local 223; Social Service Employees Union of Chicago; Timber Workers Union, Local 29; United Automobile Workers of America, Local 76; International Jewelry Workers Union, Local 1; Bakers Union, Local 507; Fur Dressers and Dyers Union, Local 140; Ohio League for Constitutional Rights; the Descendants of the American Revolution; the National Religion and Labor Foundation; the Chicago Civil Liberties Committee; Associated Musicians of Greater New York, Local 802; Furriers' Joint Council of New York; the National Emergency Conference for Democratic Rights; *Protestant Digest.*

The printed report of the addresses and discussion at the

Conference with the resolutions approved and the Constitution adopted by the delegates, occupies ninety printed pages. The report is dedicated "To those millions of immigrants from other shores who came to America in search of 'life, liberty and the pursuit of happiness,' whose efforts as part of the American people have been devoted to always insuring the preservation and extension of the democratic provisions of the Bill of Rights and of the Constitution, and who have made an inestimable contribution to the progressive economic, political and cultural and social life of this their adopted land."

The purpose of the ACPFB was explicitly defined at considerable length:

> The purpose of the ACPFB shall be to perpetuate for the foreign born the fundamental American concepts of equality regardless of race, color, nationality, creed or place of birth, and to preserve the fundamental American ideals of liberty and hospitality which serve as guarantees of democracy to all Americans.
>
> The work of the American Committee shall be to promote better relations and understanding between native and foreign born by means of education; to encourage and facilitate naturalization of non-citizens; to prevent discrimination against non-citizens or foreign-born citizens because of their nationality, political, economic or religious belief, or lack of citizenship; to prevent the destruction of American families by the threat of deportation; to maintain the traditional right of asylum for political and religious refugees in the United States; and to actively work for the solution of the problems confronting the foreign born in the United States.
>
> The American Committee shall be a non-partisan body, cooperating with all other organizations interested in any phase or phases of its program.

The content of the Committee's Annual Report amply justified the claim made in the introduction of the need for an organization such as the ACPFB which could devote all its time and energies to the carrying out of these aims. The report presented also the concrete results of the unremitting effort to achieve these aims. But the Conference itself was a significant demonstration of the fruit of the Committee's labor: a mobilization of important segments of American leadership and liberal opinion, to fight each in his own way, or together, for the essence of the program of the ACPFB, in the recognition that to do so was in the real self-interest of the American people as a whole —not simply a philanthropic favor to the foreign born; and in the realization that what was at stake was not merely the rights of a minority but the democratic way of life of all.

The co-chairmen of the Conference were Dr. William Allan Nielson, president emeritus of Smith College, and Ernest Hemingway. President Nielson presided at the first public session whose theme was "Immigration in America." He opened the Conference by reading a greeting from President Roosevelt:

> On the occasion of its Annual Conference, I am glad to greet the ACPFB. It has undertaken the task of assuring fair play to the foreign born within the United States. Every American wishes it success.
>
> Every American takes pride in our tradition of hospitality to men of all races and of all creeds. One of the great achievements of the American commonwealth has been the fact that race groups which were divided abroad are united here. Enmities and antagonisms were forgotten; former opponents met here as friends. Groups which had fought each other overseas here work together; their children intermarry; they have all made contributions to democracy and peace.
>
> Because of the very greatness of this achievement, we must be constantly vigilant against the attack of intolerance and injustice. We must scrupulously guard the civil rights and civil liberties of all citizens, whatever their background. We must remember that any oppression, any injustice, any hatred is a wedge designed to attack our civilization.
>
> If reason is to prevail against intolerance, we must al-

> ways be on guard. We welcome therefore the work to maintain the rights of the foreign born.

Archibald MacLeish read his poem *Colloquy for the States.* Then followed the first address, given by Senator Pepper:

> I do not believe in a witch hunt of Reds or Aliens, or Communists, or Baptists, Methodists, Catholics or anybody else. In certain periods of our history we have had those witch hunts [in 1798, before the Civil War, after the World War].
>
> Today, again, some people are trying to solve the problems of this country not by intelligent study of our problems, but by violent denunciation of a particular minority which they would like to make a scapegoat. . . . The aliens are not justly the scapegoat of our ills. . . .
>
> I am proud, and America is proud of what the alien has contributed to this country. I mean the aliens of each generation, for if we go back we are all aliens except the Indians. . . .
>
> [America has] a rendezvous with Destiny which cannot be kept by witch hunts, by policies based upon blind and unreasoning prejudice, by seeking a scapegoat for . . . our deficiencies.

The contributions made to America by the foreign born were recognized. James B. Carey declared, "A man or woman willing to work is an asset to this country not a liability." Representative Keller stated that we ought to be "big enough to understand that the man who chooses to live here is a better patriot than the man who was born here." Dr. Frank Bohn spoke on the contribution to democracy made by Carl Schurz.

The connection between discrimination against the foreign born and the forces of reaction was emphasized. Judge O'Brien pointed out, "After the World War, discrimination against the non-citizen arose every time reactionary forces attempted to put across political programs."

The relationship between the rights of the non-citizen and

the citizen was explicitly stated. Rep. Lee E. Geyer, in the speech already cited, declared:

> Your Conference meets at a time when non-citizen residents and foreign-born citizens find themselves the objects of discrimination and persecution in this land of traditional asylum. This attack against one section of our population is, as you fully realize, part of a more general drive against the rights and liberties of our own citizens—against democracy itself. . . .
>
> Protection of the rights of all minorities, national and racial as well as religious and political, is fundamental to our concept of democracy. And it is only in a democracy that such rights are recognized and respected. Any weakening, therefore in the general fabric of democracy threatens the citizen and non-citizen who claim protection.

Gardner Jackson was equally emphatic:

> When you have . . . a major dislocation . . . in this country, you are bound to have the representatives of the large interests try to find some scapegoat for their failure to face the economic and social responsibilities. . . .
>
> It is perfectly clear that any infringement on the rights of aliens in this country is a first step toward the infringement of the rights of every citizen. . . . The real pressure we need [in Washington] is to have you in the field to do the job. It is a local job that must be done.

Stanley Nowak stated:

> This attack on aliens is of major importance to all sections of the American people. . . . It constitutes an attack upon the best traditions of our country. These anti-alien measures indicate a rapid growth of fascism.

And James Lundaho, of the United Automobile Workers, Local 190, discussed the legislation before Congress as a means to

"Extend the Bill of Rights to the non-citizens in our midst."

A most relevant speaker at the Conference was Mr. Ralph Seward, Solicitor of the Labor Department, whose subject was "Administrative Proceedings in Deportation and Immigration." (His criticism of the administration of the immigration laws, based on inside experience, should be pondered in relation to the ways of the Department of Justice at a later period.)

Mr. Seward called the procedure "an extreme example of the concentration of great power in an administrative body with limited provision for control over its exercise." He continued,

> If we in the Service do not administer the laws wisely and fairly, few means have been provided by which we can be forced to mend our ways.

He pointed out that the decision of the Secretary of Labor was final, that the courts could review only erroneous interpretation, lack of evidence and "grossly unfair" procedure, and that the limited budget of the Service affected both the number and the qualifications of its personnel. In conclusion, he summarized the three ways in which the Committee appointed for the purpose was endeavoring to improve the Service:

> 1. Increase efficiency to lessen delays and hardships.
> 2. Insure personnel adequate to their responsibilities.
> 3. Make sure of a procedure (fitted) to insure to every alien a fair hearing in the field and a careful review of his case in Washington.

The Committee was further studying means "of divorcing the prosecuting from the judicial functions in department hearings."

Mr. Seward was followed by Edith Terry Bremer, who described the deportation procedures as she knew them:

> Because it has been held that the execution of immigration and deportation laws was "purely an administrative function," important safeguards of the civil rights of individuals which are built into the trial procedures com-

> ing before the courts have not been deemed necessary. . . . In the vast number of cases under investigation there appears to be no one to "defend" the suspected alien. . . .
>
> We have come to take deportations for granted. It is only upon special cases that question and intervention come. But it seems to me that it ought not to be so taken. Is it really "a necessary instrument of government?"
>
> America's sense of civic, national and international responsibility should be brought to bear on the whole system.

The panel on "Citizenship and Education" was chaired by Charles H. Houston of the National Association for Advancement of Colored People (NAACP), and included among other participants Federal Judge William Hastie, then Dean of the Law School of Howard University. The work done in the Americanization schools in New York and by the WPA was described and the need of many more such opportunities was stressed. The discussion bore fruit in connection with the campaign for citizenship which the American Committee undertook later in the year.

The business of the Conference, of which modifying the structure of the organization was a minor part, was centered on the passage of a number of resolutions which were to form the basis of the work of the Committee for the next year. The first group of resolutions adopted dealt with the anti-alien bills before Congress; the second with discrimination and jobs; the third with the right of asylum and the condemnation of all efforts to deport for any reason individuals who "are in danger of death, imprisonment or torture, if sent back to the country of origin." The fourth group was concerned chiefly with reforms in the naturalization laws and administration, but included various miscellaneous matters such as education (more emphasis on different world cultures), anti-German prejudice, etc. The final resolution listed bills before Congress which should be supported. But so impressive had been the presentation at the Conference of the situation of Filipino-Americans—"A Blind

Spot in American Democracy"—that a specific resolution was passed recommending the passage of Marcantonio's bill for the naturalization of Filipinos resident in the United States.

But while the Conference was a glittering reflection of the ability of people of divergent opinions to come together for common objecives, it also revealed a characteristic of liberal circles which was to retard action time and again in the critical years to come. The Conference failed to keep out a divisive note. It voted to reject one resolution which would have declared that the ACPFB was "devoted to the cause of pure democracy and opposed to forces of totalitarianism of all kinds as being essentially undemocratic." The Conference report stated that this resolution was defeated because "it was not germane to the proceedings and not within the scope of the Conference." But by many, including Rev. Herman Reissig, the chairman of the Committee, the rejection of the resolution was interpreted as a result of communist influence in the Conference. Mr. Reissig resigned from the chairmanship.

Causes for actions usually are complex and their identification difficult. There were undoubtedly communists and communist sympathizers at the Conference. The ACPFB has never rejected cooperation on the ground of political opinion. But, in the light of the rejection by later conferences of various resolutions obviously popular with the extreme left for the same reason (that they did not relate to the protection of the foreign born), the reason given in the report would seem to be valid.

Any organization like the ACPFB, engaged from its beginning in coordinating groups of different sympathies to unitedly oppose injustice to a minority group and committed to defend the rights of the foreign born "regardless of race, religion, country of origin or political opinion" can succeed only by keeping to its own work and rejecting temptations to express opinions on other matters. The difficulties of the early years had shown the wisdom of Dwight Morgan's insistence on "non-partisan." Exceptions have been made to the rule, but they have been few and reluctant.

In contrast, a pleasant example of the cooperation achieved by the Committee is offered by the back cover of the Souvenir Journal of the 1941 Annual National Conference. On the inside is an appeal for help for the Veterans of the Abraham Lincoln Brigade; on the outside is the statement of purpose of the Council for Social Action of the Congregational and Christian Churches, with an illustration of the cover of the Council's magazine, *Social Action.*

Another happy example of cooperation was achieved when the Committee decided to offer a birthday cake to Miss Liberty. On October 28, 1940, the 54th anniversary of the dedication of the Statue of Liberty, the Committee launched the "Campaign for American Citizenship and Citizenship Rights" to promote and facilitate the naturalization of non-citizens. Committee bulletins carried the heading "Campaign for American Citizenship" and "Americans All." The copies of *These United States* for October 18 and 21 stressed the preparations for the October 28 meeting, urged the holding of meetings elsewhere and by other organizations on that date. Posters and postcards to aid publicity for such meetings were offered. A model program with ten planks (the eighth was "to eliminate unnecessary red tape in naturalization") was proposed. A special New York Conference, endorsed by 125 leaders in various fields, including Prof. Franz Boaz, Leonard Covello, principal of Benjamin Franklin High School, Paul Robeson, Dr. Guy Emery Shipler, editor of *The Churchman,* Vilhjalmur Stefansson, Oswald Garrison Villard, Dr. Harry F. Ward, Thornton Wilder, met on October 19 at the Hotel Edison, New York City, approved the campaign and pledged support.

The Conference was greeted by the Honorable Stanley Isaacs, Borough President of Manhattan. A poem, *Ode in Time of Crisis,* written for the Conference by Genevieve Taggard, was read. Addresses were given by Prof. Walter Rauchenstrauch of Columbia University, by Vito Marcantonio, by Attorney Carol King. William Zuidena, a delegate from the Transport Workers Union, discussed the situation of non-citizens fired by the City's transportation systems, then privately owned. Katherine Terrill of the Council of Social Action of the Congregational Christian Churches discussed the coming ACPFB citizenship campaign. Several resolutions were passed against "anti-alien" bills and against discrimination. The organization of a special New York Committee to work under the direction of the American Committee was suggested, in addition to the formal endorsement of the citizenship campaign.

A year later the continuation of the campaign laid even more stress on national unity. The week of October 21 to 28 was designated as "Americans All Week," and was widely observed by meetings and official proclamations throughout the country. Co-chairmen of the Committee of Sponsors for the observance were Louis Bromfield and Congressman Adolph J. Sabath, dean of the House of representatives. Again the Committee could present a long list of illustrious names as sponsors. Included were F. J. Bagocius, president of the Lithuanian Alliance of America, Mayor Harry P. Cain of Tacoma, Washington, Rep. Joseph Casey of Massachusetts, Rt. Rev. John Montgomery Cooper, Hon. Edward Corsi, former District Commissioner of Immigration, Sen. James J. Davis, Dr. Albert Einstein, Rev. William Gilroy, editor of *Advance,* Charles Houston, Dr. Ales Hrdlicka of the Smithsonian Institute, Edward Lamb, vice-president of the Lawyers Guild, Bishop Francis J. McConnell, Dr. Daniel Marsh, president of Boston University, Arthur Upham Pope, Reid Robinson, vice-president of the CIO, Mrs. Eleanor Roosevelt, Prof. Edward A. Ross, president of the ACLU, and Vilhjalmur Stefansson.

The Committee believed that:

> Americans All Week [could] serve to impress upon the American people the need to defeat attacks upon the rights of the foreign born; to encourage and facilitate the naturalization of non-citizens [2,000,000 applications were then pending]; insure that the foreign born (would be) enabled to participate fully in the social, economic and political life of the country. [August, 1941]

And a "Memorandum" sent out by the Committee urging participation in "Americans All Week" described it as an "effort to contribute to the establishment of unity of the American people for the defeat of fascism both at home and abroad."

Pearl Harbor was two months ahead.

IV. THE WAR YEARS

11. Patriotism at Cost Plus

THE great Prussian military theorist, General Carl von Clausewitz, defined war as "an act of violence, pushed to its utmost bounds. . . . [It is] a mere continuation of policy by others means." (See Introduction by Hans W. Gatzke to *Principles of War* by Carl von Clausewitz, Military Service Publishing Co., Harrisburg, Pa., 1942.) Mr. Gatzke elaborated on this principle by saying, "This act of violence, moreover, is not divorced from the political life of a nation, it is not an abnormal situation, but merely the forceful realization of a political aim. . . . Therefore it must be dictated by political considerations, and military leadership of a state must be subordinated to its political leadership."

So far as this judgment is true, it follows that, if the political and economic leadership is divided, advocating contradictory policies, the conduct of the war will be confused and muddled. Although the Second World War was regarded by the American people as a war against fascism, fought in self-defense and for the preservation of freedom, in the months preceding Pearl Harbor and even afterwards, there was no such unanimity among the leaders of politics and business.

Even the date of the beginning of the anti-fascist war was subject to debate. There were those who insisted that it commenced with the Japanese invasion of Manchuria in 1931, and that its progress included the Italian aggression against Ethiopia, the Franco rebellion in Spain, the absorption of Austria, the grabbing of the Sudetenland and the fall of Czechoslovakia, the first war in Finland. For others the war began with the invasion of Poland in 1939; they approved the period of fraternization around the Maginot Line, the "Phony War," and they welcomed the slaughter on the Eastern Front as a wholesome safeguard for the future.

The date of the beginning of the struggle was more than a historian's theory. To be known as a "premature anti-fascist," supporting the Loyalist forces in Spain, or denouncing Chamberlin's Munich pact, or opposing the sale of scrap iron to Japan or Italy, could, in too many quarters of the United States, jeopardize a man's political or economic security; could, if the man were foreign born, deprive him of his right to "reside" in the United States.

Those elements in the United States who had admired Mussolini or had approved of Hitler (it is easy to forget how many and how vocal they were), had been continually urging a policy of non-intervention in Europe, and various groups on the left had urged us to keep out of an "imperialist war." Link, in the work previously cited, reminds us that during the presidential campaign of 1940 "the anti-war tide seemed likely to sweep Willkie into office"; so that on October 30, Roosevelt, speaking in Boston, promised that "Your boys are not going to be sent into any foreign wars." As Link summed up the prevailing attitude, "an overwhelming majority of persons polled [desired] to avoid active participation in the war."

Even at moments of greatest danger to the cause of freedom, after the conquest of France and the rise of underground opposition, after Dunkirk and the bombing of England, confusion did not abate. On the one hand, the extreme left in the United States, basing itself on a Soviet tactical move to buy time by signing a non-agression pact with Hitler, equated both sides in the war and adopted a "plague on both your houses" attitude. And, on the other hand, the extreme right saw in the disasters of the allies the hope of victory for fascism in Europe and the consolidation of their own power at home, and expressed their anti-democratic opinions in and out of government.

Support for the Rome-Berlin axis was not confined to any "lunatic fringe." The law firm, Sullivan & Cromwell, of which John Foster Dulles was then senior partner, drew up the incorporation papers for the America First Committee. It represented the J. H. Schroeder Banking Corporation (*Time* called it "an economic booster" of the Axis), whose main office in London helped finance the German industrialists who financed Hitler. And, after Franco controlled Spain, they represented the Bank of Spain. In 1939, immediately after the invasion of Czechoslovakia, Mr. Dulles regarded the Germans, Italians and Japanese as "dynamic peoples determined . . . to take destiny into their own hands." He protested, "I dislike isolation, but I prefer it to identification with a senseless repetition of the cyclical struggle between the dynamic and static forces of the world." Of Hitler's Germany he said, "We have to welcome and nurture the desire of the New Germany to find for her energies a new outlet." And finally he declared:

> There is no reason to believe that any of the totalitarian states either collectively or separately would attempt to attack the United States. Only hysteria entertains the idea that Germany, Italy or Japan contemplate war against us.

While the U. S. Department of Commerce was announcing in 1940 a sharp increase in the purchase of scrap metal in the United States by fascist Italy, the War Department was telling the House Military Committee that an embargo was "not necessary at the present time in the interest of national defense." In a 1940 speech, the senior elder statesman, Herbert Hoover, declared:

> The final realism is that if we are to keep cool and not stimulate war there must be an end to provocative speech by our officials. . . . It is not the province of the President of the United States to create hate, irresponsible talk in

> explosive times may bring danger. And we need remember that the day will come when we might be of service to humanity in dealing with these same men [Hitler and Mussolini] for peace.

There were more or less complacent predictions of axis victory. From Charles Lindbergh on April 19, 1941:

> This war is lost. . . . It is not within our power today to win the war for England, even though we throw the entire resources of our nation into the conflict.

From the former governor of Wisconsin, Robert La Follette, Jr., on June 6, 1941:

> Nothing that Britain can do now can pull the chestnuts out of the fire. It matters nothing to America which group controls Europe, be it in England or Germany.

And from Hoover again, on June 29, 1941, after the Hitler invasion of Russia:

> Does any sane person believe that by military means we can defeat two-thirds of the military power of the whole world in even years and years?

On June 22, 1941, Hitler's troops moved into Russia, beginning the bloodiest invasion of history. On June 24, the *New York Times* reported the Senator from Missouri, Harry S. Truman, as saying:

> . . . if we see Germany is winning the war we ought to help Russia and if we see Russia is winning we ought to help Germany; and in that way let them kill as many as possible.

Robert E. Sherwood, in his *Roosevelt and Hopkins,* reported that, when Harry Hopkins went to Moscow late in July 1941, as President Roosevelt's personal aide, to arrange for aid, "The

Wall Street Journal disapproved of the trip, saying that to rendder aid to Russia was 'to fly in the face of morals.'"

The events at Pearl Harbor stilled most of the anti-democratic voices. But as late as June 3, 1942, the then Assistant U.S. Attorney General, Thurmond Arnold, told the Illinois Bar:

> The small group of American businessmen who are parties to these international rings . . . still think of the war as a temporary recess from business-as-usual with a strong Germany. . . . It is significant that these cartel leaders still talk and think as if the war would end in a stalemate and that, therefore, they must be in a strong position to continue their arrangements with a strong Germany after the war. This is not shown by their speeches, but by the actual documents and memoranda of business policy which we find in their files.

And in the summer of 1943, describing a visit to Washington, William Allen White declared in his *Emporia Gazette*, "One cannot move about in Washington without bumping into the fact that we are running two wars—a foreign war and a domestic war. The domestic war is in the various war boards."

In 1940 the Temporary National Economic Committee (TNEC) had warned in a report:

> Speaking bluntly, the Government and the public are "over a barrel" when it comes to dealing with business in time of war or other crisis. Business refuses to work, except on terms which it dictates. It controls the natural resources, the liquid assets, the strategic position in the country's economic structure, and its technical equipment and knowledge of processes. The experience of the [first] World War, now apparently being repeated, indicates that business will use this control only if it is "paid properly." In effect, this is blackmail. . . . Business apparently is not unwilling to threaten the very foundations of government in fixing terms on which it will work. It is in such a situation that the question arises: What price patriotism?

With the entry of the United States into the war, the representatives of these dominant sections of business moved into the agencies of government, particularly those dealing with production and contracts. Big Business got into the war effort only after they were given cost plus contracts, special bonuses, fat incentives and the use of government owned plants, newly built with billions of the people's taxes. And even then the Senate Committee Investigating National Defense was obliged to complain in a report in 1942:

> This committee has repeatedly concluded that the work of the Office of Production Management and War Production Board has been hampered by the extent to which their personnel was predominantly drawn from big business groups. . . .
>
> The present grave lack of steel is the responsibility of the large steel companies which have sought to perpetuate their monopolies. Even after we were in the War, Standard Oil of New Jersey was putting forth every effort to protect the control of the German government over a vital war material. . . . Yes, it is treason. You cannot translate it any other way.

And a subcommittee of the Senate Committee on Military Affairs informed us that the "effect of various cartel agreements in strategic industries was also to prevent the development outside of Germany of a substantial production of some of the most important new materials of war." Confirming this, in 1948, officials of General Electric, International General Electric, Krupp and some of their officials, were found guilty of conspiracy and fined $53,000.

Among powerful forces in America, opinion was sharply divided. As a result, the lunatic fringe, sometimes financed by those more cautious and respectable, continued operations throughout the war. A few were indicted for sedition; fewer were convicted. Many changed their tactics to suit the occasion. What could not be done overtly was done covertly. What could not be said directly, was said in the form of carping, malicious criticism of the government war measures. It is easy to forget the extent of such propaganda; a few examples may serve as a reminder.

President Roosevelt bitterly offered the Iron Cross to John O'Donnell for his services to the enemy, but O'Donnell continued as columnist on the New York *Daily News.* The Birmingham (Ala.) *Age-Herald* reported on December 24, 1941:

> The man most frequently and approvingly quoted [on Nazi propaganda broadcasts] is a man who has made much of the word "American". . . . He is the most popular American as far as the Rome-Berlin radios are concerned. . . . His name is Martin Dies. . . .
>
> In all their quotations from Mr. Dies, no one has heard a single criticism of him by the Axis radio.

Despite this information, gathered by the Federal Communications Commission which recorded and analyzed all broadcasts coming from fascist countries, Representative Dies continued in office throughout the war, and headed that famous or infamous investigating body, the House Committee on Un-American Activities.

There were open appeals to race prejudice, anti-Semitic and anti-Negro. On July 7, 1941, Father Charles Coughlin wrote in *Social Justice*:

> Hitler has been opposed to the international godless Jew from the beginning. And from the beginning of this conflict, the international godless Jew dominated Soviet Russia, Britain and the United States. . . . Aside from the miltiary aspects involved in the Russo-German war, Hitler has won a great victory in the minds of Christians throughout the world.

And on September 11, 1941, Lindbergh said at an America First rally in Des Moines, Iowa:

> The Administration, the Jews and the American-British

> are the three major agitators for American entry into the war. . . . If any of these groups—the British, the Jewish or the Administration stops agitating for war, I believe there will be little danger of our involvement.
>
> Tolerance is a virtue that depends on peace and strength. A few far-sighted Jewish people realize this, but the majority still do not. Their greatest danger to this country lies in their large ownership and influence in our motion pictures, our press, our radio and government.

The New York newspaper *PM* reported December 22, 1942, that hundreds of thousands of copies of one leaflet, handwritten, carbon-copied, mimeographed or printed, had been distributed in such places as the Baldwin Locomotive Works, a New York shipyard, the War Production Board, a Wall Street barber shop, the Boston army base, Watertown Arsenal, Charlestown, Mass., Navy Yard, Boston City Hall and other places. The leaflet asked:

> Who was the first American to bomb a Japanese battleship? Colin Kelly. Who was the first American to detect a German spy? John Cullen. Who was the first American to bomb Japan? Jimmy Doolittle. Who was the first American to get four new tires? Abraham Cohen.

In March 1942, Parket Sage, head of the Black Legion in Detroit, an exposed labor spy, prophesied at the headquarters of the National Workers League that the Japanese would win victories and declared that "there won't be a kike left in the American nation a year after that" and "you won't be bothered by lousy niggers." In this manner, Sage continued his disruption, even after the anti-Negro riots at the Sojourner Truth Housing Project in Detroit at the end of February, in which, according to a Federal Grand Jury in Detroit, the National Workers League was implicated. As a matter of fact the government could not make it possible for the Negro families to occupy their apartments until April.

Labor unions, Socialists and Communists were bracketed together and attacked. Edward Rickenbacker attempted a divisive anti-labor campaign in 1942. In 1944, when American labor saw the absolute necessity of electing President Roosevelt for a fourth term in order to guarantee the final victory in the war, and organized to effect it, particularly through the activity of the Political Action Committee (PAC) of the CIO, a howl of protest came from the Republicans who had nominated Thomas E. Dewey, and from Southern Democrats. While 15,000 Communists were serving in the armed forces and manning the transports, receiving citations for heroism and given commissions as leaders, a group of Congressmen issued a document alleging that the Roosevelt administration was seeking to betray the country to the communists, and adding that the "red spectre of communism is stalking the country from East to West, from North to South." And Dies released a report declaring that ". . . the political views of the Communist Party and the CIO Political Action Committee coincide in every detail."

The foreign born were, of course, not exempt from the effects of such opposing currents. But in addition to meeting and facing the buffeting of contradictory policies as carried out on the domestic scene, the foreign born had a special problem that came with foreign birth, with lack of citizenship, with lack of vote, with the vulnerability of their position, and the prejudices of their neighbors, fostered by insidious elements, and expressed even by some of the respectable.

12. Rallying the Foreign Born

Most of the foreign-born citizens and non-citizens in the United States had any number of reasons for being loyal to their adopted country and strongly anti-fascist. The very act of uprooting themselves from lands where their families had lived for centuries implied admiration for their new home. The majority of the foreign born had come prior to World War I to escape from autocratic rule, economic backwardness or both. In America they had found a measure of democracy, and, even with the sweatshop, a higher standard of living. Some could even save enough, under the least favorable conditions, to bring over their families or to marry, and such a surplus was more than they could have achieved in the "old country." And withal there was a sense of security that came with a land isolated by two broad oceans from Europe and Asia, and from the tensions of national antagonisms, carefully preserved and constantly renewed, with all the consequences of military conscription, devastation and bloodshed. What was a little ill-feeling toward a "foreigner" in comparison!

After World War I, with the rise of Mussolini in Italy and the subsequent appearance of hopeful imitators elsewhere, increasing numbers came to the United States as a result of fascist persecution. They knew tyranny at first hand. Their continued contact with relatives and friends in their countries of origin kept them informed of the growth of fascist tyranny, and alert to manifestations of this political aberration in the United States.

Even those who had migrated to America earlier, and had no personal experience with fascism, were affected by mail and newspapers they received from abroad, or by reports in the foreign language press issued in this country. Nor did those who were further removed from their mother country, preserving only cultural ties with it, remain unmoved by events abroad which threatened the cultural values they prized. All this was expressed at the Tenth National Conference of the American Committee in 1943 by Chris Bohn, speaking as a representative of the Workmen's Benefit Fund, eighty percent of whose members were German born. He declared that these people

> . . . love the Germany they know, the Germany of Goethe, of Schiller, Kant, Hegel, Heinrich Heine, of Mendelssohn, Mozart and Beethoven . . . they hate Hitler who has destroyed every vestige of all that was dear to us.

As the fascist armies toppled boundaries and spread their terror across Europe and Asia, and carried out their genocidal policies against millions of "slaves," simple humanity revolted. But the emotions of the foreign born were infinitely more poignant than can be aroused by abstract principles. Their families, their friends and whole communities whom they had known intimately were under direct attack. There was hardly a foreign-born family in the United States that was not directly touched by this modern barbarism. And as their hatred for Hitler and Mussolini and their imitators grew, their devotion to the United States more than kept pace.

Undoubtedly there were elements among the foreign born who could glory in the ability of such leaders to win a false dignity for the country of their birth after years of humiliation. There was the German-American Bund, there were fascist black shirts and other such groups. But in the main, they were isolated in their own communities where, even if there was not full understanding of the issues involved, there was a strong feeling that, as new Americans or potential Americans, they had no business getting involved in something that came from abroad and that might threaten democracy. There was certainly some hesitancy about plunging into a war, but no more than in the country as a whole, and often such hesitancy was the result of pressure from outside the foreign-born community. Once the depredations of the Axis became a fact, however, once the treachery of the fascists was established in the invasion of the smaller countries and of the Soviet Union, once the United States was attacked at Pearl Harbor, the hesitation vanished. It was not difficult in the main to unify the foreign-born communities and to mobilize them for the war effort.

At the same Conference at which Mr. Bohn spoke, Louis Adamic, the distinguished Yugoslav-American author, could say:

> We must all realize—as soon and as widely and wisely as possible—that most of the new-immigrant groups have special, positive assets to enlist in winning the war and the peace. Over one-third of the men and women in the Army and Navy have such names as Kadlubowski, Levy, Suchy, Terbovec, Vlavianos, Mirkovich, Schlesinger, Romello. Names like these are appearing in casualty lists and honor rolls. They are in the majority on the employee rosters of our war industries.
>
> And there is still another, a unique service which new-immigrant groups can render.
>
> In most of the "foreign" groups, many people are passionately interested in the American war effort because they know personally or through family or friends what it is like to live under the Nazi-fascist "order." They realize not only that it must not happen here, but that the future of their homelands depends on defeating the Axis and its quislings.
>
> They are—inevitably—worried about the old countries, where Hitler is systematically exterminating the people of Poland, Yugoslavia and Greece, and tightening his murderous grip on the other countries. . . .
>
> There are hundreds of thousands of them—extraordinarily able and thoroughly Americanized immigrants and

> their sons and daughters. A few of them write to me every day, asking me where they might fit in, to whom to write in Washington, what steps to take to achieve some function that will mean something in bringing on a better world.

There was a special quality, an added asset contributed by the foreign born in support of the war. On the basis of their experiences in the Old World, and their continued direct connections with it, they dreamed and hoped—and this strengthened their loyalty to the United States—that out of this great effort would come a more democratic, secure and happy life for the people they had left behind, who had been economically and politically suppressed for centuries. Mr. Adamic continued:

> The Government must seek out the potential new leaders in our immigrant groups. It must convince them that our postwar purposes are democratic, favoring a better future for the peoples of their old countries. It must tell them that it needs their services as Americans because of their special qualifications—now to convey America's intention to enemy and occupied countries; later to help in the reconstruction. . . .
>
> The dynamic favoring a better world—a democratic world so organized that it will offer a chance of general welfare—is especially strong in the immigrant group.

All organizations in foreign-born communities—and the foreign born are highly organized—began to undertake support for the war effort as one of their main functions. New organizations arose to coordinate efforts. One of them, the American Slav Congress, formed in 1942, made notable contributions to the mobilization of vital sections of the foreign born for the anti-fascist war effort. Mr. Adamic told the Conference of another, the United Committee of South-Slavic Americans, which included Yugoslav, Bulgarian and Macedonian-Americans. Mr. Adamic, its president, listed its purposes:

> 1. To promote the dynamic unity of Americans of

South-Slavic origin and background behind the United States' and the United Nation's war against the Axis, and behind the post-war plans and operations—the latter particularly as they pertain to South-Slavic peoples.

2. To speak in the interest of South-Slavic peoples who, under the Axis which they are fighting, cannot fully speak for themselves to the American people and the rest of the world.

Our Committee's paramount concern is for the triumph —in connection with and after the war—of democratic forces in America and the rest of the world. These forces in the various countries are interdependent. They can only win together.

Certain words in Mr. Adamic's appeal for "dynamic unity" were truly prophetic, as later events have shown:

People are beginning to sense that thereafter the problems of Yugoslavia, Czechoslovakia, Poland and France are going to affect us in America quite as much as, if not more than, the developments in Ohio, Illinois, Michigan, California and New Jersey.

In the process of unifying within their organizations, and coordinating these organizations, the foreign born achieved to a high degree something that dreamers had dreamed for centuries, and that the self-interest of political partisanship and of industrial management had so often thwarted. Motivated by a positive policy, by practical self-interest and by wise leadership, the foreign born in the United States overcame the national animosities of old Europe. This was tellingly illustrated by still another speaker at the 1943 Annual Conference of the ACPFB, George F. Addes, then secretary-treasurer of the Auto Workers.

But the Slavs, the Italians, the Scotch, the Negroes, the Germans, the Hungarians, the immigrants from the mountains of Tennessee found that they were all auto workers in one industry facing the attacks of one boss. And they united in one union to build the strongest industrial organization in the history of America.

. . . It did not take the workers very long to find out that their enemy was not to be found among the workers in another department who came from the wrong side of the river in the old country. . . .

What the Ford workers learned back in 1940 and 1941, the peoples of America and the United Nations are learning today. For victory against the common enemies of humanity, unity among the peoples and governments of the free world is an indispensable weapon. . . .

Hitlerism has spelled torture, slavery and death for workers of *all* nations, of *all* creeds and *all* races. Hitlerism has sought to obliterate the national independence, the culture and the future of all nations falling under the heel of the "master race." This international offensive of Hitlerism can be met only by the fullest international unity of workers and humanity for the creation of military power sufficient to smash and forever obliterate the forces of the Axis.

The foreign born in the United States, making up a large bulk of the labor force in basic industry, which produced the instruments of war, did unite their forces, and through selfless devotion, expressed in no-strike pledges, in unremitting overtime, in union mobilizations to step up production, in suggestion boxes, in bond buying, in blood donations, in political action and in disciplined rejection of provocation, in addition to appearing in casualty lists, helped America meet the offensive of fascism, and defeat it .

As usual, the ACPFB, on matters pertaining to the foreign born, showed great understanding for their thinking, feeling, desires, problems and hopes. "Mobilizing" the foreign born for the war effort was for the Committee the immediate and necessary response to the situation. On Friday, December 12, five days after Pearl Harbor, the Board of Directors held an emergency meeting "to consider the work of the Committee in the light of the war situation." And consider it and act upon it, the

Board did with its usual vigor and persistence. A friendly critic of the ACPFB declared that during the war, the Committee "insisted on being more patriotic than the President." A few of the Committee pronouncements may give some justification for the criticism, but in the light of the war situation, especially as it affected the foreign born, the position of the Committee was understandable if not in all points justifiable.

Prior to the meeting, the chairman of the committee, Hugh DeLacey, had sent a wire to the President pledging support.

> On behalf of the American Committee for Protection of Foreign Born, permit me to voice our support and cooperation for your every effort to bring to a successful conclusion America's united war effort.
>
> Our association with, and work among, Americans of foreign birth makes us feel that every foreign-born American, naturalized and non-citizen, joins us in this expression of support for the defense of our country and our democratic and liberty-loving principles and for the crushing of the Hitler-Japanese aggression.
>
> The foreign born will come forward to assume their full responsibilities as Americans in this hour of crisis and grave danger for their adopted land, just as they have always in the past.
>
> We pledge to you the resources and wholehearted efforts of our organization to the goal of securing the complete support and participation of the foreign born for victory in America's war effort.

At the meeting, the Directors adopted a declaration of principles, and elected a special emergency committee of New York residents which could act quickly when necessary. The declaration which was immediately printed as one side of a small folder under the heading "Mobilize for Victory!" began:

> All loyal Americans of native and foreign birth are united in the defense of our existence as a nation and our liberties as a people, our very lives. . . . Only total victory

> for our country and our allies will perserve for all Americans the democratic rights guaranteed by the Constitution and the Bill of Rights.

The succeeding paragraphs were headed "Unity" (in which everything was "subordinated to the task of cementing unity for the war effort"); "14,000,000 Americans" (who were responding as did Lafayette, von Steuben, Pulaski and Mazzei); "Loyal and Devoted" (who were "producing the sinews of war"); "Expose Axis Agents" (who were attempting to create disunity). The last heading was "We Pledge," and the pledge included efforts to establish fair employment practices, to end discrimination, and to encourage naturalization. It closed with:

> As Americans, we pledge ourselves to the defense of our country and to victory in our war against Hitlerism.

The rest of the folder was devoted to the "Present Aims" of the Committee, which included the mobilization of Americans of foreign birth for victory, the promotion of unity between native born and foreign born, the encouragement of fair employment practices, and helping non-citizens to become naturalized. Together with this went seven suggestions for individual action such as volunteering for civilian defense, buying Defense Bonds, pressing organizations to make the best contribution to the war effort, reporting Axis agents and disrupters, reporting unfair employment practices—and ordered additional copies of the folder and contributing to the ACPFB.

Unity of the foreign born and contributions to the war effort were urged by the Committee throughout the war years. The Souvenir Journal of the May 1942, Annual National Conference proclaimed in large letters on the front cover: FOR VICTORY BUY UNITED STATES WAR BONDS AND STAMPS. AMERICANS ALL—FIGHTERS ALL! The back cover carried the Committee's "Present Aims."

The first item on the program of the 1942 National Conference was the reading of a message from President Roosevelt. Because of its intrinsic value, and also because the Committee has made frequent use of it in publications, we give it in full:

> So long as men and women are daring and stout of heart, there will continue to be in every country that wholesome admixture known as the "foreign born." But the community of nations at war with the axis now stands, and for the duration will stand, as the United Nations. Their fighting powers are riveted as one. And in that larger oneness there can be no "foreigners." The Chinese, the Russians, the Australians, and the Yugoslav soldiers, defending their own lands; the British Commando crossing the Channel; the Pole in Libya; the Norwegian or Greek or Dutchman on the high seas; the Yank in Australia, or in Iceland or in Ireland—all are fighters for this greater community. All are, in this larger sense, "native born."
>
> Our country expects from those who are known as its foreign born exactly what it expects from all Americans. That means, today, a willingness to give as the peoples with whom we are associated have given, to face death as they have faced it. The right to go on as free people will be the fruit of our victory. Our country expects those who are known as foreign born to be accorded that right precisely as it has been and will be accorded to all Americans.

After the Conference was welcomed by the Mayor of Cleveland, Frank Lausche, the first address was given by Commissioner of Immigration and Naturalization, Earl G. Harrison, who had only recently been appointed. This speech was printed at once by the Committee under the title *Americans of Foreign Birth in the War Program for Victory,* together with President Roosevelt's message to the Conference, an introduction by Chairman DeLacey, and a message sent by the Conference to the President. Mr. Harrison began with a look backward to 1915 and President Woodrow Wilson's speech to a group of new American citizens in Philadelphia. Then he continued:

> With a deep-seated awareness and appreciation of the real contribution of the foreign born to America and with

> supreme confidence in their loyalty and zeal for our cause, I deem it a privilege to participate in the American Committee's Conference and to bring to you the greetings and appreciation for your work, of the Attorney General of the United States.

Harold Hoskins, special assistant to the Secretary of State, followed with similar sentiments:

> We should realize that a natural sympathy of American citizens of foreign birth for the country of their origin does not indicate dual allegiance. The richness of the contribution they make to this country should be emphasized.

A whole session was devoted to "Production for Victory," which was addressed by Frank Grillo, secretary-treasurer of the United Rubber Workers, CIO, and by Hugo Ernst, secretary of the Restaurant Employees International Alliance, AFL. The Government was represented at this session by Dr. Malcolm MacLean, chairman of the President's Committee on Fair Employment Practices (FEPC) who explained its procedures.

Another representative of the government, Edward B. Hitchcock, assistant to the Secretary of the Treasury, closed his appeal for participation in financing the war with these words:

> I used to labor under the delusion that the proudest thing in existence was to be born an American. Now I think that the proudest thing is to become an American. I was born an American and so I am an American by chance. You became American and you are an American by choice. . . . This Americanism is important because it combines and comprises all the other nationalisms in the world. It is the internationalism that is Americanism that we must protect.

After the Conference the ACPFB engaged in various activities in fulfillment of the pledge made by the Conference to President Roosevelt, especially the promise:

> . . . to give of its energies without stint to enable the foreign born to increase their participation, and their sacrifice for the victory program.

The Committee's work was dramatically summed up in a flyer containing clippings from newspaper items. Among the activities reported in the language of headlines were the following:

> Rep. Thomas H. Eliot of Massachusetts honored for aid to aliens.
>
> Seven point program to mobilize loyal aliens announced by Abner Green.
>
> Special ceremonies at the Statute of Liberty to honor the ninety-third birthday of Emma Lazarus; [her] poem *The New Colossus* is inscribed at the statute's base.
>
> Investigation of foreign born participation in war effort undertaken by Abner Green.
>
> Citizenship for Filipinos urged.
>
> Survey made of situation of alien seamen; equality sought for them.
>
> U.S. Army urged to use German-born doctors.
>
> Special message by Vito Marcantonio beamed to Italian people.
>
> Naturalization of inducted aliens urged; call for speeding up of naturalization processes generally.
>
> Celebration on Bedloe's Island held to commemorate fifty-sixth anniversary of dedication of Statue of Liberty; for first time since Pearl Harbor the torch briefly relighted.
>
> Philip Murray, CIO president, hailed patriotism of foreign born.

During the war years, the ACPFB initiated or cooperated in various meetings, more limited in scope than its National Conferences but with similar aims: a victory conference of the foreign language press in January, 1943; a forum on Japanese-Americans in February; appearance at a government conference on fair employment practices at the invitation of the War Manpower Commission, in the same month. April saw a "United Nations in America Dinner," under the auspices of the ACPFB. The invitations were issued in the name of Donald Ogden Stewart, who also presided, and the program included Grace Moore and Ray Lev, Dorothy Thompson, William Allen White, Edward G. Robinson, Dr. Ira DeA. Reid, Hon. Earl G. Harrison, Hon. Vito Marcantonio, Zlatko Balokovic and Canada Lee. Guests of Honor were outstanding individuals in the theater, music, literature, art, science and education, labor and government. The list of the dinner sponsors was a roster of the illustrious. The high point of the dinner was the presentation made by Vito Marcantonio, in behalf of the ACPFB, of the Annual Award of the Committee to Earl Harrison, the U.S. Commissioner of Immigration and Naturalization.

On October 28, 1944, the American Committee again organized a pilgrimage to Bedloe's Island to celebrate the 58th anniversary of the Statue of Liberty; the program was broadcast over the New York municipal station WNYC. In a publication issued immediately after the occasion by the ACPFB, containing selections from the speeches and messages, the Statue of Liberty was reproduced with her torch held high and bearing the inscription "I'm foreign born MYSELF! The kind of men who raise the issue of who is or isn't foreign born can hardly have great liking for me or for the things I stand for."

The messages, which were also printed in the bulletin of the ACPFB, *The Lamp,* included those from Mrs. Eleanor Roosevelt, Vice President Henry Wallace, Secretary of the Interior Harold Ickes, Senators Wagner and Mead, Mayor LaGuardia, Thomas Mann and Sidney Hillman. This time a message of greeting also came from Gen. Dwight D. Eisenhower. It read:

> It is my fervent hope that soon the armies of the enemy shall have been driven completely from the soil of the country whose generosity made possible the statue on Bedloe's Island. I can think of no more fitting site where free men could gather in this momentous hour to rededicate themselves to a unified effort in the cause of human freedom and all those principles which are symbolized by the Statue of Liberty.

13. Even-Handed Justice?

ACTUALLY the unification and mobilization of the foreign born communities were inner problems. Only the foreign born could unify themselves or mobilize themselves since true unity must always be voluntary unity. They could, of course, use help from individuals of native birth, or organizations like the ACPFB.

There was, however, one problem that confronted them which the foreign born could not solve. It could only be met by the native born. The ACPFB was quick to grasp the situation and it consciously and deliberately undertook a double role. It would use its influence among the foreign born to help mobilize them for the war effort. But it would place major emphasis on persuading the government and the general public to trust the loyalty of the foreign born in order to make their effective co-operation possible.

This policy accentuated the particular responsibility the native born had for the welfare and well-being of their foreign-born neighbors. Without such principled activity much of the best intentions of the foreign-born leadership and community could not have been brought to fruition. Here, indeed, was the special, indispensable role of the ACPFB. It gave a special point to the name of the Committee, the *American* Committee for Protection of Foreign Born. Of greater significance, then, than mobilizing the foreign born, was the ACPFB's efforts to mobilize American opinion on behalf of the foreign born.

The exclusion of non-citizens from armament plants and related industries in the preceding years was evidence of the widespread doubt of the loyalty of the foreign born, many of whom still had family ties in Europe. Also, the European "governments in exile" made conflicting claims on many of the foreign born, which fed misconceptions of divided loyalties. The ACPFB persistently fought this mistrust. It took every occasion to rally public opinion on behalf of the dignity and patriotism of the foreign born. It not only spoke up itself, it made sure to encourage and to publicize statements by influential individuals and groups whose words might help establish the facts of the loyalty of the foreign born, and the need for the native born to respect and accept the foreign born.

In the very first publication it issued after Pearl Harbor, *Mobilize for Victory!*, it quoted the statement of Attorney General Francis Biddle of December 10, 1941, which said in part:

> The great majority of our alien population will continue to be loyal to our democratic principles if we, the citizens of the United States, permit them to be. We must remember, especially, that most of those who came here from other lands did so because they revere and respect the freedom which America is able to offer them.
>
> The defense of our country will be hurt, not helped, by any persecutions of our non-citizens. If we create the feeling among aliens and other foreign-born that they are not wanted here, we shall endanger our national unity. Such an impression would only give aid and comfort to those enemies whose aim it is to infect us with distrust of each other and turn aliens in America against America. To do this would be to defeat what we ourselves are defending.

Later on it publicized the December 28 statement of the Attorney General, in which he stated:

> There is no reason in the world why loyal persons, either aliens or Americans of foreign birth, should not be

> employed in American industry. . . . The Federal Government condemns such discrimination and urges all employers not to adopt such a policy.

The first publication of the Committee in the year 1942 was a pamphlet containing a radio address delivered by Mayor LaGuardia on December 22, 1941, *Non-Citizen Americans in the War Emergency.* The Mayor stated in detail the government policy for enemy aliens; but he put his emphasis on the necessity for fairness toward the alien and confidently asserted the loyalty of those "who are 'aliens' in the technical sense only," whose close family ties are in the United States, who "revere and respect the freedoms which America is able to offer them." He protested against the misunderstanding which had led certain employers to discharge German- and Italian-Americans.

The back cover of the pamphlet displayed President Roosevelt's statement of January 2, 1942, declaring that there was no law against the employment of aliens except in secret defense work, and that even there permission from the Army or Navy might be obtained. Said the President:

> To discharge loyal and efficient workers simply because they were born abroad [is] as stupid as it is unjust and on both counts it plays into the hands of the enemies of American democracy. . . .
>
> Remember the Nazi technique: "Pit race against race, religion against religion, prejudice against prejudice. Divide and conquer!"
>
> We must not let that happen here. We must not forget what we are defending: liberty, decency, justice.

A common characteristic appeared in all these pronouncements publicized by the ACPFB, and it reappeared consistently through the next four years. United effort for victory was made possible only by even-handed justice to both native born and foreign born; and victory must be won in order that freedom and democracy might survive in America. The campaign for "mobilization of the foreign born" was, like the defense of the rights of the foreign born, a part of the universal struggle for justice and freedom. The same emphasis appeared at the 1942 Annual Conference of the ACPFB, held in Cleveland. Abner Green, the executive secretary, in his report declared:

> This national conference of the ACPFB must regard its main task to be spurring with all human speed the complete mobilization of the fourteen million Americans of foreign birth for the victory effort. [The war cannot be fought effectively] if we suspect the loyalty of every third person in the United States because his parents were foreign born. All loyal Americans have a common enemy in those who would divide us.

At that same conference, in his speech already cited, Commissioner Harrison discussed especially the situation of the non-citizen and particularly of those officially labelled "enemy aliens." He stressed the increasing understanding of their difficulties which, he felt, had already had "tangible results."

> There is more confident opposition, or at least more determined action, with respect to crackpot legislation or other policies aimed indiscriminately at all aliens. It is somewhat less popular nowadays to jump on the bandwagon of the ever-present alien baiters. The work of the American Committee and many similar agencies has, indeed, borne fruit.

He concluded his remarks with:

> I have . . . confidence that the foreign born in our midst can and wish to mobilize further for victory. America, herself, deserves and needs that mobilization. In it lies her greatest strength. In my opinion we are not justified in asking or expecting full mobilization of the foreign born unless we first give them our real friendship and help. We must let them know that America and all she offers are theirs as well as ours. . . .

As the Committee's Chairman Hugh DeLacey said in his introduction to the published edition of Mr. Harrison's address, the speech was

> Evidence in itself of the . . . understanding possessed by our Government for the solution of the problems confronting the foreign born in their sincere efforts to contribute to and sacrifice for the victory program.

These sentiments seemed to be confirmed at the Conference in the remarks of Chairman Malcolm MacLean of the President's Committee on Fair Employment Practices. As Mr. MacLean admitted, complaints were many and were often justified. "Some government departments have been the worst" offenders. In processing the complaints the first consideration of the FEPC was necessarily security and here the greatest problem was "the American born fascists;" the second was production; and the third morale.

> It is the most enlightened self-interest to avoid the existence . . . of large groups of frustrated, disappointed, unemployed, angry and disturbed people.

But despite all good intentions, the situation was far from satisfactory. This was admitted first of all by Mr. Harrison, in his speech. He acknowledged that discrimination especially in employment still existed:

> All of the responsibility cannot be placed at the doorstep of industry and the employer. In spite of the . . . general statements of policy by eminent Government spokesmen [the Attorney General, the Under Secretary of War, a spokesman for the Department of State and the President], there is still a lack of uniformity in departmental practices and some employers find themselves compelled to discharge or are not permitted to employ alien workers.

In a flyer published by the ACPFB, there are reproductions of newspaper want ads of three typical days, January 24, 26 and 27, 1942, from newspapers such as *The New York Times,* the *New York Herald Tribune, The Detroit News, The Chicago Daily Tribune,* the *Los Angeles Times,* the *Cleveland Press,* the *Pittsburgh Press,* the *St. Louis Post-Dispatch.* In the cited ads, it was required that the applicants "must be U.S. citizens," "must have proof of citizenship," must state "nationality," must give "place" of birth or must indicate "racial extraction." Now obviously these are not the formulations used in all the ads in all of the newspapers in all of the typical days of all of the years of the war. But they do reflect the seriousness of the problem.

Nor was discrimination in employment the only problem. In his speech at the Tenth Anniversary Conference in 1943, George Addes spoke of the threats to unity manifest in anti-Negro riots in Detroit, in anti-Semitism, in prejudice against the foreign born in many communities, in Congress and even, in spite of the proclamation of Attorney General Biddle, in the Department of Justice, which, Mr. Addes said, "still tends to assume that hostility to the principles of democracy is characteristic of all alien groups." He declared that conferences like this one held by the ACPFB must "carry a large share of the responsibility for securing and advancing the unity among all who live and work" in the United States.

The reports at this Conference also included protests against specific manifestations of prejudice which were undermining the unity of the war effort. Dr. Liu Liang Mo, of the United China Relief, described the plight of Chinese seamen who were driven to prefer detention on Ellis Island to their status on British and Dutch ships where they were paid only half wages. He said:

> Even on the rafts after a ship was torpedoed, the Chinese don't get equal treatment. While each British or Dutch sailor will get one blanket, two or three Chinese seamen will have to share one blanket.

They were given only half as much from the emergency rations. Meantime, the United States left unrepealed the Chinese Exclusion Act, "an insult to the Chinese people." Even if it were repealed the Chinese quota would be only 105 a year.

Mr. J. Austin Daly of the U. S. Treasury Department added a postscript to Dr. Liu's speech.

> I want to say Amen to everything Dr. Mo has said. . . . The Chinese are almost as good people as we are [sic], and when you get to know them you kind of feel that they are a little bit better. They are a little bit older. Their civilization gets down into the soil a little bit deeper than ours. They have a philosophy that you wonder at. . . . And when you come back [to America], you wonder why we ever let these politicians misguide us into passing this obnoxious Act.

Dr. Charles Petioni, the President of the Carribean Union, and a member of the Board of Directors of the ACPFB, told the story of some 900 workers brought in from Jamaica to harvest crops in the war labor shortage who refused on arrival to sign a Jimcrow agreement. They were turned over to the Immigration and Naturalization Service and were promptly jailed in Miami, Tampa and the Florida State Penitentiary. Ernest May, a torpedoed seaman, declared that in the lifeboats they had learned that there was no difference between black and white and his plea for rights for the Negro people was echoed by New York State Assemblyman Hulan E. Jack.

The annual report of the Secretary, Abner Green, printed with the title *United Nations in America,* dealt chiefly with the forces at work to divide the foreign born and the means of counteracting these forces. "Dividing the population has always been one of the favorite tactics of reactionary American politicians." There were those even in the State Department who supported anti-United Nations propaganda and aided in the spreading of anti-Semitism. "The foreign born need but to look to Europe to see how Hitler used Jew-baiting to divide the people and communist-baiting to scare them," Mr. Green declared.

The crassest example of divisive action was committed by the government itself in complete contradiction to the ideals extolled daily by all the leading spokesmen of the country. What happened to the Japanese-American community was inexcusable; but liberals and progressives in general made no protest against it.

A succinct and thoughtful account of "relocation" is given by Carey McWilliams in his book, *Brothers Under the Skin,* published in 1943 by Little, Brown & Co, Boston. Early in 1942 the military authorities on the West Coast decided to remove the Japanese-American communities from the West Coast. Between March 2 and June 8, 112,353 Japanese-American men, women and children were moved into temporary assembly centers, and between June and November they were moved again to relocation centers in California, Arizona, Idaho, Utah, Wyoming, Colorado and Arkansas. According to Mr. McWilliams, all the Japanese-Americans except a few who were institutionalized, were either removed from the West Coast or were placed in "protective custody" in centers located in California. Of the number so treated, 41,000 were foreign born, but 71,000 were American-born citizens. Says Mr. McWilliams:

> The civil liberties of upwards of 71,000 American citizens have been suspended without due process of law; property losses running into the millions of dollars have been sustained; and the government, at an initial cost of $70,000,000, is now attempting to resettle these evacuees.

The Japanese were suspect as foreigners from the first day of their arrival on the West Coast of the United States in the late 1880's. Mr. McWilliams reports:

> With the exception of only a few years . . . the Japanese in California were constantly involved in a rapidly developing international crisis. Under an increasing barrage, they were kept constantly on the defense. . . .

> For forty years on end, crisis followed crisis; one investigation succeeded a prior investigation; one campaign ended only to find another launched; and the newspaper attack was continuous and remorseless. They were discriminated against in almost every walk of life; no session of the legislature passed without the introduction of some anti-Japanese bills. Sounding off about the Japanese became a legislative pastime in California. One legislator called them "a bandy-legged set of bagaboos—miserable craven Simians—degenerate rotten little devils"; they were "skulking," "servile," "immoral," "treacherous," "sneaking," and "insidious." While they were never physically mistreated as were the Chinese . . . nevertheless the atmosphere in which they lived became poisonously prejudiced against them.
>
> . . . the Californians continued to repeat the dogma, "Once a Jap, always a Jap," and to urge the contention that they were biologically unassimilable.

The anti-Orientals did not hide their motives. The author of an Alien Land Act in California, which was passed in 1913, had stated quite clearly at the time, that "the fundamental basis of all legislation upon this subject has been, and is, race undesirability."

In spite of this the Japanese-Americans had tried their best to establish themselves as Americans. To avoid misunderstanding as a result of sensational "picture bride" stories in the press, California Japanese in 1919 "voluntarily petitioned the Japanese government to deny further passports to Japanese women," which the Japanese government carried out. Japanese workers asked and received higher wages for farm labor and other services, so as not to depress wages. They undertook self-discipline and achieved the lowest criminal record among all the foreign born. They renounced dual citizenship and forced the Japanese government to release all those born after December 1925, from a claim to Japanese citizenship. Despite the existence of vernacular schools, the U.S. Army discovered that only 15 percent of the younger generation could speak Japanese and only 5 percent could pass a test in reading and writing. They even disassociated themselves from other persecuted groups, such as Negroes, and "some Japanese were not above slandering Chinese, Negroes, Filipinos, Indians, and Mexicans. In retrospect it cannot be said that the strategy was particularly effective."

A picture of the Americanization process of the Japanese, cited by Mr. McWilliams, was given by one Michio Kunitani to the Tolan Committee which investigated the West Coast Japanese situation in February and March, 1942.

> We are Americans, not by virtue of our birth in America, but by virtue of the social and cultural forces in America. . . . We are Americans, not by mere technicality of birth, but by all the other forces of sports, amusements, schools, churches, which are in our communities and which affect our lives directly. Some of us are Yankee fans; some of us are Dodger fans; some of us like to sip beer; some like to go up to the Top of the Mark (the Mark Hopkins Hotel); once in a while we enjoy Jack Benny; we listen to Beethoven; and some of us even go through the Congressional Record.

Milton Eisenhower, formerly director of the War Relocation Authority (WRA), testified before a Congressional Committee that in spite of what the Nisei (American born of Japanese descent) had suffered, 80 to 85 percent of them were loyal to the United States. He added, "I just cannot say things too favorable about the way they have cooperated under the most adverse circumstances." In fact, only about 1,250 of those removed from their homes signed with the WRA for repatriation.

We have gone into this detail because there is a major lesson to be learned from this experience of the Japanese. At the 1942 Conference of the ACPFB, the secretary's report spoke of the evacuation program for the Japanese on the West Coast, and could only say, "It is our responsibility to insure these loyal Americans against unnecessary hardships growing out of their relocation." The long report on the Japanese relocation which followed simply summarized in some detail the findings of the Tolan Committee of the House of Representatives and conspicuously refrained from any expression of independent opinion. The Conference passed a rather elaborate resolution accepting the necessity of the relocation and commending the self-sacrificing cooperation of "the thousands upon thousands of loyal Americans of Japanese descent, both citizen and non-citizen"; but offering only the recommendation that Loyalty Hearing Boards be established to examine the loyalty of non-citizens of German, Italian and Japanese birth individually, and that jurisdiction should be transferred from the War Department to the Department of Justice.

The Committee was not alone in its acquiescence. The relocation was undertaken by the Army whose Commander-in-Chief was President Roosevelt. Even Mr. McWilliams wrote in 1942 "It would also serve no purpose to debate the question of whether or not mass evacuation should or should not have been ordered. The fact is that the decision was made by the military and it is to be presumed that it was dictated by good and sufficient reasons." Also "there were many sincere and fair-minded citizens of California who supported the anti-Japanese movement because they wanted to prevent a race problem from arising in the state." It is true that the action finally broke up the Japanese ghettos and integrated their residents into the rest of America. But regardless of the military exigency and of whatever good results may have followed, the violation of the rights of American citizens and non-citizens is undeniable.

The American Committee and Mr. McWilliams at that time missed the point entirely. That there were spies and saboteurs in the Japanese community may have been a fact. And the U.S. Army and the government had the right, the duty and responsibility to round these elements up, to isolate them and to put them out of mischief's way. But here was an action taken not against individuals, but against an entire community, punishing the overwhelming majority for what were the anticipated sins of the few. The action was, both in its intent and manner of execution, not only insulting, humiliating, unjust and painful to the community; it had also the character of Hitlerite collective punishment and race prejudice. No other concentrated community of foreign born from enemy countries of origin were similarly treated.

For the American Committee, engaged as it was in a campaign to win the unity of the foreign born and to win the confidence of the native Americans in the foreign born—an indispensable condition for such unity—the failure to protest the treatment of Japanese-Americans was especially inconsistent. It could not fail to weaken the ACPFB's campaign. The Committee had become so wrapped up in the exigencies of the war situation that it completely lost sight of the fact that its position on the Japanese evacuation was in contradiction to its policies and to the very aims inherent in its war position.

The action by the government against the Japanese-American community encouraged the racists in the land, encouraged discrimination and anti-foreign born legislation. By 1943, Carey McWilliams could report in *Brothers Under the Skin*:

> Already a movement is under way to exclude the Japanese altogether from the United States after the war. This movement has taken two forms: a rather vague expression of an intention to deport all Japanese; a more specific plan to deprive the second generation of American citizenship, if necessary by constitutional amendment. A bill introduced by Senator Stewart of Tennessee purports to authorize the detention of all persons of Japanese descent for the duration of the war; a bill by Senator Holman of Oregon seeks to deprive the Nisei of American citizenship.

Not only did the fascist publicists make hay out of the American treatment of the Japanese-American, but foreign born other than the Japanese-Americans felt the consequences of this action, which could be justified by no political or military policies.

14. The Fruits of Unity

No government and no organization functions without error. But there is a difference between making mistakes and having a mistaken aim. It must be said that the Roosevelt administration, individual officials notwithstanding, conducted by and large a consistent war against fascism. So also it is true of the ACPFB that the general consistency of the total record of its activities in defense of human rights makes the inconsistency of its attitude towards the relocation of Japanese-Americans the more conspicuous.

The difficulties of its work in the war years were increased by special problems arising from the national emergency. At its 1941 Annual Conference, the officers elected were: Congressman Hugh DeLacey as chairman; attorney Pearl M. Hart, Edward Lamb, Rev. Edgar A. Lowther, Hon. Stanley Nowak, Prof. Walter Rautenstrauch and Dr. Max Yergan as vice-chairman; Curt Swinburne as secretary; Irving Novick as Naturalization Aid Director; and Abner Green as educational and legislative director.

But immediately after the Directors' meeting of December 12, 1941, the Committee had to meet a personnel crisis. Prof. Rautenstrauch of Columbia University, a consistent pacifist, felt obliged to resign from the vice-chairmanship and from the Board of Directors, and his resignation was accepted at the meeting of December 29, with expressions of regret and of appreciation for his cooperation and help in the work of the Committee. Several members of the office staff desired to undertake other work, including Secretary Swinburne and Naturalization Aid Director Novick. The secretary of the Italian-American Committee was slated to join the armed forces.

The Board of Directors elected Abner Green, who in the preceding six years had been publicity, educational and legislative director, to serve as secretary. This office he has continued to hold for sixteen years—with one enforced six month vacation, a prison sentence. These years have been crucial in the work of the Committee, and its continued existence is in itself a tribute to his unswerving, courageous and able leadership.

The stress of the final period of the war made necessary some further changes in the leadership of the Committee. In 1943, Hugh DeLacey felt that he could not give adequate time to the chairmanship and became one of the vice-chairmen. The other vice-chairmen in 1943 were Meyer Adelman of Milwaukee, director of the United Steel Workers District 4, Pearl Hart, Edward Lamb, Arthur Upham Pope and Dr. Max Yergan. In 1944 Joseph Muzio of San Francisco was added. Isidore Englander was elected treasurer, and Carol King, who had for years been an outstanding attorney, particularly in the field of immigration and naturalization law, was elected general counsel of the Committee.

What the ACPFB meant to the foreign born, what impact it made in the nation, became apparent at its Tenth Anniversary Conference held in New York in 1943. It was not what was stated in the many tributes to its work in the speeches or in the messages, including one from Secretary of State Cordell Hull, and another from Governor Leverett Saltonstall of Massachusetts. It was rather its program and the bill of particulars about its work that told the story.

The general emphasis of the Conference was the same all-out unity which was the theme of the 1942 Conference. But there was a somewhat less complete absorption in the war effort. "Since the beginning of the war our Committee has devoted itself exclusively to promoting the mobilization of the foreign born for a United Nations victory," the secretary's annual report stated. But it is significant that three of the five "Aims of the Committee" for 1943 were not specifically related to the war effort, and two-thirds of the "greetings" refer chiefly to the general work of the Committee for the past ten years. In part this was due to the anniversary spirit of the Conference. But in part it was due also to the continued vigilance of the Committee and of its friends for the welfare of those with whom it was particularly concerned—the foreign born.

The real story is told in a brief summary of the ten years work of the ACPFB given in a leaflet asking for funds, which was printed immediately after the Anniversary Conference. The summary is significant not only for the work of the Committee but for the situation in which the foreign born had found themselves. In that decade, the ACPFB had handled 4,520 application for citizenship; 3,542 cases to regularize the status of foreign born in order to prevent the separation of families; 3,814 cases of citizenship problems; 768 immigration problems; 524 cases of political or religious refugees; for naturalized and non-citizens, 2,006 cases of discrimination in employment; 2,574 problems of status and similar difficulties; 1,461 miscellaneous problems of relatives of foreign born. It had distributed over five million copies of pamphlets; had issued about 240 different leaflets on special problems; had conducted 62 radio programs. It had held eight national conferences and twenty-seven regional conferences. It had participated in 26 public hearings before Congressional committees. It had furnished special material to periodicals, newspapers and radio commentators. It had initiated annual observances of Statue of Liberty Day and had inspired the national celebration of "Americans All" Week.

But the Conference was concerned not primarily with what the Committee had done in its specialized field in the past ten years, but with what it was doing right then. The regular work of the Committee had not ceased during the war years because it could not. "Anti-alien" bills were still presented in Congress and although there was more general opposition to them, the

Committee could not neglect its legislative activity. There were fifty such bills before the 77th Congress alone. And with all its efforts for mobilization for unity, with all of its educational activity, the ACPFB did not, of course, lessen its defense of individual foreign born.

Settling "citzenship problems" was often a laborious, long-drawn out process, as the letters in the ACPFB files show. Anthony Palagin of Grand Rapids, Michigan, who came to the United States in 1914, was denied citizenship on September 1, 1942, because, as he wrote the Committee, he was "a member of the I.W.O. and read the Russian newspapers." His letter asks in a postscript, "Shall I send a letter to someone in Washington to tell them what the examiner has told me about Russia and Hitler?"

The Committee sent a copy of Palagin's letter to Commissioner Harrison who replied that he was asking for a report on the case from the District Director in Detroit. Meantime, the Committee began looking for an available lawyer in Palagin's vicinity and getting necessary papers prepared in New York so that an appeal could be filed within the required time limit. On September 22, Palagin wrote:

> All this thing makes me dizzy. I am of poor health and now all this do make me lots of trouble. . . . First of all that I am afraid of, that "they" [newspapers] will "smear" my name and that will "push" me of my job. Please, Mr. Green, try to make it best.

When no lawyer was found in Grand Rapids—one refused the case and another wanted $100 telegraphed to him as a "retainer" before he would begin – the Committee decided to handle the case from New York and the papers were sent to Mr. Palagin for signature and filing. The next letters report his various difficulties in getting the papers accepted. The October 10 letters ends: "I wonder if it is not too hard to understand my writing, please tell me." (As a matter of fact his handwriting is both legible and unusually well-formed.)

A letter of October 14 from Commissioner Harrison reported that the report from the Detroit office was still "being awaited." On November 9, the Committee again wrote the Commissioner, from whom nothing more had been heard, reminding him that the appeal must be made before the end of the month. On November 12, Mr. Palagin wrote that on October 28 a "new examiner" called him and asked many questions. "Since October 28 I don't hear anything from no one. . . . I know they try to impose communism on me, but I don't know why." On November 18, Commissioner Harrison wrote that he had directed the Detroit office not to oppose a re-hearing of the case.

In March of the next year, the Judge agreed in writing that the denial of citizenship would be set aside; and Mr. Green sent a copy of the letter to Mr. Palagin. But on March 22, Mr. Palagin had heard nothing and wrote, "Don't you think that there is some mistake about all this news?" And he was still more in need of reassurance when he was told to appear for a "hearing" on April 14.

The file closes with his letter of April 15:

> Your advice and your persistency gave me willingness to fight for my right, and I believe that you are happy to hear that at last I get my citizenship papers.
>
> I am happy very much and I can't find no words to express my thanks for your sincere help.
>
> THANK YOU VERY MUCH.

Eight months of Committee effort—letters, telegrams, telephone calls, a lawyer sent from New York to Grand Rapids—and one man is "happy very much" to have won his citizenship.

The letter files are full of so-called "human interest." A lady complained that she was denied citizenship because another lady (with whom she had had a quarrel) had testified that she was known as "red Tillie," although no witness who knew the nickname was produced. Also the accuser, who was herself known to have been a bootlegger, was given *her* citizenship.

There was the man who read the *Daily Worker* "because it speaks for labor" and was "pushed around" because "They disapprove of that kind of literature and cannot demand me not to read it"; and a wife, wanting to do war work in a defense plant, whose papers were held up because her husband, a barber, had told the examiner that he studied "Philosophy Economics." But even the file of the California woman at whose hearing three social workers testified that she was "demanding," closes with a letter of gratitude to the ACPFB. Her papers were given her a year later.

Deportations were of necessity halted by the war situation but not completely. In March, 1944, habeas corpus had to be used for the first time since the war began to halt a deportation. Martin Charasch was a German Jewish seaman who had fled from Germany to Italy and then to Palestine. He continued as a merchant seaman and was torpedoed three times. In 1942 he was given a sixty-day stay in the United States. He joined the United States Army and was discharged after two months and twenty-seven days, just three days short of the time required for naturalization. He was arrested at once and brought to Ellis Island. Such cases, however, were few.

But difficulties in obtaining citizenship still presented themselves, although less frequently under Mr. Harrison, about whom Abner Green said at a 1943 Conference, "Due to the capable administration of the Hon. Earl Harrison, most of the serious naturalization problems have been eliminated." The Committee's Naturalization Aid Service, however, was still interviewing on the average of seventy-five people a week, and handling the naturalization of about a third of them.

The Anton Lerich file is informative. The first document is a letter sent in November, 1942.

> I have difficulty in obtaining the Citizenship Paper, here in Wadsworth, Ohio, reason for not getting the Citizenship Paper up to this time I don't know, despite the fact that I wrote two letters to Immigration and Naturalization Service, Cleveland, Ohio, asking for reason why I

> don't get the Paper, and I never got no answer from that office.
>
> It was in April 30, 1931 that I file petition . . . and at that day I past exesamination O.K. everything was all right, paid my 5 dollars but got nothing more. [He was a member of the IWO and the AFL "and nothing more."]
>
> I'm in this country since 1911 and I have a family. I have a son in the army. Never was arrested no charge of any kind against me.

The Naturalization Aid Director wrote various letters. A reply from Commissioner Harrison dated December 30 states that he has asked Cleveland for a report; another of January, 1943, reports that the investigation is in progress. But a letter to Mr. Harrison in August asks if the report has been received. The final letter in the file is from Mrs. Lerich and is very brief. "Well I am sorry, the case has to be dropped because Mr. Lerich has been dead over a year."

A number of the officials in different parts of the country denied naturalization to members of the International Workers Order. The Committee files include other protests against similar delays. The Committee raised the specific question with Mr. Harrison who ordered an investigation, and on December 8, 1943, wrote to Abner Green that instructions were being sent to the field offices of the Service not to object to any petition for naturalization solely on the ground of membership in or affiliation with the IWO. The full letter appears in a tiny seven page folder, *ABC of Naturalization and Citizenship,* which the Committee prepared the next year especially for members of the IWO.

The "happy endings" of most of the files of the war years were due largely to the attitude of Commissioner Earl Harrison, who consistently regarded his task as a real *service* to *foreign-born Americans* and not as an instrument to be used to serve other interests, economic or political. Unfortunately, there was no way to guarantee that his successors would hold the same opinion.

But the final decision in the case of William Schneiderman, which was carried to the Supreme Court, has been, in spite of all efforts by the Department of Justice to nullify its force, for the past fifteen years a protecting wall for the foreign-born citizen.

William Schneiderman was a year old when he was brought to the United States from Russia in 1908. At eighteen, he applied for citizenship and received his papers when he became 21 in 1927. He was later a candidate for office on the California State Communist ticket, and afterwards was the California state secretary of the Communist Party. In 1939, twelve years after his naturalization, proceedings were brought in the Federal District Court in San Francisco to cancel his citizenship on the ground that his membership in the Young Workers' League and the Workers' Party showed that he was not attached (as he had said) to the principles of the Constitution. Federal District Court Judge Roche ruled for the Attorney General.

Early in 1940, the Board of Directors of the ACPFB had sent a letter to Attorney General Jackson protesting against the suit on the ground that the Department's

> . . . interpretation of the naturalization laws establishes a precedent that jeopardizes the freedom of belief and the civil rights of naturalized Americans.

The Board issued with the protest a public statement which declared:

> We have no desire to defend Mr. Schneiderman's political, social or economic views. At the same time we have every desire to defend Mr. Schneiderman's right to retain his American Citizenship; and to defend his right as an American of foreign birth to hold whatever views or social opinions he desires.

The statement also emphasized the twelve-year interval between the naturalization and the suit to cancel it, and the implication involved in the charge that unasked-for information not considered relevant at the time of naturalization must be volunteered by the applicant.

The legal brief in Schneiderman's defense declared that the government's interpretation of the law would bar all political activity to non-citizens, who would not be able legally to express approval of any suggested amendment whatever; and quoted Justice Holmes' dissenting opinion in the Schwimmer case:

> If there is any principle of the Constitution that more imperatively calls for attachment than any other, it is the principle of free thought—not free thought for those who agree with us, but freedom for the thought we hate. I think we should adhere to that principle with regard to admission into as well as life within this country.

When the 1941 Conference of the ACPFB met, the Schneiderman case was on appeal to the U.S. Circuit Court, and there was general recognition of the fact that the Justice Department's interpretation created two classes of American citizens. This aspect was especially stressed before the Conference:

> Heretofore, naturalized citizens have received the same punishment for violation of our laws as native born citizens. . . . Now, if the American people lose the Schneiderman Case, naturalized citizens face an additional threat. . . . Thus the issues in this case have far wider implications than the personality of William Schneiderman or the fact of his membership in the Communist Party. What is being defended is the American democratic principle of one citizenship for all our people, one set of rights for all our citizens. To create divisions, to permit two classes of citizens . . . is to deny democracy, to render it a mockery which belies its name.

The Conference pledged

> . . . its full support to the defense of William Schneiderman . . . [the cancellation of whose citizenship] is con-

trary to law and the Constitution of the United States which draws no distinction between naturalized and native born citzens.

But the U.S. Court of Appeals affirmed the cancellation on the ground of illegal procurement of citizenship, and the appeal was carried to the U.S. Supreme Court. Here Wendell L. Willkie, Roosevelt's presidential opponent in the 1940 election, associated himself with Carol King and argued on behalf of Schneiderman before the nation's highest court. The cancellation was reversed. This decision had such significance for the future, and is so important in the immediate present that excerpts from the majority decision must be included in any work on the foreign born, or in any account of the work of the ACPFB.

> The Government seeks to turn the clock back twelve years after full citizenship was conferred on the petitioner by judicial decree and to deprive him of the priceless benefits that derive from that status. In its consequences it is more serious than a taking of one's property, or the imposition of a fine or other penalty. . . . It would be difficult to exaggerate its value and importance. . . .
>
> Whatever attitude we may individually hold towards persons and organizations that believe or advocate extensive changes in our existing order, it should be our desire and concern at all times to uphold the right of free discussion and free thinking to which we as a people claim primary attachment. To neglect this duty in a proceeding in which we are called upon to judge whether a particular individual has failed to manifest attachment to the Constitution would be ironical indeed. . . .
>
> Security of the status of our naturalized citizens must not depend upon the political temper of majority thought and the stresses of the times. . . .
>
> It may be doubted that the founders of the Constitution intended to create two classes of citizens, one free and independent, one haltered with a lifetime string tied to its

> status. . . . [The latter would be] not admitted to liberty—his best course would be silence or hypocrisy.

The court also, in contrast to later court actions, gave careful consideration to ambiguities and variations in the statements of the Communist Party and insisted that there was no justification for "imputing the reprehensible interpretation" to a member of an organization when no overt act could be found. One could wish that the Supreme Court decision in the Schneiderman case were required reading for all Americans.

But the year 1943 not only brought this outstanding victory for the foreign born, for national unity and for the war effort; it also brought the first rumblings of another struggle for which the people had to be rallied in the interests of national unity, the war effort and the coming peace, in the interests of the American people as a whole as well as the foreign born. The shadow of the presidential election of 1944 began to be felt as early as the 1943 Annual Conference of the ACPFB. It was the subject of a Sunday afternoon panel, where "the Southern oligarchy" and "political bosses of the big cities of the North" were credited with attempts to "blackmail" the President. It was noted that the government account of the European situation had contained no statements by either Ambassador William Dodd (Germany) or by Claude Bowers (Spain). It was necessary for Americans who believed in democracy "to risk everything rather than tolerate compromise with fascism as the keystone of foreign policy." Roosevelt must remain in office "because his win-the-war program has brought us the greatest victory the people of this country have ever seen, the diplomats of America and England sitting down with the diplomats of Russia." He must be kept in office to insure the peace of the world and "the demolition of reactionary forces in this nation."

It is easy to forget today how strong were the pressures for an early and separate peace; and how strong was the Republican opposition to the re-election of President Roosevelt. In the effort to defeat the President, specific appeals were made to win the support of various groups of the foreign born. Their nature can be understood from a group of quotations from the foreign language press, which the Committee used to give urgency to its campaign for unity.

> Democracy is only where it serves the interest of Great Britain. *Bulletin of the Pulaski Foundation.*
>
> America and England today are fighting not for the freedom of all nations but for the salvation of the British Empire and for turning over to the Asiatic Communists of Europe or at least some part of it. *Dirva* (Lithuanian).
>
> When Germany will be defeated, there will be no other nation existing to prevent the Russians from becoming the predominant power of the continent. And this would be an extremely annoying situation for Great Britain. *Staats-Anzeiger* (German).
>
> The longer Germany and Russia fight the better for all peoples who love freedom. . . . As two gigantic serpents, they bleed each other. *Ausma* (Latvian).

It must be repeated again, that this last statement and the other statements quoted, were made with impunity not *before* the attack on Pearl Harbor, nor *after* the hostilities had ended; but in the midst of the most bitter bloodshed, when the fate of the United States and of its democratic institutions was at stake. Nor was such subversion expressed only in words.

The secretary's report to the Board of Directors in March, 1944, told of the increase of anti-Negro and anti-Semitic propaganda among foreign language groups; of attempts to set Greek-Americans against Italian-Americans, Serbs against Croats; of attempts to influence foreign policy by the threat that six million Polish votes might be lost to Roosevelt. In fighting these divisive attempts, said the secretary, "The Committee's aim is not political. Ours is a non-political organization, but we must fight for unity and democracy." Insofar as the Committee implied that unity and democracy were obtainable *only* through a Democratic party victory in November, a contrary judgment might be made. However, the emphasis was certainly on unity rather than on support of the Democratic Party.

The year 1944 was marked by a series of "Campaigns for Unity." A "Declaration of Unity" was published at the beginning of the year and prominent individuals were asked to sign it. It read:

> The historic conferences at Moscow, Cairo and Teheran laid the foundation for a working unity between democratic nations. The outline for victory in the war and the peace established by leaders of Great Britain, the Union of Soviet Socialist Republics and the United States is an inspiration to all peoples in all lands who seek security, democracy and peace for generations to come.
>
> These great perspectives, however, must be won. They will not come as a grant. The future of mankind holds great promise as a result of the international unity of purpose which has been established in the course of this war by the leading democratic nations of the world. But, disunity on our home front can turn this promise into a mockery. The hope for the future which is being won by America's fighting men can become meaningless until and unless racial, religious, sectional and national group prejudices are eliminated from our land.
>
> Anti-Semitic, anti-Negro and anti-foreign born prejudices are subversive of our American democracy. They can and will hamper our efforts for victory in the war. They can and will prevent a democratic people's peace.
>
> Our sons and brothers, together with the soldiers of our allies, are giving their lives in this just war against the military forces of the Axis, which has always served as a monstrous inspiration to the anti-Semites, the advocates of white supremacy and national chauvinism. We must as certainly and as determinedly destroy these evils at home. Anyone who spreads the Hitlerite doctrines of hatred and prejudice is guilty of the highest possible treason to the United States, and to the American people.
>
> Our country has a proud heritage. "All men are created equal. They are endowed by their Creator with certain

> inalienable rights." This concept helped to bring freedom to the world. Our nation was born and grew strong in struggle against tyranny. The contribution of its Negro, Jewish and foreign born citizens helped it become great. Americans—all must become fighters—all against any form of prejudice or discrimination that would serve to divide our ranks and weaken us before the onslaught of the fascist enemy. The American people, to be victorious in this war, must mobilize to defeat fascism at home as well as abroad. Let us go forward, strengthened by understanding between all peoples and tolerance between all men, to even greater glory.

Reading these ringing words today, after the years of the "cold war," one may wonder whether this was blind optimism or a vision of what might have been. But in 1944 the challenge was immediately accepted. Among the signers were Dr. Herbert Davis, president of Smith College, Hon. Adolph Sabath, Judge George L. Quilici of Chicago, Professors Louis C. Karpinski and Kasimir Fajans of the University of Michigan, Mrs. Louis Brandeis of Washington, D. C., and they were joined by others of equal standing.

"Emergency Unity Conferences" were held in various cities—the first in New York on March 18. A letter announcing this conference and suggesting that others should be held in cities with large foreign-born groups described the situation.

> We in the American Committee are concerned with the activities of fifth columnists, quislings and other reactionaries among the foreign born. From reports reaching us it is clear that the opponents of Teheran, the enemies of the United Nations concept are busy spreading confusion. . . . They raise questions based on old world differences and prejudices. They spread anti-Semitism and anti-Negro propaganda. They pander to all the worst prejudices they can find and invent new ones. . . .
>
> In New York we have already begun by calling an Emergency Conference on American Unity.

> it is now when the crucial moments of the war are rapidly taking place.

The speakers were Wisconsin leaders of the German American Society, the American Jewish Congress and the CIO.

The call for the Detroit conference on May 28 was headed by President Roosevelt's statement:

> In this war, we have been compelled to learn how interdependent upon each other are all groups and sections of the population in America.

The second page gave the reason for calling the conference. "The foreign born have demonstrated their devotion and loyalty," but a fifth column "employs every divisive method, cultivates all prejudices and seeks to misuse the . . . ties of the foreign born to their homeland. They are planning especially to utilize the 1944 presidential election as one chief means for destroying unity." They are particularly active in Detroit. The conference is a part of the effort "to expose and defeat" such activities.

The conference formally pledged its support to the President:

> We support without reservations your win-the-war program.
>
> We are united in our approval of your policy for the development of the full United Nations coalition warfare.
>
> We condemn any attempt to utilize the coming 1944 election to spread disruption in our country.

The resolutions passed call for: unity for winning the war; naturalization for all over fifty who had lived fifteen years in the country; citizenship after three months in the armed services; right of asylum for refugees; defense of Fox and Bridges, deportation victims. One resolution praised Earl Harrison as Commissioner of Immigration; another (somewhat prematurely) praised the Justice Department for instituting the sedition trials of Father Coughlin and Gerald L. K. Smith.

Just after the Detroit conference, the ACPFB issued an appeal for funds, carrying reproductions of stories on the conference from both English and foreign language newspapers. The appeal ran:

> United—our nation will go forward to the destruction of the evil we are fighting. But if we permit ourselves to become disunited—if we permit bigotry and prejudice and the evils of racism and division to develop, then we have fallen short of our responsibilities to our fighting men and to our fighting allies.
>
> It was in order to combat the menace of disunity that the ACPFB sponsored the Detroit Emergency Conference on American unity. . . . A good deal of the fifth column activity calculated to divide us was concentrated among foreign-born Americans and in their communities.
>
> We are sure you will want to help us carry on . . . against this insidious enemy which utilizes blind prejudices and bigotry to attain his ends.

The 1944 Annual Conference of the ACPFB was to have been "The National Unity and Victory Conference." But when the Government requested that unnecessary travel be curtailed, the conference was cancelled, and numerous area conferences were held in different parts of the country instead. The purpose of the conference as stated in the call before it was cancelled, embodied the policy of the ACPFB as the war drew towards its close.

> The central purpose of this Conference will be the development of a program for:
>
> 1. The solution of the remaining war-time problems confronting the foreign born, including naturalization, discrimination in employment, fifth column activities.
>
> 2. The fullest possible participation of the foreign

born in determining the character and role of the United States in the post-war world.

For dealing with these two problems the Conference was badly needed and in cancelling it, the ACPFB once more sacrificed its basic concern for the sake of promoting the war effort. But for the immediate problem of national unity the conference was not necessary. The American people were in overwhelming majority united in the determination to win the war, to defeat their fascist enemies, to guarantee the continuation of the United Nations. For these considerations of national policy they temporarily laid aside all other differences. And so clear were they in their goals, that all divisive, high pressure propaganda again failed, and President Roosevelt was reelected for an unprecedented fourth term. Unity once again bore fruit.

15. "Man's Intolerance of Man"

THE unity manifested in the election of 1944 did not last long. By the death of President Roosevelt on April 12, 1945, the United States and the world lost the leader on whose insight and influence that unity in large measure depended. By his awareness of international realities and his sensitivity to the needs of all sectors of the American people, President Roosevelt had preserved cooperation among the allies and achieved a working coalition of the various interests within the United States. After his death, only the need to finish the war quickly delayed the immediate triumph of divisive forces.

Although hostilities in Germany did not formally cease until the signing of the armistice on May 8, 1945, in one sense the end of the war was in sight once the long-delayed invasion of Northern Europe was successfully begun on D-Day, June 6, 1944. Among the innumerable cables of good wishes to General Eisenhower was one from the ACPFB, expressing the enthusiastic loyalty of the foreign-born Americans. And the Commtitee files still contain the cable reply: "All ranks of the allied forces sincerely thank you for your message of good wishes. Eisenhower." After the collapse of Hitler's last effort in the Battle of the Bulge from December, 1944, to January, 1945, the only serious question was the kind of peace which would be made.

Even in the months immediately following the election of November, 1944, the difficulties which would face the foreign born when peace was declared became increasingly clear. The nature and the seriousness of those difficulties are obvious from the sudden changes in the activity of such an organization as the American Committee for Protection of Foreign Born, changes which were the necessary response to the increasing needs of the foreign born for protection of their rights.

In the period between D-Day and the presidential election, the Committee had continued to work unceasingly for unity at home and for support of the United Nations in Europe. But a decided change of content and emphasis appears in the January, 1945, issue of *The Lamp* where the Committee's eight point program for the coming year was presented. The abolition of racial discrimination was the first point, and the rest of the program was almost wholly concerned with changes in the laws dealing with naturalization and in the procedures followed in administering the laws. The changes would provide special consideration for those who had been in the armed services and for their families, and for those who had served three years in the U.S. Merchant Marine. The abolition of the literacy test for older people who had come here before 1930 was urged. The eighth point was a demand that naturalization be made an administrative procedure with the right of appeal and with the decision in contested cases left to the Federal courts. This would curtail the almost absolute power over the fate of individuals exercised by the Immigration Service, which has too often illustrated Lord Acton's famous dictum: "Power corrupts; absolute power corrupts absolutely."

The Naturalization Aid Service of the Committee had in the preceding year interviewed an average of sixty people a week (beside answering questions and giving advice by letter). This Service not only forced awareness of the growing danger upon the Committee, but also provided the experience necessary to prove how badly particular changes in law and procedure were needed. It was to spread this awareness to broad sections of the people, to inform those who might need the Service that help was available, and to establish the need for the changes its program advocated, that the Committee issued at this time a telling four page folder entitled "A Typical Day at the ACPFB."

The cover reproduced a calendar sheet, showing an 8:30 A.M. appointment to take a victim's children to Ellis Island; a 10:00 A.M. call to a lawyer on another case; a 10:00 A.M. call to Detroit on the Weiss case; an 11:00 A.M. call to Washington on the McClure case; a 1 P.M. visit to the Department of Justice on the Marino case, this encircled in red; a 9 P.M. conference. Inside the folder, is the reproduction of the Guiseppe Marino file card, which is so illuminating in its terseness that it is reproduced in full:

> Entered U.S. legally 1907; laborer for construction co. 1916 —left U.S. to join Allied army in Italy—1920 ret'd under Wilson proclamation for allied Veterans. Brought wife to U.S.—1934—has 6 Am. born children. 1936 was arrested for deportation on grounds of conviction of felony on circumstantial evidence 1909 (aged 19) served 6 mos. 1/15/37 Released $500 bail. 2/6/37 Conference with Immig. Auth. in Wash. D.C. 4/2/37 Atty's recomm. Congress'l action. 4/12/37 Private Bill introduced in Cong; deportation postponed. 3/5/38 Hearing before House Comm. considering bill, Marino and attys appear. 12/1/38 House group defeats bill. 1/15/39 Immig. Auth. resume deportation proceedings. 2/17/39 Last minute personal appeal to Auth. by family. 10/2/39 Applic. made for Presidential pardon. 12/6/39 Mrs. Marino naturalized. 11/3/40 President'l pardon granted. 12/1/40 Deportation proceedings dropped. 1/5/41 Application for citizenship filed. 11/21/44 Marino sworn in as American citizen—Closed.

Among other services, we are informed, the Committee secured bail, sent its counsel to Washington, appeared before the House Committee hearing, took the Marino family to Washington, applied for the Presidential pardon, at a total cost to the Committee of $310.17, and at no cost to the Marinos.

Other problems also faced the foreign born. Consistent with the program published in *The Lamp*, a New York "Legislative Conference" was held by the ACPFB in New York on January

20, 1945. It centered around an immediate situation—the practical disfranchisement of large numbers of naturalized citizens in the New York State elections. New York State Senator Herman Greenberg, the first speaker, had introduced two bills to remedy this injustice by making it easier to prove naturalized or derivative citizenship. Max Torchin, the executive secretary of the American Labor Party of King's County, also spoke in favor of the bills, support for which was voted by the Conference as "important in promoting the widest possible participation by foreign-born Americans in the political life of our state."

Still another barrier to the voting of the foreign born was the literacy test for first voters. This was discussed by Cyril Graze of the Teachers Union of New York City. There were too few examiners, in too much of a hurry, and no efforts were made to reassure the often nervous first voter. On the contrary, the passages to be read and the questions asked were sometimes made deliberately confusing. For the sentence, "The building is topped by a large dome which terminates in a statue known as the "Torch of Science," the question was, "What is on top of the building?" What would be the correct answer: dome, statue or Torch of Science?

Mr. Graze suggested various remedies, including classes offering preparation for the ordeal, dread of which kept many from registering to vote. A concrete result of the Conference was the mailing by the ACPFB of a letter calling attention to the voting rights of naturalized citizens and including samples of the literacy test previously used and the affidavit form needed when naturalization papers could not be found.

The third topic considered at the Conference was discrimination against minority groups in employment in New York.

Except for the specific bills before the New York legislature, these matters had been concerns of the ACPFB since its early years. During the war they had been subordinated to the war effort, and they were again to be subordinated to the more pressing problems of the foreign born which arose as peace drew nearer. By the time the war in Europe was officially over on May 8, the Committee knew, the foreign born were directly informed, and the public in general had to be made aware that the chief threats to the security of the foreign born were once again deportation and persecution. The situation began to resemble in many ways that which had originally called the Committee into existence in 1933.

On January 18, 1945, testifying to a Congressional committee on the Justice Department Appropriation Bill, the Commissioner of Immigration and Naturalization, Ugo Carusi, declared:

> We have at the present time approximately 16,000 warrants of deportation that have not been executed because of our inability to deport to Europe.

Also, as a result of the Alien Registration Act, 500,000 cases of what might be illegal entry had been found. About one fifth of these were probably deportable. No legal bar to deportation could be raised in most of these cases; but it was possible to get special consideration for those with American-born families, and on the basis of special circumstances for some others.

On May 1, the Gripsholm carried the first installment of 1,150 deportees back to Europe. Many of these had been seamen in the merchant marine; for them, as for war-contract laborers from Mexico and the West Indies, no exceptions were made.

Other organizations besides the ACPFB felt the effects of these deportations. Most important among them was the National Maritime Union, which held its Fifth National Convention in June, and to which the ACPFB sent a formal statement of its work and aims. This statement is especially significant as the first expression of concern over the deteriorating situation, and of the Committee's understanding of its work in postwar America. First in the statement stood the Naturalization Aid Service. Second was defense—with specific mention of the cases of Ernest Fox and Harry Bridges, and of the special problem of contract laborers. Third was education, with special reference to *The Lamp* and to published pamphlets. Fourth was legislative activity—the support of pending bills to eliminate the bar to citizenship for Filipinos, for natives of India, Burma, etc., and opposition to four "anti-alien" bills.

Circumstances forced the Committee back to its pre-war job!

The two cases cited to the National Maritme Union convention and reported at length in current issues of *The Lamp* were like the other cases chosen at various times by the ACPFB for national publicity—cases which could establish precedents.

Ernest Fox was born in Germany and was three years old when he was brought to this country by his family in 1909. He grew up in Seattle where he became a seaman. From 1935 to 1937 he was a member of the Sailor's Union of the Pacific and served as a member of the Central Labor Council, AFL. During the West Coast maritime strike he was chairman of the North-West Strike Committee and in 1937 he became the Washington State organizer for the CIO. Shortly after Pearl Harbor he answered the call for men to serve in the merchant marine, but just as his ship was leaving for the war zone, he was arrested for failing to register as an alien. (He had been an American for thirty-two of his thirty-five years!)

His punishment was the extraordinary one of "internment as a dangerous enemy alien" for the duration of the war. The fight for his release in which hundreds of organizations (mostly trade union locals) took part was led by the ACPFB. The legal battle was carried on by George Andersen of San Francisco and Carol King, counsel for the Committee. In June the Committee featured Fox's jubilant telegram: "Your splendid organization made possible my release on parole today. A million thanks."

The attempt to legalize internment of militantly anti-fascist, pro-labor, foreign-born Americans brought this statement from Carol King: "When Ernest Fox gets into trouble because he did not register as a German, we have no issue with the Government. But when Fox is interned as a dangerous enemy alien merely because he is an active trade-unionist, I think we did have a real complaint against the Attorney General."

In the case of Harry Bridges the ACPFB filed an *amicus* brief with the U.S. Supreme Court, contending that the deportation statute under which the proceedings against Bridges were brought was unconstitutional. The court's decision for Bridges was made on other grounds. But such were the circumstances surrounding the Bridges case both in the background, facts and court decision, such was the importance of it as a reflection of the general atmosphere of the country and of the interplay of forces, and issues, that special attention must be paid to it in any study of the foreign born.

While the court based its decision on other grounds, the concurring opinion of Justice Frank Murphy dealt specifically with the question of constitutionality. His words are a defense without reservation or equivocation of the American tradition of equal justice and equal rights. This concurring opinion was printed by the American Committee with a brief introduction by Carol King. The situation of the foreign born was never so succinctly and fundamentally put, the position of the Committee on the rights of the foreign born had never been better stated, nor does any publication better illustrate the purpose of its work. A few paragraphs from Carol King's introduction are essential for an understanding of the nature of the problem.

> There are two opposing schools of thought concerning non-citizens in this country.
>
> One school believes that the Federal courts cannot interfere with the sovereign power of the government over aliens; that aliens are 'guests' in America, no matter how long they may have lived here, and that the Constitution does not protect their right to remain here.
>
> The other school believes that aliens, as legal residents in this country—and future citizens—have the same constitutional rights as all other persons; that the Constitution must apply to all within our borders or else it will eventually apply to none. . . . Justice Murphy in his opinion . . . presents its argument eloquently. . . .
>
> These differences have always existed in our country, even during the first days of the American Republic. Then, one school sought to limit democratic rights, to prevent fulfillment of the American Revolution, and to place

> power in the hands of native reactionaries. But the people fought and won inclusion of the Bill of Rights in the Constitution. . . .
>
> The case of Harry Bridges was one of the battles fought in our day to preserve and extend American democracy. While the Bridges case is won, the basic democratic issues are not settled. These issues, while affecting only aliens directly, affect indirectly the democratic rights and welfare of all Americans. . . .
>
> Justice Murphy's opinion . . . tells in the measured and stern words of impartial justice what has been done to a man in the name of enforcing our deportation laws. . . . It challenges the right of Government under our Constitution "to make hollow mockery" of the right of free speech, press and assembly by depriving an alien of their protection in a deportation proceeding. . . .
>
> The ACPFB must rally all Americans to secure the repeal of this un-American provision in our deportation laws. . . .

The opinion of Justice Murphy begins with one of the sharpest denunciations of injustice and intolerance in Supreme Court history:

> The record in this case will stand forever as a monument to man's intolerance of man. Seldom if ever in the history of this nation has there been such a concentrated and relentless crusade to deport an individual because he dared to exercise the freedom that belongs to him as a human being and that is guaranteed to him by the Constitution.
>
> For more than a decade powerful economic and social forces have combined with public and private agencies to seek the deportation of Harry Bridges, who came to this country in 1920 from Australia. Emerging from the Pacific Coast maritime strike of 1934 as a recognized labor leader, Bridges incurred the hatred and hostility of those whose interests coincided directly or indirectly with the "vicious and inhumane practices toward longshoremen" [144 F2d 927, 928] that Bridges was combatting. His personal view-

> point on certain matters also antagonized many people of more conservative leanings. Agitation for his deportation arose. . . .
>
> This opposition to Bridges' presence in the United States has been as persistent as it has been undaunted by temporary setbacks.

The facts which justify the forceful statements of Justice Murphy can be briefly summarized. Shortly after the strike in 1934 and 1935, the first efforts to "get" Bridges through deportation were made. He was investigated by the San Francisco police and by the District Director of Immigration and Naturalization in San Francisco, who concluded in a report that

> The investigation of the alien referred to above has failed to show that he is in any manner connected with the Communist Party, or with any radical organization . . . whenever any legal ground for the deportation of Bridges has been brought to the attention of the Department of Labor, it has been investigated, but invariably it has been found that he was in the clear, and that his status as an immigrant was entirely regular.

In 1936 a House Committee undertook the first congressional investigation of Harry Bridges, during which the Commissioner of Immigration and Naturalization testified to facts:

> He has a perfect legal right to be in this country. The San Francisco police followed him unremittingly for years, and our men have also. . . . The facts are that there is no shred of evidence in our files . . . or police files . . . to indicate that he is in any way subject to the provisions of the immigration law because of his radical views.

In 1937 Secretary of Labor Perkins succumbed to intense pressure and put Bridges under oath in still another investigation. But George D. Reilly, then Solicitor of the Labor Department, dropped the matter on the ground that there was no basis for action. In spite of this, a resolution was introduced in Congress to impeach Secretary Perkins for failure to act on Bridges. This time she did "act" by issuing a deportation warrant against him in March, 1938. In July there commenced eleven weeks of hearings during which 7,742 pages of testimony were taken before James M. Landis, dean of Harvard Law School and former chairman of the Securities and Exchange Commission. In December, 1939, Dean Landis decided that

> The evidence . . . establishes neither that Harry Bridges is a member of nor affiliated with the Communist Party of America.

The Labor Department accepted the verdict, cancelling the deportation warrant.

But the reactionary anti-labor forces in Congress were not satisfied. In June, 1940, the House of Representatives passed the Allen Bill, clearly a bill of attainder and therefore thoroughly unconstitutional. The bill ordered the Attorney General ". . . notwithstanding any other provision of the law" to arrest and deport Bridges "whose presence in this country the Congress deems hurtful." Attorney General Jackson objected strongly that for the first time in American history "an Act of Congress has singled out a single named indivdual for deportation," and the bill died in the Senate. Congress retaliated fifteen days later by passing the Smith Act amending the deportation law, and stipulating that an alien could be deported if at the time he entered the United States, or any time thereafter, he was a member of or affiliated with an organization advocating the forceful overthrow of the government. Congressman Hobbs proudly announced in the *Congressional Record*:

> It is my joy to announce that this bill will do, in a perfectly legal and constitutional manner, what the bill specifically aimed at the deportation of Harry Bridges seeks to accomplish. This bill changes the law so that the Department of Justice should now have little trouble in deporting Harry Bridges and all others of similar ilk.

But in essence under its new guise, it was still a bill of attainder.

In February, 1941, a new warrant of deportation based on the Smith Act was issued against Bridges. In March hearings began before Presiding Inspector Charles B. Sears. This time they lasted ten weeks, and produced 7,546 pages of testimony from thirty-three witnesses (one more than in the Landis hearings). Judge Sears, accepting the testimony of only two witnesses, one admittedly "strongly biased" and the other denying what the FBI claimed he had told them, found Bridges deportable. However, a four-man Board of Immigration Appeals unanimously overruled him in January, 1942, with the verdict that

> We find that the evidence in this record does not establish that Harry Bridges was at any time a member of or affiliated with any organization proscribed by the statute.

But on May 28, 1942, something happened which had no precedent in immigration history. On that day, for the first time, Attorney General Biddle, forgetting his former advocacy of justice towards the foreign born, overruled his own Immigration Appeals Board without giving Bridges prior notice and therefore denying him an opportunity to prepare argument in defense. Furthermore, Biddle denied a petition for a hearing before him, and Bridges was ordered deported. Six hundred prominent Americans were sufficiently outraged to appeal to the President to rescind the Biddle decision, declaring:

> In the last few days we have given careful consideration to the far-reaching effects of the Attorney General's order. To the best of our ability, we have analyzed the public response, and have found organized labor shocked and concerned, government production chiefs and patriotic industrial leaders deeply disturbed, many newspaper editors and columnists critical—and the appeasement, anti-war forces of the country, along with the official Axis propaganda bureaus, delighted by the decision. . . .

Mr. Biddle's decision was described by one commentator as "the blunder for which pro-Axis propagandists have been waiting." It is exactly that, through its negation of the cause for which we are fighting and its contradiction of your pledge that all loyal residents of our country would find a place in this fight. . . .

Because the decision rendered by Mr. Biddle in the case of Harry Bridges can only serve to undermine our national morale, and because it has already been used to create distrust of aliens and of labor leaders, we urge upon you the necessity of directing reconsideration. We make this plea not alone in justice to Harry Bridges, alien and labor leader, but in justice to Harry Bridges, fighting leader of the men behind the fighting lines, forceful asset to our war effort, vigorous spokesman for unity behind the war. . . .

We believe, therefore, that you must offset the dangerous aspects of the Attorney General's order by a positive and immediate reaffirmation of the rights of labor, and of all loyal racial, religious and political groups, to full participation in the war.

In June, 1942, Bridges appealed to Judge Martin Welsh of the District Court, who upheld the Biddle order in February, 1943. In March the appeal was carried to the U.S. Circuit Court of Appeals for the Ninth Circuit. On June 26, 1944, the court upheld the ruling of the Attorney General by a vote of 3-2. Judge Healy, in his dissent, declared:

It is notable that the alien, in one fashion or another, has been under almost continuous investigation for a period of more than five years. Prior to and during the course of the second trial the Service has enlisted the powerful cooperation of the Federal Bureau of Investigation. The country has been scoured for witnesses, every circumstance of Bridges' active life had been subjected to scrutiny, and presumably no stone was left unturned which might conceal evidence of the truth of the charges which the alien so flatly denied. The most significant feature of

> the inquiry, as it seems to me, is the paucity of the evidentiary product as contrasted with the magnitude of the effort expended in producing it.

He also stated that

> The evidence before Judge Sears would be condemned and proscribed without hesitation by any American court. . . . the crucial finding in the case was arrived at in reliance upon incompetent evidence—evidence, moreover, received and considered in violation of a regulation of the Department designed to insure fair hearings and safeguard the rights of aliens.

On July 26, 1944, Bridges appealed for a rehearing. On September 27, the court denied the rehearing. On December 27, Bridges filed with the Supreme Court of the United States a petition for a writ of certiorari. On June 18, 1945, the Supreme Court reversed the lower court, and held that the warrant of deportation against Bridges was unlawful. It was in this decision that Justice Murphy wrote this concurring opinion:

> It is not surprising that the background and intensity of this effort to deport one individual should result in a singular lack of due process of law. Much of the evidence presented by the Government has been described by the Attorney General as "untrustworthy, contradictory or unreliable. . . ."
>
> But the Constitution has been more than a silent anemic witness to this proceeding. It has not stood idly by while one of its subjects is being excommunicated from this nation . . . When the immutable freedoms guaranteed by the Bill of Rights have been so openly and concededly ignored, the full wrath of constitutional condemnation descends upon the action taken by the Government. And only by expressing the wrath can we give form and substance to "the great, the indispensable democratic freedoms" (Thomas v. Collins) to which this nation is dedicated.

[The] assumption underlying the statute is that the "plenary" power of Congress to deport resident aliens is unaffected by the guarantee of substantive freedoms contained in the Bill of Rights. . . .

I am unable to believe that the Constitution sanctions that assumption or the consequences that logically flow from its application. The power to exclude and deport aliens is one springing out of the inherent sovereignty of the United States.

. . . But once an alien lawfully enters and resides in this country he becomes invested with the rights guaranteed by the Constitution to all people within our borders. . . . None of [the provisions of the Bill of Rights] acknowledges any distinction between citizens and resident aliens. They extend their inalienable privileges to all "persons. . . ." [They] make no exception in favor of deportation laws.

Any other conclusion would make our constitutional safeguards transitory and discriminatory in nature. Thus the Government would be precluded from enjoining or imprisoning an alien for exercising his freedom of speech. But the Government at the same time would be free . . . to deport him for exercising that very same freedom. . . . I cannot agree that the framers of the Constitution meant to make such a hollow mockery of human freedom. . . .

The deportation statute completely ignores the traditional American doctrine requiring personal guilt rather than guilt by association or imputation before a penalty is inflicted. The doctrine of personal guilt is one of the most fundamental principles of our jurisprudence. . . . Yet the deportation statute on its face flatly disregards this rule. It condemns an alien to exile for beliefs and teachings to which he may not personally subscribe.

It is no answer that a deportation proceeding is technically non-criminal in nature. . . . The impact of deportation upon the life of an alien is often as great if not greater than the imposition of a criminal sentence. A deported alien may lose his family, his friends and his livelihood forever. Return to his native land may result in poverty, persecution or even death. . . .

> We as a nation lose part of our greatness whenever we deport or punish those who merely exercise their freedoms in an unpopular though innocuous manner. The strength of this nation is weakened more by those who suppress the freedoms of others than by those who are allowed freely to think and act as their consciences dictate.
>
> Our concern does not halt with the fate of Harry Bridges. . . . The liberties of the 3,500,000 other aliens in this nation are also at stake. . . . Only by zealously guarding the rights of the most humble, the most unorthodox . . . among us can freedom flourish and endure in our land.

It might be well to add here a few words from Justice William O. Douglas, who delivered the majority opinion:

> Freedom of speech and of press is accorded aliens residing in this country. So far as this record shows, the literature published by Harry Bridges, the utterances made by him were entitled to that protection. They revealed a militant advocacy of the cause of trade unionism. But they did not teach or advocate the subversive conduct condemned by the statute.

The Bridges decision could well be claimed as a vital victory not only by the foreign born but by the American people as a whole. But the Bridges case was not yet finished and its continuance is a necessary part of the story of the fight for the rights of the foreign born. Immediately after the Supreme Court decision, Harry Bridges became a "new" American in a hurry. On June 23, Bridges filed for citizenship—something which more than a decade of hounding had prevented him from doing before. On September 17, he faced a naturalization court in San Francisco and before the Hon. Thomas M. Foley the government counsel said there was no objection to naturalization. Harry Bridges became an American citizen at last.

Armed with his citizenship papers, fortified by the Supreme Court decision, Bridges could now dream of enjoying in future the freedom and security guaranteed to United States citizens under the Constitution and the Bill of Rights. But his dream and his enjoyment were short-lived. Not even the sharp words of Justice Murphy had lessened the prejudices of his persecutors.

In May, 1949, Bridges and his two character witnesses were indicted on three counts of criminal fraud and conspiracy. Count one claimed that they had conspired to defraud the United States, impairing, obstructing and defeating the proper administration of the naturalization laws by having Bridges fraudulently petition for and obtain naturalization. Count two claimed that Bridges made a false statement when he answered the question about Communist Party membership. The Government claimed that Bridges had committed fraud when he had sworn he did not belong to the Communist Party. The Government alleged he did belong from 1933 to September 17, 1945. Count three claimed that the two character witnesses assisted Bridges in receiving a fraudulently obtained certificate of naturalization. And the merry-go-round was on again.

In moving for dismissal, Bridges claimed that the matter had already been adjudicated by the highest court, that this indictment was double jeopardy, and further, that the three-year statute of limitations made criminal indictment void. James Lawrence Fly, former Federal Communicaions Commission chairman and attorney for Bridges, declared that "There has never been a more melancholy record in American legal history. . . . One seeks in vain for a comparable case. . . ." What was perhaps more melancholy was the evidence of subservience to and connivance with the reactionary forces on the part of the Department of Justice and some sections of the judiciary. For in June, 1949, Bridges' union was engaged in a longshore strike in Hawaii. And on June 26, the then U.S. Attorney General Tom Clark, now Justice of the U.S. Supreme Court, made a speech before the American Relief for Germany Committee in Milwaukee, in which he stated:

> If we are successful in our present prosecution of

> Bridges, it may be that we can break the Hawaiian situation without any other intervention.

Melancholy indeed!

On November 1, 1949, Bridges and his two witnesses went on trial before Federal Judge George B. Harris in San Francisco, during which the judge took on at times the role of prosecutor. When attorneys for the defense objected vehemently they were threatened with contempt of court. On April 4, 1950, Bridges and his two co-defendants were found guilty. Bridges was sentenced to five years, his two character witnesses to two years each. And the attorneys were imprisoned on contempt charges. Bridges was released on $25,000 bail pending appeal. But when the Korean war broke out the government demanded the revocation of the bail on the ground that Bridges proved himself a menace to national security when he proposed at a union meeting that the San Francisco local go on record for an immediate cease-fire and the settlement of all issues through United Nations negotiations. U.S. Prosecutor Donahue insisted that Bridges be jailed because

> In this common cause . . . there can be no minority opinion, for we are not fighting for more security; we are fighting for survival.

Thus the "police action" in Korea required a degree of conformity greater than demanded even during World War II.

Judge Harris obediently complied. Bridges' bail was revoked and he went to jail for twenty-one days. The bail question was appealed to the Ninth Circuit Court, which overruled the lower court, and Bridges was again released. The majority opinion written by Judge Healy (Judge William Orr concurring) declared:

> There was a period in English history when high judges prostituted themselves to the role of mere instruments for carrying into effect the arbitrary will of the

> Crown. . . . It was in part owing to those unhappy experiences [that] the judiciary was set up as an equal [and independent] branch of the government. . . . The conception of the founders was of an unfettered judiciary standing whenever necessary, between the individual and the exercise by the state of arbitrary power. But it is one thing to refrain from interference [where public safety is involved] and quite another for the courts to become themselves tools of the military; and we say now . . . it is the duty of the courts to set their faces like flint against this erosive subversion of the judicial process.

The Circuit Court then proceeded to sustain Judge Harris on the conviction of Bridges and his two witnesses. On May 4, 1953, the appeal from the Circuit Court decision was argued before the U.S. Supreme Court. And on June 15, the Supreme Court announced its decision. The verdicts of the District Court and the Circuit Court were set aside, and Bridges was restored to citizenship. But even this did not restore a sense of decency to "judicial prostitution" or remove "erosive subversion."

It appeared that the 1949 trial was a double action: a criminal charge of fraud and a civil action to revoke citizenship based on the alleged charge of fraud. Before Judge Harris, the government elected to go to trial on the criminal charge. When the Supreme Court reversed the criminal conviction, the government asked that the case be put on the calendar for the fall of 1954. Bridges' attorney contended that the civil action to denaturalize and then deport was illegal. But the court again sustained the government. And on June 20, 1955, Harry Bridges faced his fifth proceeding on the same charge – quintuple jeopardy – making up a total of eleven and a half years of engagement in trials out of twenty-one consecutive years of consistent and persistent investigation and persecution. *The Lamp* of July-September, 1955, reports that on July 29, Judge Louis E. Goodman of the Federal District Court in San Francisco denied the petition of the Justice Department for the revocation of the citizenship of Harry Bridges.

V. THE COLD WAR

16. Turning the Clock Back

WHEN Congressman Edward Livingston spoke in the House of Representatives against the Sedition Act of 1798, he was not so much predicting the future as describing a pattern of behavior which under certain circumstances would always be repeated with only minor variations. Said Congressman Livingston:

> The country will swarm with informers, spies, delators, and all the odious reptile tribe that breed in the sunshine of despotic power. The hours of the most unsuspected confidence, the intimacies of friendship, or the recesses of domestic retirement, afford no security. . . . Do not let us be told that we are to excite fervor against a foreign aggression to establish a tyranny at home; and that we are absurd enough to call ourselves free and enlightened while we advocate principles that would have disgraced the age of Gothic barbarity.

If von Clausewitz is correct in his definition of war as "a mere continuation of policy by other means," then peace is the establishment of the policy which war continues. But if the policies of those supporting the war are confused and divergent then the peace which follows will either be confused, or will reflect the particular policy which happens to be dominant by the time the war ends.

President Franklin Delano Roosevelt had solemnly written:

> We seek peace—enduring peace. More than an end to war, we want an end to the beginning of all wars—yes, an end to this brutal, inhuman and thoroughly impractical method of settling the differences between governments. . . .

Such a peace was never attained. For on the day after these words were written, President Roosevelt was dead; and in his place came Harry S. Truman.

How could two individuals lead a nation in such diametrically opposite directions both at home and in international relations? The answer is relatively simple, and it must be taken into account if the course of later events is to be even partially understood. It was not so much the individuals, as the forces each represented that made the difference. This was symbolized by the fact that within a brief period of time Washington was swept clean of the Roosevelt type of bi-partisan officials and advisors, who were replaced by men of very different background and convictions.

What this shift of forces meant internationally is made quite clear by Albert Z. Carr, who was a special assistant to President Truman, in his book, *Truman, Stalin and Peace.* In May of 1945, only one month after Roosevelt's death, Carr said:

> A complete diplomatic rupture with the Soviets, with war not far off, was then privately predicted by certain Washington officials—one of them, at least, on the White House Staff.

This seems a surprising attitude to take toward an ally, who was at that very moment, with the knowledge of Truman, preparing to enter the war on our side against Japan. There is ample evidence that men who were in a position to know believed from 1946 to 1952 that Russia neither wanted nor would provoke war. Compare for example the judgments of Forrestal, General Lucius Clay, and the ambassadors to Russia, Averell Harriman and General Bedell Smith (*Forrestal Diaries*) and for

1950-52, George Kennan (*Readers Digest,* March 1950), the heads of NATO (*N.Y. Times,* Nov. 1951), Admiral Kirk (*U.S. News and World Report*, Dec. 1950), General Gruenther (*Chicago Tribune,* March 13, 1952) and Herbert Hoover (*N.Y. Times,* Jan. 6, 1952).

Yet anti-Soviet policies and propaganda persisted; and the attempt to charge Russia with the responsibility for everything that went wrong either in the United Nations from its founding in San Francisco onwards, or anywhere else in the world, was largely successful, in spite of occasional voices reminding the United States that mistakes were also made elsewhere. Sumner Welles in his book *Where Are We Heading* published in 1946, wrote:

> . . . It has become the tendency in the Western world to place the entire blame for the tragic collapse in peace-making at the door of the Soviet government. It would seem to me far more realistic to admit that the blame for the present disaster should be shared by the government of the United States.

And in the *Saturday Review of Literature* of March 8, 1947, the industrialist, Robert R. Young declared:

> Russia showed not the remotest sign of aggression . . . prior to our interest in her border states Poland and Manchuria coincident with gratuitous and undiplomatic insults. Every move she made has been a counter-move.

The Cold War became and has remained the accepted policy of the government. For obvious reasons, it has been generally supported by "Big Business." Consider the comment in *U.S. News and World Report*, May 26, 1950:

> Government planners figure they have found the magic formula for almost endless good times. They are now beginning to wonder if there may not be something to perpetual motion after all. . . . Cold War is the catalyst.

> Cold War is an automatic pump-primer. Turn a spigot, and the public clamors for more arms spending. Turn another, the clamor ceases. Truman confidence, cockiness is based on this "Truman formula." Truman era of good times, the President is told, can run much beyond 1952. Cold War demands, if fully exploited, are almost limitless.

The end of the war brought changes within the United States as well as in external relations. While fighting lasted, the labor unions had patriotically refrained from the use of strikes to enforce their demands; but in 1945, faced with rising prices and stationary wages, three and a half million men went on strike; in 1946, four and a half million. The president of General Electric declared that the problems of the United States could be summed up in two words: "Russia abroad and Labor at home." In 1947 Congress passed the Taft-Hartley Act against the latter, an act which, according to the ACLU "put many of [Labor's] hard won rights . . . in a legal strait-jacket."

It is difficult to say how much conscious and intentional relation existed between the direct effort to curb labor and the government's "cold war" attack on so-called "subversive elements." Certainly the same forces and many of the same individuals were involved in both. And the activities of the House Un-American Activities Committee and the procedures under President Truman's Loyalty Order, which were imitated in many places, fostered disunion and suspicion in labor as elsewhere. An atmosphere had been created in which every variety of demagogue could flourish.

The increasing antagonism between the U.S.A. and the Soviet Union (U.S.S.R.), and the increasing influence of those forces in America which wished to repudiate the domestic policies of the "Roosevelt era" were rapidly generating in the United States the "second Red Scare so reminiscent of the hysteria of the years after the First World War," as Professor Link puts it in the work previously cited. The fear of Russia and Communist "infiltration" in America increased steadily with the succession of investigations and trials: Amerasia (1945), the Canadian Royal

Commission exposure (1946), the Chambers-Hiss controversy (1948), the trial of Hiss (1949), Elizabeth Bentley's "revelations" (1948) and the Judith Coplon charges (1949). This backward trend was encouraged, fed and "legitimatized" by Truman's Loyalty Order and by the Congressional Taft-Hartley Act. That Truman himself fell into the pit which he had dug and was later accused of "twenty years of treason" was both ironic and inevitable.

In such a situation, what security had the foreign born, particularly the non-citizen? All the factors that made possible the persecution of this vulnerable section of the population were present in the highest degree. The mounting tension found a vent in ever-increasing attacks on the foreign born, and on organizations which might plausibly be labelled pro-communist because they continued to work for justice and the protection of the law for all—including those accused of communist "affiliations."

And to this was added one more factor, a direct result of the Cold War. For events in Europe created their confusions and tensions in the foreign-born communities. With the approval of the State Department, and with its direct and indirect financial assistance, refugees from East European countries poured into the United States. To a large degree they were business people, professionals, intellectuals—articulate people who came here to find refuge from social and political systems which they did not like. Once here, they stirred up dissensions and divisions among the related groups already established here, in their effort to support and influence American Cold War foreign policy. Their divisive influence was reflected in the foreign language press and in foreign-born organizational life. And with the axes they were grinding, they hewed to pieces the war-time unity of the foreign-born communities.

17. Tension Tightens

TOM CLARK, who was U.S. Attorney General immediately after the end of the World War II, could well stand as the symbol of repression to the foreign born. What Palmer was to 1920, Clark was to the mid-forties, and more. He not only made his own direct contribution to the reactionary anti-democratic acts of terror, he instituted departmental policies and procedures jeopardizing the constitutionally guaranteed freedoms of the individual whether native or foreign born—policies which his successors consistently followed. Without the precedents set by Clark, the objective of Herbert Brownell to eliminate nonconformists would have been more difficult to implement.

Whereas Palmer after 1920 sank into political oblivion, except for the association of his name with the infamous acts of tyranny, Clark went upward to the U.S. Supreme Court. Nothing better reflects the change in the political atmosphere in the country; nothing more fully exhibits the corroding influence of Cold War politics and psychology.

When the Immigration and Naturalization Service was transferred from the Labor Department to the Justice Department in 1940, misgivings were expressed about the future handling of immigration problems. These misgivings were laid aside for a time because of the fair-mindedness and humanity of Earl Harrison in the post of Commissioner. With the accession of Clark to the Attorney-Generalship, however, the worst fears showed themselves to have been fully justified.

Against the unanimous recommendation of the Board of Immigration Appeals, Clark denied a visa to a British Labor Party leader and former member of Parliament because he had been a communist until 1937. In a speech at the national conference of federal attorneys in September, 1946, Clark called for an intensive drive against the foreign born. "If any alien in your district engages in Communist Party activity, there is no place for him in the United States," he announced. Fifteen months later, on January 15, 1948, in an address to the Cathedral Club of Brooklyn, New York, he declared: "Those who do not believe in the ideology of the United States shall not be allowed to stay in the United States." *The Lamp* posed at the time, the pertinent question: "Did the Attorney General mean the ideology set forth in the Bill of Rights?"

The procedure under which residents in this country here without legal entry (mostly refugees) had been permitted a pre-examination followed by departure to Canada and a return with a proper visa, was discontinued. Attorney Isaac Shorr, in an article in *The Lamp* of December, 1945, correctly characterized this change as "a first step in the direction of a general attack on immigrants and foreign-born citizens, to be followed by other and even more far-reaching oppression." Mr. Shorr's foresight was backed by a quarter of a century experience with American immigration laws.

Citizenship was refused more and more often to any who had been prominent in labor unions or who were members of unpopular organizations. The ACPFB reported a steadily increasing number of requests for investigation of such denials. The government attorney had used against Anthony Goncharevich the files of the House "Un-American (Dies) Committee." The ACPFB protested such usage both publicly and by letter to Ugo Carusi, Commissioner of the Immigration and Naturalization Service. The citizenship of Spero Evanoff of Lebanon, Pa., had been held up for four years. When after an investigation instigated by the ACPFB, it was finally granted in December, 1945, Mr. Evanoff wrote, "It was a great day for me—for which

I have long waited. . . . I will be eternally grateful." John Wasilewski had been originally arrested for deportation in the Palmer Raids of 1920, and the twenty-five year old warrant was held to be a bar to his application for naturalization. This decision was reversed by the Federal District Court in February, 1947, and the reversal was sustained by the Circuit Court.

Citizenship was also won for Thomas Scarpone, whom the Committee had saved from deportation in 1936, and for a Cuban, who had served three and a half years in the army (two years overseas). A two year fight against the Justice Department's efforts to get rid of Humberto Silex, of El Paso, Texas, a leader among the Spanish-speaking people of the Southwest, was won in the Federal District Court in Texas. The Justice Department had first tried to deport Silex because of a thirty-minute visit across the Mexican border. When that failed, they opposed the granting of citizenship on the ground of "immoral character." The only evidence offered was his plea of guilty to a charge of aggravated assault for which he had been fined $35, and for which he had later been granted a full pardon by the Governor of Texas. He was married and had eight American-born children. The court, on the basis of testimony from "reputable, credible witnesses" found that there existed no evidence of "immoral character" or of hostility to the United States and ruled him eligible for citizenship. But not every non-citizen denied naturalization could seek justice in the federal courts.

As a matter of fact, the whole situation with regard to naturalization grew progressively worse. At the October, 1945 Conference of the ACPFB the question was dealt with at a single session from the point of view of speeding the naturalization of 3,000,000 non-citizens as the most obvious defense against both deportation and discrimination. Ways of facilitating naturalization were suggested and the special hardships encountered by seamen and contract laborers were emphasized.

But less than a year later the situation had so deteriorated that, even while the American Committee was still attempting to keep its emphasis on unity and on united efforts to preserve the American liberal tradition of justice for all, it was compelled to hold a special conference on American citizenship. And its call to this conference in April, 1946, stressed the "drive being made to deprive naturalized citizens of their rights," the increasing difficulties confronting those seeking naturalization, and the denial in the naturalization and deportation laws of freedom of speech and freedom of thought to non-citizens.

The year 1947 was marked by one of the most flagrant and widely publicized instances of the abuse of power by the Immigration Service. Farrell, in the steel producing area of Pennsylvania, was a town of about 20,000, mostly Yugoslav-Americans who had been in the country some thirty-five years. In January, two leaders in the community, both citizens, were called to the Youngstown, Ohio, office of the Immigration Service, questioned separately for three hours, and threatened with revocation of their citizenship. According to a folder on the case issued by the ACPFB:

> They were insulted by insinuating questions concerning their private lives. They were harangued. They were threatened that, unless they cease their progressive activities in the Yugoslav-American community, their American citizenship would be revoked.

Naturalization was refused to a dozen or more applicants, including two women whose sons had fought in the U.S. armed forces overseas. People in the community were told that membership in various organizations—the Aria Singing Society, the Croatian American Civic Club, the local branches of the Croatian Fraternal Union, the IWO or even the sending of aid to friends and relatives in Tito's Yugoslavia—would bar them permanently from citizenship. The Belgrade newspapers reported this example of "American liberty," and the United States press in general got its first information from Belgrade. The ACPFB, however, had issued two folders, one on the situation in general, the other featuring a letter to Commissioner Carusi, signed by sixty prominent women, including Mrs. Eleanor Roosevelt, Dr. Mary McLeod Bethune, Hon. Jane M. Bolin, Genevieve Taggard, protesting the denial of citizenship to the two women. Organizations across the country joined in the protest, and the Youngstown office changed its ways.

However, another problem, that of deportation, came to absorb in ever-increasing measure the attention and energies of freedom-loving people and of such organizations as the American Committee. The situation of alien seamen in particular had involved tragedy for many from the moment hostilities ceased. Of their services in the war, Craig S. Vincent, Atlantic Coast representative of the War Shipping Administration, had said:

> Alien seamen were a crucial factor in keeping American flag vessels sailing during the most difficult period. Over 3,000 assignments were made to Panamanian and Honduran flag vessels [owned by American shipping companies]. Forty-three nationalities were represented by the seamen who were assigned. Alien seamen are deserving of full measure of praise for that service which they performed so courageously and skillfully in the fight against Fascism.

U.S. Senator Pepper had said:

> Men from countries overrun by the enemy who have lost family and friends found it possible to contribute to victory as members of the American merchant marine.

General Eisenhower had said:

> When final victory is ours there is no organization that will share its credit more deservedly than the Merchant Marine. We count upon their efficiency and their utter devotion to duty as we do our own.

And President Roosevelt had declared:

> They deserve, and receive from all of us, our thanks for the job they have done.

But no gratitude was forthcoming from Attorney General Clark's Justice Department and Commissioner Carusi's Immigration Service. For, despite their contribution to the war effort (in the course of which they had been attacked in mid-ocean by bombers, submarines and torpedoes), they were ineligible for residence in the United States and faced deportation regardless of the fact that many had American wives and children dependent upon them. For instance, a Swedish seaman, twice torpedoed during the war, had not been permitted to see his wife and child in the United States for eight years, since he could not apply for legal entry. This provision had worked similar hardship for many.

Such was their plight and American ingratitude, that *The New York Times* editorialized upon it on July 22, 1945:

> Barred in many cases from a return to their own countries, ineligible for residence here, they have continued . . . going to sea and into the world's dangerous war zones on United States flag ships.
>
> Under our present . . . laws, these men who have served faithfully and tirelessly for the last three and a half years are ineligible for United States citizenship until they have served five full years at sea. . . . Time in port . . . does not count. . . . There are some 15,000 now sailing under the American flag.
>
> It would seem that if five years' service in peacetime qualified a man for citizenship, then three years in time of war should suffice, or one year for that matter. As a token of gratitude this country should feel for services rendered—and keeping the supplies flowing was certainly a great and vital service—favorable consideration by Congress is in order.

The ACPFB, in a folder entitled "Is This the Way to Treat Heroes?" listed the bills under consideration by Congress, one by Sen. Pepper granting legal entry after one year's war-time service, and one by Sen. George L. Radcliffe and one by Rep. DeLacy granting American citizenship after three years' war-time service. Neither bill was acted upon by the 79th Congress and the fight for fair treatment of alien seamen continued.

But it was not only alien seamen who faced deportation. The Attorney General's bias was manifested in many ways. Ten trade union leaders were among the first picked up for deportation, an attack aimed at the United Shoe Workers, the Transport Workers Union, the Upholsterers Union, among others. A native of Holland, legally resident in the United States, a charter member of the Marine Cooks and Stewards Union, CIO, was put forcibly on board ship in Galveston, Texas, on verbal orders from Clark, and after the boat had sailed was given his choice of going along as a prisoner or as a member of the crew.

Two young men in their early twenties, one Rumanian the other Polish, had been together as Jewish prisoners in Buchenwald. Their families had perished; their only surviving relatives were in America. In their eagerness to leave the horrible past behind them, they came as stowaways to the United States. On arrival they were turned over to the Immigration Service. The Board of Immigration Appeals by a 3-2 vote sustained their exclusion and the Attorney General gave the order. The ACPFB managed to delay their departure and started a publicity campaign in their behalf. The *New York Herald Tribune* published in March, 1946, the message sent to the Committee by Albert Einstein:

> I heartily agree with your efforts on behalf of the two Nazi victims. Here is an occasion to show that the mentality of the United States is essentially different from Nazi mentality.

Special bills for the admission of the two young men were speedily introduced in Congress by Rep. Adolph Sabath, but they were opposed in the House Committee on Immigration by the Attorney General, who also refused to release the two while Congressional action was pending. The American Jewish Congress requested that the case of the young men be handed over to it, and the responsibility of the ACPFB ended.

Rabbi Ruttner, a native of Rumania, came to this country with a Red Cross passport. He was held at Ellis Island because his papers were not in order. A congregation in Newark was ready with a contract for his services. The Justice Department refused any reconsideration of the exclusion and all efforts to gain permission for him to go to Canada and re-enter failed. He finally accepted asylum offered him in Cuba.

Rabbi Feierlicht and his wife, "displaced persons," had come to this country on visitors' visas. Mrs. Feierlicht was expecting a child and the Jewish holidays were at hand. But the Justice Department refused extension of the visa. The refusal was publicized by the ACPFB and the resulting protests from various organizations finally won for Mrs. Feierlicht the three months' extension needed.

Arrests for deportation multiplied, deportation orders were issued with no opportunity given for legal defense. Men and women were arrested for deportation and held without bail. Ellis Island in New York harbor and Terminal Island in San Pedro became virtual concentration camps. For 1946 and 1947, *The Lamp's* reviews of the year chronicled those ordered deported month by month. But by 1948, the cases were too many. In April, 1948, forty "political" deportees were listed (nineteen of whom were active trade unionists). By the end of the year, the list had grown to seventy-one. The United Press reported that for 1949 the Justice Department was planning 482 new arrests on political grounds. *The Lamp's* review of the year 1949 gave a total of 140 held in nineteen states.

Who were these people? The names called the roll of the world: Steve Tandaric, John Nabeshka, Peter Harisiades, John Greenberg, Charles Doyle, Benoit van Laekan, Katherine Hyndman, Eula Figuerido, Anna Taffler, Michael Salerno, James Mackay, William Heikkila, Sayad Hasan. Their arrests covered the United States from San Francisco to Boston. Some of them were labor leaders. Some of them were or had been members of the Communist Party. And the Justice Department began its heresy hunt. That the heresy was economic and political rather than religious made no difference in the procedure. Ideas, not actions, were on trial.

Steve Tandaric of Indiana was born in a section of Austria-Hungary which became a part of Yugoslavia. He came to the United States in 1911. In 1937 he went to Spain as a member of the International Brigades. The deportation order was on the ground of illegal entry on his return from Spain. From the federal penitentiary in Indiana, serving a sentence for false claim of citizenship he wrote:

STATUE OF LIBERTY

Oh, ye indentured slaves and your kind of the days gone by,
The trail you left from across the pond to follow and leave
 tyranny behind!
You gave us Lincoln, emancipation with joy, to build, to grow
 forever on.
America, the home of the brave on the Atlantic.

Now again a homestead we must find.
We travel across a land so wide, in sail-less schooners, not a
 pond.
The humble, welders of a nation so great, connect the Pacific
 with the Atlantic so blue.
The nation is forged, a melting pot of people from all over the
 world.

The invitation stands in perpetuity, grand old lady with the
 torch so high.
The torch that guides us to your shore is like a rainbow in the
 sky, it ends at your door.
New Americans, your task is great, answer the call.
To our forebears that gave their lives we dedicate ours to
 carry on.

The two-year prison sentence given him seemed an excessive penalty for his false claim of American birth in order to work in a war industry. An organized campaign of letters of protest to Washington, of Christmas greetings sent to Tandaric in prison, of petitions and mass meetings, finally resulted in his release on parole, and new hearings in the deportation case. Steve Tandaric remained and worked in this country. In November, 1948, he wrote to make reservations for the Bill of Rights Dinner at the Fifteenth Anniversary Conference, and added, "It will be a pleasure seeing you again, am happy our meeting date is not far off." (In 1957 Steve Tandaric was again ordered deported by the Justice Department under the terms of the Walter-McCarran Act.)

While there were congratulatory messages and speeches at the Fifteenth Anniversary Conference in Chicago in 1948, the immediate problems tended to crowd out reminiscences and congratulations. The "kit" handed out to each of the delegates contained the list of sixty-six men and women facing deportation for political reasons, giving their ages and the length of time they had been in the United States. One man had spent 45 of his 47 years in this country; a woman 43 of her 48. Only three on the list had been here less than ten years. The oldest was 69; the youngest was 32. More than 50 of them had applied for citizenship.

Carol King's report to the Conference summed up the deportation procedures of the Department of Justice. She cited arrests with public fanfare of prominent union leaders like Michael Obermeier of the Hotel and Restaurant Workers Union; the use of highly unreliable informers like George Hewitt who had a warrant against him for perjury in the State of Washington. She said:

> The question in all these cases is substantially identical. The constitutional rights, and particularly the right of free speech and free association, to which non-citizens are entitled under our laws and the Federal Constitution. . . .
>
> Attorney General Clark stated quite openly that he was arresting "leaders." He has been doing this with various nationality and trade union groups. By these tactics the Department of Justice unnecessarily terrorized various groups in the community.

Mrs. King went on to speak of the cooperation of the Justice Department with the House Committee on Un-American Activities in the case of Alexander Stevens; of the refusal of bail to those picked up for deportation until the challenge of five determined men on Ellis Island brought thousands of protests.

Abner Green began his report with what he called "a message to the Conference" from Attorney General Clark—the newspaper report published on the anniversary of Pearl Harbor that the Justice Department was investigating 482 non-citizens and preparing deportation cases against them, and that the Department was preparing to denaturalize 228 citizens because they were communists. He summarized briefly the achievements of the Committee in its fifteen years and went directly to the problem of deportations.

> If you take the . . . figures issued by the Justice Department and . . . put them together, it is clear that we have a minimum of 4,000 non-citizens facing deportation.
>
> We have seen . . . during the past year what chaos, terror and havoc the Justice Department created with a mere sixty-six arrests. Imagine what will happen if they go ahead and arrest only the 482 mentioned in the United Press. That alone would mean one half million dollars in bail.
>
> About a year and a half ago, Tom Clark spoke of 124 deportation cases. We have [had] more than seventy. That is about sixty percent. Well, sixty percent of 4,000 is about 2,500. . . .
>
> The Justice Department is trying very hard to give the impression that its sole concern is with aliens and with communists. The first part is obviously false because they have announced that they are going to try to take away the citizenship of 228 naturalized Americans.
>
> The second part is equally false. Our Committee defends non-citizens who are communists. But a great number of these non-citizens who face deportation are not communists. Sixteen of the sixty-six deportees deny that they were ever members of the Communist Party. William

> Weber came from Germany in 1938. He hated Hitler and he joined the Communist Party here. He went to one meeting and decided that they were interested in too many things for which he had no interest. He never went to another meeting. Heinrich Nawrocki did join the Communist Political Association, but when the Communist Party was formed in the United States, he did not join it. There are others like them.
>
> Not one [of the sixty-six] is charged with committing any crimes against anyone. Not one of them need be reluctant to defend himself, or need they be in the slightest bit ashamed of the years they have spent in this country. They have been useful, hard-working, democratic people.

But even the determined Tom Clark was not always invincible. In a battle with five men who would not yield and who had the courage to take a stand to win mass support, Clark emerged second best, despite the power of his office.

Charles A. Doyle was forty-three at the time of his arrest for deportation. A native of Scotland, the youngest of eleven children in an Irish worker's family, he came to the United States in 1924. He was married and the father of four American-born children. So devoted and efficient were his activities on behalf of his fellow unionists, that he was unanimously elected in convention as international vice-president of the United Chemical Workers of America, CIO. While giving leadership to a strike in Niagara Falls, N. Y. in 1947, he crossed over to Windsor, Ontario, to attend the international convention of his union. He had, of course, obtained a valid border crossing card before leaving; but on his return he was barred from re-entry. He came back illegally, was arrested on February 20, 1948, on a deportation warrant, taken at once to Ellis Island and held there without bail.

Gerhart Eisler, brother of the famed German composer, Hans Eisler, was fifty-one. During the defense of Spanish democracy against the Franco civil war in Spain, he was one of the Germans who joined other anti-fascist forces in the International

Brigades fighting Hitler's protege. He spent a number of years in concentration camps and prisons because of his fight against the German Nazis. He came to the United States on his way to Mexico, but was not permitted to proceed further. But his case took a peculiar twist. From the first moment that it became possible he sought by every means to return to his native land but American authorities refused him exit, apparently anxious to keep this "alien" in America. It would appear then that his arrest for deportation was a sign that the administration's left hand did not know what its right hand was doing. But this opinion would be a grave injustice to Tom Clark. The arrest of Eisler for deportation when the State Department would not allow the refugee to leave the country, was all too plainly intended to keep him indefinitely—perhaps for life—inside prison walls.

Then there was Irving Potash, at 45 manager of the Furriers Joint Council of New York and vice-president of the International Fur and Leather Workers Union, CIO. Born in Russia, he came to the United States in 1913, eventually marrying an American citizen and becoming the father of an American-born daughter. Twice he applied for citizenship, which was denied each time because of his union and political activities. For Potash, it seemed, did not merely investigate racketeering, gangsterism and racketeer-management relations in industry. He fought it at a time when fighting it meant literally risking one's life, and when fighting it meant involvement in city politics in which racketeers had their fingers manipulating politicians, police and "civic"-minded public figures, as well as corrupt labor leaders.

Ferdinand C. Smith came up the hard way in a rough industry. A native of Jamaica, British West Indies, he came to the United States in 1918. At fifty-four he was married, the father of an American-born daughter and the grandfather of an American-born citizen. His application for citizenship, filed for the last time in 1946, was pending at the time of his arrest. He had shipped out as a seaman for nineteen years. In recognition of his leadership of the struggle of seamen for decent and humane conditions, he was elected secretary of the National Maritime Union, became a member of the executive board of the national CIO, and a trustee of the Sydenham Hospital in Harlem. On the night before his arrest, he sat on the same platform at a meeting in Harlem with Henry A. Wallace, formerly vice-president of the United States, who later that year was to be a candidate for the presidency on the Progressive Party ticket.

John Williamson was the 45-year-old trade union secretary of the Communist Party and a member of its national board, with over twenty years of organizing, writing and speaking activity behind him. Trade union leaders of varying political shades respected him highly for his contributions to the building of a powerful labor movement in the United States. Married to an American citizen he was the father of two American-born children, one of them an infant of less than a year at the time of his arrest.

The five were arrested at different times during February, 1948, and kept in solitary confinement on Ellis Island, compelled even to eat their meals alone. As a result of their protests, they were finally put together into one cell, which was locked day and night. Still worse was the denial of bail, an unwarranted action, carried out, the prisoners were informed at the time of their arrest, at the special order of Tom Clark. In the whole procedure, the real purpose of the Attorney General seemed clear. Here was an attempt to strike directly at trade unions through the use of his deportation powers against their leadership. Here was an effort to apply the red label to the entire labor movement by including Eisler and Williamson in the group. And here, finally, was the beginning of an endeavor to establish without specific legislation an American concentration camp in which deportees could be held at the pleasure of the Attorney General. Court decisions, due process of law, the Constitution itself could be set aside by the head of the Department of Justice!

Their personal liberty was important to the five imprisoned men. But as leaders in the labor movement who had long participated in social and political activities, they also recognized fully the importance of the principles of democracy and civil liberties involved. They were convinced that justice was on their side and their experience on picket lines and in social struggles had instilled in them confidence in the decency and love of democracy of the American people when once issues were clearly understood. Legal pleas having failed, the five decided on drastic action. On March 1, 1948, at breakfast, the five went on a hunger strike to continue so long as they were kept in prison without bail.

The action taken by the five was understood by the American people, as they had guessed it would be, and the reaction was prompt. Thousands of New Yorkers picketed the Immigration and Naturalization Service building and then marched down Broadway to Times Square in a body. A picket line marched in front of the White House. Mass protest meetings and picket lines were held in Chicago, San Francisco, Detroit, Los Angeles, Pittsburgh, Cleveland and elsewhere. Labor unions took official action condemning the abrogation of the Bill of Rights, sending telegrams and resolutions to Tom Clark. Newspapers like the *New York Post,* the *Chicago Star,* periodicals like *The Nation* spoke out. In the courts, a group of attorneys pressed the fight.

On the third day of the strike, Potash was released in $5,000 bail, pending an appeal to the Circuit Court. On the fourth day, the remaining four were taken to a room in the Marine Hospital on Ellis Island. On the fifth day, they left their hosptial beds, weakened though they were, to travel to the Federal Courthouse in Manhattan, where they sat for five hours without water, while the attorneys were conducting the fight for their freedom against the opposition of Clark's federal attorneys. Then they returned to their hospital beds to await the judge's decision. But on the afternoon of the sixth day, they were suddenly informed by the assistant director of Ellis Island that they were to be released on bail and could leave by the last ferry at 4:15 P.M. Official lawlessness had met its match.

And Tom Clark was to be blocked by American democratic tradition once more. On May 5, 1948, District Judge Alan Goldsborough of the District of Columbia agreed to the request of attorney Carol King of the ACPFB for an injunction against the Attorney General and the Commissioner of Immigration and Naturalization, enjoining them from proceeding with deportation hearings until they complied with the Administrative Procedure Act, requiring that the hearing officers must be under civil service, selected in rotation, and other such elementary regulations.

But Tom Clark was not willing to accept such a defeat as final. On May 27 he called for a law under which he could jail indefinitely non-citizens ordered deported but undeportable to their countries of origin, and advocated the passage of the Hobbs Bill (restored to life by the Cold War climate after its death in 1941). And in June, 1948, the Attorney General put on the "Subversive List" the organization active in both defeats, the American Committee for Protection of Foreign Born. Twenty-eight years before, in the days of the Palmer Raids, twelve attorneys, including Felix Frankfurter, Roscoe Pound and Zechariah Chafee, had made the public declaration:

> For the Attorney General to go into the field of propaganda against radicals is a deliberate misuse of his office.

In the atmosphere of the Cold War, the Department of Justice moved rapidly to intensify its campaign against those of foreign birth who had records of "radicalism" of any kind; and sections of the public press, influenced by conservative pressures from many directions, aided the general repression by rousing the general fear of "conspiracy." The Bill of Rights failed to give protection for freedom of thought, speech or assembly.

18. The Fight for Public Opinion

THE Ellis Island hunger strike was in itself a courageous and dramatic action, and the immediate response of the American people showed that such an appeal to the American democratic tradition could still be effective despite the increasing Cold War propaganda. But the hunger strike was by its very nature an act of desperation which was a very distinct warning of danger. The necessity for such an act was evidence of a deliberate and high-handed increase of repression. It also demonstrated how far the initiative in defense of the foreign born had still to be taken by the foreign-born victims themselves; how little the native born were aware of their responsibilities.

The ACPFB was one of the groups that had accepted, long before the hunger strike, the responsibility of the native born for the welfare of their newly arrived and therefore more vulnerable neighbors. From the day of its origin the Committee had insisted that in a democratic society the problems of the foreign born were the concern of the entire people; and both before and during the war had had as a special objective the achievement of the unity of native and foreign born, of citizen and non-citizen. Toward this end it directed its educational material, publicized and encouraged the participation of native born in defense of the foreign born either through collaboration with the Committee or in independent activity.

This two-fold approach, defense of the foreign born and

appeal to the conscience of the American people, had given the Committee its unique character; and both aims were kept clearly in mind at the war's end. To continue to "zealously guard" the rights of the foreign born, the Committee, which had cancelled the 1944 Conference at the request of the government to curtail travel, decided to hold its 1945 conference in New York City. Since travel was still somewhat restricted, attendance from a distance was, again in accordance with governmental regulations, limited to fifty, and a special provision was made for "participation by mail." The "National Conference on the Foreign Born in Post-War America" was duly held at the Hotel New Yorker on October 20-21, 1945.

The need for such a conference was forcibly expressed by Lt. Comm. U.S. Navy (retired) Charles S. Seely of the Board of Directors of the Chicago Civil Liberties Committee, in a letter to Hon. Stanley Nowak, chairman of the ACPFB:

> Now, more than at any other time in our history, our foreign born need the protection America can and should give. The war is over, and our enemies have been defeated abroad, but our enemies in America—the reactionaries—are still as strong as ever. . . . It is clear that the reactionaries will in one way or another seek to set one group of foreign born against another and also to set non-foreign-born Americans against the foreign born.

The number and character of the greetings sent to the Conference were not merely a courteous tribute to the ACPFB. They gave evidence of a widespread recognition that the special defense of the foreign born was closely intertwined with the defense of freedom and democracy elsewhere, and that there was particular need for the continued existence of an organization like the ACPFB. A cross-section of American life was represented. Senator Wagner lent the breadth of statesmanship to his comment:

> Americans of foreign birth are especially concerned with the continuing strength and health of our democracy.

They want to do everything possible to assure a post-war America with full employment and full production without discrimination because of race, color or national origin. They also see clearly the need for our helping the stricken people of Europe reconstruct their countries along democratic lines. I am sure that your National Conference will help in formulating constructive plans for achieving these objectives.

From Louis Adamic, recipient of the Committee's award for 1944:

Your Conference meets in a period when important decisions are being made . . . that will control the character of the peace. The American people have a great responsibility in helping to shape the future world along democratic lines. . . . The so-called minority groups in America, comprising as they do the majority of the people, can make an outstanding contributing in this direction. . . . We have everything in common. Only reaction and stupidity can keep us divided.

Sen. James M. Mead also laid stress on the aims for which we had fought:

Your Committee is to be congratulated upon its splendid record and we must each pause to rededicate ourselves to the principles of the Four Freedoms so that our victory will not be an empty one and the peace will be a permanent and lasting one.

From Rep. Sabath:

I want to assure you of my appreciation of the splendid work which your Committee is doing on behalf of our foreign born citizenry.

From Michael J. Quill, president of the Transport Workers:

The Transport Workers Union of America heartily en-

> dorses the Conference called by your organization on the subject of the foreign born in Post-War America. It is hoped that your Conference will focus attention on the sore spots and danger signals in our treatment of non-citizens and minority groups and in this way will strengthen democratic processes for all within our borders.

From Richard T. Frankensteen, vice-president of the United Auto Workers Union, and a candidate for mayor of Detroit:

> Here in Detroit we see very clearly the need for such work as you are doing. Those who want us to go backwards do not depend upon reason or decency. They appeal to prejudice, bigotry, disunity. As our economic situation worsens, we can expect increased poison of the Gerald L. K. Smith variety. The work of your Committee is a vital counter-weapon against intolerance and fascism.

There was explicit approval of the two-fold character of the work of the Committee from Thomas G. Finucane, chairman of the Board of Immigration Appeals:

> It is true that there has been and still is among a segment of our population a very definite feeling of hostility against all foreign born or the foreign born of certain races. . . . Extolling the virtue of charity is a slow way to remove prejudice and bias from the hearts of men. A realization of the truth is the surest way to wipe out intolerance. . . . The work of your Committee in fostering understanding of and just treatment for the foreign born demands the respect and appreciation of us all.

Henry A. Wallace, then Secretary of Commerce, came perhaps closest to expressing it.

> Your organization can do much by reminding the nation forcibly of its debt to the foreign born, and by bringing the pressure of opinion to bear in the normal

> democratic way to make certain that we do not build a wall of exclusion along our borders and foster a program of hate within.

The silence of the years of McCarthyism had not yet begun. Included among those sending messages to the Conference were: Secretary of Labor Lewis Schwellenbach, U.S. Supreme Court Justice Hugo Black, Philip Murray, Mrs. Eleanor Roosevelt, Earl Harrison, then a member of the faculty of the University of Pennsylvania Law School and general chairman of the United War Chest Campaign; from Senators Elbert Thomas, Brien McMahon, Joseph Guffey; from various members of the House of Representatives, from trade union officials and from university professors.

There was one greeting, however, that brought the Conference face to face with the complexities of the time. It came from the Philippine Islands, sent jointly by Go Kin-Seng, chairman of the Philippine Chinese Anti-Japanese and Anti-Traitors League, and Huang Chieh, commander of the Philippine Chinese Anti-Japanese Guerilla Forces. "We feel our comradeship with you," said the message, "in the world-wide fight of national minorities for a full place in their nations." But the letter made two complaints: discrimination against Chinese residents and Moros, and the growing domination in the government "due to the leniency of the United States army" of "Japanese collaborators and fascist elements." A letter written in August by Ira Gollobin (an attorney who before the war had defended victims of deportation, and was then serving with the U.S. Army in Manila) had referred to the discrimination against minorities in the Philippines and suggested that this was a legitimate concern of the Committee.

The Conference at once responded to the appeal by voting to call on President Truman for an investigation of the charges of leniency to collaborators and fascists; and to send a reply to the greeting condemning discrimination against minorities and stressing the importance of defense of democratic rights in the

Philippines "to the unity and well-being of the democratic world." The answer to the appeal to President Truman came from the chief of the Division of Philippine Affairs in the State Department and stated merely that collaborators were to be tried by a special Peoples Court and that the Department believed that "justice would be meted out."

It was, of course, hard to keep any post-war conference confined within limits either of geography or subject matter. But the need of concentration on the specific purpose of the Conference was fully understood and firmly stated by Abner Green, the executive secretary, in his greetings on the first page of the Souvenir Journal.

> During the war, our attention was devoted exclusively to the mobilization of foreign-born Americans for victory. Now our attention must turn to the problems of peace and to the problems which could not be considered during the war without disrupting our national unity.

He mentioned specifically "the widespread fascist propaganda —anti-Negro, anti-Semitic, anti-United Nations"—in the foreign-born communities of the United States and the support of anti-alien legislation by a coalition of "poll tax" Democrats and reactionary Republicans. In his report to the Conference, he faced squarely the difficulties ahead:

> The ACPFB was established twelve years ago. It is concerned with all the problems that confront foreign-born Americans as a result of their foreign birth. These include naturalization, citizenship, immigration, discrimination. . . .
>
> We must face the prospect that the problems . . . will be intensified in the period ahead. . . . As long as the correct solutions are delayed, these problems will become . . . more widespread. . . .
>
> The strength of reactionary elements in our national life—especially in Congress—interferes. . . . But we will find support for the program we adopt in all sections of the American people.

Congressman Emanuel Celler, the first Conference speaker, emphasized one problem, "the huge volume of poison propaganda that has been spilled into this country by the Hitlerite jackals," whose effective weapon has been arousing racial and religious intolerance. He listed various apparently respectable organizations whose "hate-sheets" reached every corner of the land.

Of special and permanent value for insight into the recurring relation between attacks on the rights of the foreign born and the abrogation of civil liberties in general were the comments of attorney Isaac Shorr, who had defended some of the foreign-born victims of the Palmer Raids in 1920-21. Mr. Shorr analyzed the situation of 1945 in comparison with that of twenty-five years before, an analysis equally applicable to the present days of the Walter-McCarran Act.

> There are in this country certain elements who do not like our free institutions. They do not like organized labor. They do not like our public educational system. These elements are always on the lookout for a chance to hit these institutions and to destroy them, if possible. So that, whenever this country finds itself in difficulties, these elements get busy. They create an issue of the foreign born, usually accusing them as a class of being too radical—or too prominent in strikes—or taking jobs away. In support of that anti-alien agitation, they put in motion our immigration and naturalization laws.
>
> This happened after the First World War when the law enforcement branch of the government became the greatest single violator of our laws. Without any warrants, without any accusations, without any real issues, they rounded up thousands of immigrants, legal residents in the United States, as well as citizens and threw them into jails, immigration stations, police stations—denied them bail, refused relatives and friends any access to the prisoners, beat them and actually tortured them. This is history. It was so raw that it forms one of the blackest parts in the history of the United States, and will be known forever as the Palmer Raids.

> Now we are emerging from the Second World War. If, as an aftermath of the recent war, this country finds itself in some difficulties, we, the foreign born, cannot rule out the possibility of a similar attack upon us as a stepping stone for an attack on America's free institutions. . . . It is certain that, if the attitude of the government towards immigrants becomes as it was in 1920, we may find ourselves confronted with the same problems as we were at that time.

And as though to offer further proof of the truth of his analysis, Mr. Shorr is once more defending against deportation under the Walter-McCarran Law of 1952, some of the very same foreign born he defended in 1920.

The government's attitude towards immigrants in 1945 was indicated in an address to the Conference by Jack Wasserman, member of the Board of Immigration Appeals of the Department of Justice, in which he demanded "the elimination of racial discrimination in our immigration and naturalization laws." Mr. Wasserman elaborated:

> We are still the only country in the world prescribing racial disqualifications for citizenship. We are likewise . . . one of a minority of countries which provides a racial test for admissibility of immigrants.
>
> The racial provisions of our laws provide administrative officials with an unwelcome headache. In the cases of persons of mixed blood, we must determine whether they are more or less than fifty percent of racially eligible blood. . . . We are still trying to find out who are white persons.
>
> Now I believe that it is morally wrong to brand an individual with the stigma of ineligibility. Such discrimination is not based upon the inherent worth of the individual. It is not grounded upon respect for the dignity of man. It preaches a doctrine of unequal justice instead of equal justice. . . .
>
> We fought a war to discredit the Nazi myth of racial superiority and we buried that myth upon the battlefields of Europe and in the Pacific at a cost in blood of all races.

> Today the ghost of that myth of racial superiority still rises to haunt us whenever we look at our immigration and naturalization laws.
>
> We proclaimed that all men are created equal in our Declaration of Independence. We guaranteed all men equal protection under our Constitution. . . . We cannot remain true to our American ideals . . . and at the same time permit the retention of laws which contain the corroding influence of racial discrimination.

In confirmation of this opinion, at a panel entitled "Defend and Extend American Democracy," the deliberate attempt to arouse inter-racial hatreds, pitting national group against national group, and the native born against the foreign born in Chicago and Gary, Indiana, was described by Ira Latimer, executive secretary of the Chicago Civil Liberties Committee. Some aspects of the fascist activity among the foreign born were reported by Albert Kahn. The anti-alien, anti-freedom activities of certain members of Congress were condemned: John Rankin of the House Committee on Un-American Activities, Congressman O'Konski, Senator Bilbo. On the doings of the last named, Edward Bykowski, a Polish war veteran, holder of the Purple Heart, had been scheduled to speak. Unable to attend the Conference, he telegraphed: "Bilbo forgets that the 'original American' is the Indian and when he slanders a . . . group because of national origin, he negates everything this wonderful country has always stood for."

The content of the report of the addresses and discussions at the 1945 Conference shows that it did not wholly escape the bewildered confusion of the post-war world. And the resolutions adopted give further evidence of the prevalent desire to solve all problems at once. They deal with the rehabilitation of Europe and the Far East, with the nation's foreign policy, with Jewish refugees in other countries, as well as with the foreign born in the United States. But in spite of the wide scope covered in the resolutions and an occasional confusion in the minds of the speakers between the rights of the foreign born and the adoption of their own cherished ideas, concern for foreign-born Americans predominated. The net result of the Conference was the adoption of an amended Constitution which reiterated the purpose of the ACPFB "to perpetuate for the foreign born the fundamental American concepts of equality . . . and to preserve the fundamental ideals of liberty and hospitality." And the future work of the Committee was defined:

> To promote better relations and understanding between native and foreign born by means of education; to encourage and facilitate the naturalization of non-citizens; to prevent discrimination against non-citizens or foreign-born citizens because of their nationality, political, economic, or religious belief or lack of citizenship; to prevent the destruction of American families by the threat of deportation; to maintain the traditional right of asylum for political and religious refugees in the United States and to actively work for the solution of the problems confronting the foreign born in the United States.

Of the six point summary program for the coming year, five dealt specifically with the defense of the rights of the foreign born. And from all the addresses delivered, the Committee chose for printing the one by Jack Wasserman, under the title "Unequal Justice." The Commtitee began to work at once on the program formulated by the Conference. And work there was!

From February to April 1946, the House Committee on Immigration and Naturalization held hearings on the Gossett Bill, one section of which cut immigration quotas by fifty percent. The Committee sent out a letter urging immediate action to defeat the bill, and accompanied the letter with the statement to be made by Abner Green for the Committee at the hearings, a list of organizations on record opposing the bill, and a page reproducing various newspaper clippings against it. In April the Committee published, as a public service, the statements made at the hearings by the AFL and CIO.

Contrary to expectations, as a result of the aroused opposition, the bill which had been ardently supported by the American Legion and by many America First and anti-alien organizations, was defeated in Committee 7 to 5. At the same time, the campaign in favor of bills permitting the naturalization of natives of India and the Philippine Islands came to a successful conclusion. In a letter to the signers of a public statement in favor of these bills, which was prepared by the Committee in February, Abner Green could happily report the end of a six-year fight.

Successful also was the protest made to the Attorney General, personally, by a delegation headed by Abner Green and Carol King and including representatives of Italian-American organizations against the returning of Italians to Italy without the formality of passports. The Italian Ambassador had stated that about 1,500 Italian-Americans, including a few hundred with criminal records, had been "dumped" in Italian ports controlled by the U.S. Army, with entire disregard of the sovereignty and independence of Italy.

The annual celebrations of the anniversary of the Statue of Liberty had become an important avenue for making the American people conscious of their obligations towards the foreign born. Furthermore, they helped extend the influence of the Committee into the general liberal movement, where awareness of the problems of the foreign born was essential if the native born were to assume responsibility for the solutions. The "60th Anniversary Dinner" on October 27, 1946, and the ceremonies at Bedloe's Island the following day, continued the tradition. Presiding at the dinner was the novelist, Fannie Hurst.

Earlier in the year, Fannie Hurst had described the work of the Committee in a broadcast beamed by the Office of War Information (OWI) to New Zealand and Australia, which began:

> Does it strike you as extraordinary that there is need for such an organization in a country that is practically

> made up of people whose forebears, one or two generations back, were practically all foreign born?

She went on to tell of the filling of America with those seeking all sorts of freedoms and to describe some of the contributions made by the 80 million who came between 1812 and 1930, and she concluded with a reference to the difficulties of language, of cultural adjustment and with legal red-tape which made an organization like the ACPFB necessary. The Committee

> knows how bewildering these procedures can be. And so they circulate educational material to help the foreign born, and to encourage non-citizens to become citizens and enjoy the incomparable benefits of such citizenship. And since human nature persists in being human nature, the Committee realizes that even in a democracy, pitfalls lurk for the newcomer and so it seeks to prevent discrimination in employment or in any other sphere of social or economic activity, against persons because of their national origin or non-citizenship, by fostering legislation which will afford such protection.
>
> The Committee stands guard over the inalienable rights of the foreigner. . . . It also encourages America to live up to her ideals by granting these newcomers the full rights of free men.

American traditions of democracy are vigorous, and the sincere upholders of these traditions are not easily intimidated. Amid the increasing post-war tensions and the increasing fear of incurring "guilt by association," the work of the Committee went on, and was recognized on its merits. The list of 120 sponsors of the Statue of Liberty 60th Anniversary Dinner, with Thomas Mann and Fannie Hurst as co-chairmen, included names famous in literature, art, music, the church and the political world. There were some 400 people present. The chief speakers included Senator Herbert Lehman; Arnold Wapler, representing the French Ambassador; Charles Marshall, superintendent of the Statue of Liberty National Monument. A special tribute to Sidney Hillman was presented by Eugene Cotton, assistant general counsel of the CIO.

The annual national conferences of the Committee were held regularly, sponsored as before, by men and women prominent for achievement and character. But increasingly a note of urgency crept into the conferences. The Call to the 1947 Conference held in Cleveland, Ohio, stressed "the attempt to terrorize the foreign born" by discrimination, deportation and denial of citizenship. The order in which the resolutions were adopted reflected the relative immediacy of the threat to the foreign born. The first dealt with "Deportation for Political Opinion."

> The civil rights of the American people and our democratic institutions are endangered by any attempt to deny non-citizens the equal protection of the Bill of Rights. Whereas the Department of Justice is attempting to use the deportation laws as a political weapon against legally resident non-citizens . . . resolved that this Conference go on record condemning any attempt to deport . . . any citizen on the ground of political opinion or membership in the Communist Party.

The second resolution dealt with naturalization, then came revocation of citizenship, the immigration quotas, the racial provisions of the immigration and naturalization laws. These were followed by asylum for displaced persons, legislative activity and finally a number of specific resolutions dealing with individual cases or specific recommended actions.

As already indicated in the previous chapter, the 1948 Fifteenth Anniversary Conference spent little time on celebration, reserving its main energies for protest against the rising tide of terror against the foreign born begun under the administration of Attorney General Tom Clark. The very title of the 1949 Detroit Conference, "Against Deportation Hysteria" was symbolic of the deterioration of the situation.

The Attorney General was now Howard McGrath, and Rev.

John Darr, Jr., chairman of the ACPFB's Board of Directors, invited him to attend the Conference,

> . . . Since this deportation program was initiated prior to your assuming the office of Attorney General [and] we feel that you should in all fairness examine the effect of these deportations on the lives of Americans.

The invitation was not accepted. He should have been there, for both the formal speakers and those who took part in the discussions were for the most part, those directly affected by the deportations—either representatives of trade unions whose leaders had been arrested, the deportees themselves, or members of their families. And if Mr. McGrath had accepted the invitation, he might have learned enough of that truth which Mr. Finucane, of the Board of Immigration Appeals, had declared to the 1945 Conference to be the only remedy for intolerance and prejudice, so that he might have altered the policy of his Department.

An individual or an organization wholly devoted to a cause becomes attuned to currents that not only touch the immediate area of special interest, but that affect the national life as a whole. The fact that those directly affected by the deportations dominated the 1949 Conference was a barometric registration of stormy weather ahead, indicating that reactionary, anti-democratic propaganda and action had begun to have their effect on American society, and were corrupting and intimidating public opinion. This was expressed with particular sharpness by Ralph Filiccia, vice-president of Local 51 of the United Automobile Workers, CIO.

> At the outset I want to pay tribute to the ACPFB and the distinguished group of citizens who are sponsors for this important Conference. In my judgment the ACPFB and the individual sponsors are a great group of patriots and champions of democracy, contrary to what has been said by attorney generals and other reactionary forces.
>
> I regret the fact that the entire labor movement does

not see the same way as my local union in giving full support to this type of meeting and conference.

I maintain that the attack and witch hunts against the foreign born and naturalized citizens is an attack against democracy in general and it strikes at the heart of labor in particular.

I feel that the so-called native Americans cannot feel secure if the attack against the foreign born continues. This attack against the foreign born is not an isolated matter. It is part of the whole cold war drive. It is part of the Taft-Hartley Slave Act which was instituted against labor. It is part of the drive against the living standards of all labor.

In our own local union we have felt the effect of the so-called drive by the Immigration Department and the Department of Justice. Our educational director, Sam Sweet, who has been working in the labor movement for eleven years, who has served the Plymouth workers faithfully and helped to organize the auto workers, is being haunted and attacked.

Throughout the nation we find that individuals in the ranks of labor are being attacked and haunted.

It is rather interesting to remember that there isn't a labor representative in the Immigration Department, while there are representatives of corporations. I know that Chrysler, General Motors and Ford have much to say about the conduct and operation of the Immigration Department. I know, for example, that in Chrysler's Plymouth plant there is an individual who decides many cases on whether individual workers shall or shall not receive citizenship papers.

We have learned from our own hard experience what it means when employers and government agents begin to class individuals as subversives or communists. In our experience in the union anyone who dares to speak for better wages, better conditions, is being classed as a subversive or a communist.

We also know that the cry of communism by reaction will not put food on the table. We know that the cry of communism will not pay the rent. We know that the

> cry of communism will not buy clothing and provide medical aid for our children.
>
> The same forces who are attacking the foreign born are attacking the Negro people. They are responsible for anti-Semitism. They are responsible for lynching.
>
> Therefore I maintain that the battle for protection of the foreign born is a battle for democracy and the protection of all those whose civil rights are being threatened today.

Poignancy and dignity were added to these sharp words of Mr. Filiccia by the statement presented for the deportees by Mrs. Ann Ganley, herself one of them.

> We, the undersigned, are not yet citizens of this country. We want to become citizens of this land of our adoption. But instead of being granted citizenship, we have all been arrested and face deportation from the United States because of our political opinions.
>
> We are not criminals. Not one of us is charged with the commission of any crime or of any act that might endanger the welfare of the American people. Not one of us seeks to harm in any way the people of this country. Indeed, we face deportation because we have tried—each in our own way—to improve the living standards and the democracy of the American people.
>
> We came to this country as immigrants. Some of us came here almost half a century ago. We came here, like millions of other immigrants have come, seeking a new life in a better country for ourselves and our families. Europe to us during the early part of this century meant oppression and wars and starvation. And here the Statue of Liberty greeted us, held out a hand of welcome and a promise of freedom and liberty and equality.
>
> Through the years, we have lived useful lives. We have worked in the factories and in the mines. We have helped build the roads and the cities. We have raised families and paid taxes. We have helped build unions. During the depression, we fought for relief and unemployment insur-

ance, and during the recent war we did our utmost for victory over fascism. We fought against Jim Crow, discrimination and anti-Semitism.

We are a part of America. Our lives and our fortunes are in the soil of America. Most of us know no country other than the United States. We belong here with our families and our friends and we are fighting to remain here where we belong.

The Department of Justice seeks our deportation on the ground that we advocate "the overthrow of the government of the United States by force and violence." That is nonsense. Not one of us believes in or advocates—or has ever believed in or advocated—"force and violence" and we challenge the Justice Department to support its charge with one iota of proof.

We feel that there is a sense of decency and a sense of fairness that guides the overwhelming majority of the American people, which false charges and hysteria cannot destroy. Today we appeal to all fair and decent-minded Americans. We who have lived with and among you for thirty-five and forty and fifty years face exile from your midst. We face enforced separation from our children, from our wives and husbands, from our fathers and mothers.

We look to the American people to defeat our deportation and to demand that we be provided with an opportunity to become citizens of the United States. We are confident that the American people, guided by our democratic traditions, will prevent our deportation and will defeat this disguised attack on the Bill of Rights and the liberties of all Americans.

The statement was adopted by the Conference and the delegates present took a solemn pledge:

We have heard with mounting indignation reports of the treatment suffered by legally-resident non-citizens at the hands of agents of the Department of Justice.

We are shocked by the callous and inhuman manner in which the Justice Department is hounding non-citizens and naturalized American citizens and depriving them of their rights.

We protest the attempt by the Justice Department to forcibly separate from their American families and to exile from the United States men and women who have devoted their lives to the building of this country and to defending the welfare of the American people.

We condemn without reservation the attempt to deport these good and honest men and women as a vicious distortion of the laws of our land and as a disguised attack on the rights and liberties of all Americans, native as well as foreign born.

We associate ourselves with the position, taken by the late Supreme Court Justice Frank Murphy, when he declared: "There is no justifiable reason for discarding the democratic and humane tenets of our legal system and descending to the practices of despotism in dealing with deportation."

These men and women who face deportation have made this the country of their conscious choice. They are good Americans and are not yet citizens because they have been prevented from becoming citizens by the Justice Department and through no fault of their own. In the name of American decency and in keeping with the glorious traditions of democracy, we extend our hand in fellowship and pledge to these victims of hysteria:

We will never relent in our determination to defeat your deportation and to enable you to remain in this country, where you belong, with your families and your friends.

We will support with all our resources the fight against your deportation to the end that you will become American citizens and continue in your efforts to advance the well-being of the American people.

Special measures were required to meet the situation. National conferences were not enough since they were intended primarily for the determination of policy for the ACPFB and for enlisting, in carrying out that policy, the cooperation of those who already knew and approved the Committee's work. Other means were needed to give the general public some understanding of what was being done. To check, if possible, the mounting flood of prejudice, to rouse sympathy for the deportees, and gain general support for legislative action in their behalf, a series of emergency conferences was held in various parts of the country. The greatest need was to alert people who were not immediately concerned with the Justice Department's program.

Already, in May, 1947, a call for a Midwest Conference to be held at Hull House in Chicago, had been issued by Stanley Nowak, national chairman of the ACPFB, and attorney Pearl Hart, of Chicago, chairman of the conference, "to defend the rights of the American people and their organizations by protecting the liberties of foreign-born Americans." Religious leaders and leaders in other fields recognized publicly the need for such a conference. Dr. Abraham Cronbach, of the Hebrew Union College, Cincinnati, Ohio, stated:

> Most social disorders arise from the belief—or rather from the attitude prompting the belief—that we can benefit ourselves by hurting somebody else. Any step which challenges that assumption or forsakes that attitude marks a social gain. Herein lies the significance of the American Committee for Protection of Foreign Born. We must steadily controvert the fallacy that, by injuring foreigners, we help Americans.

Rev. Karl Baehr, of the United Congregational Church of Chicago, declared:

> Again we are facing a crisis in democracy. A wave of hysteria has been drummed up by selfish groups who are afraid to trust the thinking ability of the public. They want to sift ideas, blacklist thoughts and burn books. But it's not easy to sift ideas and blacklist thoughts. In order to accomplish that one must sift men and blacklist those harboring strange thoughts. And for this, what better method can be found than to deport those who think strange thoughts and at the same time don't happen to be citizens of the United States?

> It is unjust, undemocratic and unthinkable . . . to call for the deportation of men whose only crime is birth in a foreign country along with the exercise of freedom of speech in America—a crime our forefathers (foreigners) came to America to make legal. I hope and pray that the American people will be big enough and have faith enough to resist these hysterical efforts to put democracy into a straight-jacket and make it goose-step to the tune of the Dies, Rankin, Thomas Committee.

The authority of historic experience of the past was added to democratic expression and compassionate humanity in the words of Bishop R. R. Wright, Jr., secretary of the National Fraternal Council of Negro Churches in America:

> America's greatest development is the result of the foreign born and their children from the humble slave in the South who helped make cotton king there, to many of our ablest scholars, scientists, religious, business and political leaders.
>
> In this day when hate and racial prejudice are on the upward trend, may we all who believe in the true America cooperate and work harder for our treasured ideals.

The same sentiments moved Judge Arthur LeSueur, of Minneapolis, Minnesota, to state:

> I am well advised that this movement is an important one and is not premature by any means. Too often the average person, if there is any such person, forgets that when civil rights are attacked and minorities deprived thereof, the next step is to deprive all common citizens of their rights.
>
> I personally had a very considerable part in stopping the Palmer Raids, and I know that those who engage in such activities as your Committee is now beginning, are always charged with fighting the government of the United States. That is utterly false. The Government of the

> United States is the Constitution of the United States and the principles on which it is founded.

The nature and extent of the immediate danger to the foreign born was presented to the Conference by Abner Green in a report later printed by the ACPFB under the title, "The Fight for the Rights of Foreign-Born Americans."

> . . . the pattern set by Hitler and the Nazis in Germany . . . is being copied closely and carefully by the enemies of the American people. . . . It was in this atmosphere of . . . red-baiting and labor-baiting that the Justice Department launched a series of deportations and denaturalization cases—several hundred—in all parts of the country.
>
> More than 124 non-citizens face deportation [on the grounds of] their political beliefs. [Not all the 124 were former Communists, though many were.]
>
> Naturalized citizens are far from secure. . . .
>
> These cases . . . are all one case. It is the case of the people of this country against [those] who want to erect concentration camps for those who disagree with their views.
>
> We have convened this Conference to consider these problems and to consider what can be done to organize an effective fight in the Midwest on these issues.

The immediate result of the Conference was the establishment of the independent Midwest Committee for Protection of Foreign Born with attorney Pearl Hart as chairman.

Other conferences followed, some of them centering around individual cases, but all planned to arouse public protest against the procedures of the Immigration Service in general. On September 18, 1947, in New York City, the chief emphasis was on the deportation of leaders of trade unions, with representatives of a dozen or more union locals and some union national officers present. In January, 1948, a legislative conference was held in

Washington, with fifty-seven organizations represented from California, Illinois, Maryland, Michigan, New York, New Jersey, Ohio, Pennsylvania and the District of Columbia. The conference discussed pending legislation, went in groups to confer with their Congressmen and passed a series of resolutions condemning specifically sixteen House and five Senate bills and expressing support for thirty-three bills before the House and twelve pending in the Senate.

In April, 1948, after the successful conclusion of the Ellis Island hunger strike, a conference was held in New York City under the general slogan, "In Defense of the Bill of Rights." In February, 1949, the Committee called an "Emergency Conference on Deportations," after the newspapers had reported that the Justice Department was preparing to arrest some 500 noncitizens and hold them for deportation because of political opinion.

The Washington Mobilization of March, 1949, brought to the nation's capital many American-born members of the families of those facing deportation, to confer with the Justice Department, with officials of the Immigration Service and with their Congressmen. Special press interviews were held; the "mobilization" was reported on local radio and on one national hookup. The group included Peter Warhol's wife from Minneapolis with three children, aged ten, four and one; Leon Callow's wife from Niles, Ohio, with their eight children, ranging in age from sixteen to four; the wife and seventeen-year-old daughter of James Mackay of Gary, Indiana; a large group from New York and many others. The entire delegation marched in front of the White House (the Callow children were especially appealing) with signs calling for an end of the deportation drive. Bishop Arthur W. Moulton, of Utah, honorary co-chairman of the ACPFB, and the Rev. John Darr, co-chairman, called at the White House and left an Open Letter signed by fifty prominent men and women protesting against the threatened destruction of American families by the Justice Department. The group gathered at the Lincoln Memorial where

Bishop Moulton began an address to the group. It was finished at the final meeting later in the afternoon.

In April three women, Prof. Dorothy Brewster, Uta Hagen and Fredi Washington, initiated a luncheon meeting of women. The situation which moved them to action was vividly presented to the audience by the first speaker, Anita Alvarez, the dancer:

> The dance has always afforded me my share of self-expression and I have never had the desire . . . for speech-making. What underlines most the seriousness of the situation we face, is the fact that I am standing here . . . speaking to an audience. Those of you who know me realize that nothing short of a catastrophe could have brought this about.
>
> In a land founded on freedom and justice . . . a woman takes her child to school and is picked up by government agents and dragged away. A mother of a war veteran is aroused in the morning and torn from her home. A father of a dead war hero is waylaid on his way from work and snatched away from his family. . . .
>
> What is their crime? Where is the evidence? The accusation is "You believed—you thought—you spoke."

Miss Alvarez concluded with an appeal to fight to prevent the erection of a tombstone with the inscription, "Here lies personal freedom, born 1776, died 1949, plagued by fiends and deserted by cowards."

The Cold War had not entirely silenced the voice of freedom.

VI. THE ATTEMPT TO SILENCE AMERICA

19. The Free and the Brave

THE pressure to silence all opposition to and criticism of government policy and action continued relentlessly. Nor did it affect the foreign born only. On March 17, 1948, Joseph and Stewart Alsop could say in their New York *Herald Tribune* column, "The atmosphere in Washington today is no longer a post-war atmosphere. It is, to put it bluntly, a pre-war atmosphere. . . ."

This atmosphere was created not alone by the irresponsible "inevitability of war" talk, by the constant calls for preventive war. Concrete measures taken by the government itself to facilitate the carrying out of its new policies aggravated the situation.

In May, 1947, President Truman submitted to Congress an Inter-Continental Defense Plan. In July, he signed the National Security Act, setting up a National War Council and unifying the armed services. In January, 1948, the President, in his budget message, called for expenditures which, according to the *U.S. News and World Report,* "directly related to war make up 79 per cent of the budget." In May, the Senate authorized a seventy group air force, presumably against what Senatory Henry Styles Bridges termed America's "only possible foe," the Soviet Union. In June, Truman signed into life the first peacetime military draft in American history. In November, the Civilian Defense Plan was announced.

In June, 1949, Truman's signature established the Central

Intelligence Agency, with duties so secret that not even Congress was informed of all the details, and with powers so sweeping that *The New York Times* worried about its being "a legislative catch-all with very broad . . . implications, which under improper administration or spur of hysteria could lead to grave abuses of freedom." In July, Truman signed the North Atlantic Pact, on which a *New York Daily News* editorial commented with enthusiasm, "Let's stow the baloney and doubletalk, and admit there is a treaty creating a military alliance which contemplates war on Soviet Russia." In September, Truman himself announced that Russia had set off an atomic explosion. In October, the Justice Department, with what has seemed to many (including two Justices of the Supreme Court) a deliberate disregard of the First Amendment to the Constitution, won the conviction of eleven leaders of the Communist Party on a charge of conspiracy to *teach and advocate* the overthrow of the government by force and violence.

In January, 1950, Truman ordered the speediest possible development of the hydrogen bomb. In June, the Korean conflict broke out and two days later Truman ordered a "police action" involving United States air and sea intervention, without even waiting for the approval of the UN Security Council which the Soviet Union was boycotting.

All these actions were by their very nature highly controversial. And there was controversy. We shall note only some highlights. In 1948, the Northern Baptist Convention called for the establishment of a World Peace Movement. In that year, too, there suddenly emerged a new third party, the Progressive Party, with a clear-cut peace program and a Rooseveltian New Deal orientation, headed by former Vice-President Henry Wallace and U.S. Senator Glen Taylor as presidential and vice-presidential candidates. *The Churchman* in its 1948 Christmas issue said: "So, because the Christmas song of 'Peace on Earth' haunts Protestantism, it is subversive and identical with communism! We suggest that all the 50,000,000 American Protestants be jailed."

In March, 1949, a Cultural and Scientific Conference for World Peace was held under the auspices of the National Council of the Arts, Sciences and Professions and sponsored by more than 600 outstanding Americans, culminating in a Madison Square Garden meeting attended by 20,000 people. In April, an American Sponsoring Committee of the World Congress of Fighters for Peace was formed by 300 well-known individuals. In September, over 200 delegates from the United States attended the American Continental Congress for Peace held in Mexico. In October there was held a National Labor Conference for Peace, with more than a thousand delegates from twenty-eight states. And in early 1950, there began the door to door collection of several million signatures to the Stockholm Peace Petition. Discussion of the national policy and declared disagreement with it still survived.

But the next two years showed that, in America, as in Germany 20 years earlier, public opinion could be altered and opposition silenced by a skillful mixture of propaganda and penalty. The situation in March, 1952, was described by Professor Zechariah Chafee, Jr., of the Harvard Law School. His lecture given at Columbia University under the auspices of the Roger N. Baldwin Civil Liberties Foundation was published by the Foundation under the title *Thirty-Five Years with Freedom of Speech.*

In Professor Chafee's judgment:

> The most striking difference from the earlier Period of Struggle [1917-1920] lies in the subtlety of the suppressions now employed.

The formula was simple enough, as all good propaganda campaigns should be if doubt and suspicion were to be overcome. First came the emphasis on the ambition, ruthlessness and power of the Soviet Union, which had begun almost before the end of World War II. By 1952, fear of Russia as an immediate international menace had become so great that any individual who during the war years had had a good word for Russia's contribution to the anti-fascist war effort was denounced and ostracized. As Professor Chafee said:

> All the water that ran under the bridge for a quarter of a century after 1917 is now coming back under the bridge in waves of intolerance.

The complementary part of the formula was, using "international communism" as a bridge from the Soviet Union and espionage as a direct link, to create the "clear and present danger" of communism and the Communist Party on the domestic scene. This campaign was furthered by a series of international spy trials, the Hollywood investigation and contempt convictions, the Foley Square trial, the Hiss conviction, culminating in the Rosenberg case, in which for the first time in peace time execution was the judicial sentence for "espionage."

Now America was ready for McCarthyism and similar reactionary efforts to discredit all ideas opposed to official policy, regardless of their source, as part of communist ideology or a communist plot; and to link all individual opponents, regardless of their political positions, to the Communist Party. Having achieved this atmosphere, it was a simple matter to give the consequent suppression an aura of legality. This is what led Professor Chafee, in evaluating the results of a contempt case involving Eugene Dennis, general secretary of the Communist Party, to say:

> This is to me the most disquieting feature of the Dennis case. It cut down the First Amendment to mean about this: "Congress shall make no law abridging the freedom of speech and of the press unless Congress does make a law abridging the freedom of speech and of the press."

And furthermore, in the words of Professor Chafee,

> Anything which is found to be "subversive" can be

> penalized in some way or other, and "subversive" is rapidly coming to mean anything which the powers that be don't like.

A frightened and subservient Congress could pass bills which included "built-in" verdicts of guilt. Nor were the Courts immune to the general psychological atmosphere, as Professor Chafee plainly recognized:

> Determination of guilt in a criminal prosecution is made by a jury and reviewed by judges; and the test of guilt is defined in a statute with considerable clearness. All these safeguards are conspicuously lacking in the novel methods of suppression which have recently sprung up. . . . There is ever so much more suppression today through proceedings which have no juries, no substantial supervision by judges, and vague definitions of wrongdoing. . . .
>
> Run rapidly over some of the current methods of suppression and see what persons do the deciding and penalizing instead of jurymen. In legislative investigations, the denouncing and ousting from jobs is done by legislators with an eye on reelections and party axes to grind. Loyalty programs in federal and state governments are run by administrative officials, who can drive men out of their chosen careers and often make it hard for them to get any private work. If loyalty programs are extended to industry, the decision is made by businessmen who are often afraid of losing government contracts. In public schools and universities, the loss of a career is inflicted by educational officials, who are sometimes threatened by a statute with being severely punished themselves if they decide the teacher is innocent and are afterwards ruled to have been mistaken. Many efforts are made to extend the same system to private schools and colleges. Books are weeded out from schools and colleges by officials. The extensive outlawing of organizations contemplated by the McCarran Act will be done by a board of five men specially selected as watch-dogs of sedition. Administrators can also stifle organizations by choking off the financial contributions

> which are essential to their existence; they can deprive potential givers of exemptions from income taxes and sometimes threaten them with prosecution if they give money to a red-listed group. The denial of passports is chiefly left to the uncontrolled discretion of one official whose name is unknown to the public. If a war or declared emergency exists, administrators will decide who shall be sent to concentration camps under the McCarran Act. And over and above all these penalties imposed on American citizens by officials is the constant smearing of them by single speakers on the floor of the legislature and single columnists, who now exercise the power to take away any man's good name and blackmail his customers and sponsors with threats of boycott and very likely ruin his chances of supporting himself, his wife and his children.
>
> Not only do jurymen have almost nothing to do with the suppressions just listed, but judges too are pretty much out of the picture.

And there was no certainty that the judges, if given opportunity, would exercise a controlling influence. The record, indeed, shows that some judges ignored their judicial function in order to insure due penalty to the "disloyal" who had dared to disagree with authority. The Bill of Rights, especially the First and Fifth Amendments, were in practice nullified; and the behavior of the judges encouraged legislators to ignore existing law. Professor Chafee commented:

> . . . There is as yet no evidence that a majority of the Supreme Court Justices will give any protection to freedom of thought and expression from legislative investigations, loyalty programs, purges of teachers, and test oaths. . . . If judges cannot or will not review suppressions, then legislators and officials are left free to penalize speech and even thoughts as much as they may desire, and they desire a great deal.

Furthermore, to make conviction doubly sure, an old and sordid trade was raised to a highly respectable and lucrative profession. The informer, the spy, the secret agent, the renegade, the stoolpigeon, who told their tales and pocketed their pay, were eulogized in many places as self-sacrificing patriots, Professor Chafee testified:

> I am disturbed by the growing inclination to turn spies into heroes. One of the earliest lessons learned by children is, as I have already said, that tale-bearing on one's comrades is a dirty business. . . . Spies sometimes become agents provocateurs, who incite the very crimes they are hired to report. . . . A still more pervasive evil of spies is the breakdown of confidence in social and family life. Intercourse is poisoned when one never knows if his fellow-guest at dinner is going to report his casual statements to the secret police. . . .
>
> The worst spy of all is the renegade. He has already doublecrossed the community by engaging in wrongdoing and then doublecrossed his associates by deserting them and helping to punish them. After such an experience, truth-telling does not come naturally. The renegade has to make a good story in order to obtain immunity for his own admitted misconduct. Hence there is a great temptation to exaggerate or falsify the behavior of his former associates. . . .
>
> The political spy can send human beings to prison or deprive them of a job, and he may have strong motives to warp his story for personal reasons or to shield himself. . . . The very nature of a spy's work requires lying. He has to deceive his associates into thinking him one of themselves. . . .
>
> The trouble is not that you can be sure a spy is lying. The trouble is you cannot be sure he is telling the truth. The risk of false testimony is tremendously increased.
>
> Therefore, the fact that it is hard to obtain convictions for political crimes without the use of spies is not an argument for using spies. It is an argument against having political crimes.

In the end, the collapse of this Hooverville of falsehood was inevitable. The very character of the informers themselves betrayed them. Some were confined in mental institutions; others were sent to prison for crimes of various kinds. Indictments for perjury dogged them. Recantations of evidence impeded the prosecuting attorneys who had helped prepare the original statements. And courts began to question the value of evidence from this stable of professional informers in government pay. But their diminishing effectiveness did not undo the injustices to which they had contributed.

The whole situation in this period of course offered a wide open door to ambitious seekers after publicity and influence. J. Parnell Thomas, later convicted of misuse of government funds, headed the House Committee on Un-American Activities with its prestige enhanced by President Truman's approval. Senator Joseph McCarthy found his unfailing road to more and more headlines. Few then had the courage to oppose him—although an editorial in the Roman Catholic *Commonweal* questioned (August 17, 1951):

> If West Point cadets are to be tried for cheating (at examinations), why not McCarthy? Has he done less than these cadets to debase the integrity and honesty of our national life?

The disregard of the rights of individuals by Congressional investigating committees and the like disregard by the numerous little "Un-American Committees" which flourished in states and cities across the country, the spectacular success of Senator McCarthy's methods, the autocratic rule of administrators involved in "security" and "loyalty" matters, were accompanied by an increase of lawlessness across the country. To give only a few items: In November, 1947, a Progressive Citizens of America rally in Philadelphia was broken up by young hoodlums and men wearing American Legion and Catholic War Veterans insignia. A little later in California, a meeting of the La Cresenta Democratic Club in session in a private home was broken up by American Legion men wearing official caps. "Are we on the verge of storm trooper incidents throughout America?" asked Rep. Chet Holifield of California.

In March, 1948, in Columbus, Ohio, a mob wrecked the house of a local Communist Party official. A few weeks later, a National Maritime Union official was stabbed to death in Charleston, South Carolina, by a vicious anti-communist who had threatened to "fix . . . that nigger lover and Wallace stooge." In September, 1948, two thugs attacked a national leader of the Communist Party in New York, and two months later, his eight-year old daughter was subjected to a terrifying experience at the hands of a morally degenerate private detective and ex-labor spy who did not like communists and wanted to give her father "a hard time." Throughout 1948, political rallies and local headquarters of the Progressive Party were the scenes of violence.

In August, 1949, an ugly mob broke up and assaulted the audience at a Paul Robeson open-air concert on a private picnic ground in Peekskill, New York. Stickers pasted on cars and buses read: "Communism is Treason, Behind Communism—the Jews! Therefore: For My Country—Against the Jews." A week later, the plans for the concert were successfully carried out as a result of the mobilization of a large defense guard. But a large, unruly protest parade organized by local veteran organizations waited until after the concert and then with the overt and covert aid of state police viciously attacked the departing audience. Commenting on the incident, the *Christian Science Monitor* declared: ". . . . if a community like that could produce the tyranny of riots which denied constitutional rights of free assembly and free speech, few cities in America can feel safe. . . ."

There were isolated murmers of protest here or there from a public figure, from the press or even from an official. But in the main, a pall of conformity settled over the country.

Surely there must have been many more like Professor Chafee who were "disturbed by the gradual erosion of many fundamental human rights which were cherished by the Americans of 1791"; by the "abominable" practice of investigating bodies who insisted that decent Americans betray their friends; "by the growing use of perjury prosecutions to bypass the Statute of Limitations"; by the grave impairment of the traditional right to a fair trial; "by the common assumption that deprivation of a job connected with the government is not a substantial loss of freedom"; by the strong tendency to establish an American party-line" to which all must adhere—or else! Surely there must have been many more in public life who could say with Professor Chafee, "Hounding a man [like a Bridges or Remington] after he is cleared may be constitutional, but it is not the way I was brought up."

But there were few who made public protest. The difference between the reaction of liberal, democratic America to the Palmer Raids of 1920 and to the suppressions of the '30's has already been noted. Professor Chafee made the comparison with the early '50's.

> . . . Although the reasons for suppression are weaker today than during the Red Menace [of 1919-20], resistance to suppression is weaker too. Alistair Cooke remarks [in *A Generation on Trial]* that "liberty is not in our time a markedly American passion." [People like] Samuel Gompers and leading newspapers spoke out against the federal sedition bills of 1920, but the Smith Act met with no similar opposition and the McCarran Act sailed through without any conspicuous protesters.

As a matter of fact, the newspapers, which did on occasion protest mildly and hesitantly, for the most part cancelled their editorial protest by their own headlines and first page columns. Their expert reportage spread before the public the most outrageous and unproved charges and included the names, addresses and places of employment of the victims before they had opportunity for defense. And defense was difficult. For the American bar, except for a handful of courageous attorneys who faced loss of clients, sentences of contempt and even disbarment, played on the whole a negative role in this crisis of American law. No Clarence Darrow rose to the occasion. Professor Chafee could find no dozen prominent attorneys such as he had found in 1920 to join him in speaking out. Also, as a whole, organized labor was intimidated or disoriented and silent.

What was perhaps more disturbing than the actual suppression, which was serious enough, was the revelation that the American democratic tradition, deep rooted though it was, could temporarily become so paralyzed in defense of its institutions and of the very principles that nourished it. The proud American sense of fair play seemed to desert the people.

A depressing sense of helplessness began to permeate the land. And that, too, took its toll. In November, 1947, John Gilbert Winant, former Ambassador to England, committed suicide in New Hampshire. In June, 1948, Morton E. Kent, who had been an employee of the State Department and had been accused of contacting a Soviet agent, cut his throat. In August, Harry Dexter White, former Assistant Secretary of the Treasury, died of a heart attack, after a session with the House Committee on Un-American Activities. In December, Laurence Duggan, former State Department official accused of being a communist, jumped from a New York office building. In the same month, Mrs. Minnie Gutride, a New York school teacher under investigation for communist activity, committed suicide. In February, 1950, Mrs. Emily Anderson preferred death by throwing herself before a train, to life under the threat of the hydrogen bomb. In April, Professor F. O. Mathiessen, of Harvard, an outstanding liberal, jumped from a hotel window. The same month, N. W. Robertson, a Washington newspaper correspondent, committed suicide. Nor is this the total roll call. Nor is this the only way in which tragedy manifested itself.

But democracy, too, has its reserves. While "quality" may have deserted their posts, the "common people," the "little man," held the fort against the day when they could bring reason back to the land.

20. McCarran Un-Americanism

In accordance with the precedent set in 1798, the foreign born were the group most easy to attack.

On October 20, 1950, the Internal Security Act, commonly known as the McCarran Act, went into effect.

On October 22, 1950, at 2 A.M., the Immigration Service began a series of arrests in New York, Duluth, Los Angeles and Seattle. Between that date and November 2, further arrests were made in other major centers of the country. During that period, the Justice Department, using the FBI to supplement the activities of the Immigration Service personnel, patrolled office buildings, posted guards before apartment houses, even used search warrants to suggest that the "aliens" they were seeking were hiding from justice.

The purpose of all this cloak-and-dagger activity was apparently publicity rather than efficiency. Six men whom an especially spectacular "search" allegedly failed to locate, appeared at the immigration office promptly in response to letters sent them through the United States mail! This public display of police techniques was meant both to impress the American people with the alertness of the Immigration Service and the prowess of the FBI, and to inspire the foreign born with sufficient fear of the effects of the new law to stifle all opposition.

Presumably for the latter purpose, bail which had already been allowed was cancelled, and the Justice Department publicly declared its intention to deport 3,400 for their political beliefs immediately. The same purpose was implicit in the statements of federal attorneys in Chicago and New York that according to the new law, "wherever you have an alien, you have an enemy alien. . . . He should be treated accordingly"; and that the law "gave the Attorney General the unreviewable right to hold 'enemies' without bail if they were not citizens."

As the Cold War continued, "anti-alien" legislation before Congress had become more and more threatening. Again, as in 1940, the Hobbs Bill with its grim reminder of Hitler's concentration camps took the center of attention. In the 1949 hearings on the measure, the Commissioner of Immigration and Naturalization himself had appeared in its favor and had read an approving statement from Attorney General Tom Clark. The bill, allowing the Attorney General to hold certain non-citizens indefinitely without bail, passed the House 326 to 15, in spite of Rep. Celler's argument that it was clearly unconstitutional since even a dope peddler or a murderer had a right to trial by jury. Fortunately, the Senate had some doubts about the constitutionality of a similar bill.

Absorption in defeating the Hobbs Bill (again as in 1940) may have distracted attention from an equally dangerous bill. The bill actually passed in 1950 was the worst anti-alien law since 1798. It is perhaps true that the Hobbs Bill would have become law, despite the opposition, if its supporters in the Senate had not realized that in the McCarran Act they had a more satisfactory and definitive measure to curb American liberties.

In April, 1950, Senator Pat McCarran, an outspoken admirer of Franco's regime in Spain, offered the Senate an omnibus bill of 248 pages, which not only included most of the provisions of the Hobbs Bill and the Judd Bill, but also (to quote *The Lamp*) "incorporated every un-American proposal on immigration and naturalization ever advanced in Congress." *The Lamp* listed nine of its provisions:

1. Annual publication by the Attorney General of a

list of organizations which he considers subversive to the national security.

2. Present or former membership in any organization so listed to be ground for denial of citizenship, for deportation of non-citizens and for exclusion from the United States.

3. Exemption of deportation hearings from the Administrative Procedure Act.

4. Authority to hold for life without bail non-citizens ordered deported.

5. Yearly reporting by mail by all non-citizens.

6. Denaturalization for membership in any listed organization within five years of naturalization.

7. Establishment of a "central index" of all non-citizens, to include all relevant information and to be available to the FBI and the CIA.

8. Authority for the President to stop all immigration at any time.

9. Limitation of immigration from the British West Indies or any other colony or dependency to 100 a year.

The omnibus bill was apparently too crude, its legality too questionable to be swallowed at once by Congress, even in the midst of the Cold War. But McCarran reduced his measure to forty-seven pages and presented it as Senate Bill 1832. He eliminated, for instance, the third provision listed above; but exemption from sections 5, 7 and 8 of the Administrative Procedure Act was granted to the Immigration and Naturalization Service on the grounds of economy (in a rider attached to the Appropriation Bill for the Department of Justice in September). On August 2, the McCarran Bill was favorably reported by the Judiciary Committee of the Senate, without hearings, and was passed without debate on August 9. A similar bill was passed by the House, and differences were quickly ironed out by a Joint Committee. The Internal Security Act of 1950 became law when it was passed in amended form on October 20, over the veto of President Truman.

One example of how the Act deals with a constitutional

question may serve to illustrate its entire approach. In order to avoid being declared unconstitutional as a bill of attainder, the measure does not name the specific organization, the Communist Party. It speaks instead of the "Communist movement" in the United States. But, by eliminating the specific and dealing with the general, the Act really enlarges the dragnet. On the basis of the definitions as established in the Act, anyone who does anything, says anything, thinks anything or associates with anyone condemned by spokesmen for the government readily falls into the "communist" category. And, by establishing such broad generalizations as "Communist action groups" and "Communist front organizations," the Act can be used against all organized opposition to any economic, social, political, administrative, legislative or judicial procedures that are unwise or unjust. To paraphrase Professor Chafee, this may make the Act constitutional, but that is not the way the American people were brought up. But, unfortunately, the American people did not do credit to their upbringing for they failed to demonstrate their opposition to the Act before it was passed.

The Act, having declared by legislative fiat that the communist movement in the United States is a subversive conspiracy, a clear and present danger determined to overthrow the government by force and violence, then defines who is a communist and what is a communist action or front organization in the broadest and vaguest terms. It goes on to prohibit the employment of members of such "communist" organizations in certain categories, and denies them passports. It calls for the registration of such "communist" organizations, their officers and membership, and establishes punishment for failure to register. It sets up a Subversive Activities Control Board (SACB) before which the Attorney General may cite organizations he believes to be subversive. Since the verdict of guilt against any organization is written into the Act, the maintenance of the board is sheer misappropriation of public funds.

Once these restraints are placed upon American citizens, the Act then proceeds to deal with non-citizens. It provides for the deportation of non-citizen members of proscribed organizations. It provides for the holding of those under deportation proceedings without bail "at the discretion of the Attorney General." It requires annual registration by aliens. It facilitates denaturalization of all foreign-born citizens who fall into the McCarran dragnet.

President Truman in vetoing the bill, stated that it

> Would put the government of the United States in the thought control business.
>
> It would give government officials vast powers to harass all of our citizens in the exercise of their right to free speech.
>
> No considerations of expediency can justify the enactment of such a bill as this, a bill which would greatly weaken our liberties and give aid and comfort to our opponents.

These were strong and true words that the President uttered. But the Cold War atmosphere in which the President himself had issued his own Loyalty Order closed the minds of Congress to their truth.

The dangerous implications of the Act both for the foreign born and for the American people as a whole were fully recognized and forcibly presented by the Executive Secretary of the ACPFB, precisely because of his years of experience in the struggle to defend the rights of foreign-born Americans. In his annual report to the National Conference of the ACPFB in New York City on December 2, 1950, Abner Green dealt chiefly with the McCarran Law and the procedures of the Department of Justice since its passage. Every page of the report, which was immediately printed under the title *The Deportation Drive vs. the Bill of Rights,* was ablaze with the incredulous indignation of an American who fully understood both the immediate effects of the law in terms of human tragedy and the threat to the future of the American tradition of freedom, embodied in the Bill of Rights.

It was not that the contents of the law was novel—its provisions were all too familiar from the Mundt-Nixon Bill, the Reynolds Bill, the Hobbs Bill and scores of others (not to mention the laws of Nazi Germany). But those bills had not become law. Nor was it that the procedures of the Immigration and Naturalization Service in November 1950 were novel—they were those of the Palmer Raids of 1920, of the "Deportation Special" of the 1930's, and of the deportation drive that followed the end of World War II. What McCarran's Internal Security Act did was to make provisions formerly rejected as tyrannical and un-American a part of the law of the land; and to authorize precisely those practices of the Immigration and Naturalization Service that had been condemned by the courts in the 1920's and the years following.

Abner Green opened his report with a quotation from a speech to the UN made by the American delegate Warren Austin:

> "We must never forget that internal terror and aggression have, in the past, led to external aggression and war."

He went on to describe the "internal terror" which began October 22.

> [The Justice Department took] one sentence of this forty-seven page law. Forty-eight non-citizens were arrested and held without bail. . . . We do not claim that having to go to jail is the worst thing that can happen to a person. It is no shame to be in jail when you are fighting for your rights and the rights of the American people. The shame is on the jailer. . . .
>
> The only way a police-state measure, such as the McCarran Law can be put into effect is with the use of police-state methods. . . .
>
> The McCarran Law makes it possible for the Justice Department to try to deport many more than the 3,400 non-citizens [of its announcement]. The law provides for the deportation of any non-citizen who engages "in activi-

ties which would be prejudicial to the public interest or would endanger the welfare or safety of the United States."

Who is to determine which activities are prejudicial to the public interest? The Attorney General.

Who is to determine which activities endanger the welfare and safety of the United States? The Attorney General.

Therefore this infamous law, in police-state fashion, gives the Attorney General the power to decide who shall live in the United States.

[Striking, picket lines, even membership in a union may be prejudicial to the public welfare.] Any non-citizen, communist and non-communist, who engages in or who ever has engaged in any democratic and progressive cause seeking to advance the welfare of the American people [may be included].

The law has a few additional nightmares. It grants the Justice Department the right to deport non-citizens to any country that will accept them. It grants the right to imprison any non-citizen for six months without bail after a deportation order has been issued. After six months it can release him under "supervision" [with regular reporting and with the requirement that he give information on anything which the Attorney General deems it proper to ask about]. Failure to comply means a fine of $1,000 or one year in prison or both.

It will not be just the non-citizen who will suffer. These deportations reach into every phase and facet of American life. Of the 160 arrested in deportation proceedings to date, more than twenty-five are women—wives, mothers, grandmothers of American citizens; more than thirty are leaders of trade unions, two are leaders of the Negro people, three are important leaders of Jewish communities, and more than 100 are active members and leaders of national group communities throughout the country. These deportations cut into the very heart and soul of the American community because the non-citizen is an integral part of our society.

These non-citizens have lived all their lives in this country. They have no place to go. This is their land. This is where they grew up. Their families are here in this country. They are fighting to remain where they belong. . . .

Does any one have any idea what a McCarranized deportation hearing actually is like? [They] are degrading in their sheer bias and in their treatment of human beings. They are police-state hearings. The Attorney General makes the charges [which] serve as the basis for the hearing. . . . [There] is a prosecutor. He works for the Justice Department. . . . There is a stenographer, also paid by the Attorney General. Then there is the hearing officer—the supposedly fair and unbiased judge. . . . This unbiased hearing officer works for the Justice Department. . . . [His] recommendation goes to the man who makes the decision . . . also fair and unbiased, except that he is the Commissioner of Immigration and Naturalization, . . . works for the Department of Justice and gets paid by the Attorney General. Now, the Commissioner's decision can be appealed to the Board of Immigration Appeals . . . five men, all of whom work for the Justice Department and get paid by the Attorney General. . . . This is a lot of hokum. It is not democratic procedure. . . .

. . . With three employees of the Justice Department sitting in judgment—they bring in witnesses. And who are these witnesses? All employees of the Justice Department . . . a retinue of informers and paid agents who take the stand . . . for a weekly salary or a fee of $25 a day. . . .

There is one thing for which we can be grateful. We cannot select the people we defend against deportation since the selection is at the whim of the Attorney General. But the Attorney General has some very good judgment. The non-citizens he selects are always the kind that have devoted their lives to fighting for the rights of the Negro people, against anti-Semitism and for labor's rights.

The first arrests were illegal in spite of the broad powers accorded the Attorney General in the law. The arrests were made and bail was denied *before* deportation had been actually ordered. Refusal of bail was a denial of the fundamental right, recognized long before the first settlers came to Jamestown and Plymouth. It is recognized in the Eighth Amendment to the Constitution. Protests arose. Thirteen Federal District Court judges condemned the action as an abuse of the Attorney General's discretionary power. Of the forty-eight foreign-born Americans first held, all but eight were released on bail during the month of November.

But while any kind of victory in times of stress is welcome, this kind of victory does not alter the content of a law. And the very essence of the McCarran Law was a rejection of the Bill of Rights. The new Law could be fought in two ways: (1) by persuading Congress to repeal the law, or to change it fundamentally; (2) by testing the constitutionality of its provisions in the courts.

Both ways presented difficulties. The temper of the times was such that a total rejection of the fundamental thesis of the Act implied in repeal or in basic change was highly improbable. The temporary, panic-inspired apathy with which important sections of the American people faced the passage of the bill could not be changed abruptly into the energetic revolt against it, which would be required to compel Congress to reverse itself. It was obvious that quick results could not be expected.

Senator McCarran was still not satisfied with the results of his anti-democratic machinations. Supported by McCarthy and his followers, McCarran went to work again, this time in collusion with Rep. Francis E. Walter of Pennsylvania. By January, 1952, they had ready the Immigration and Nationality Act of 1952, better known as the Walter-McCarran Act. And once again the Senate and House overrode President Truman's veto on June 27. And the Act went into effect—adding irony to bitterness for the foreign born—on Christmas Eve, 1952.

The (presumably deliberately) vague but all-inclusive wording of many of its provisions, the extraordinary absolute and arbitrary power which the act puts into the hands of the Attorney General, the obvious intention to make conditions difficult for the foreign born—all presented new barriers to any effective defense of the rights of the foreign born. The law had been presented to Congress as a codification and clarification of the mass of existing legislation on immigration and naturalization; and this characterization was partially correct. But, to quote Prof. Oscar Handlin, of Harvard University, "The Law brought to light the unlovely residue of outworn prejudices" together with "the burdensome provisions under the old laws . . . extended to the point of meanness." (*Atlantic Monthly* May, 1953, p. 27.)

Again it is Abner Green who gives us in his pamphlet, *The Walter-McCarran Law, Police State Terror Against Foreign Born Americans*, published in May, 1953, both a blistering denunciation of the law and a keen analysis of its content.

> This Law . . . negates the principles enunciated in the Declaration of Independence and in the Bill of Rights of the United States Constitution.
>
> It would extinguish the torch of freedom so proudly held aloft by that immigrant from France, the Statue of Liberty, in New York harbor. . . .
>
> [The] fight will never cease until the Law is repealed and the Justice Department's deportation and denaturalization hysteria is ended.
>
> This is part of the fight against the reactionary drive to fascism and war. It must be seen as such if it is to be won.
>
> All forms of repression must be defeated. Otherwise, no minority—and therefore, no person—in the United States can feel secure from attack by these advance guards of American fascism.

In spite of the pamphlet's somewhat lurid cover, with its barbed wire squares and the sense of outrage, its pages convey throughout a specific and accurate appraisal of the different sections of the law, combined with concrete illustrations of the effects of its provisions, both on individuals and on the nation as a whole. For the author added to a passion for justice and a knowledge of the subject his daily experience with the tragic insecurity of the foreign born in this "land of the free."

1. *The Powers of the Attorney General.* In admitting and in excluding immigrants, "determination and ruling by the Attorney General shall be controlling." He may expend such amounts as may be necessary "for establishing quarters for the detention of aliens" (concentration camps). He can deny residents the opportunity to adjust their status on the basis of undisclosed information. He becomes virtually a dictator over non-citizens.

2. *Status of the Non-Citizens.* The violations of the rights of non-citizens, incorporated in the Act, are complete and tyrannical. The non-citizen can be arrested without warrant, and held without bail. He can be deported for exercising freedom of speech or belief. He can be deported by an *ex post facto* law for action which was legal when it was carried out. He can be deported by a bill of attainder. Hearings against him can be held *in absentia.* He can be deported to any country which will accept him, even to a country like Spain, where fascist rule may mean his death. He can be jailed for ten years for wilfully failing to deport himself. "It thereby creates a community of 3,000,000 people without rights, whose lives are bound up with the fate of all the people."

3. *Registration of Non-Citizens.* Deportation may follow failure to comply with the provisions. This is a reversal of the attitude of the Justice Department itself, in 1941, which opposed a similar law in Pennsylvania, as making non-citizens "subject to constant threat of intrusive surveillance by the state police."

4. *Preliminary Investigations.* The lack of safeguards makes investigation a ready weapon for strike-breaking, anti-union actions, or personal spite. A man can be, and often is, discharged by his employer simply because he is being "investigated."

5. *The Right to Bail.* When arrested, the non-citizen can "be held without bail or released under such conditions as the Attorney General may prescribe." Mr. and Mrs. Fradkin in Los Angeles were released on bail under bond not to associate with anyone affiliated with any affiliate of the Communist Party. Since both were former members, they apparently would have to separate or go to jail.

6. *Deportation Hearings.* There are no rules of evidence, hearsay testimony is admitted. The Special Inquiry Officer, worse than Lewis Carroll's cat, Fury, is not only "judge and jury," he is also prosecutor. The President's Commission reported, "The present hearing procedure in deportation and exclusion cases fails to conform to the now generally accepted standards of fair hearings."

7. *Deportation.* No statute of limitations is recognized. The length of residence or date of offense is immaterial. Deportation is possible if the Attorney General knows "or has reason to believe" that the man had intended to act against the public interest, or for two crimes after entry, or for membership or affiliation at any time with the Communist Party or with any organization required to be registered under the Subversive Activities Control Act. Once this law is in force, "there will be no need of thought control, for there will be no such thing as a thought left in this country to control."

8. *Self-Deportation.* Failure to make "timely application in good faith" for necessary documents is a crime punishable by ten years in a federal penitentiary. Two men, one from Austria, fifty-one years old, resident in the United States for forty-nine years, and one of fifty-five from Russia, in this country for forty years, had already been indicted.

9. *Supervisory Parole.* After six months the non-deportable non-citizen must make a private concentration camp for himself and live under close supervision for the rest of his life. Breaking regulations can bring a $1,000 fine and a year in jail.

10. *Naturalization.* "What was once conceived as an act of transformation from alien to citizen now becomes the grant of temporary license, revocable for what may be no more than an indiscretion." (Sen. Herbert Lehman.) Fraud has become "concealment of a material fact" and various acts like refusal of information to a congressional committee or affiliation within five years of naturalization with any organization considered "subversive" are grounds for denaturalization.

11. *Immigration.* Quota provisions dictated by race preju-

dice remain, denial of visas or of entry may be refused if the Attorney General "has reason to believe," etc. The token immigration of 100 a year from Japan, Korea, India, etc., is a sort of "democratic fig leaf" which fails to hide the racial prejudice of the law clearly shown both in the retention of the old quotas and in the refusal to count West Indians and people of mixed race in the British quota.

12. *Alaska Cannery Workers.* Exclusion is allowed for non-citizens returning from Alaska, Hawaii, Puerto Rico, etc. Re-entry permits may be cancelled after they have been given without opportunity for the holder even to hear the charges.

13. *Mexican-Americans.* Mass deportations are authorized. In the first three months of 1953, 204,767 were deported.

14. *Exchange of Information.* The Commissioner of Immigration and Naturalization is directed "to maintain direct and continuous liaison" with the FBI and the CIA "for the purpose of obtaining and exchanging information. This obviously provides a "master black-list."

Abner Green, in the pamphlet, calls for the necessary separation of the Immigration and Naturalization Service from the Justice Department. It "should function as a social service agency of the government to encourage and facilitate the naturalization of non-citizens and help the immigrant." The Justice Department inevitably develops "a police attitude and police point of view. . . . The Service has become an agency for repression and oppression."

This was the Walter-McCarran Act. This was McCarranism, the statutory codification of McCarthyism. The McCarran Act and the Walter-McCarran Act both violate the American way of life. They ignore the tradition of welcome to the stranger and the oppressed so often expressed by the Presidents of the United States, from George Washington to Franklin Roosevelt, and the tradition of individual liberty embodied in the Constitution and the Bill of Rights. Only the pressures of the Cold War (analogous to the fear of France in 1798) could have made the acceptance of such legislation possible.

21. Direct Attack

In all sections of the country there were individuals and groups who condemned the two McCarran Laws as a whole, or who objected to specific provisions, as the 2,000 page report of the Presidents' Commission on Immigration and Naturalization shows. A national committee, set up "to repeal the McCarran Law" of 1950, changed its name to the Committee to Repeal the McCarran Acts. But most of the opposition was unorganized and the general public was concerned with other matters. Press and radio ignored the threat to freedom.

One group determined to fight the laws, in collaboration with all liberal forces if possible, but alone if necessary, was the American Committee for Protection of Foreign Born. The ACPFB had failed to prevent the passage of the McCarran Law but it was prepared to fight for its repeal, to defend its victims and so far as possible to unify its opponents. The call to battle was sounded by Abner Green in the report which he gave to the ACPFB Annual Conference to Defend the Bill of Rights, December 2, 1950:

> We will never relent in our determination to end this disgraceful treatment of honest and decent people who, by accident of birth, are not citizens of this country and who, because of the reactionary anti-labor administration of the naturalization laws of the United States, have been prevented from becoming American citizens so that today they are targets for the reactionaries who prevented them

from becoming American citizens. We will fight against their deportation and we will fight to obtain American citizenship for them in this country. . . .

At the same time, we who are citizens must realize that only by defeating these deportations can we preserve our own rights as Americans. Only by ending the harassment of non-citizens can we advance and strengthen our liberties and our freedom, because the treatment accorded non-citizens today will be measured out to citizens tomorrow—but measured out in much larger doses. The only way in which we can enjoy democracy in the United States is to guarantee that all of us—native and foreign born, Negro and white, Jew and Gentile, men and women—live in full equality, live in dignity as free men and women without discrimination and without distinction. To that goal we dedicate our unceasing efforts.

The Conference, attended by 365 delegates and observers, with 163 organizations represented, elected as officers for the following year Thomas Mann and the Rt. Rev. Arthur W. Moulton as honorary co-chairmen, Abner Green as executive secretary, Harriet Barron as administrative secretary and Carol King as general counsel. The constitution was amended, leaving unchanged the statement of purpose but making the executive secretary and the elected officers directly responsible for carrying out the program adopted at the Conference. The Conference voted a formal statement of policy and objectives and listed the issues for action.

The National Conference to Defend the Bill of Rights was called to consider the dangers to the existence of the Bill of Rights of the United States Constitution caused by the widespread attack on the democratic rights of foreign-born Americans, naturalized and non-citizens. The Conference, in devoting itself to the rights of these Americans, recognizes that reaction in the United States seeks to use the foreign born as scapegoats, and seeks by acting against the foreign born to provide legal and political precedents for attacking the civil rights of all Americans.

The issues on which the Conference is resolved to act are:

The Justice Department's announcement that it will arrest and deport more than 3,400 non-citizens on the basis of the deportation provisions of the McCarran Law.

The Justice Department's announced intentions to revoke the citizenship of more than 1,000 naturalized American citizens.

The difficulties the Justice Department has placed in the way of thousands of non-citizens who have been trying for years to become American citizens without success.

These issues create serious dangers to the civil rights and freedom of every American, native as well as foreign born. This Conference, therefore, in order successfully to accomplish objectives of common concern, calls for support of its program of action by all Americans and all American organizations, regardless of political or social beliefs, or differences, that recognize the defense of the rights of foreign-born Americans as being essential to the preservation of democratic liberties in the United States.

The Conference reaffirms its attachment to the democratic aspirations of the American people, to the United States Constitution and to its Bill of Rights. It appeals to all sections of the American people to join together in defense of the rights of all non-citizens—regardless of their race, color, creed, national origin, or political belief—who have become, or may become, the victims of the McCarran Law hysteria.

The resolutions passed dealt almost exclusively with the procedures of the Justice Department in deportation and naturalization. The stress was on the denial of constitutional rights: refusal of bail, illegal arrests, the infringement of freedom of opinion and association, and of due process of law in hearings which were "a travesty of justice and bring into mockery law, constitutional rights and every concept of democratic procedure and decency." It was decided to observe March, 1951, as "Fight Deportation Month," during which a special delegation would go to Washington; protest meetings would be held across the country. In accordance with this decision, the Committee issued special bulletins and a folder, *1798, Thomas Jefferson Fought the First Deportation Drive*. Special meetings were held from Chicago to Portland, Oregon; several in Greater New York —the last New York meeting was a "send-off" for those going to Washington.

The attitude of the government toward these activities was reflected in the reception given the delegation. It was composed of some forty American citizen members of families of deportees, coming from eleven states: California, Illinois, Indiana, Massachusetts, Missouri, New Jersey, New York, Ohio, Oregon, Pennsylvania, Washington. They called on Senators and Representatives, they picketed the White House briefly. A delegation of seven veterans of two World Wars delivered a letter to the President with the signatures of prominent Americans. Appointments had been made with Attorney General McGrath and with the Commissioner of Immigration.

The Attorney General, however, refused to see more than one member of the delegation in company with Clemens France of Providence, Rhode Island, who led the group. (Mr. France had been a civil rights attorney since the days of the Palmer Raids and had been State Director of Social Welfare of Rhode Island when Mr. McGrath was governor.) The Attorney General refused to discuss the policy of the Immigration and Naturalization Service, but William Sentner of St. Louis did protest the holding of deportees without bail and spoke of the hardship of expensive legal proceedings for the families of deportees, who were for the most part working people. Mr. McGrath advised that the Committee "would do better to use their funds for legal defense instead of the publication of literature." (Seven years later, the Attorney General of New York State enjoined the ACPFB from using its funds for legal defense, and ordered it to use them for education only.)

In spite of an appointment, the Commissioner of Immigration was not available. Mr. Kelly, acting for him, listened to each member of the group, taking copious notes. Temporarily at least, he and other members of the Service present showed some understanding of the serious effects of the Service policy on the lives of American citizens as well as on the foreign born.

Clemens France's words at the delegation press conference re-echo the astonished anger expressed at the 1950 Conference at the essentially "un-American" character of the McCarran Security Law.

> You cannot import fascism and at the same time export democracy. Just as the lion and the lamb cannot lie down together—unless of course the lamb lies inside the lion's stomach. The enactment of the McCarran Act was a direct and overt act of fascism, the most subversive act ever perpetrated in the United States. . . .
>
> It is a basic thesis of Marxism that democracy on a capitalistic base is a wolf in sheep's clothing, a hypocrisy, a mask which is immediately shed when Capitalism is placed under stress and strain. Therefore the McCarran Act wiping out the safeguards of the First and Fifth Amendments [and other amendments also] to the Constitution proved to hundreds of Marxists both in front of and behind the Iron Curtain that our Bill of Rights was just such a facade. . . .
>
> Our grandiloquent protestations that the United States is the world champion of democracy . . . never sat well with European nations. Now . . . its verity is under serious question.
>
> In stressing the serious impact of the McCarran Act on "friendly nations" (President Truman), I do not minimize the human fact of this deportation business. For these families on this pilgrimage my whole being is stirred to indignation. As an American I feel a sense of degradation. . . .
>
> These victims of fascism—McCarran style—are just "little people" who have lived their lives working at humble tasks in industry and trade, yet devoting their lives to the betterment of the lot of their fellows—Negro and white.
>
> Thought control has no limits. Today these non-citizens,

> tomorrow any citizen who has a new idea. . . . For nearly eight hundred years Europe lived in what history records as the Dark Ages, a period of stagnation, a period of thought control. It is conceivable that we in the United States can inaugurate our own era of the Dark Ages. . . .
>
> These families here on this pilgrimage, whether they realize it or not, are symbols of all pilgrims. A Pilgrim is defined as one who travels far to visit some sacred shrine. This, our Capitol, is the sacred shrine of all our history of social progress, of freedom, of independence. It is the place for victims of a fascist law to be. Here they are. If they return from their pilgrimage empty-handed, the shame is ours. The degradation is ours—not theirs. The graveyard of democracy we prepare is ours—not theirs.

The experiences of the delegates at the offices of the Attorney General and the Commissioner of Immigration brought again into clear light one of the reasons for the frequently expressed judgment that the Immigration and Naturalization Service should be an independent department, not a section of the Justice Department. Two years earlier, when the Supreme Court had ruled that the Administrative Procedure Act was violated in deportation hearings, Rev. John Darr, Jr., then chairman of the ACPFB Board of Directors, had written to President Truman:

> The Department of Justice has been found guilty of violating the law passed by Congress and ignoring basic democratic principles. . . .
>
> The Justice Department has used the deportation laws for the purposes of political persecution and in order to create hysteria against the foreign born. . . .
>
> We call on you to . . . remove the Immigration and Naturalization Service from the Department of Justice and establish it as an independent agency.

And in April, 1950, the ACPFB had initiated a nation-wide

petition to the President with the same request. Truman took no action.

In March, 1952, the Attorney General specifically refused to discuss matters of policy with a delegation because, as he said, they were the concern of the Immigration and Naturalization Service. But the representatives of the Service were equally insistent in their statement that policy was not theirs to determine—they were merely carrying out the orders of the Attorney General. (A year later, a group sponsored by the ACPFB had difficulty in seeing anyone from the office of the Attorney General and were told that they should go to the Immigration Service on the other side of the city. Meantime, the delegation which was at that moment making an appeal to the Immigration Service was meeting the same denial of responsibility.) Such a situation in itself goes far to nullify the right of petition specifically guaranteed to the American people in the Bill of Rights.

Various conferences to rouse public opinion or to raise funds for court proceedings or for both purposes were held in many parts of the country. In June, 1951, to coordinate the fighting of all groups that had sprung up, and to make it possible for each locality to benefit from the experiences of all the others, a "Conference of Deportee Defense Committees" was held in Chicago, with the Midwest Committee for Protection of Foreign Born as host. Reports of their work were given by the Los Angeles Committee, the Minneapolis Joint Committee Against Deportation, the Midwest Committee and the Michigan Committee; and written statements were sent by the Northwest Committee and the Northern California Committee. Reports were made also by committees organized to defend individuals or to defend those with a common national background: the Tonie Sentner Defense Committee of United Electrical Workers Union, District 8 (St. Louis), the Resnikoff Defense Committee, the American Polish Committee, the Committee for the Protection of Greek Americans, the Finnish American Freedom Committee, the Lithuanian American Committee, and the Czechoslovak Committee. Reports were read from the Hungarian American Committee, the American Yugoslav Committee and the Harisiades-Taffler Neighborhood Defense Committee of Brooklyn, New York.

These committees, separate and independent, had come into existence at various times to meet specific emergencies and the nature of their relationship to the ACPFB had varied according to circumstances. But the McCarran Internal Security Act made very obvious the need for active cooperation. Similar yearly conferences for the pooling of experience were held so long as the deportation drive continued.

Some concepton of the activities of these committees can be gathered from the reports and from the problems they faced. The Midwest Committee reported that when, in October, 1950, six non-citizens (James Keller, Vincent Andrulis, James MacKay, Moses Resnikoff, Fred Lichota and Peter Kushnir) were arrested in midnight raids and jailed, it immediately called an emergency conference which was attended by representatives of eighty organizations. Within ten days, 10,000 protests were sent to Washington. Five special protest meetings were organized, 900 attending the meeting protesting the arrest of Andrulis. A series of meetings, large and small, was held involving unions, nationality groups and interested friends of those arrested. During "Fight Deportation Month" of March, 1951, a Conference and banquet brought together 600 people. Arrangements were made for groups to attend deportation hearings which were held as often as two in one day. Two hundred trade unionists attended a reception to congratulate Joe Weber on the reversal of his conviction for falsely claiming United States citizenship. Five thousand people sent protest cards against the holding of four deportees without bail on Terminal Island on the West Coast, thus giving active evidence of the increasing realization of the value of concerted action and a recognition of the fact that defense of the foreign born in one area can succeed only if there is national cooperation.

A special report on denaturalization came from the Michigan Committee. There were four cases in Detroit, and six elsewhere, brought on the ground of "fraud." (The answer "no" had been given during the naturalization proceedings to the question of membership in an organization advocating the overthrow of the government by force and violence.) The Department of Justice was obviously attempting to obtain a reversal of the Schneiderman decision. The government was waiting, before continuing the prosecution, for the conviction of the eleven Communist Party leaders in the first Foley Square trial.

Meantime, the FBI and the Immigration Service were busy questioning citizens in their homes and at places of employment. Official letters were being sent to naturalized citizens inviting them to visit Immigration and Naturalization offices "to clear up your citizenship status." Once the decision, as anticipated by the government, was given at Foley Square, the groundwork was laid for renewed activity against the naturalized citizen. The number of cases would increase, perhaps to a thousand. Preparation needed to be made to carry a test case to the Supreme Court. (The cases of Stanley Nowak and Mrs. Rebecca Maisenberg were not accepted by the Supreme Court until 1957.)

With the increase of Justice Department activity in deportation and denaturalization and the corresponding increase in local action in behalf of the victims; and with the growing burden of costs for all manner of defense, it was inevitable that some misconceptions and misunderstandings should arise about the relationship between legal defense and mass activity. There were some who would rely only or primarily on mass activity as the sole agent of victory, and considered legal defense an illusion and a waste of time and money. Others, doubtful of mass response in a period of hysteria and fearful of the consequences of mass activity, placed their complete reliance on legal procedures, and sought to discourage and prevent mass action. Each side reflected a growing lack of confidence in American justice, the U.S. Courts and the protection afforded them by the Bill of Rights—a mood not confined to forces around the American Committee.

Abner Green dealt with this question at a special session. He reminded his hearers that, for all the mass activity, the fight for bail in October and November 1950 might not have been won had not some thirty-five lawyers stood their ground and fought for the constitutional rights of non-citizens. "There is no conflict between legal and mass defense . . . the lawyer and the defense committee have the same objective . . . one must supplement the other." The legal issues must be correctly understood and integrated into the mass campaigns, for confusion on the legal issues will disorient the campaign." However difficult it was both for lawyers and campaign leaders to find the time, both must realize that "through discussions, a complete understanding of the lawyers' problems and mutual respect," which were essential, could be achieved. As to fees, some lawyers volunteered their services, but for many this was impossible. "They must pay rent and stenographers . . . their time and their experience is their stock in trade. . . . It is the responsibility of defense committees to secure the funds needed for legal (and all other) expenses."

The true significance of the defense effort in relation to the preservation of the rights of all Americans was emphasized forcibly in Abner Green's report to the Defense Committee's Conference:

> For the past month, no political deportees have been held without bail Of the forty-eight held without bail in October, forty-eight are now free. Your defense Committees shared the work and the costs of winning these forty-eight victories and your committees are to be congratulated with special commendation to the Los Angeles Committee for Protection of Foreign Born, for the leadership it displayed under Rose Chernin, in winning the release of the Terminal Island Four. . . .
>
> The ACPFB defends the rights of foreign born Americans because we are concerned with the status of the democratic rights of all of the people of this country . . . [This is] the basic guide for our defense and educational

work and has been the basis . . . through the nineteen years of our existence. . . .

What confronts us? We are faced with not just a deportation drive, not just an attack on bail, not just a Karasek or Chew case. We are a part of the fight against American fascism which has selected as one of its first victims the non-citizen and the naturalized citizen. . . .

Today there is a general assault on the rights of the American people. . . . As a part of this general attack, the minimum of democratic rights possessed by the non-citizen is . . . threatened with obliteration.

What rights would a non-citizen have if the immigration and naturalization section of the McCarran Law became the accepted law of the land? None at all. And the absence of all democratic rights means fascist conditions of living. That is what we are fighting. If we do not understand that danger we miss the whole point of our mass defense work. . . .

We are only at the beginning of our fight. This session must provide us with many weapons for this fight. . . . We must continue to mold and develop additional weapons. We share a great responsibility. But we are confident that we will make a good fight—and we are confident that we are going to win this fight.

Our confidence is based on the knowledge that we are in the right, that justice and humanity are on our side. . . . Our confidence is fed by the great democratic tradition which is a part of the American people and which no Justice Department official can brutalize or destroy.

Our confidence is nourished also by the indomitable spirit of the victims of hysteria, of those we defend, who remain firm in their devotion and attachment to the cause of democracy and peace. . . .

In the tradition that is America, in the spirit that has guided the people of this country and has left an indestructible residue, an imperishable attachment to the democratic faith—we set forth to win for all persons in this country the human right to live in dignity, in equality, in democracy and in peace.

And then the blow struck! The persistent activity of an organization like the ACPFB, utilizing to the utmost—and skillfully—the legal avenues of defense, rallying and organizing active mass support for the victims of deportation and denaturalization, could not continue to hamper and often defeat the attacks of the Immigration and Naturalization Service on the foreign born without provoking a direct attack on the Committee itself. Already in 1948, Tom Clark, then Attorney General, had placed the American Committee on the "Subversive List." But at that time no law added punitive measures to the vindictiveness of the listing; and the ACPFB weathered the annoyance and went on its forceful way to fight for the rights of the foreign born.

There was something of a problem in attacking a force like the ACPFB. Its sole guilt was an active defense of a vulnerable section of the American population—the foreign born, which touched directly a major section of the American people. Its efforts to establish in the national mind the role and contributions of the foreign born had been successful among broad sections of the population. Its campaign for unity was widely known. These campaigns—culminating in the annual Statue of Liberty celebrations—as well as its vigorous defense of the foreign born against persecution had met with the approbation of men at the highest level in the government and among public-spirited citizens of prominence in all walks of life. This had been publicly expressed in statements that were widely publicized at home and beamed across the seas by government radio. To attack the ACPFB at the very moment when the hounding of the foreign born increased—and thereby involved directly increasing numbers of the American people—might rouse serious opposition. It might outrage the American traditional sense of fair play. And, instead of winning support for the un-American campaign against the foreign born, it might win sympathy for the ACPFB.

The government, therefore, bided its time, waiting for the opportunity to strike when it might cause the least reaction.

That opportunity came, in the opinion of the government, when four defendants in the Foley Square trial of the eleven Communist Party leaders failed to surrender in July 1951 after they had lost their appeal to the U.S. Supreme Court. The four thereby forfeited their bail, which had been posted by the Bail Fund of the Civil Rights Congress of New York, an independent organization having no connection with the American Committee for Protection of Foreign Born. This, together with the jumping of bail in 1950 by the deportee, Gerhart Eisler (whom the government would not allow to deport himself to Germany, his country of origin), made direct action against the Committee easy. On the theory that cutting off the head could destroy the body, the government decided, while investigating the Bail Fund, to "get" the Committee's executive secretary who was one of the trustees of the Bail Fund. The issue of *The Lamp* for August-September, 1951, carried as its first item:

> On July 27, Abner Green was imprisoned because he refused to submit the names of thousands of contributors to the work of the ACPFB to the Federal Grand Jury in New York.

Whatever reason was given for the arrest, the motive behind it was plain. As early as January 1950, a full ten months before the passage of the McCarran Act, Abner Green had published his pamphlet, *The Deportation Terror—A Weapon to Gag America.* Its first edition was sold out within a month, and it was translated and published in Greek and Finnish and printed serially in the New York *Daily Compass.* The "gag" which the author had so clearly recognized and so effectively described was now, a year and a half later, applied to him.

The Grand Jury investigating the Bail Fund subpoenaed Abner Green to produce the books and records of the Bail Fund. While he was a Trustee of the Fund, Green was not in possession of the books, nor could he turn them over; the secretary of the Fund, Frederick V. Field, was already in prison for contempt for refusing to produce them. At his appearance before the Grand Jury, Green was ordered *also* to produce the records, including the names of contributors to the ACPFB, which were obviously not pertinent to the investigation. Clearly, the "investigation" was, in part, a "fishing expedition" for names, in order to intimidate, to harass and to establish "guilt by association." Abner Green refused to turn over the records of the ACPFB, demanding that they be subpoenaed, so that he could challenge the subpoena in court. The Grand Jury refused and Judge John F. X. McGohey, who had only recently been promoted to the judgeship (after having "successfully" prosecuted the eleven Communist leaders at Foley Square), sentenced Abner Green to six months in prison. An additional sentence of six months, to run concurrently, was imposed for being unable to produce the books of the Bail Fund.

This first direct attack on the ACPFB was a severe blow. Abner Green in his years of association with the Committee had become an expert in the field of civil rights for foreign born. Since 1941 he had been executive secretary of the Committee, giving it vigorous, perceptive and imaginative leadership, with a doggedness and persistence that cut through apathy, ignorance or bias, and brushed off hysteria and persecution. The seriousness of the loss, even though temporary, was fully recognized by his associates and the supporters of the Committee. Their response was swift. The same issue that announced Green's arrest also carried two open letters to President Truman, one signed by the Sponsors of the ACPFB, the other by a group of American citizens which included Florence Converse, Mary Van Kleeck, Muriel Draper, Rev. Lee Ball, Dr. Preston Holder, Rockwell Kent, Father Clarence Parker, Prof. Daniel Levinson, Prof. Robert J. Havighurst and others. The main point of both letters was the same. That from the Sponsors ran:

> As Sponsors of the ACPFB we are alarmed at the persecution and imprisonment of Abner Green, who has been executive secretary of the Committee for the past ten years. . . .

> We have sponsored the work of the Committee for the past year because we believe that the protection of the rights of foreign-born Americans is a fundamental right.
>
> We protest the unwarranted and unconstitutional attack on the ACPFB. We urge that you use your good offices to intercede in behalf of Abner Green so that he may continue his work in defense of the civil rights of foreign-born Americans.

The paper also carried the notice of a protest meeting to be held in New York on September 15.

But the blow, serious as it was, did not halt the Committee's activities. The two pages of *The Lamp* also contained notices of the Los Angeles banquet to honor California attorneys involved in deportation cases, and of the California Conference to be held on October 27; of the Midwest Committee's annual festival in Chicago on October 6 and of the Michigan Committee's Conference on October 27. There was space, too, for the announcement of a new folder on the right to bail, and of post cards to commemorate appropriately the 65th Anniversary of the Statue of Liberty. And on the bottom of the first page was the large type announcement of the 20th Anniversary National Conference to be held in December.

This was not only important evidence of the temper of the Committee. It was also evidence of a fact that the government persecutors had failed to grasp—that the life of a movement answering a fundamental need of large numbers of people, and inseparably bound to the welfare of a whole nation, does not depend on one head, on one individual, invaluable as his contribution may be, but on the mass of the people that movement represents. Here was hydra-headedness that was an evil—only to reaction!

22. A Year of Defeats

THE 20th Annual Conference of the ACPFB was held in Chicago as scheduled on December 8 and 9, 1951. The spirit of the Conference was expressed in the first greeting read at the opening session, which was from Dr. W. E. B. DuBois: "At eighty-three greeting twenty with all the spirit and love and fight of fifteen." And "fight" was an immediate necessity. The Committee's executive secretary was in federal prison in Danbury, Connecticut, serving his sentence. The Rev. John Darr, who had been chairman of the Board of Directors until 1949 and the Committee's co-chairman from 1949 to 1951, had accepted a position which took him to Europe.

As for the foreign born themselves, the Conference Call described their situation:

> The knock at the door—the cruel breaking up of families—the galloping terrorism—not in some faraway "totalitarian" country—but here in the United States. That knock has been heard in hundreds of homes of foreign-born Americans.
>
> Today we find:
>
> Thousands of non-citizens threatened with deportation after living in the United States from twenty-five to fifty years.
>
> Other thousands investigated and hounded with the objective of taking away their citizenship.
>
> Thousands more prevented from becoming citizens be-

> cause they belonged to or took part in the activities of progressive organizations.
>
> This is no longer a quiet raid on a few homes. Senator McCarran wants to clear from the United States from 3,000,000 to 5,000,000 foreign born whom he calls "rabble."

The Conference had an attendance of 347, from 289 organizations: trade unions, national groups, fraternal orders, women, youth, peace, civic, defense and church groups and committees; from thirteen states, California to Massachusetts. The first business was the presentation by the co-chairman of the ACPFB, George B. Murphy, Jr., of the statement of policy, which was later adopted unanimously.

> This 20th Anniversary Conference of the American Committee for Protection of Foreign Born has convened in one of the crucial periods of American history. Today the issue is clear—peace and equality or war and repression.
>
> Today, all sections of the American people are under attack. The Negro people, the Jewish people, cultural workers in Hollywood, teachers, government workers, trade unionists. All are facing abrogation of their civil and human rights.
>
> This Conference recognizes the scope and seriousness of these infringements. However, we are assembled to deal with one phase of this attack. Protection of the rights of the foreign born.
>
> We condemn and reject McCarran and Smith Act tyranny and oppression no matter where it strikes and are primarily concerned with the manner in which these twin measures of repression are used to destroy the rights of foreign-born Americans.
>
> Our only task here is to concern ourselves with the civil rights of the foreign born. We are here to ensure adequate defense of all foreign born—naturalized citizen, non-citizen—regardless of race, color, creed, national origin or political belief—who have become or may become victims of McCarran or Smith Act hysteria.

Attorney Pearl Hart, general counsel for the Midwest Committee, gave expression to the fighting mood of the Conference.

> We are gaining strength . . . picking up and fighting back. . . . The right to bail will be won; by the end of 1952 many sections of the McCarran Act will be declared unconstitutional and the rights of the foreign born will be permanently established. . . .
>
> We can stand erect and be proud because we fight in a constitutional way. . . .
>
> I say to you that if we stand together, we can be optimistic about the future. We are here to fight together . . . and long after the name of Mr. McGrath is forgotten, the name of our national executive secretary, Abner Green, will be remembered.

The same fighting spirit animated the chief speaker at the meeting Saturday evening, William Hood, recording secretary of Ford Local 600, UAW-CIO:

> I am here to join hands with you to help keep America democratic. . . . I am here with the foreign born in America today and expect to stay here until . . . every man, woman and child will have equality, be free to think as he wants to and to more abundantly enjoy the fruits of his labor. . . .
>
> We must do like Paul Revere did in the early days of this Republic. We must get off our seats. We must get on our horses. We must warn America of what is happening.

There was increased recognition that the special difficulties faced by immigrants from the West Indies were an integral part of the national problem and not merely of local interest. Ewart Guinier, who spoke of the unfair discrimination practiced against the people of the West Indies, began by quoting from Justice William O. Douglas:

> The great danger of this period is not inflation nor the national debt nor atomic warfare. The critical danger is

> that we will so narrow the range of permissible thought and discussion that we will become like the man on the toboggan, who can ride it but can neither steer it nor stop it.

And he concluded:

> It is to the credit of this Committee that it has stood fast and has shown the way. We have learned the lesson that our problems are not separate, they are united. If we in our own communities unite, no matter on whose problem (foreign born, West Indian whose relative is excluded by the quota, a person arrested because of political belief), we are going to win and make America the land of the free and the home of the brave.

Equally the concern of all were the accumulating difficulties met with by the Mexican-Americans of the southwest and California, whether immigrants or native born. The situation confronting them was presented to the Conference by Ralph Cuaron of Los Angeles. Mr. Cuaron gave practical expression to his demand for united action—which was stressed also by Mr. Guinier—by urging that the resolutions of the Conference should deal with all Spanish-speaking Americans together, rather than as separate groups.

The Annual Report of the ACPFB was given by Harriet Barron, administrative secretary of the Committee, whom Mr. Murphy introduced as one who had given "twenty-four-hours-a-day leadership to the Committee in the absence of Abner Green." Mrs. Barron stated in part:

> We are here today despite the fact that the Justice Department has attempted to destroy the work of the Committee by the imprisonment of our executive secretary. . . .
>
> We are meeting despite the new wave of terror which is sweeping the foreign-born communities. . . .
>
> When the American people fully understand what deportation means in the life of an individual . . . they will

surely fight to end it. Deportation is worse than prison. It means the destruction of homes and families. It means starting a new life in a new country with a language that has long been forgotten, under new conditions. To the old and sick, deportation means the end of everything. . . .

At the outset of the deportation drive, the Justice Department indicated that it sought to deport 3,400 non-citizens. These are only the political deportations. Many in recent months have been brought under arrest on warrants dating back to the early thirties and several on warrants issued during the infamous Palmer Raids. . . .

Congress . . . eliminated part of the Administrative Procedures Act from deportation hearings. . . . A recommendation for deportation is written by the hearing officer. The recommendation is sent to the Commissioner; he orders the deportation. . . . You may appeal before the Board of Immigration Appeals. An attorney is sent to Washington to argue before the Board—but to no avail. The decision comes down "ordered deported." A number of these cases have reached this stage and we are confronted with court actions to keep these people from deportation.

You all know the story of the midnight McCarran Law arrests [and the denial of bail] . . . Then began a series of court actions. We won most of them in the District Courts. But John Zydok sat for five months in a filthy county jail in Detroit, Knut Heikkinen for almost five months in a similar hole in Duluth, and the "Terminal Island Four" remained there for more than six months. The Justice Department [has] appealed these cases to the Supreme Court.

On August 2, bail of some thirty-nine non-citizens was cancelled, presumably because it had been posted by the Bail Fund of the Civil Rights Congress of New York. When the families and friends appeared with new bail, they became victims of a new inquisition. The money was "tainted." "Who are the friends who left you the money? What organizations are you a member of?"

And sweeping through every city, especially in indus-

> trial centers, terror and harassment continue in the form of letters [from the Immigration and Naturalization Service]. . . . We have no statistics on the number of those subjected to this form of persecution. We know only that daily in the offices of our Committee and in the offices of the Midwest, Michigan and Los Angeles Committees, people come—old people and sick people—people who for the past ten, fifteen, twenty or more years have not attended a meeting of anything that could be called remotely progressive, people who are or have been members of the IWO or other such fraternal, insurance or social organizations. . . .
>
> A new "crime" has been invented in the United States, the "crime" of failing to deport yourself. When you are ordered deported . . . it is a crime if you just don't want to. If . . . after six months you are still living with your family, you are to be indicted for failure to depart and you can then go to prison for ten years. . . . . We already have two such cases.

After summarizing briefly various other oppressive features of the law and the procedures of the Justice Department, Mrs. Barron turned to forces opposing them. The CIO and UE had urged repeal of the law. Ford Local 600 had formed a defense committee and hundreds of organizations of many kinds were becoming aware of what was happening. She mentioned some of the many new defense committees, the Michigan Committee, the Yuditch Defense Committee, the Lithuanian Defense Committee, the Rose Nelson Defense Committee.

Her conclusion was less optimistic and more in agreement with the experience of the next years than attorney Pearl Hart's prediction, but no less determined.

> We have a growing feeling that the battle ahead can be won. It will not be easy. It has not been easy these past years and it will grow more difficult in the period ahead. But we have great confidence because the past months have shown that millions of individuals and many organi-

> zations are beginning to understand that the attack on the foreign born is an attack on themselves.
>
> You cannot remove the progressive segment of this great group of our population without removing a vital part of all that is America in its truest and finest sense. If a Peter Harisiades, a Katherine Hyndman, a Claudia Jones, a Benny Saltzman, a David Hyun, and Ernesto Mangoang is deported . . . if they deport them—they are deporting an important part of America.

The reports from the different defense committees gave ground for confidence. The Ukrainian Committee reported:

> The deportation drive is no longer a drive against individuals . . it has broadened into a drive against organizations. He [Dmitryshyn] was charged with being a member of an organization that was second cousin to an organization that advocated violent overthrow of the government by force and violence. The witnesses of the Immigration Department did not know him and were not known by him. One witness said he saw him at a meeting. At that trial Dmitryshyn was the forgotten man. It was the IWO that was on trial, not he. . . . The American Committee for Protection of Foreign Born fights for the rights of all foreign born—not only defends some people. . . . The Committee has done a good job.

A defendant declared:

> Each deportee is a symbol of the hope of every immigrant who came to this country to escape persecution of their native countries.

The Czechoslovaks reported:

> The Czech Committee is only two weeks old. We never organized anything as easily as we did this committee.

And the pageant produced at an evening session emphasized

the welcome that the real America gave to the foreign born, and the contribution they made to the country's welfare.

The determination of the delegates did not falter before the acute problems that lent urgency to the Conference. In preparation for the business session at the close of the Conference, the delegates had in their hands a mimeographed list of 205 noncitizens from eighteen states facing deportation, presented in order of the countries to which the government wished to deport them, from Albania to Yugoslavia. The oldest was seventy-two; he had lived in the United States for forty-five years and had five dependents. Many had been residents of the United States for forty years or more; only eleven of the 205 for less than twenty-five years; only six for less than twenty.

With this list before them, with the reports of the midnight arrests, of struggles to raise bail, of refusal of bail, of threats of loss of citizenship and accounts of the loss of employment fresh in their minds, the delegates planned the Committee's program for the next year: the raising of funds, the organization of protests to the Attorney General and to members of Congress, the setting up of special committees to deal with the problems of Mexican and West Indian immigrants, the preparation of publicity campaigns for the repeal of the McCarran and Smith Acts, the exertion of increased efforts against the refusal of bail. And to give leadership in the implementation of these plans, the Conference elected as officers: Bishop Arthur W. Moulton as honorary chairman, George B. Murphy, Jr., and Prof. Louise Pettibone Smith as co-chairmen; and by standing acclamation, Abner Green as executive secretary.

The year 1952 began with a series of banquets held across the country to greet and honor Abner Green who had finished his sentence at Danbury on December 24. The first of the series, held in New York City on January 12, also honored for his long fight against deportation Peter Harisiades, who had recently been released on bail by decision of Federal Judge Leibell of New York. The banquet was sponsored by seventeen defense committees of the Greater New York area and attended by some four hundred people. So many of those present had, like the Committee's executive secretary and Harisiades, served prison sentences at one time or another for their defense of the Bill of Rights that the rest of those present found themselves rather in Emerson's position when Thoreau in Concord jail put to him the unanswerable question, "What are you doing outside?"

It was well to have had so good a beginning for the year. For despite the spirit and the will to fight, and despite continuous battles, the year 1952 was one of disappointed hopes and serious defeats. The McCarran Internal Security Law was not repealed; on the contrary, the immigration and naturalization bills of Sen. McCarran and Rep. Walter became law in spite of President Truman's veto. In February the *Vulcania* carried one hundred and eight deportees back to Europe. In March the U.S. Supreme Court (the chill of the Cold War had penetrated its sheltered halls, too) affirmed, in the case of the "Terminal Island Four," the right of the Attorney General to detain non-citizens arrested in deportation proceedings without bail. This was a most serious setback to civil liberties in the U.S.

In March 1952 also, the U.S. Supreme Court affirmed the deportation of Peter Harisiades. The history of this case throws a spotlight on the elaborate, prolonged, tortuous and costly legal path to civil liberties which a foreign-born working man or woman had to travel, a path which did not necessarily lead to "equal justice" despite all reliance on the Constitution, the Bill of Rights and the Supreme Court. For this reason as well as because the issue itself is so important, a detailed account of the Harisiades case is essential.

The ACPFB had undertaken the case of Peter Harisiades in 1947 because, as a leaflet stated at the time:

> The ACPFB takes the position—which has been upheld by the United States Supreme Court—that all the guarantees of the Bill of Rights of the United States Constitution gave protection equally to all residents of this country, non-citizens as well as citizens.
>
> The ACPFB intends to make a principle of this issue

> and to fight to the end the use of the Immigration and Naturalization Service by the Department of Justice as a political weapon against legally-resident non-citizens of this country.
>
> The case of Peter Harisiades will determine the status of the democratic rights of all the people of this country.

Peter Harisiades was born on the Island of Samos, Greece. He was thirteen years old when he came to the United States with his father in 1916. He worked first as a water boy, then in a machine shop for the Illinois Central Railroad; then in a foundry in Beloit, Wisconsin; in a rubber factory in Akron, Ohio; in steel mills in Ohio and in New Castle, Pennsylvania where he took out his first citizenship papers. He went next to Boston and in 1928 to New Bedford, Massachusetts. There he joined the Textile Workers Union and was active in the strike.

His second papers were not filed, at first because of his frequent moves, and later because of the prejudice against the textile strikers. In 1925, in Boston, he joined the Communist Party and remained a member until 1939. From 1931 to 1933, he was a Communist Party organizer and became in 1933 the secretary of the Greek Bureau. Seven years later he joined the staff of the *Greek-American Tribune*. He married an American citizen and they had two children—obviously "American-born."

When he applied for his second papers in Brooklyn in 1944 (on the basis of his wife's citizenship), he was arrested by the Justice Department on a warrant issued in 1930 and ordered deported. The first hearing was held October 15, 1946, and a second hearing at the end of January, 1947.

The Lamp for February, 1947, carried this heading, "Committee Opposes Deportation Based on Political Opinions," and announced the decision of the Committee to carry the case further. The March issue outlined the beginning of the national campaign—a special six page folder, a tour by Abner Green and Harisiades through Pennsylvania, Ohio, Michigan and Illinois in March, and an "Action Conference on the Case of Peter Harisiades" set for April 27, in New York City.

The April issue reported the formation of a "Neighbors' Defense Committee for Peter Harisiades" and listed labor union protests from the West Coast to Boston. The first item in the May *Lamp* was the account of the sixty-five page opinion of the Immigration and Naturalization Inspector recommending deportation. This was followed by the announcement of printed post cards of protest prepared by the ACPFB to be sent to the Commissioner of Immigration and Naturalization, Ugo Carusi. More protesting organizations were listed and the report of the April 27 conference followed.

The *Memorandum for Peter Harisiades,* submitted to the Department of Justice on July 4, 1947, by Carol King and Isidore Englander, was published and distributed by the Committee. Its forty-four pages set forth various questions of fact and law, including the change of the 1930 warrant from "present" to "past" membership, Harisiades' residence and work in New York since 1933 and his registration under the Act of 1940 which make clear that the original warrant could have been served at any time since 1930.

The real and permanent value of the pamphlet, however, lies in the direct and documented discussion of the practice of "guilt by association" and of the charge that the Communist Party in the United States, under the dictates of the Communist International, which was dissolved in 1943, was preparing the overthrow of the United States government by force and violence. This clearly reasoned, unemotional presentation of evidence is important to all who desire to evaluate honestly later court decisions and congressional actions. Surviving copies will be treasured as indispensable by future historians who deal with the mid-twentieth century in the United States.

In the *Review of the Year* 1947, which was printed in January, 1948, activities in the fight against political deportation, are listed, usually as the first item for every month except August. All through 1948 the hearings—and the work of the Committee—went on. In July a second adverse decision, 308 pages this time, was given by the presiding inspector. In November, Carol King argued the case before a special three-man board, appointed by the Commissioner of Immigration. On December 16, the Commissioner ordered deportation. The next step was a hearing before the Board of Immigration Appeals. This was set for March, 1949. The decision of the Board, sustaining deportation, was given on May 13 and Peter Harisiades was arrested and held on Ellis Island without bail.

Not until then could the case be carried to the Federal courts. It reached the District Court in August; bail was not allowed until July 22 of the following year. The District Court decision sustaining deportation was given on February 9, 1950, and was appealed eleven days later to the Court of Appeals. Bail was set again at $5,000. Certain questions on the application of the Administrative Procedures Act, with records and brief, were filed with the court on July 1; but the hearing was delayed until October, and then at the request of the government, was further delayed until January 1, 1951.

The Lamp (June-July 1950) had summarized the issues:

> Whether non-citizens in the United States are fully protected in their liberties by the Bill of Rights of the United States Constitution;
>
> Whether non-citizens, as legal residents of the United States, do in fact possess freedom of speech and freedom of belief;
>
> Whether non-citizens can be deported because they belong to organizations that do not have the approval of the Justice Department;
>
> Whether non-citizens have the right to belong to organizations of their free choice.

The Court of Appeals in January, 1951, sustained the deportation but ordered the Attorney General to investigate the possibility of persecution in Greece. An appeal for *certiorari* was made to the U.S. Supreme Court and a hearing on the appeal was set for October 5. Meantime in anticipation of the hearings on persecution in Greece, the Committee issued a special leaflet,

Deportation Means Death, and sent a special brief to the Board of Immigration Appeals asking them to reconsider the constitutionality of deportation provisions.

On October 8 the Supreme Court agreed to review the case and hearings began on November 11. The ACPFB had hoped the Supreme Court, in spite of the Cold War, would hold to the concurring opinion of Justice Murphy in the Bridges case and assert that the Bill of Rights protected all legal residents of the United States. But on March 10, 1952, the deportation was sustained by a 6-2 decision. The First Amendment did not apply, the majority held, nor the prohibition of *ex post facto* legislation, "since deportation is not a punishment." They admitted the hardship—"that aliens remain vulnerable to expulsion after long residence is a practice that bristles with severities." But apparently the practice did not "bristle" enough to prick the conscience of the majority of the Court. For the Court held that the hardship could be justified by the international situation. The Cold War could freeze even the Constitution into impotence.

A rehearing was denied in April and, on May 29, Peter Harisiades was again a prisoner on Ellis Island. All that remained to be done in his case was to win for him asylum in some land other than his "country of origin" as an alternative to the island prisons of Greece. Poland offered sanctuary, and in November he left with his American citizen wife and his two American-born children.

The two March Supreme Court decisions on bail and deportation were serious blows. The Los Angeles Committee for Protection of Foreign Born was prompt in its reaction on the bail question. It issued a flyer headed:

THE U.S. SUPREME COURT HAS DECIDED
The Right to Bail for Non-Citizens Is Abolished
THE PEOPLE MUST NULLIFY THIS DECISION!!

And it continued:

We must above all defeat the immediate effects of the

> decision by compelling the Attorney General to admit the Terminal Island Four to reasonable bail at once.

Justice Frankfurter's agreement with Justices Black and Douglas on the question of bail was stressed and his statement on the purpose of bail quoted:

> It is not a device for keeping persons in jail until it is convenient to give them a trial; on the contrary, the spirit of the procedure is to enable them to stay out of jail until a trial has found them guilty.

The ACPFB was equally prompt in its reaction to both the Carlson and the Harisiades decisions. It immediately issued a protest petition headed by a map of the United States, illustrating the geographical spread and the number of other pending deportations. In addition, it published a folder with full excerpts from the minority opinions of the Supreme Court in both cases, and printed a discussion of the various issues involved in the fight to defend the rights of the foreign born, as a supplement to the April 9, 1952, issue of the *National Guardian*, one of the last remaining newspapers with which such cooperation in the interests of civil liberties was still possible.

From Justice Douglas the following was quoted on the Harisiades case:

> We have long held that a resident alien is a person within the meaning of the Fifth and Fourteenth Amendments. He therefore may not be deprived either by the national government or by any state of life, liberty or property without due process of law. Nor may he be denied the equal protection of the laws. . . . Guarantees of liberty and livelihood are the essence of the freedom which this country from the beginning has offered the people of all lands . . . the right to remain here has a like dignity. Unless they are free from arbitrary banishment, the "liberty" they enjoy while they live here is indeed illusory.

And from Justice Black on the bail case:

> The denial of a right to bail [in these cases] strikes me as a shocking disregard of the following provisions of the Bill of Rights: Eighth Amendment's ban against excessive bail; First Amendment's ban against abridgement of thought, speech and press; Fifth Amendment's ban against depriving a person of liberty without due process of law. . . . To put people in jail for fear of their talk seems to me . . . in flat violation of the First Amendment. . . . My belief is that we must have freedom of speech, press and religion for all or we may eventually have it for none. . . .
>
> The Eighth Amendment [as construed by the majority] is reduced below the level of pious admonition.
>
> I deeply regret that the Court now adds the right to bail to the other Bill of Rights guarantees that recently have been weakened to expand governmental powers at the expense of individual freedom.

The ACPFB added its own determination to continue its work to win rights for the foreign born of America.

> Since the Supreme Court majority has failed to sustain its responsibility to the Bill of Rights, it becomes the duty of the American people and their organizations to reaffirm allegiance to the democratic principles on which this country is founded. . . . The American people must give expression to their support for the views expressed by the Supreme Court minority in defense of a democratic . . . treatment of non-citizens. We publish excerpts from these minority views. It becomes the responsibility of every American who believes in civil liberties to win support for these views . . . to re-establish the rights of non-citizens and end the threat to the American right to bail.

And the ACPFB, accepting such responsibility for itself, summarized again the reasons for repealing the McCarran Act, and for offering a five point program for the foreign born with which to replace it.

23. Carol King

Civil rights in America in general and the foreign born in particular, received yet another blow in 1952. Carol King, for ten years attorney for and General Counsel of the ACPFB, died on January 22. From the beginning of her legal practice, she had been one of that long line of outstanding liberal lawyers who used their talents, knowledge and physical resources to guard jealously the liberties of the American people; who made justice a living reality to countless oppressed and persecuted; and who helped check the efforts of recurring forces to pierce the protective armor of the Bill of Rights of the U.S. Constitution and to nullify the civil rights guaranteed in it.

Carol King was born and educated and practiced law in the City of New York. Her father, Samuel W. Weiss, had been a lawyer and, after her graduation from Barnard College, she decided to follow his profession and entered the Law School of New York University. She received her law degree in 1920. The next year she joined the law firm of Hale, Nelles and Shorr in New York. In 1917 she married the writer, George Congdon King, who died in 1930. Their son was just two hours old when the law firm of Shorr, Brodsky and King was formally established on January 1, 1927. In 1948, Carol King joined forces with Blanch Freedman, to form the law firm of King and Freedman. Mrs. King was a charter member of the National Lawyers Guild. She held the office of secretary of the International Juridical Association and was responsible for the issuing of the International Juridical Association Bulletin.

One of the most satisfying events of the post-war years was the dinner on March 5, 1948, honoring Mrs King for her "twenty-five years of service as an attorney in defense of human rights in the United States." In that quarter of a century, she had served in the Sacco and Vanzetti case; in the case of Benjamin Gitlow, sentenced for distributing revolutionary literature; in the Scottsboro case; in the Herndon and de Jonge cases; the Bridges case; the Schneiderman case and other famous civil liberties cases. In time, she had become the outstanding authority on immigration and naturalization law, both because of her mastery of its intricate content and by her continuous defense of countless victims of anti-foreign born legislation. Between 1920 and 1948 reaction had given attorneys who were so inclined plenty of opportunity to become expert in that special field.

Co-chairmen for that Dinner were attorney Nathan Green, Charles W. Houston, and Donald Ogden Stewart (the last acting as toastmaster). The speakers included Isaac Shorr, Lee Pressman, O. John Rogge, Abner Green, Irving Potash, Isidore Englander and Clara Binswanger. The tributes of Lee Pressman, former general counsel of the CIO, and O. John Rogge, formerly Assistant Attorney General of the United States, were printed in full in *The Lamp*:

> Over the last twenty-five years . . . [when] some harassed general practitioner or bewildered labor lawyer finds himself entrusted with an immigration or deportation matter, there is only one way out—get Carol King! She has labored day in and day out, in bad Palmer Raid days and in good New Deal days in a field which offers very limited material rewards. . . . I think it fair to say that no lawyer of our generation has made such enormous contributions in a specialized field and that no civil liberties lawyer has made such personal sacrifices. . . .
>
> [The present] chapter in the history of the American bar will be illuminated only by the records of those few who like Carol King, love people more than they love safety, comfort and respectability. (Lee Pressman)

> These are dark days for our civil liberties. . . . We are returned at one blow to mediaeval days when the individual had no rights and could be punished without trial. . . . We are told to conform, these days. . . .
>
> With new courage let us go forward to win the battle that Carol King and other brave souls have been waging—the battle for peace and progress, this great fight for human freedom. (O. John Rogge)

Both speakers stressed the difference between the silence of most of the bar in 1948 and the reaction of the bar to the Palmer Raids in 1920 when "the lawyers of the country played the important and honorable role which lawyers in a democracy should play."

Innumerable messages of congratulations were received. But it was typical of Carol King and her way of life that they came from both the great and the lowly, from Henry Wallace, Thomas Mann, Robert Morss Lovett, J. Allen Frankel, Bartley Crum, Lion Feuchtwanger, Professor F. O. Mathiessen, I. F. Stone, Roger Baldwin; and from "your friends on Ellis Island," from four "admiring friends" in Hammond, Indiana, Steve and Stanley Tandaric, Mrs. Genovesa and Mrs. Perrone. For it was characteristic of Mrs. King once or twice a week, after leaving late at night a gathering of prominent friends and colleagues or a speakers' platform, to rise early the next morning to catch the first ferry to Ellis Island for her regular visits to her "client-friends" to comfort them, to reassure them, to bring them family greetings and gifts, and to consult with them on their plight.

Henry Wallace's message read:

> Over the past twenty-five years your steady defense of the civil liberties of both native and foreign born constitutes a great service to the cause of freedom for all Americans. . . . I join with you in your fight to preserve and enlarge the frontiers of American democracy.

A letter from the San Francisco lawyer, George Andersen, expressed the hope "that you will sort of unveil Carol at this dinner so that without any bushel over lights, all those in attendance will be able to fully appreciate the splendid job that she has done during these many years." The ACPFB rejoiced in that unveiling, and four years later had reason to be more thankful that it had been done.

Carol King fought hard and brilliantly for the foreign born to the very end, and she died in the midst of the battle for civil liberties, human decency and dignity. The January, 1952, issue of *The Lamp,* which announced her death, said of her:

> Carol King's courage and brilliance will long be remembered and will remain indelibly marked in the record of the fight for civil rights in the United States. Her leadership especially in the field of the foreign born has left a tradition which is an inspiration to all who knew and worked with her.
>
> Carol King used her great knowledge of the law . . . not for personal gain but with boldness and imagination in the defense of thousands of people, important and "little," who came to her for advice and assistance. . . . The memory of her achievements in behalf of the American people can be perpetuated only in the struggle to end the deportation hysteria and the harassment of the foreign born and to win full victory in the fight to preserve the Bill of Rights.

Expressions of sorrow and mourning were many. From Justice Jane M. Bolin of the Domestic Relations Court, City of New York:

> The legal profession has suffered a great loss in the passing of Mrs. Carol King. She devoted her life to the protection of civil rights and stood out radiantly as a courageous, sincere upholder of the tradition of our profession to protect the legal rights of accused persons no matter how unpopular or disapproved their conduct has been. Her example, it is hoped, will inspire all lawyers to

rededicate themselves to this professional and democratic ideal.

From Robert J. Silberstein, executive secretary of the National Lawyers Guild:

> With the untimely passing of Carol King, the cause of civil liberties, especially for the foreign born, has suffered the loss of an eminent legal champion.

From the *New York Guild Lawyer*:

> The death of Carol King has taken from our midst a magnificent personality of unique quality and great distinction. With her passing the American Bar has lost one of its outstanding figures, liberty one of its most courageous champions, the poor, the oppressed and the foreign born, their most eloquent defender.

From attorney Paul O'Dwyer, emphasizing her attitude to the Constitution:

> The death of Carol King marks the passing of one who practiced in the noblest traditions of our profession. To her the Constitution was indeed a living thing. She refused to regard it as a collection of pious phrases to be more honored in the breach than in the observance.

From Clifford J. Durr:

> Carol King's ability, courage and cheerfulness will be badly missed. Her devotion to the cause of human liberty has been equalled by few lawyers of this generation. I doubt if any have surpassed it. The rights of all of us are more secure because of Carol King.

The passing of a person like Carol King demands more than words of sorrow and mourning. Her unceasing devotion to the preservation of justice and individual freedom, the importance of her special contribution to that continuing struggle, required and received full recognition. On February 18, 1952, more than

400 friends of Carol King met to honor her memory. An authoritative evaluation of her character and her work was made by Professor Thomas Emerson of the Law School of Yale University. His address was printed in the *Lawyers' Guild Review* and we are most grateful to this journal for permission to reprint the speech, which is much more than a tribute. It follows in full.

* * * * *

When Carol King graduated from New York University Law School in 1920 she faced a world that seemed bent upon trampling into forgotten dust the entire tradition of American liberty. In the years just passed hundreds of persons had been sent to jail for political utterances opposing official policy in the conduct of the war. Already federal and state legislative committees—led by the Lusk Committee—were whipping up public hysteria against the imagined menace of Bolshevism. In January of the very year that Carol graduated, the federal government had launched the infamous Palmer Raids—inhumanly rounding up, mostly in the middle of the night, over 4,000 allegedly dangerous aliens. It was in that same month that Victor Berger had been excluded, for the second time, from the seat to which he had been elected in the House of Representatives; that five other members of the Socialist Party had been refused their seats in the New York State legislature; that Benjamin Gitlow had been sentenced to hard labor from five to ten years for distributing the Left Wing Manifesto. For several years more the panic was to continue.

It is hardly surprising that Carol King—a rebellious, courageous and warm-hearted spirit—should have plunged into the task of defending the dissenters, the underprivileged, the despised ones who were the immediate objects of these attacks. Not long after her graduation she became associated with Hale, Nelles and Shorr, then the leading liberal law firm of New York. And from that time on she devoted her great energies and talents to safeguarding the basic democratic rights of the common man—and through him the rights of all free men.

It must be remembered that when Carol started in the practice of law many of the legal principles that are now recognized as fundamental to the democratic process were unsettled and unformed. Thus in the famous Schenck case of 1919, in which Justice Holmes first formulated the clear and present danger test, the application of the First Amendment to dissenting political utterances received from the courts as a whole merely cursory attention. It was only during the next two and a half decades that there gradually emerged a series of important doctrines which give fuller and more explicit meaning to the concept of liberty in a modern industrial nation.

In this period the courts came to recognize that freedom of speech, press or assembly could be restricted only upon showing clear, present and imminent danger of some serious evil the government had a right to prevent; that the guarantees of the Bill of Rights enjoy a preferred position in the hierarchy of constitutional values; that legislation impinging upon political rights must be framed in sufficiently definite and precise language so that the citizen may know and understand the limits of any restriction; that under our system of law guilt is a personal matter, not to be imputed from association with others. It was likewise in these years that the Fourteenth Amendment, applicable to state governments and state officials, was held to prohibit infringement by state action upon the right to freedom of speech and to a fair and orderly trial; that certain rights of the working man, including the right to picket, were brought within the protection of the First Amendment; that important rights of Negroes and aliens were recognized and vindicated. And, in the early years of the New Deal some of these rights were implemented and extended by legislation.

Throughout this development—a proud chapter in American democracy—Carol King played a vital role. She herself participated in many of the actual court battles—perhaps in more than any other single attorney. She carried a substantial part of the load in the Scottsboro cases, in Herndon *v.* Lowry, in Kessler *v.* Strecker, in the repeated trials of Harry Bridges, in the Schneiderman case. And, equally significant, she was instrumental in bringing other lawyers into the struggle—Walter H. Pollak, who handled the Gitlow case, the first Scottsboro cases, and others; Whitney North Seymour, who argued the Herndon case and the Strecker case in the Supreme Court; Wendel Willkie, who won the Schneiderman case in the same tribunal. Her influence permeated this whole era of tremendous constitutional advance.

At the same time Carol was active on another front. In 1932 she organized the International Juridical Association Bulletin—a monthly publication devoted to legal problems in labor, civil liberties, Negro rights and similar fields. For ten years—until it merged with the Lawyers Guild Review in 1942—Carol saw to it that the I. J. A. *Bulletin* came out month by month. She coaxed, cajoled and coerced a number of highly skilled lawyers to edit and contribute, but Carol was the heart and soul of the project.

Scholarly, reliable, imaginative, the I.J.A. *Bulletin* disseminated information and ideas throughout the legal profession in a period of rapid and critical development of the law. Its influence was widespread. Its National Committee contained many outstanding scholars and practitioners. Its subscription list included the names of two justices of the Supreme Court, a score of other judges, half a hundred teachers in the law schools, and many others. Among the testimonials to its standards of workmanship and to its value to the profession I shall mention only two. A dean of one of the nation's leading law schools wrote of the *Bulletin*:

> [It] is by far the best legal publication in this country in the fields of labor law and civil liberties, and is extremely useful to law students and teachers in those fields. I do not think, for example, that any first-rate course in labor law would be complete without frequent reference to the *Bulletin* on the part of both teacher and student.

And a distinguished lawyer, now a member of the Supreme Court, declared:

> In the course of my occupation as a legal scholar, I have read regularly the monthly *Bulletin* issued by the International Juridical Association. On the basis of this experience I have no hesitation in saying that the monthly *Bulletin* is an indispensable publication for all students of the law in the fields with which the *Bulletin deals,* to wit, labor law and the law pertaining to civil liberties.

In 1945 the tide started to turn and the courts began to gloss over, to avoid, or to repudiate many of the principles that had been established in the previous decisions. Hence in the last few years Carol found herself fighting to stem a retreat. Her task became even more onerous. She found it harder to get support from her fellow lawyers; more difficult to obtain a sympathetic hearing from the courts; impossible to rally adequate public backing. But Carol would not, and did not, yield an inch. She carried on with the same inspired zeal she had shown in more favorable days. At the time of her death she was pressing vigorously, and not without some success, a series of crucial cases under the bail provisions of the McCarran Act.

Thus Carol bore her share—and far more than her share—of the struggle to create a liberal law, fit for a growing democracy.

Any appraisal of Carol King's contribution to the law must, of course, take special note of her work on behalf of aliens. That Carol should have devoted so much of her life to this field is entirely characteristic of her. The alien within our country, or seeking admission to our gates, has always tended to be the object of mistreatment, exploitation and oppression. This was particularly true in the 1920's when Carol commenced the practice of law. It was the alien who bore the brunt of the hysteria at that time. For Carol it was intolerable that any human being should be treated so shamelessly. It was in her nature to go to his defense. And she became his able, ardent and indefatigable champion.

Carol's work with aliens eventually made her the outstanding authority on immigration and naturalization law. She handled many of the most significant cases of the period. In the National Lawyers Guild it was always Carol to whom everyone turned for the latest and most authoritative discussion of developments in the field. She knew more about immigration and naturalization law than any other attorney in the country. And she was always ready to assist any person who came to her in need. It was not in her power to refuse a call for help.

Carol's contribution in the field of alien law has a deeper significance than may appear on the surface. The alien is the first to feel the sting of reaction, but he is not the last. The restrictions imposed upon his rights inevitably spread to encompass the rights of others. It is not an accident that the Smith Act—the first peace-time sedition law since 1798—was incorporated into a statute termed the Alien Registration Act and ostensibly directed at aliens. No country which continues to treat any group within its borders unfairly or cruelly is likely to retain that moral stamina—that fighting will to achieve human decency—which is essential to the preservation and advancement of real freedom. And hence Carol, in pledging so much of her life to the cause of the alien, was actually contributing far more to the rest of America than even to the alien himself.

I must add one final thought. It concerns an aspect of Carol's legal career which is hard for me to put into words, but which I may perhaps describe as Carol's impact upon the tone of the legal profession. Carol was, above all else, direct, honest, overwhelmingly committed to the basic moral values which represent the best in American society. She could not stomach cant, evasion, lip service. She could not accept sham on any terms. And this quality of openness and integrity created an atmosphere around her which enlivened, refreshed and stimulated many of her colleagues throughout the legal world. Perhaps, in the end, this was the most important contribution of all.

For Carol King really believed the things that too many of us just talk about. She really believed in justice for the poor and powerless. She really believed that the voice of the underpriviliged should be heard in the land. She really believed that a growing democracy must be bold, dynamic and forward moving. Carol King took the great moral and social principles of American society seriously. Her life was as simple, yet as subtle and as glorious as that.

* * * * *

Those who were most closely associated with Carol King in the last decade of her life had learned well the lessons of her life. Much of her work had centered primarily around the American Committee for Protection of Foreign Born, whose constant inspiration she was. Her death at a time of special stress in the midst of all the new problems presented by the Walter-McCarran Act might well have discouraged the Committee's leaders. But the memory of her unceasing and gallant fight became rather one more reason for continuing the unremitting struggle for the rights of the foreign born. It is fitting that the final tribute to Carol King, expressing especially her lasting influence, should be given by the American Committee. In the *Souvenir Journal* of the National Conference to Defend the Rights of Foreign Born Americans, sponsored by the ACPFB and held in Detroit, Michigan, on December 13 and 14, 1953, there is this "Tribute to the Memory of Carol King":

> The American Committee for Protection of Foreign Born takes this opportunity to honor the memory of Carol King.
>
> Carol King was the most competent and outstanding attorney in the country in the field of immigration and naturalization law. Her loss is felt most by those who are engaged in the fight to preserve the rights of foreign-born Americans and by the thousands of foreign born who were defended by her.
>
> Carol King hated oppression and discrimination whenever and wherever it was expressed. Fearless herself, she had no tolerance for those who faltered or wavered in the fight for democratic rights and dignity of mankind.

Carol King devoted her life to the cause of justice and freedom. In her lifetime, she was an inspiration to thousands as a result of her fearless and tireless devotion to the fight for the Bill of Rights and the liberties of the American people. Her memory can best be honored by continuing the work to which she devoted her life.

The American Committee for Protection of Foreign Born pledges that it will not cease in its efforts to safeguard the rights of the foreign born, to defeat the current deportation hysteria, and to defend the welfare of the millions of immigrants who live in the United States. This, we feel, is the best tribute that can be paid to the life and work of Carol King.

VII. THE FIGHT-BACK

24. The Opposition Mounts

In a nation like the United States, rich in democratic tradition, a nation whose history began and continued as a history of the struggle to win and preserve liberty, the will to oppose violation of the rights of individuals may appear for a time timorously ineffective or even paralyzed. But reaction against oppression is never impossible, as events in 1958 have proved.

Far too many non-citizens had been summarily removed from the United States by the Immigration and Naturalization Service without opportunity to notify family or friends, given no possibility of establishing legally their right to remain in the country; and no effective protest had been made. But the nation-wide disgust at the kidnapping of William Heikkila raised a storm of wrath in press, radio and the judiciary itself against the "gestapo like procedure" of the Immigration officials, and Heikkila was brought back at once. The investigative methods of the FBI agents had brought trouble and panic and economic disaster to many homes, but public criticism was rare. In 1958, the industrialist Cyrus Eaton denounced over TV the disastrous effect of such "police-state" hounding and snooping.

It is a commonplace that reaction takes the offensive in times of economic stress or political crisis. But that is obviously an over-simplification, since many other factors—historic, psychological and social—contribute. The causes leading back to democratic sanity are even more complex. But one factor stands out as essential, the courageous activity of people, sometimes of well-known and influential people but more often and more necessarily the activity of the "little people" who persist through all difficulties, even after they are temporarily forsaken by their accepted leaders.

Perhaps the beginning of the break in the apparent apathy of the nation as a whole occurred with the opposition to the Walter-McCarran Act—the Immigration and Nationality Act of 1952.

Condemnation of the law came almost immediately from all quarters once its content was known, regrettably not until after the law was in force. Articles in law journals assailed it as unconstitutional and contrary to the established principles of American jurisprudence. Among them were the *Columbia Law Review, Leland Stanford Law Review, University of Chicago Law Journal.* Labor unions, AFL, CIO and independent, passed condemnatory resolutions against the Act. Religious organizations of all kinds expressed their opposition to the Act. In fact, so strong and articulate was the protest that President Truman set up on September 4, 1952, the President's Commission on Immigration and Naturalization to hold hearings and to report to him not later than January 1, 1953.

We have already summarized in a previous chapter the content of the Walter-McCarran Act. The measure revealed itself as being obviously against the national interests of the United States. It exposed plainly its crassly anti-democratic objectives. By codifying every scrap of anti-alien legislation hitherto passed, it emphasized how shabbily and unfairly the foreign born had been treated. And by its all-embracing attack on the foreign-born Americans and on potential immigrants, it directly affected a substantial section of the American people.

For a thorough examination of this blot on American statute books, nothing matches the work of the President's Commission. Its membership was composed of the following: chairman, Philip B. Perlman, formerly Solicitor General of the United States, formerly city solicitor of Baltimore, secretary of the

State of Maryland, Assistant Attorney General of Maryland; vice chairman, Earl G. Harrison, attorney, formerly United States Commissioner of Immigration and Naturalization, formerly dean of the Law School of the University of Pennsylvania; Monsignor John O'Grady, secretary of the National Conference of Catholic Charities; Rev. Thaddeus F. Gullixson, president of the Lutheran Theological Seminary of St. Paul, Minnesota, chairman of the Minnesota State Displaced Persons Commission; Clarence E. Pickett, honorary secretary of the American Friends Service Committee; Adrian S. Fisher, legal advisor to the State Department, formerly general counsel of the Atomic Energy Commission and solicitor of the Department of Commerce; Thomas G. Finucane, chairman of the Board of Immigration Appeals of the Department of Justice.

The Commission held hearings in eleven major cities from coast to coast. It listened to and questioned 400 persons who testified before it and studied the statements of an additional 234. These 634 witnesses constitute a roster of outstanding individuals in the economic, political, social, religious, educational and organizational life of the United States, representing not only themselves, but an overwhelming majority of the American people. Their testimony comprised some 2,100 printed pages. The Commission's own report filled 300 pages, published under the title, *Whom We Shall Welcome*. The authoritative character of the Commission's report is unquestionable; both criticisms and recommendations are worth careful study. The close connection between the lot of the foreign born and the welfare of the nation is explicitly recognized.

The hearings produced a most extraordinary outpouring of public opinion too long silent on matters even remotely connected with "security." Furthermore, the testimony given reflected a degree of unanimity which, as the report shows, surprised the Commission itself.

> The Commission was surprised to learn of the widespread and rather determined opposition to the act of 1952. . . .

> The dominant theme of those who appeared to testify or file statements was criticism of the act of 1952. Some objected to the specific aspects, but most witnesses opposed the basic theories of the new law. . . .
>
> The nation's greatest and most powerful groups in welfare activities were reaching agreements on vital issues within their own organizations, and with each other. . . . [The hearings disclosed] instances indicating increasing unity of study and thought throughout the country on problems relating to immigration and naturalization. They indicate a trend of the greatest possible importance toward the growth of cooperation and good will among the people of the United States. . . .
>
> Comparatively few of the organizations and individuals appearing before the Commission were in favor of the act of 1952. However well-intentioned, the statements of approval were generally without documentation of any sort, and were seemingly the result either of special benefits conferred by that law or of emotion and deep-rooted fears and prejudices.

The act was attacked from every conceivable angle: economic, political, social, moral, legal, humanitarian, diplomatic, scientific, national self-interest. We can include only a few samples of the valuable data and scientific appraisals presented, which the Commission considered "of great importance and permanent value."

From the most Rev. Richard J. Cushing, Archbishop of Boston:

> The above indicated discriminatory and undemocratic features of the McCarran-Walter Law are to my mind a grave potential threat to our domestic development and our international leadership.

From Rev. Walter W. Van Kirk, executive director of the Department of International Good Will, National Council of Churches:

> The immigration and naturalization law of 1952 . . . is at some points not compatible with the spirit and intent of the principles set forth by the National Council of Churches, principles which are dictated alike by consideration of Christian justice and love of country. . . . We do not pose as experts on the question of immigration and naturalization. But we do feel very strongly that the law placed upon the statute books in the last session of Congress is an affront to the conscience of the American people.

From Rabbi Gunther Plaut, representing the Minnesota Jewish Council:

> We further respectfully submit that distinctions between native-born and naturalized citizens in our immigration laws must be eliminated as contrary to the spirit of the Constitution. In a democratic republic such as we are building in America, there is no room for any form of limited citizenship. . . . But Public Law 414 flouts this time-hallowed principle. It introduces a note which should have been forever repugnant to American practices, even as it is repugnant to American ideals.

From Governor Paul A. Dever of Massachusetts, calling for

> . . . an examination of our immigration laws to eliminate the possibility of action in respect to admission, exclusion, or deportation, based upon the mere opinion of an administrative official apart from sustained burden of proof or the weight of factual evidence and without an established tribunal for appeal. Our Constitution protects all persons from being deprived of life, liberty, or property without due process of law.

From United States Senator John O. Pastore of Rhode Island:

> Our immigration and naturalization laws need not only overhauling but virtual replacement. The heart of our

> present immigration system is the national origins quota system. It is a vicious system—bigoted in concept, discriminatory in operation, and self-defeating in execution.

From Congressman John F. Kennedy of Massachusetts:

> The example, however, we have set in passing the Walter-McCarran Immigration Act is unfortunate. This bill is un-American and discriminatory.

From Walter White, secretary of the National Association for Advancement of Colored People:

> Both with respect to a more just and sane immigration policy, free of dangerous racial connotations, I recommend strongly to your committee that it urge immediate revision of our immigration and naturalization laws to eliminate all distinctions based on race, sex, language or religion.

From Helen M. Harris, testifying in behalf of the National Federation of Settlements and Neighborhood Centers:

> We are opposed to many of the current immigration and naturalization policies in Public Law 414 and we believe they should either be eliminated from the law or liberalized. (a) First, we urged the elimination of the national origins quota systems as a basis for selection of immigrants. . . . (b) Also, we consider vicious and self-defeating the clauses in the McCarran-Walter Act that discriminate against Catholics, Jews, Negroes and Asiatics. (c) We deplore the deportation clauses which arbitrarily place in jeopardy both naturalized citizens and resident aliens. . . . (d) We particularly protest the extension of the policy that differentiates in its penalties for conviction for contempt between naturalized and native-born citizens. (e) From our experience with this matter, we feel that annual re-registration is both unnecessary and too costly to continue. . . . (g) We are concerned with the powers given immigration officers and employees in Pub-

> lic Law 414 and believe they set a new precedent that could seriously affect our civil liberties. . . . (h) We note other precedents in the section, "information from other departments and agencies" which we believe to be equally dangerous. The opening of the records of any Government agency or department to the Attorney General for the purpose of identity and location of aliens seems a different concept of the use of Government records from that which we have traditionally followed in this country.

From Jack Wasserman, legislative representative of the Association of Immigration and Nationality Lawyers:

> We believe that many—all too many—of the provisions of Public Law 414 are unfair, unwise, unworkable, unjust, unreasonable, un-American and unconstitutional. As attorneys, we believe in and support the letter and spirit of the Constitution of the United States. Accordingly, we recommend its repeal.

From Dr. Arthur H. Compton, chancellor of Washington University, St. Louis:

> Speaking in all seriousness, it seems to me that the Walter-McCarran Act is damaging greatly the welfare of the United States, and is endangering our national safety to a critical degree.

From Prof. Alfred de Grazia, executive officer of the Committee for Research in Social Science:

> A naturalized American will never be able to rest secure that he will not be deprived of his nationality. He is restrained from political activities a native American might engage in. He is encouraged by the act to become an hysterical patriot before he has learned to be a simple patriot. Or else he is encouraged to passivity. This is one more contribution to the political sterilization of the American population.

cultural and public figures and labor leaders, reaching from coast to coast. The letter concludes with the statement:

> Endless police-state procedures have been initiated against the foreign born, the aim of which can only be to make all ideas subject to the discretion of the Attorney General. Freedom of thought, speech and association are being denied to all foreign born in this country.
>
> We, the undersigned, respectfully urge that on this, the final day of your hearings and on the 66th Anniversary of the dedication of the Statue of Liberty, you do your utmost to guarantee that there shall be a new policy of immigration and naturalization—a policy which makes no distinction between native and foreign-born citizens, a policy which accords to all native and foreign born liberty and freedom as guaranteed under the Constitution of the United States, and a policy which ends discrimination against the peoples of the world.

The conclusion arrived at by the Commission from the testimony submitted to it is not in the least ambiguous:

> The Commission believes that our present immigration laws flout fundamental American traditions and ideals, display a lack of faith in America's future, damage American prestige and position among other nations, ignore the lessons of the American way of life. . . .
>
> The Commission believes that our present immigration law should be completely rewritten. . . .
>
> The immigration and nationality law embodies policies and principles that are unwise and injurious to the nation. It rests upon an attitude of hostility and distrust against all aliens. It applies discriminations against human beings on account of national origin, race, creed and color. It ignores the needs of the United States in domestic affairs and foreign policies. It contains unnecessary and unreasonable restrictions and penalties against individuals. It is badly drafted, confusing and in some respects unworkable.
>
> It should be . . . revised from beginning to end.

Opposition to the Walter-McCarran Law continued to grow and spread. On February 5, 1953, Abram L. Sacher, president of Brandeis University, condemned the restrictive immigration provisions of the Walter-McCarran Law. On February 9, the New York State Assembly, by a vote of 133 to 2, approved a resolution urging Congress to revise the law, just as the previous month the City Council of Philadelphia had adopted a similar resolution. On March 21, Governor Theodore R. McKeldin of Maryland asserted that the law created "second-class American citizens" and that it "opens the way to harsh treatment of aliens." In April the Welfare Planning Council of Los Angeles charged that the law was working unnecessary hardship on American families, and the Council's president, Walter S. Hilborn, announced that the organization's board of directors had decided to work for amendments to the law, including reasonable limits on the grounds for deportation.

The opposition mounted high enough to reach even the halls of Congress. Hope was kindled that the first year's efforts to win repeal of the law might be successful. Two bills had been introduced, one by the Republicans, Senator Ives and Representative Javits; the other by the Democrats, Senator Lehman and Representative Celler, supported by thirty-two other members of Congress. The latter measure, in spite of certain provisions narrowing the non-citizen's right of appeal, corrected many of the abuses of the Walter-McCarran Law. For instance, exempting from deportation those who had lived in the United States for twenty years or had entered before the age of fourteen. A comparison of the Lehman-Celler bill and the Walter-McCarran Act in parallel columns, which was issued by the ACPFB, was used by many interested groups including church social action committees in all parts of the country. A campaign demanding public hearings on the bill was initiated with postcards, petitions and letters. President Eisenhower's campaign pledge, "We must have decency and fairness among all our citizens. We must repeal, for example, the unfair provisions of the Walter-McCarran Law," promised presidential support for revision at least.

But on September 24, 1953, the *New York Times* reported that an agreement existed between Senator McCarran and the Republican leaders that Congress would not consider any amendment to the law in 1954. The Lehman-Celler bill would be tabled in Committee without public hearings. Protests began anew. An open letter to the members of Congress, prepared by the ACPFB, was signed immediately by 114 prominent individuals, among them Dr. Frank Aydelotte (Princeton, N. J.), Dr. Alice Hill Byrne, Rev. Raymond Calkins, Dr. Abraham Cronbach, Dr. Alice Hamilton, Rev. Clarence Herriot (Berkeley, Calif.), Rev. Fleming James, Sr. (New Haven, Conn.), Prof. Vida Scudder, Prof. Leroy Waterman. It stated in part:

> The provisions of the Walter-McCarran Law have been condemned by the overwhelming majority of the American people. We welcome therefore the action taken during the first sessions of the 83rd Congress by thirty-two members of Congress in sponsoring the Lehman-Celler Bill (S. 2585 and H.R. 6280) for repeal of the Walter-McCarran Law, as a step toward returning this nation to the road of a fair, positive immigration and naturalization policy.
>
> We are exceedingly shocked, therefore, to have learned from a report in the *New York Times* of a Congressional pact to bar repeal, revision or any amendment of the Walter-McCarran Law in the forthcoming session of Congress.
>
> We regard this pact as a conspiracy violating democratic procedures. We call upon Congress to schedule public hearings on the Lehman-Celler Bill immediately after Congress reconvenes in January, 1954.

At the Annual Conference of the ACPFB in December, 1953, the stress of most of the speakers was naturally laid on the oppressive nature of the provisions of the Walter-McCarran Act as they had been enforced in the first year of its administration. According to Rev. Joseph Evans of the Community Church of Chicago:

> The liberties we have striven so long to obtain in this United States of America, those principles of government we so highly appreciate and in defense of which many have died, must never be threatened nor endangered by unwise doings nor robbed of their luster by anything that would seek their despoilment. . . . At this time there is before us the enactment of a bit of legislation known as the Walter-McCarran Law. It is held to be un-American by many who have studied its provisions. It is evidently discriminatory . . . and would therefore militate against our welfare as a nation. It stands in the way of the accomplishment of the good we seek. . . .
>
> Any legal or governmental institution that strikes at the heart of our national welfare, any action that sets up legislation that is not in harmony with our institutions, with the true spirit of our national and international relationships necessary for the promotion of the common good, that tends toward shaming our national prestige before the eyes of the rest of the world, should certainly meet with stubborn opposition on the part of all the liberty loving.

And Dr. Anton J. Carlson, the world-famous scientist, stated:

> The aspect of the law that has struck my brain most is this: You have come from foreign lands, you have been admitted and you have been made citizens. Then if you transgress—like any citizen born here may do—then you can be denaturalized and deported back to your country where you were born. In other words, it creates two classes of citizens—something like the class distinctions in old India. . . .
>
> I have been an American citizen more years than most of you who were born here. I have been an American citizen for fifty-seven years and I owe our beloved USA more than I can pay because it gave me an opportunity for work. But in 1896 or '97 I was arrested on the Midway in Chicago—for riding a bicycle more than ten miles an hour! I was arrested and fined. Under the Walter-McCarran Law I could have been sent back to Sweden.

> I think we owe it to ourselves, we owe it to our forefathers who created our principles and our traditions to do what we can to eliminate this stupid law. . . . If I know anything of the nature of man, I call this law stupid, stupid, stupid.
>
> I have been around most of the countries of this world, I hope with my eyes and ears open. . . . This kind of law which makes two classes of citizens belongs back a thousand years, two thousand years. It does not fit in with our great American traditions.

Throughout the country, opposition to the law continued to find expression. Section 19 of the 1954 platform of the Democratic Party of Massachusetts declared:

> We pledge continued revision of our immigration and naturalization laws to do away with any unjust and unfair practices against national groups which have contributed some of our best citizens. We want no second-class citizens in free America. We are unalterably opposed to and we demand repeal of the iniquitous Walter-McCarran Immigration Act.

On September 21, the California State Bar, by a two-thirds vote, adopted a report based on a two-year study, urging legislation "to eliminate from the Act those provisions which are capable of being administered arbitrarily and capriciously." The report condemned especially the provision authorizing the Attorney General to hold non-citizens without bail. The 1954 national convention of the AFL was urged by the Brotherhood of Painters, Decorators and Paperhangers to go on record for repeal, and the International Ladies Garment Workers Union urged it to support revision. The CIO 1954 convention reaffirmed "its stand in favor of a liberal immigration policy for the United States and for revision of the Immigration and Nationality Act of 1952 to that end."

The 1954 program of the Methodist Federation for Social Action declared, "We deplore the injustices and cruelties of a law such as the Walter-McCarran Act, which President Truman labeled in his veto message to Congress on June 25, 1952, as 'worse than the infamous Alien and Sedition Act of 1798.' We call for its repeal. . ." In connection with a minor change made in the law, the *New York Times* stated editorially on September 7, "Our country only injures itself by this kind of law. The sooner it is revised the better." While the *Boston Post* declared on September 8, "this revision is a reminder of the many others that have been called for since the enactment of the omnibus law, and of the dismal failure of Congress to act on them. . . . [The act] needs not just a patch here and there but a major overhaul."

In a letter to the *New York Times* on February 4, 1955, Irving M. Engel, president of the American Jewish Committee, declared that "Only fundamental revision can bring the act into consonance with American democratic principles." And February 25, Dr. Louis Hacker, dean of the School of General Studies of Columbia University, deplored present immigration policies especially as they affect foreign scholars and scientists. In Detroit, Rev. Henry Hitt Crane made public a joint request by seventy-three prominent Michigan citizens that Congress hold immediate public hearings. On June 1, Adlai Stevenson charged that a "misguided" immigration policy had choked the flow of new talent and energy to this country. On June 2, in San Francisco, before 4,000 social workers attending the National Conference of Social Work, who also heard a panel of experts on immigration brand the law as the kind of legislation "native fascism always thrives on," Edward Corsi, former Commissioner of Immigration, called for the scrapping of the law. On June 21, the Gallup Poll announced that 53 percent of those asked supported changes in the law, of whom 68 percent supported liberal changes. Only 15 percent opposed changes.

Finally, Sen. Harley Kilgore, chairman of the Senate Judiciary Committee, began hearings on legislation pending before the Senate for repeal or revision of the Walter-McCarran Law. (Rep. Walter, of course, could and did block any such hearings in the House.) During the first session the Subcommittee on Immigration and Naturalization heard from representatives of the AFL, CIO, the National Council of Churches of Christ in America, the Synagogue Council of America, the National Lutheran Council, the National Catholic Welfare Conference, scientific and learned societies, in support of repeal or revision. Only one organization, the American Legion, supported the law as it stood. But, in 1956, the prospects for congressional action darkened again. The sudden death of Senator Kilgore had ended the hearings and there was small prospect of Judiciary Committee action while the Dixiecrat Senator Eastland of Mississippi was its chairman. But by this time the general atmosphere in the country had changed for the better. There was a much wider knowledge of the content of the law, and red-baiting was less often given front page publicity. Slowly but surely the will of the people was once more beginning to exert influence.

25. Mitigating Interpretations

THE overcoming of the political apathy was general. The stark reality of the Walter-McCarran Act seemed to act as a catalyst, stimulating, together with other factors, reappraisal of democratic attitudes. Its more immediate effect was, of course, in the field of the foreign born, which the Law directly concerned. Decisions in cases carried to the Federal courts began to offer some protection against the rigors of the Law.

The first issue of *The Lamp* for 1953 hailed the 8 to 1 decision of the Supreme Court declaring the two-year imprisonment on Ellis Island "on the basis of confidential information" of the seaman, Harry Chew, to have been illegal and unconstitutional, and requiring that he be given a hearing. Chew, married to an American citizen, had left the United States as a seaman on an American vessel and was barred from the country when he returned. The decision was not much immediate help to Chew himself, since the Justice Department rearrested him on the charge of perjury while he was in the act of posting the bail allowed him by the Supreme Court. But the two-year fight by Chew to rejoin his wife, conducted by the ACPFB through attorney Ira Gollobin, which succeeded in winning a proper hearing, held out hope for other seamen in the future.

Also in 1953 came the decision of the Federal Court of Appeals in San Francisco in the case of Ernesto Mangaoang, of Seattle, who had been arrested for deportation to the Philippine Islands on the ground of past Communist Party membership. The court ruled that, since Mangaoang had entered the United States as a "national" prior to the independence of the Philippines and not as an alien, he was not deportable, and the U.S. Supreme Court in November refused to hear the appeal of the Justice Department. This decision affected all those who came to this country from the Philippines before 1934. In June of the next year, the Supreme Court heard the somewhat similar Gonzales case. Gonzales was ordered deported because he had been convicted of two crimes involving moral turpitude after entry. The Supreme Court ruled, 6 to 3, that Filipino-Americans who came here before 1934 could not be deported because they had never "entered" the United States, they had merely moved from one part of the United States to another. Some 70,000 Filipino-Americans were thereby freed from the threat of the Walter-McCarran Law.

Ernesto Mangaoang was the business agent for Local 37 of the Cannery Workers Union. Two weeks after the Federal court decision another provision of the Walter-McCarran Law was set in motion against the union, which since its formaton had raised wages from $30 a month to $250, and made important changes in working conditions. Members of the union returning from seasonal work in Alaska were denied re-entry at the border, this time not as communists but as criminals. (One of them had been jailed for stealing a chicken when he had been a "teen-ager" in the depression!) The Walter-McCarran Law had made Hawaii, Alaska and the Virgin Islands foreign countries from which the non-citizen could be denied re-entry. The fight against this threat to the Cannery Workers Union was begun jointly by Local 37 and the Washington State Committee for Protection of Foreign Born, Marion Kinney, secretary.

In 1954 the Supreme Court refused to hear the case on the ground that injury was only threatened, although the dissenting opinion of Justice Black recognized that the "wearisome routine of immigration procedure" to which the cannery workers were subjected was itself an injury. In May, 1955, however, the Federal Court of Appeals reversed an earlier District Court decision in the case of Alec Alcantra and declared that Alcantra, returning from work in Alaska, could not be excluded on the basis of violations of law in the 1930's. This decision re-established Alaska and Hawaii as integral parts of the United States and made it possible for the members of the cannery workers union to continue their work without fear of exile.

Victory was again achieved in 1955 in a fight begun in 1950, when the Justice Department held for deportation Dr. Krishna Chandra, born in India, and Andrew Dmytryshyn, born in the Ukraine, solely on the ground of membershp in the International Workers Order. In 1943, Earl Harrison, then Commissioner of Immigration and Naturalization, had stated officially that such membership was not a bar to naturalization. But in 1948, Dr. Chandra, married to an American citizen and the father of three American-born daughters, had been told that such membership might prevent him from becoming a citizen. He immediately gave up his insurance and discontinued his membership in the IWO. But two years later the Immigration and Naturalization Service began deportation proceedings on the basis of past membership.

In 1951 the ACPFB printed a folder on these cases which included a protest to the Commissioner of Immigration and Naturalization, signed by some twenty educators and other well-known Americans, including Prof. Emily Brown of Vassar, Dr. John A. Kingsbury, the Rt. Rev. Walter Mitchell, Prof. Philip Morrison of Cornell, Prof. Robert Morss Lovett of the University of Chicago, Mrs. Muriel Draper, the Hon. Elmer Benson, former governor of Minnesota:

> It is inconceivable that the Justice Department should attempt to deport long-time residents of this country and forcibly separate them from their families because they insured themselves and their families in an organization that may not have the approval of the Justice Department.
>
> It is shocking to see the Justice Department attempt to use the deportation laws in order to harass and intimidate non-citizens because of mere membership in the Interna-

> tional Workers Order or any other legally constituted organization.
>
> We call on you to end these deportation proceedings since they are completely contrary to the American principles of freedom of belief and association, violate all concepts of democratic procedure and jeopardize the constitutional rights of all Americans, native as well as foreign born.

Dr. Chandra's case finally reached the Board of Immigration Appeals in August, 1953; its final decision was given in December: mere membership in a "communist front organization" was not a ground for deportation. The ruling was accepted, obviously with reluctance, by the Attorney General. On March 14, 1955, Dr. Chandra wrote to Abner Green:

> This is just to let you know, although I am unable to express it in proper words, that I am very grateful to your organization for having taken my case in the most depressing years of my life and for having fought my case to a successful conclusion. On behalf of my family and myself, may I thank you all from the bottom of our hearts for what you have done.
>
> I hope, pray and I know your organization will win its fight. May God bless you all.

The Chandra case illustrates clearly the relation between the defense of individual cases and the defense of democratic rights. Thousands of people all over the country held insurance policies in the IWO. Many young people had been insured in childhood by their parents. But the legality of such threatened deportation could be tested only through the case of an individual whose rights were infringed. The mere financial cost of such an appeal is beyond the resources of most individuals. And those who might be able to provide the money lack the experience necessary to carry on a successful defense.

Once a case is won, uncounted other foreign-born Americans are safe from that particular threat to their security. The wording of the Walter-McCarran Law had not been revised, but its interpretation by the Justice Department had been altered.

Danger from a very different section of the law was mitigated when the U.S. Court of Appeals in Philadelphia reversed on April 28, 1955, the conviction of Mike Gates for failure to report his address in January, 1951 and 1952. Mr. Gates had been sentenced to serve six months in a federal penitentiary for allegedly failing to register under the registration law of 1940 and for allegedly failing to report his address in January, 1951 and 1952. Mr. Gates had been sentenced to serve six months in a federal penitentiary on the testimony of the Justice Department that no record could be found of his annual reports. The Circuit Court held that conviction under the 1940 Act was impossible since it had been replaced by the Walter-McCarran Law, and that the absence of a report card from the government files was not in itself evidence that no card had been sent. The ACPFB press release notes with relief:

> The rights of all 3,000,000 non-citizens are strengthened, since if Gates' conviction had been upheld, any non-citizen could have been framed [on a charge of failure to report].

In another area victory was slow in coming. Nowhere has the "administrative meanness" noted by Prof. Handlin been more conspicuous than in the treatment of those foreign born who are undeportable because their "country of origin" no longer existed politically or refused to accept them. The procedures have differed in different sections of the country but in the beginning the parolees were required to report regularly (in New York once a week at Ellis Island) and answer detailed questions on their activities. Among them were "Where did you buy your groceries? How long did you stay in the store? Whom did you talk to? Do you know X? Or Y? When did you last see him? What paper do you read? What movies have you seen?" They were ordered to cease all association with any organization on the Attorney General's list, or with members of such organizations (which might well involve separation of husband and wife). Further, if the parolee had previously been released on bail, the government retained possession of the bail after parole.

The first victory was won on the return of bail. On December 4, 1953, the District Court in Minneapolis ordered the Justice Department to return to Charles Rowoldt the $4,000 bail it was holding. The Justice Department appealed, claiming that it could hold the bail indefinitely. But in June of the next year the Court of Appeals in St. Louis sustained the District Court's decision, just in time for the war veteran son of a parolee in New York to cut the year's coupons on the bonds he had deposited for his father.

The fight against the "house arrest" provisions of supervisory parole started independently in three cases: Chicago (the cases of Keller and Witkovich), St. Louis (the case of Mrs. Antonia Sentner) and in New York (three defendants). The challenge of the Justice Department's action in the Federal court in New York on October 13, 1953, and in St. Louis on October 22, resulted in a temporary stay only. But in May, 1954, proceedings were begun in New York in behalf of eleven additional defendants (the Nukk case). The Justice Department demanded trial by a three-judge court, and the decision, delivered by Judge Medina, refused to take action on the ground that there was no substantial issue involved and "no one was being harmed." In January, the Supreme Court accepted the appeal and in October, 1955, ordered the case to be returned to the three-judge court on the ground that there was a substantial constitutional question involved.

In November, 1955, James Keller and George Witkovich were indicted in Chicago for "wilfully failing to answer and reply to" a series of questions on their associates and activities. In February, 1956, Judge Sullivan of the Federal District Court dismissed the indictment in the Witkovich case, ruling that only questions relating to the availability of the deportee for deportation were admissible. The Justice Department's appeal to the

Supreme Court was accepted in October. In the same month the three-judge court in St. Louis rejected in the Sentner case the contention of the Justice Department that it could maintain rigid political and physical (i.e. refuse travel permission, etc.) control of parolees. Such an interpretation, the court ruled, would involve "grave constitutional questions" which Congress could not have intended. The court held also that the sole purpose of Supervisory Parole was to guarantee the deportee's availability in the event travel documents were obtained for his deportation, that parole was a part of the deportation process and could not be used for any other purpose. The Justice Department appealed this decision also to the Supreme Court.

Final decision had to wait until 1957. On April 29, the decision in the Witkovich case was delivered by Justice Frankfurter. The decision affirmed the judgment of the District Court that questions should be limited to matters related to the availability of the undeportable alien and emphasized that the supervision of such a person may well be a life-time problem. In May, the Supreme Court also affirmed the judgment of the three-judge court in the Sentner case, basing their refusal to review on the Witkovich decision. In these circumstances, since issues touching liberties that

> . . . the Constitution safeguards, even for an alien "person" would fairly be raised on the government's view of the statute, the path of constitutional concern in this situation is clear.

The denaturalization provisions of the Walter-McCarran Law are somewhat less subject to the arbitrary will of the Immigration and Naturalization Service officials and the Attorney General than are the provisions affecting non-citizens. Denaturalization is a court procedure and requires the use of "due process," rather than a hearing in which the Justice Department is both prosecutor and judge. However, under the pressures of the Cold War, due process often proved insufficient protection, especially since the government had plenty of paid witnesses to testify to the Communist Party membership of the foreign-born citizen. "It seems queer that what took you five years to get can be taken away from you in four hours," commented one newly made "ex-citizen." But even in the Cold War, due process and the insistence by many fair-minded judges on the production of valid evidence in support of the Justice Department's action slowed up the denaturalization drive.

The case of Ettore Zucca, begun in 1954, reached the Supreme Court in 1956. The court ruled that all petitions for denaturalization must have attached an affidavit showing "good cause [which] is a procedural prerequisite to the initiation and maintenance of the proceedings." More than half the petitions in the political denaturalization proceedings had never had such affidavits. The effect of the decision was seen immediately in the withdrawal by the government from a number of cases already begun.

A party to raise funds for the defense of Charles Tuteur of Chicago, unexpectedly became a victory celebration. Charles Tuteur had to flee from Nazi Germany because of certain books which were found on his shelves. And he lived to face surprisingly similar treatment in democratic America where he was threatened with the loss of his American citizenship because he had not mentioned receiving certain publications through the mail when he applied for citizenship. Also in the next month after the Zucca decision, the Federal District Court in Brooklyn dismissed the Justice Department complaint in the case of Gaetano Luchese and, on July 27, the Federal court in Los Angeles did the same in the case of David and Freeda Diamond. Both decisions were based on the Zucca decision.

But even such a victory as the Zucca case did not end the struggle. There was still a difference of opinion in the lower Federal courts as to the exact requirements of a proper affidavit, and cases dismissed by the Justice Department might be reopened later; but the government at least had to be prepared with something more than statements by paid informers that so-and-so was once seen at a Communist Party meeting; or that the government witness had once been told that so-and-so was a Party member.

Nonetheless, although the Justice Department finds denaturalization more difficult to accomplish, and although cases brought to trial have been lost by the government—notably that of Rose Chernin, the executive secretary of the Los Angeles Committee for Protection of Foreign Born—the Department could not be accused of not trying, particularly under the leadership of Herbert Brownell. It was still aiming at a reversal of the Schneiderman decision and the conversion of naturalized citizenship into a "temporary certificate revocable at the pleasure of the Attorney General." The battle was not over. In 1956 the Supreme Court accepted *certiorari* in the cases of Stanley Nowak and Mrs. Rebecca Maisenberg of Detroit. The case was placed on the 1957-1958 calendar.

The fight for the right to bail clearly guaranteed by the Fifth Amendment continued even after the Supreme Court affirmed in 1952 the right of the Justice Department to hold the "Terminal Island Four." Martin Young remained on Ellis Island for a year, from October 1951 to October 1952. His "birthday party" was celebrated in Manhattan, with the birthday cake prominently displayed, ready for his wife to carry it to Ellis Island the following day. In 1953-54, Boris Sklar was held on Ellis Island for eight months. On May 20, 1954, Nick and Mary Karman were arrested and held on Ellis Island without bail, leaving a fourteen-year-old son at home. Steve Tsermegas was held for more than a year in Cook County Jail in Chicago and Katherine Hyndman for ten months in the county jail at Crown Point, Indiana.

The Justice Department was extending the March 1952 decision by the Supreme Court in the Carlson case which held, 5 to 4, that non-citizens arrested in deportation proceedings can be denied the right to bail at the discretion of the Attorney General, and which allowed the holding of "active communists," so that it would permit the holding of past communists. Mrs.

Goldie Davidoff, charged with having been a member of the Communist Party in Canada, was arrested the morning of April 23, 1953, after her husband, a returned GI, had left for work. Her two-year-old baby had to go to Ellis Island with her. (The government witness against Mrs. Davidoff, by the way, was Harvey Matusow of whom in the words of a radio commentator "only one thing is certain; he has lied like a rug on the floor." He is the same Matusow who later created a sensation by publicly recanting his lies. But Mrs. Davidoff had already been deported to Canada.)

But on the other side of the ledger were grants of habeas corpus and orders to set bail by judges who still believed that the right to bail was a fundamental right which could not be ignored.

Early in 1954, Felix Kusman was released on *habeas corpus* in New York City; and in Los Angeles David Hyun, aided especially by the protests of the Methodist Church in which his father was a retired pastor, also won release. The Justice Department apparently played a kind of "cat and mouse" game, granting bail when adverse publicity threatened their procedures and cancelling bail again when the opposition died down. In June, 1954, there were five deportees, defended by the ACPFB, held on Ellis Island and one in the West Street House of Detention.

One case of imprisonment had so many implications with regard to immigration and naturalization policies and democratic rights—of which bail was an important factor—and so clearly revealed the reactionary purposes of Attorney General Brownell's Justice Department, that it might well claim our attention at this point. This is the case of Cedric Belfrage, then editor (now editor-in-exile) of the *National Guardian.* Belfrage, British born, came to the United States in 1926, as a journalist, and became a permanent resident in 1937, taking out his first citizenship papers immediately. But between 1942 and 1944, when Belfrage became eligible for citizenship, he was not in the United States. In 1941, before Pearl Harbor, he became active on a war assignment which the British Government considered important and for which British citizenry was mandatory. As he explained his quandary:

> It was hardly thinkable that I should quit just to satisfy my personal desire for U.S. citizenship; and I had no doubt that the matter would be completed without difficulty as soon as the war ended.

In 1944 and until near the end of 1945 Belfrage was in Europe serving in Germany directly under Gen. Eisenhower's Supreme Headquarters as a member of the Army press control teams charged with denazifying the German press and working under the directives of Eisenhower's U.S. Army. When he returned in 1946, he immediately informed Washington of his desire to complete his citizenship. But he was informed that he had overstayed his time abroad and would be required to go through the five years waiting period all over again. Belfrage decided against submitting to such an indignity. Whether this was a mistake is questionable,

> . . . for in the light of what has happened since, none will seriously suggest that I could have obtained citizenship in 1951.

The following year, under a Guggenheim fellowship, Belfrage wrote a book about his experiences in Germany which was considered so "hot" politically that he could not find a publisher until 1954, when it appeared under the title *Seeds of Destruction*. In 1948 he helped found the *National Guardian* of which he became editor. The *Guardian* supported the Progressive Party and Henry Wallace. It fought against injustice and McCarthyism, and for peace, and followed generally a non-communist, left-progressive and socialist position, as Belfrage has stated,

> . . . which Washington is so anxious to have Americans think does not exist, [and which] is an accepted feature of

> the political scene in every other Western country. . . . The position of the *Guardian* which the witch-hunters cannot tolerate is that you do not have to be a Communist to accept the facts of life in our time.

On July 19, 1950, Belfrage was summoned to Immigration headquarters in New York and told that he was being "investigated," and asked if he would answer questions on his "views, associations and writing." He declined and heard nothing further. But on May 8, 1953, he was subpoenaed by the House Committee on Un-American Activities where he refused to answer questions on the basis of the Fifth Amendment. On May 13 and 14 he was compelled to appear under subpoena before Senator McCarthy's investigating committee. Belfrage answered specific questions about his work in Germany but declined to answer questions on his personal beliefs. At a closed session McCarthy directed that an official of the Immigration Service be present at the public session the following day, and Brownell's Justice Department dutifully complied.

On May 15, Belfrage was arrested in the office of the *Guardian* on a deportation warrant and was taken to Ellis Island. It was June 10 before he was ordered released in $5,000 bail in a *habeas corpus* proceeding, but his movements were restricted to the New York area. This did not satisfy Brownell. But on December 14 the government's effort to revoke bail was rejected by a Federal judge, and on April 9, 1954, the Federal Court of Appeals, on the government's appeal, reaffirmed Belfrage's right to bail. Belfrage's comment to all this was stated ruefully:

> They never discussed whether I should have been arrested, only whether they could keep on holding me.

Deportation hearings began on August 20 and were concluded on October 12. The charge against him was former membership in the Communist Party. The evidence against him was all bought and paid for by the government from professional informers and witnesses, and none was corroborated. Defense evidence by experts on handwriting was minimized and testimony on mental illness with regard to the star government witness was completely ignored, while obvious perjury by government witnesses as to time, place and circumstances was simply disregarded. On December 9, deportation was ordered, and an appeal was announced.

On May 13, 1955, even before the Justice Department's final decision had reached his attorney's office through the mail, Belfrage was again arrested for deportation without warning. Held without bail in the Federal Detention Center in New York, Belfrage went on a three-day hunger strike to get out of solitary confinement. District Court Judge Dawson sustained Belfrage's deportation and an appeal, as well as application for bail, was taken to the Court of Appeals. On June 11, the *New York Times* criticized his imprisonment without bail. His appeal was denied; and after being held without bail for three months, Belfrage decided to accept deportation when bail for his release was again denied. On August 15 he was shipped to England after having lived in the United States for twenty-nine years. Considering the facts of the case and the treatment accorded Belfrage, there is merit to his comment:

> When the men with the shears in Washington considered the *Guardian,* an obvious place to begin trimming without nakedly assaulting "freedom of the press" presented itself: the editor was an alien.

Thus having resuscitated the Alien and Sedition Act of 1798, the McCarthyites in and out of government turned the clock even further back and resurrected for further victimization John Peter Zenger, the heroic colonial editor whose historic fight for the right to dissent established the concept of freedom of the press in America.

It is of some significance that, in 1958 in the Bonetti case, the Supreme Court ordered deportation cancelled since Bonetti had been a member of the Communist Party from 1934 to 1936 and last entered the country in 1938. The Court's decision was based on the fact that an immigrant's last entry into the country has always been regarded as his date of entry and the law provides for the deportation of non-citizens who are members of proscribed organizations after entry into the United States.

The Belfrage case was fought on the same grounds as the Bonetti case. But, because of the hysteria and Belfrage's mistreatment and jailing, no real test could be made of the issue in his case. The evidence is clear that Belfrage's deportation was a rank miscarriage of justice and an open violation of United States law since his last entry into the country was 1946 and even the false testimony of government witnesses claimed that his membership in the Communist Party pre-dated 1946.

But there came a change in the treatment of deportees. On November 11, 1954, Attorney General Brownell announced the closing of Ellis Island, Terminal Island and the detention centers in San Francisco, Seattle, Boston and Hawaii in an "economy move." Those held for deportation would henceforth be lodged at government expense in county jails. The decision raised a storm of protests from all directions. County jails were not places in which men and women convicted of no crime should be properly confined.

The novelist, Pearl Buck, who had Chinese friends under deportation order, was horrified by the surroundings in which she found them. Her indignant letter to the *New York Times* was published on November 17, severely criticizing the treatment non-citizens received in county jails. "Their food is inadequate, their bed mattresses dirty. They have little opportunity to get fresh air. . . ." On November 18, the *New York Times* supported her protest, declaring editorially:

> Persons convicted of no crime who are detained by the immigration authorities may not be entitled to board and lodging at the best hotels; but, even if few in numbers, they certainly don't deserve to be thrown into jail.

On November 24, while publishing a callous and insensitive defense of the policy by Edward Shaughnessy, district director of the Immigration Service, the *Times* returned to its criticism, declaring that despite the alleged "high" standards of county jails, a jail

> is still a jail. The accommodations, the food, the amount of freedom and number of visitors are only those customarily given to persons under punishment for serious violations of law. But detained aliens haven't even been accused much less convicted, of anything. . . .

Such individuals and organizations as Averill Harriman, Jacob Javits, the American Civil Liberties Union, joined in the protests. As a result, on December 11 the Justice Department was compelled to change its procedure—the use of jails for detention of deportees was to be discontinued; the Department would provide suitable quarters.

Since then bail has no longer appeared regularly in the headings in *The Lamp,* and in the various special bulletins issued by the ACPFB. Certain other specific court decisions were undoubtedly factors in bringing about the change. Instead of waiting, as had been formerly required, until the deportee was actually in custody in order to challenge the deportation order by *habeas corpus* proceedings, review could be instituted in Federal court at any time after the final order of deportation or, when the non-citizen received an order to surrender for deportation. In April 1955, in the Pedriero case, the Supreme Court held that it was not necessary to bring such proceedings to Washington since the Attorney General was not an "indispensable party" to the proceedings. The next year in connection with the Ceballos case, which dealt with suspension of deportation, the Solicitor General announced the Department's acceptance of the applicability of the Pedriero decision.

But the change was due much more to the increasingly vocal and widespread condemnation of the violation of a right recognized by statute as far back as 1275.

Another gain achieved in the general fight to maintain the traditions of American justice deserves to be mentioned. That is the increasing skepticism with regard to the reliability of the testimony given by what is often in a disrespectful mixture of metaphors referred to as "the government stable of stoolpigeons." In the struggle in defense of the foreign born many contributions were made by the ACPFB over the years toward this well-justified skepticism. The inaccuracy and irrelevance of much of such evidence in the hearings before the Subversive Activities Control Board was exemplified and emphasized in Abner Green's "Report from Washington." (I shall deal with the SACB in greater detail soon.)

The essential unreliability of a Matthew Cvetic was made clear by the physician's certificate obtained in Pittsburgh by a representative of the Western Pennsylvania Committee for Protection of Foreign Born; and the deportation proceedings of Matthew Brzovich were terminated by the Court of Appeals in Chicago on the ground that Cvetic's testimony was "evasive and conflicting." (*Lamp,* May-June, 1955) The next issue of *The Lamp* reports an incident in the career of Paul Crouch who, in 1954, appeared as the only government witness against the man who had previously saved the lives of Crouch and his two children. The deportation proceedings in the cases of Costas Athos of Charleston, West Virginia, and of Charles Soldo of Coverdale, Pennsylvania, were ordered terminated by the Board of Immigration Appeals in 1955 because the testimony of John Lautner was judged insufficient.

The proper curbing of the use of paid informers is a battle still to be completely won. But a beginning has been made, to which the ACPFB is proud to have given some aid.

26. A People's Movement at Work

Direct contributions to a people's movement are hard to chronicle and difficult to estimate. A victory or a defeat in an individual case is not simply a single victory or a single defeat to be added together for a numerical total of defeats versus victories. A victory or a defeat has repercussions far beyond the particular case, even beyond other similar cases, which affect attitudes, opinion and policy. The work of the American Committee for Protection of Foreign Born has had such repercussions.

This work has not been easy. With the end of World War II, the ACPFB constantly had to meet new difficulties arising from and in an atmosphere of prejudice and unreason created by the Cold War and McCarthyism. Also in meeting the new legal complications of the 1950's the Committee no longer had the advice of Carol King, whose wisdom and initiative had so long found paths over and around difficulties. It is no disparagement of the courage and legal acumen of those who have carried on her work since 1952 to recognize how great was the loss of her guidance. There were, in addition, the problems arising from the sheer physical weariness of the men and women working under extreme pressure and carrying a load far beyond normal human endurance. No less serious were the complications caused by enforced withdrawals of individuals because of threatened danger to relatives or associates. But in spite of all difficulties, the cumulative effect of the victories has been amazing. If the size of the shadow cast by the Walter-McCarran Law has shrunk perceptibly since December, 1952, it has been due directly and indirectly in no small measure to the work of this Committee.

Since December 25, 1952, the work of the ACPFB, difficult enough under the preceding laws, has had to be carried on against the administration—too often unreasonable if not vindictive—of the baffling, all-inclusive, arbitrary and oppressive provisions of the Walter-McCarran Law. The repeal of the Law has, therefore, necessarily been a major objective—although an objective shared by many other organizations. From year to year the fight for repeal continued. But in line with the flexibility of the organization, the form and emphasis of the campaign varied in conformity with the necessities of the changing situation. The Calls to its successive Annual Conferences show both the unchanging purpose of the Committee and the variation in methods of procedure.

The Annual Conference, meeting in Chicago, December 12 and 13, 1953, was called "To Repeal the Walter-McCarran and Defend Its Victims."

> The fight for an immigration and naturalization law that would respect the liberties and traditions of the American people merits the support and consideration of all persons concerned with the preservation of democratic rights.
>
> Public opinion must be informed and mobilized to change the immigration and naturalization law and to defend those victimized under the existing law.
>
> Therefore the ACPFB is convening a National Conference to repeal the Walter-McCarran Law and defend its victims. . . . To this Conference we invite all organizations and individuals interested in developing a program of action to establish an immigration and naturalization policy that would re-affirm the people's attachment to the Bill of Rights of the United States Constitution and to the cause of human liberty.

In the 1954 Conference (New York City, December 11-12), the emphasis had shifted because of the increasing number of victims of the Law and because of the consequent demands on the Committee's resources to meet emergencies. The Conference was called to "Defend the Rights of the Foreign Born"; but a "speedy repeal" of the law was a necessary part of the defense.

> The treatment of foreign-born Americans is an obvious violation of our democratic traditions. At the same time the attacks on the rights of the foreign born endanger the liberties of all Americans. . . . It will be the purpose of this Conference to discuss and develop ways to promote adequate defense of the rights of non-citizens and naturalized American citizens, as well as to seek a speedy repeal of the Walter-McCarran Law when the 84th Congress convenes in January, 1955.

In the Call to the 23rd Annual Conference (Detroit, December 10-11, 1955), "revision" of the law is for the first time coupled with repeal.

> Current efforts to bring post-war tensions to an end make it essential that the government and the people of this country take a fresh look at the treatment accorded to non-citizens and naturalized American citizens. The manner in which foreign-born Americans are being treated by the Justice Department serves only to maintain an atmosphere of intolerance that interferes seriously with achieving peaceful and democratic relations at home as well as abroad. . . .
>
> These anti-democratic activities are being conducted by the Justice Department in an effort to legitimatize the provisions of the Walter-McCarran Law despite the fact that the Law, a product of post-war tensions and passed over President Truman's veto in 1952, has been criticized and condemned by a majority of the American people as harsh, discriminatory and unjust.

> If post-war tensions are to be fully eliminated . . . the Walter-McCarran Law must be revised basically or repealed, as provided by forty bills which have been introduced in Congress this year and which are to be considered when the 84th Congress reconvenes in January, 1956.

The Call to the 1956 Conference, Los Angeles, (December 8 and 9) declared that "repeal of the law" was essential before "an atmosphere of true democracy can be established."

> It is urgent that ways and means of working towards this goal be discussed and worked out.

But revision was included as an alternative aim. Especially imperative were the following:

> Eliminating of racial discrimination from the immigration laws.
>
> Discontinuing the attack on the citizenship rights of naturalized Americans to re-establish full liberty and equality before the law for all.
>
> Ending the harassing methods used by the Immigration and Naturalization Service in its treatment of the non-citizen.
>
> Ending the threat of deportation and exile for lifetime residents of this country.

The same themes are re-echoed in the annual reports to the conferences and permeated the discussions and plans of action. Abner Green declared in his annual report to the 1953 Conference:

> The Walter-McCarran Law seeks to use the non-citizen as a scapegoat in order to legitimatize police state conditions of living for the American people. . . . In the hands of the Justice Department it is an inhuman law—brutal and indecent.

> One phase of its operation was illustrated in the discussion before the Senate Appropriations Committee. Mr. Kelly [of the Immigration Service] was asked by Senator Ellender, "Is there anything under the law you can do so aggravating that they will *want* to leave the country?" Mr. Kelly replied that the Justice Department was trying to do exactly that by holding non-citizens in detention. Senator Ellender's final comment was, "I thought the law gave the Department full power to make conditions so distasteful they would not want to live in the United States. . . ."
>
> Yesterday, Mayor-elect Wagner of New York City, condemned the law as an "ugly monument to theories of racism and isolation." Last month the CIO National Convention went on record for repeal of the law.
>
> To date, 300 non-citizens have been arrested in political deportation proceedings. Ninety-three are over the age of sixty and have lived in this country forty to fifty years.

Much of the report was devoted to individual cases, illustrating the sufferings of the individuals involved. Refugio Martinez, deported after twenty-seven years, dead at forty-nine from a heart attack two days after he reached Mexico. Norman Tallentire, thirty-three years in this country, retired after a heart attack, died in the midst of the court fight against his deportation. Francesco Costa, eighty-three, arrested for deportation because he refused to give the Justice Department the information it wanted for deporting his son. The report emphasized that

> . . . the fight against the Walter-McCarran Law if it is to be successful, must be conducted on two fronts—in a repeal movement and in a defense movement. These two constantly supplement and strengthen each other. The broad repeal movement that has developed during the past year has aided immeasurably in winning support for those victimized under the Law. And exposure of the effects of the Law [on individuals and families] has made the repeal movement constantly more significant and vital.
>
> While hundreds of organizations have spoken out

> against the Law, the ACPFB is the only national organization in the country that defends those victimized, while fighting for repeal. It is only natural therefore that this Committee should give special consideration to the defense of those attacked as an integral part of our fight for repeal.

The first press release after the Conference outlined the two-front campaign planned by the Conference (which had been attended by 321 delegates representing various organizations).

> A program of action, adopted through resolutions, called for winning public hearings on the Lehman-Celler Bill; and an all-out effort to assure full protection to all against whom Walter-McCarran Law proceedings have been initiated.

Although the title of the New York Conference of 1954, for which the New York Committee for Protection of Foreign Born was host, stressed the "second front" of the Committee's fight, the need to work for the repeal of the Walter-McCarran Law was the first item on the agenda at most of the sessions and panels. The first bulletin sent out after the conference (December 17) was wholly concerned with the repeal campaign, offering, as a result of the conference deliberations, six concrete suggestions for rousing individuals and organizations of various kinds to take action. The final section announced the calling of a legislative conference and a lobby in Washington in March, 1955, in accordance with a decision of the Conference, and urged that plans be made for participation.

When the 23rd Annual Conference met in Detroit, December, 1955, Sen. Kilgore had already opened hearings. The executive secretary declared in his report:

> Our Conference must set for itself as its major responsibility to campaign and work to re-establish the democratic and constitutional rights of non-citizens and naturalized American citizens.

> The main point on any such program is self-evident—the speedy repeal of the Walter-McCarran Law and its replacement by a new immigration and naturalization law that will deal with the potential immigrant, the non-citizen resident and the naturalized citizen as human beings entitled to equal justice under law, to democratic consideration and to democratic rights.
>
> The first major step in this direction are the public hearings just recessed and scheduled to be resumed in January by the Senate Judiciary Subcommittee on Immigration and Naturalization. . . .
>
> All organizations should concentrate on securing action by the Senate Judiciary Committee in reporting a bill for action as speedily as possible [especially because Rep. Walter as chairman of the House Committee serves as a major obstacle to any change]. The builder of the prison hates to see his dungeon torn down. [The only approach available in the House was the Discharge Petition introduced by Rep. Victor Anfuso.]

Abner Green also urged, that although repeal was the ultimate objective, a program of minimum alternatives should be prepared. The Conference agreed on a five point program: Naturalization after two years legal residence, no deportation after five years residence, naturalization to be cancelled for fraud only and proceedings must be begun within five years, immigration without discrimination as to country of birth, race, color, creed or political belief, full protection of the Bill of Rights for non-citizens, especially the right to bail and to freedom of belief, speech and association.

The annual report to the 1956 Conference still listed as the first concern of the Committee "An immigration and nationality law to replace the Walter-McCarran Law." But the second point was "The need for a statute of limitations in deportation and denaturalization." If the Law could not be immediately repealed, attention could be concentrated on an amendment putting an end to one of its worst features, the banishment of foreign born who have lived and worked in this country for years. Stress was laid also on publicizing the contributions of the foreign born to the growth and culture of the country, on winning a wider basis of sympathy and understanding, and on circulating more widely knowledge of the undemocratic procedures of the Justice Department in dealing with the foreign born.

The dominant theme of the Conference was the effect of the law on the people of America: the foreign born, the native born, the various minority groups, Chinese, Korean, Mexican, Negro, on trade unions, on the freedom of the press.

During the years, not only were the programs of the National Conferences followed consistently in spite of difficulties; new methods of work were devised to meet the increasing complications. Special conferences were held in all parts of the country, called by the ACPFB, by local groups or by defense committees interested in special cases. In 1954, for example, a conference "to map a program to defend Walter-McCarran Law victims" was held in New York in February, another in Cleveland in March, in Philadelphia in April and a conference of defense committees in New York in June. The officers of the Committee crossed the country, holding meetings and conferences and interviews with leaders of churches and labor unions, of organizations for social welfare and for civil rights.

Conferences and meetings were only a part of the Committee's work. A month after the President's Commission submitted its report on the Walter-McCarran Law, the ACPFB published and distributed in February, 1953, a pamphlet containing thirty pages of extracts from the testimony of 111 witnesses before the Commission, with an introduction by Abner Green and with an open letter, which had been sponsored by the ACPFB and signed by prominent people from coast to coast, presented to the Commission on the last day of the hearings. And on December 10 of the same year, the fifth anniversary of the United Nations' Declaration of Human Rights, the ACPFB issued a press release charging the Justice Department with the violation of five articles of that Declaration in its administration of the Walter-McCarran Law: Article 7, all are equal before the law; Article 9, no one shall be subject to arbitrary arrest, detention or exile; Article 10, everyone is entitled to a fair public hearing by an independent and impartial tribunal; Article 18, the right to freedom of thought, conscience and religion; Article 19, the right to freedom of opinion and expression.

In addition, leaflets and pamphlets and petitions were printed and distributed, both by the ACPFB and by the independent area committees. Reprints of articles were distributed, such as "Deportation Deliriums" by Laurent B. Frantz from *The Nation* of March 26, 1955, and "The Rusted Gate" from the November 26 issue of the same periodical—the latter was included in the "kit" for the delegates at the 1956 conference. Probably the most effective publication was Abner Green's *Under the Shadow of Liberty*, a forty-six page account of twenty-three typical Americans out of the over 400 with whom the Committee was concerned, and whom the Justice Department had ordered deported.

The interest aroused by the human appeal of this pamphlet is again evidence of the close interrelation of the Committee's "two fronts." Proof that the provisions of an act of Congress contravene the accepted rules of judicial procedure, or that they are contrary to the Constitution of the United States is obvious ground for repeal or revision. But the number of people outside the legal profession whose feelings are outraged by such contradictions is never large. Justice in the abstract is almost universally praised (Hitler, of course, decried it as "a mere sociological concept") but like all abstractions it invites to admiring contemplation rather than to action. When an act of Congress deprives men, women and children of the right to live with their families and to enjoy the normal freedoms guaranteed by the Constitution, the incentive to fight actively for repeal or revision is provided. But the American Committee in 1952-56 recognized, as it had done from its very beginning, that the legal defense of the rights of individuals was indivisible from the fight for just laws.

From 1952 to 1954 especially, the lists of those in jeopardy steadily lengthened. But mere numbers alone do not explain why an organization such as the ACPFB which devoted itself so unsparingly to the defense of the foreign born, has won such trust and deep affection. There is, of course, the political aspect, the fight for civil rights, for the democratic way of the American people. But together with this, inextricably intertwined, is the human element, the human emotions, the human relationships, the tragedies, the hopes, the frustrations of men, women and children.

The most detailed statistics do not serve to depict this human element. But short of a biographical study of each of the victims, which would require space far in excess of what is possible here, statistics may give some notion of what is involved. When the main brief in the Rowoldt case was submitted to the U.S. Supreme Court on September 7, 1956, it was accompanied by an Appendix which contained a study, conducted under the supervision of Anne Fagan Ginger, based on 307 political deportation cases. For the first time an overall picture of the people the Justice Department wanted to deport was given. It was summarized in *The Lamp* of September-October 1956, from which excerpts are taken.

One of the impressions the Justice Department seeks to create is that those facing deportation are "aliens." But one of the harshest aspects of the political deportation drive is that deportees have spent their adult years in the United States and that trying to begin life anew in another country promises to be difficult at best. Of the cases studied the following ages are recorded:

	Number	*Cumulative Percentage*
Over 65 years of age	74	25
55 to 65 years of age	122	66.4
45 to 55 years of age	80	90
35 to 45 years of age	17	99.3
Under 35 years of age	2	

The length of time they had lived in the United States is:

	Number	Cumulative Percentage
More than 50 years	35	11
41 to 50 years	143	60
31 to 40 years	83	87
21 to 30 years	20	94
11 to 20 years	10	98
Less than 10 years	6	

The study further reveals that the overwhelming majority entered the United States early in life. Ages of the deportees at the time of entry were:

	Number	Cumulative Percentage
Less than 1 year old	8	2.6
1 to 5 years old	15	7.7
6 to 10 years old	34	19.1
11 to 15 years old	35	31
16 to 20 years old	86	60
21 to 30 years old	100	93.5
31 to 40 years old	16	99.7
Over 40 years old	1	

And it is also worth noting that of all the 307 cases considered, only fifteen were retired and three others unemployed, the rest were gainfully engaged either in the professions or business, in farming or as workers.

But there is information of even greater significance. Of 286 who replied to the question, 225 are or have been married, and of these, 127 married American citizens, 169 have citizen children and 92 have citizen grandchildren. On the other hand, 173 have no close relatives living in their countries of origin to which it is planned to deport them, and only 75 have one or more close relatives living in those countries; 62 are totally unable to speak or read the language of the country of origin; 170 are able to speak or read it in some degree.

Sixty-seven of the deportees are women, 58 of them have lived in this country 30 years or more. Forty-four have citizen children, 33 citizen grandchildren. Are close family ties to be broken or are the American-born children to become exiles from their native land?

The contemptuous comment is often made that, if these people loved the United States so much, they should have become citizens. The facts give sufficient answer. Of the total number of cases studied, 173 tried to become citizens before the initiation of deportation proceedings, an additional 78 had applications for citizenship pending at the time of their deportation arrest. Of those who had made no effort to achieve citizenship one could not apply for citizenship because of national origin, nine had been citizens but had lost their citizenship by denaturalization or marriage to non-citizens, and five had believed they were citizens by birth, marriage or derivation before the commencement of deportation proceedings. As to the fifty odd others, there are too many legal reasons for the refusal of naturalization—including inability to meet the sometimes unduly difficult literacy test, or the requirement of continuous residence in one place; prison sentences imposed for picketing or "disorder" during strikes; also the many attempts to obtain from an applicant information about the doings of his neighbors—to make it possible to use failure to become a citizen as a criterion of love of country.

Legally, deportation "is not punishment"; but to most of these men and women deportation is banishment from the only country they know. In the ancient and medieval world, banishment was, next to death, the penalty most to be dreaded. And now as then, "it can deprive a man of all that makes life worth while." What the *threat* of deportation means in terms of insecurity, anxiety, grief and dread, only those fighting to remain in the United States and the members of their families understand. For four people this fight began before 1920; for two, between 1920 and 1929; for 24 between 1930 and 1939; for 8 between 1940 and 1945; for 50 between 1945 and 1949; for 164 between 1950 and 1956.

Such is the human side of the deportation story. It is clear why the non-citizen so desperately requires a competent, experienced and honest defense, and why the ACPFB has placed so much stress on this aspect of its work. Some deportation warrants have been cancelled; about 200 are still pending. But that they are "pending" instead of executed, that these 200 foreign born are still in the country of their choice is largely the result of the defense work of the ACPFB.

But on the defense front there were also defeats, which the annual reports were forced to record. Intense personal pressure, the feeling of legal hopelessness, the extreme danger of physical persecution in fascist "countries of origin," induced nine deportees to accept "voluntary" departure. An additional twenty-seven were deported. Among these some were the result of defeats in court. The Supreme Court decision in the Galvan case in May, 1954, recognized the power of Congress to legislate almost anything it pleased concerning non-citizens. The immediate question decided, deportation for former Communist Party membership, was not materially different from the Harisiades case.

There was great disappointment in the case of sixty-five-year-old Giacomo Quattrone of Boston, resident of the United States for forty-five years (the last year and a half in the East Boston detention center). He was not charged with Communist Party membership but with "affiliation" with the Communist Party. He had answered truthfully, in the confidence that he had nothing to hide, when he was questioned by immigration officials. "Yes, I went to Communist Party meetings in my district once in a while." "Yes, I read the *Daily Worker* sometimes." Had he ever given money to the Communist Party? "Well, they pass around the hat and you just can't let it go by you." Since at the end of the long court fight the Supreme Court refused to to take the case, Quattrone had to return to the country he had left forty-five years before. "I don't know anybody in Italy any more," he said. "Everybody I care about is here." (He had eight American-born children, most of them married now with children of their own.) "But the worst is, I love America and what shall I say when they ask me in Italy about freedom and justice in the United States?"

The decision in the Jay case in 1955 might also be listed among the defeats since the majority decision allowed the use of confidential information to serve as the basis for a denial of suspension of deportation. But the four dissenting justices spoke so vigorously and so cogently against any such practice by the Department of Justice that, on October 31 of the same year, the Department announced a change of policy. Abner Green's report at that year's Annual Conference therefore counted it with the victories.

There were, however, undebatable and decisive victories which the Committee could chronicle, some of the most significant of which were recorded in the previous chapter. These victories were attained through the laborious and money-consuming method of carrying individual cases through to the Board of Immigration Appeals and through the Federal courts, step by step, and sometimes retracing steps. The victories, while won in individual cases which were the responsibility of the ACPFB, set general precedents which affected cases not directly the responsibility of the ACPFB, such as the Bridges case. The same was true in the defeats, which had their effect on non-ACPFB cases such as that of Belfrage. But the defeats served an additional purpose: they indicated points where even greater concentration was needed to shatter the judicial justification of unjustifiable, anti-democratic, un-American legislation.

How unjustifiable, how anti-democratic, how un-American—and how "mean" and subversive!—we shall see in a moment. For apart from the two-front battle against the Walter-McCarran Law and in defense of the foreign born, the Committee has been forced also to undertake a third front in recent years—"the defense of the right to defend," which the Attorney General attacked under the McCarran Internal Security Act of 1950.

27. Punitive Measures

THE ethical standards governing the actions of many of those concerned in the drive to enforce conformity—which has characterized the period since the end of World War II—are not easily justifiable. Even the un-American assumption that disagreement with the current government policy is disloyalty or treason does not in itself excuse procedures in which ordinary honesty appears secondary to prejudice or to personal triumph. How reconcile the difference between Attorney General Brownell's public lauding of the safeguards of individual freedoms in the Bill of Rights and his disregard of those same safeguards in relation to the foreign born?

Cyrus Eaton's forcible criticism in May, 1958, of the methods of investigating agencies, including the FBI, has already been mentioned. The comment of the present Attorney General, William P. Rogers, was: "Such reckless criticism is an insult to the men and women who are devoting their lives to a career of service in the law-enforcement profession." And Rep. Walter hastened to serve a subpoena on Mr. Eaton, by television, to appear before the House Un-American Committee to answer for his criticism.

Which is "reckless?" The criticism or the activity of agencies who send investigators into homes and neighborhoods to ask questions too often impertinent rather than pertinent, to use the telephone as an instrument of terror, to advise employers to fire certain individuals and hint that it would be well not to mention the FBI in connection with the firing?

It is not only the foreign born whose rights are endangered by government investigating agencies' procedures. Those who would defend the rights of the foreign born are also vulnerable. After ten years of attack on the foreign born, the power of the Government was directed also against the one national organization that sought to defend them.

In 1948, as has been already noted, Tom Clark placed the ACPFB on the Attorney General's subversive list. In 1951 came the attempt to paralyze the ACPFB by the arrest and imprisonment of Abner Green and by the demand for the names of contributors.

However, the ACPFB did not cease its work and that work won increasing public response. The Committee's persistence in carrying cases to the courts began to pay dividends in an increasing number of victories which threatened to tear the complex web of anti-foreign born legislation. Further action against the ACPFB was clearly indicated.

The McCarran Internal Security Act of 1950 provided for a Subversive Activities Control Board, and gave that Board all the legal paraphernalia for the registration of communist "action" and "front" organizations. This is obviously not the place to give either a general history of the proceedings under the SACB nor to evaluate its work. I. F. Stone, the journalist, described SACB's job caustically, "to play ideological nursemaid and flatfoot to the American people by registering radicals and labelling their writings." But it is more than that. A more accurate evaluation by Laurent B. Frantz appeared in the civil liberties issue of *The Nation* in December, 1953, under the title, "Tooling Up for Mass Repression," reprints of which were distributed "as a public service" by the ACPFB. Mr. Frantz's judgment was later confirmed by an ex-member of the SACB, Harry Cain, who declared that the result of the law under which the Board functioned was to "perpetuate an atmosphere in which loyalty oaths, purges of governmental workers and heresy trials remain a continuing blot on our national life. . . . Legislation which imposes disabilities on a harmless group is bad and should be repealed."

Attorney General Brownell, however, found the act useful and lost little time in applying to the SACB to require the ACPFB to register as a "communist front" organization. On March 17, 1953, he had made public his intention of deporting 12,000 non-citizens and denaturalizing 10,000 for political opinions. On April 23, he presented his petition for the registration of the ACPFB. The relation between his deportation-denaturalization program and his petition was obvious.

Abner Green's brief announcement of the Attorney General's action in *The Lamp* of March-May, 1953, declares:

> The ACPFB is the only national organization which defends non-citizens against deportation and naturalized citizens against the threat of denaturalization. The Attorney General's petition . . . is filled with false statements. One of the charges, however, is based on the fact that the ACPFB opposed the Hobbs "Concentration Camp" bill, the Mundt bill and the 1950 McCarran Act—all predecessors of the 1952 Walter-McCarran Law.
>
> The ACPFB has opposed this legislation and condemned the Justice Department's support of this legislation. (A 48-page pamphlet now being published details the Committee's objections to the Walter-McCarran Law.)
>
> The ACPFB will defend itself against the Attorney General's unwarranted charges and we hope that, with the support of the American people, this attempt to destroy our organization after twenty-one years of work on behalf of the foreign born will be defeated.
>
> We expect to be able to go on working until the Walter-McCarran Law is repealed, a democratic immigration and naturalization policy adopted, and the Justice Department's deportation and denaturalization hysteria ended.

The next issue of *The Lamp* devoted the last page wholly to the impending hearings before the SACB. A statement signed by the Honorary Chairman of the Committee, Bishop Arthur Moulton of Salt Lake City, and the two co-chairmen, George B. Murphy, Jr. and Prof. Louise Pettibone Smith, was published as a leaflet, bearing on the front cover Franklin Delano Roosevelt's greeting to the Committee on March 2, 1940, "We welcome the work to maintain the rights of the foreign born," with comments on the Committee and its work by Oswald Garrison Villard, the *New York Times,* former Secretary of State Cordell Hull, former Secretary of the Interior Harold L. Ickes, former U.S. Supreme Court Justice Frank Murphy, former president of the CIO Philip Murray, former U.S. Attorney Francis Fisher Kane, former Commissioner of Immigration and Naturalization Earl G. Harrison and former Republican presidential candidate Wendell L. Willkie. The leaflet included also the list of the Committee's sponsors, a brief history of the Committee's work since 1933, and five suggestions for help in the fight to maintain and extend the rights of fellow-Americans of foreign birth. The officers' statement said in part:

> The work of the American Committee is a matter of public record. It has long stood as the only national organization defending the democratic and constitutional freedom of the foreign born. . . . [It] has opposed the Justice Department publicly as well as in the federal courts whenever that government agency has attempted to deprive non-citizens or naturalized American citizens of their rights.
>
> We stand firm in our conviction that the work of the American Committee has served the best interests of all the American people.
>
> The new assaults planned against the foreign born, coupled with the attack on the American Committee are reminiscent of the police state. . . . Today's attacks are one with the Alien and Sedition Laws of 1798, the infamous Palmer Raids of 1920 and all other efforts over the years to legalize prejudice and terror against minorities in the United States. . . .
>
> We shall defend the ACPFB. With the help of all

> Americans, we will defeat this attack by the Attorney General . . . and make our contribution to maintaining the Bill of Rights . . . and the liberties of all persons, native born as well as foreign born.

On June 30, the statement received the public endorsement of ninety leaders of religious and secular thought in America.

Various legal procedures followed. Motions were offered by the attorney for the Committee and were denied by the SACB with unswerving regularity and undeliberate speed. The Committee's Answer to the Attorney General's petition was prepared for filing on September 3. Then the Attorney General decided to amend his petition, which might have necessitated changes in the Answer. (Since the main amendment was a 600-word description of the Communist Party, the purpose of which could only be to arouse prejudices, as it had nothing to do with the ACPFB, no alteration in the content of the Answer was needed.) The Answer was filed on October 30 by the co-chairman, Louise Pettibone Smith.

The hearings began in Washington on June 21, 1955. Abner Green's opening statement was printed by the Committee as a pamphlet, *In Defense of the Right to Defend Foreign Born Americans*. The statement summarized briefly the purpose and history of the Committee, and promised to disprove certain false assumptions of the Attorney General and to demonstrate his reasons for trying to end the work of the Committee. There is space here for only a few essential paragraphs.

> The right of Americans to join together to defend the freedom of their fellow Americans is under serious attack. . . . This is not a privilege which some benign public official allows the people to enjoy out of the generosity of his heart. This is a right possessed by the people which the Attorney General today is trying to take away. . . .
>
> A part of America is on trial here. . . . The American Committee expresses that body of public opinion which feels that in the spirit of the Declaration of Independence

> all persons have a right to share in the country's advancement as they share its burdens and tribulations.
>
> The American Committee symbolizes that area of American thought which feels that the Bill of Rights can survive only if all residents enjoy its benefits, regardless of race, color, creed, national origin, descent, citizenship or political beliefs.
>
> The American Committee believes in the democratic principles voiced by leaders in our national life since the days of the American Revolution and given expression recently by Supreme Court Justice Hugo Black: "We must have freedom of speech for all or we will in the long run have it for none but the cringing and the craven."
>
> It is this sentiment which is on trial here. . . .
>
> As long as there is one non-citizen threatened with exile or jail for some harmless offense, or questioned illegally and terrorized by Justice Department agents, there will be an organization like the ACPFB. As long as there is a Walter-McCarran Law, there will be a movement of people unswerving in their determination to revise or repeal it.
>
> As long as there are decent Americans, there will be organized efforts to defend the democratic and constitutional rights of foreign-born Americans. As long as there is a breath of democratic spirit left in the American people, there will be opposition to the spread of hatred and oppression.

The chairman of the Board in 1953 was Thomas Herbert, a former Governor of Ohio, with a record of having used state troops to break a strike in 1948. In September, 1952, he had publicly defended Sen. McCarthy and his committee: "The overall results of his committee's labors need no apologies." One of the members of the SACB was Watson B. Miller, who as Commissioner of Immigration had initiated deportation proceedings against a hundred or so non-citizens defended by the Committee. A third was ex-Senator Harry Cain whose voting record in Congress (on fifteen key issues his vote had been anti-liberal) gave no indication of his future criticism of the security law. In October, 1953, Francis Cherry, ex-governor of Arkansas, became a member of the Board. In 1954, according to Drew Pearson, he charged Governor Faubus, of later Little Rock fame, with "communist leanings"—a judgment which might raise the question of sanity. The Board is an expensive luxury; a member's salary is $15,000 a year. In 1952 the Board spent $204,105; the next year over $300,000 and estimates for the following year were $400,000.

The muttering of one spectator at the opening hearing on June 30 presumably expressed the opinion of many: "Waste of money to defend yourself before these people—waste of money —sheer waste of money!" But waste of money or not, there was no possible alternative for any organization which wanted to continue in existence. And defense required not only money in large quantity, but also an enormous expenditure of time and energy. Carrying on the work of the Committee while defending its existence has been an amazing achievement in itself and conclusive evidence of the Committee's viability.

The presentation of the case for the Attorney General at the hearings before Edward Morrissey, the appointed hearing officer for the Board, consumed four days a week for three weeks, then recessed to be resumed on September 8. The Justice Department finished its case on November 29, taking in all thirty-nine days, in which it offered seventeen witnesses whose testimony filled 3,500 pages. Week by week Abner Green's "Report from Washington" chronicled the witnesses and the substance of their testimony, 80 percent of which the ACPFB would have been willing to stipulate, since it dealt with the defense of the rights of the foreign born (mostly against deportation or denaturalization), and with efforts to defeat bills which threatened their rights. But to have permitted the stipulation of these facts would have reduced the cost of the hearings and that was not in the interest of the government or of the government-employed informers. So the testimony went on. Many of the witnesses were unacquainted with the ACPFB and testified either concerning proceedings of the Communist Party or about the independent defense committees. The information which might have been pertinent was shown on cross-examination to be incorrect. Ten of the witnesses were Justice Department employees or spies employed by the FBI.

In the first of the Washington Reports, Abner Green quoted from the decision of Judge Anderson of the Federal District Court in Boston, rendered in a deportation case at the time of the Palmer Raids in April, 1920:

> I cannot adopt the contention that government spies are more trustworthy or less disposed to make trouble in order to profit therefrom, than are spies in private industry. Except in time of war, when a Nathan Hale may be a spy, spies are always necessarily drawn from the unwholesome and untrustworthy classes. A right minded man refuses such a job. [The spy system] destroys trust and confidence, it kills human kindliness, it propagates hate.

Judge Anderson's judgment apparently applied to the testimony of the second government witness before the SACB, when he named various residents of Pittsburgh as members of the Communist Party but admitted under cross-examination, that he did not know the difference between "support" and "membership." The same witness stated that he had seen Abner Green at a "closed" communist meeting in Pittsburgh in December, 1949—a month during which records show that Green could not possibly have been in Pittsburgh.

The second report opened with a quotation from an editorial in the *New York Times* of July 8, 1954, just a year earlier:

> The process of informing is—as Justice Holmes once said of the not unrelated art of wiretapping—a "dirty business." The tattletale of children becomes in adult life the gossip, the tipster, the informer, the keyhole peeper, the agent. Paid or unpaid, it is a distasteful occupation, and one that does not well become a free society. It implies accusation without proof, defamation without responsibility. . . . The informer smacks of the police state.

The report closed with a second extract from the same editorial:

> It is reasonable to suppose that the professional, paid informers, such as those on the rolls of the Justice Department, who can be said to make their living at this game, feel the necessity of continuing to "produce" if they are not to give up their lucrative occupation.

As illustration Green cited testimony of four witnesses for the Justice Department offered in the first two weeks. John Hardin testified concerning two non-existent organizations, the Nationality Committee of the Communist Party and the American Committee for Protection of Foreign Born in Western Pennsylvania. James Glatis testified about a non-existent organization, the New England Committee for Protection of Foreign Born in 1950—a New England Committee was not organized until May 1952. John Lautner testified about a non-existent meeting in 1942. Carl Hacker testified about a period of time before the ACPFB was in existence.

The list of misstatements, of totally irrelevant information, chiefly about the relation of the informers to the Communist Party, lengthened with each issue of the report. One witness was shown to have testified that she had volunteered to work from patriotic motives and had received only her expenses; but a sworn statement of the Justice Department (November, 1952) proved that she had received $24,026.45 of which only $149.00 was for expenses. Another had received $18,000; others were paid at the rate of $100 to $150 a day.

The government relied heavily on the connection alleged to exist between the ILD in the early days of the ACPFB and on one check from the Communist Party as a contribution toward legal expenses.

The cumulative effect of the impression made by the government witnesses was described in the secretary's Annual Report for 1955:

> I sat through each one of those thirty days, listened to

> all of the testimony, and I must share with you my complete bewilderment.
>
> The only thing the Justice Department proved in the course of those thirty days is that the ACPFB since the first day it was organized in 1933, has consistently defended the democratic rights of foreign-born Americans; fought deportation and denaturalization and discrimination; opposed alien-baiters like Dies and Reynolds, Walter and McCarran; defended the rights of the foreign born regardless of race, color, creed, national origin or political opinion.
>
> The Justice Department does not seek to illegalize our Committee because we are a "communist front" organization. They never proved it—and they couldn't prove it. The Justice Department seeks to illegalize our Committee because we have never swerved from our avowed purposes, which are in every sense of the word legal and unassailable.

The ACPFB began its defense in New York City on December 20. Joseph Forer of Washington, D. C., stated at the opening of the ACPFB defense:

> We will produce the facts about the Committee. We will show what it does and how it does it. Our witnesses will be people who participate in and support the work of the American Committee. Unlike the Attorney General's witnesses they will not be professional witnesses earning their hire by giving testimony which they agilely adjust for each case in which they appear. Our witnesses will not be political informers, renegades, spies or agents provocateurs. None of them will have stolen papers [a reference to the testimony of Marion Miller who had volunteered office help and removed certain records] for the FBI or anybody else, or lived a life of deception. They will be honorable men and women, many of them of great distinction.

The first witness was the honorary co-chairman, Prof. Louise

Pettibone Smith. As the report for December 28 summarized:

> Prof. Smith [made] clear that the ACPFB defended the rights of foreign-born persons regardless of their race, color, creed, national origin or political belief. She stated clearly and simply that the ACPFB governing body is the National Conference, where the Committee's program is examined and adopted each year; that all officers are responsible to the National Conference and not to any other body or to any person.
>
> Prof. Smith declared that the ACPFB is not controlled or dominated by any other organization and that the Attorney General's charges are completely false. Prof. Smith made clear the ACPFB policy of accepting cooperation and support from any group, organization or individual—so long as the cooperation and support are extended for the purpose of the ACPFB and not for any other purpose.

Prof. Smith testified for three days, after which the hearings were held in Washington, beginning January 4, 1956.

Other witnesses for the ACPFB included: Prof. Anton J. Carlson, appointed to the faculty of the University of Chicago in 1904, in 1940 appointed Fred P. Hixon Distinguished Service Professor Emeritus; Horace Meldahl, law degree from the University of Louisville in 1917, practicing law in Charleston, West Virginia; Rev. Charles A. Hill, pastor of the Hartford Avenue Baptist Church in Detroit, Michigan; Rev. Harvey McArthur, professor of New Testament, Hartford Seminary Foundation, Hartford, Connecticut; Bishop Arthur Moulton, whose testimony was taken at Salt Lake City; Mrs. Sadie Saltzman, the wife of a New York deportee; Peter Soldo, the son of a Carverdale, Pennsylvania deportee.

The testimony of these witnesses on file in Washington is well worth reading for the light thrown not only on the work of the Committee but also on the ways of a government investigation and the procedures of the Department of Justice. Prof. Carlson when asked if he was being paid for his testimony, responded, "Paid with money? No. I am being paid because I think that I am doing my duty to the human race." (He had remarked earlier that "the communist is a human being, sometimes at least in Russia he is very superficial"; but the communist like any other citizen, should be judged on the basis of actions rather than on his pretended beliefs.)

Mrs. Saltzman's husband had applied for citizenship in 1944. In 1948 she said "they sent a man to arrest him."

> Q. Did they arrest him? A. They did.
>
> Q. Where did they pick him up? A. In the house.
>
> Q. Was there previous notification? A. No, nothing, just came and they took him. . . . Oh, sure we talked. We wanted people to know. . . . He shouldn't be deported. He is a very honorable American person. . . .
>
> The American Committee was proven to be very good friends. They gave us very warm feeling, and also they gave us legal and moral support because we were very panicky when my husband got arrested, because we didn't expect that.
>
> [He was] forced to apply for passport . . . to Russia, but Russia don't accept him, which we wouldn't wish Russia would accept him.

Questioned on the word "forced," she answered, "Yes, he would be punished if he wouldn't." On supervisory parole she said:

> I don't go with him there. What I know is they always pressure him where he goes and what he does, and it is a lot of particular nonsense that he is very much annoyed by.

Asked whether the reporting really mattered, she replied,

> Of course, it matters. He is very upset about it, I would say. When he works he loses a day and then it is a disgrace to have a man like my husband to come like a criminal to report.
>
> Q. Do you work for the Committee for nothing? A. I do it not for nothing. I don't get paid but I get a good

> feeling to do that. I feel the American Committee is helping so many people, including myself, and I feel like I got to help them.

She was questioned on the Washington "pilgrimage" of 1949 and about the others who were there.

> Mrs. Callow is a very nice young lady and she had a big family with her—some very small kids and one after another until the oldest one which was sixteen. [The oldest son was in the army and Leon Callow was still fighting deportation to Greece in 1957.]

Mr. Meldahl testified,

> The only thing the American Committee . . . has ever attempted to do is to help foreign born protect such rights as they have under the Constitution and the laws of the United States and the States wherein they reside.

But the chief witness for the Committee was its executive secretary who testified for six weeks—four on direct testimony and two under cross-examination—presenting the complete history of the American Committee since he became associated with it in 1936.

When the 1956 report was made to the Annual Conference in Los Angeles, Edward Morrissey had not yet given his decision—not that there was any doubt as to what it would be, so thoroughly was the verdict built into the Act, the procedure and the mentality of the Board. The SACB has never yet refused to comply with the requests of the Attorney General. As Harry Cain declared, in giving the decision on the Washington Pension Union, the Law as written makes an acquittal by the SACB impossible. And nine months later Mr. Morrissey submitted his decision to the Board, recommending that the ACPFB be ordered to register as a "communist front" organization. So neither the ACPFB nor Harry Cain had been mistaken. Certainly twenty-seven witnesses, 518 exhibits and 7,095 pages of testimony were not needed for such a decision. A successful defense before the Federal courts is a different kind of battle. But that fight, with all that it entails in energy, time and money, still lies ahead.

Although the Los Angeles conference did not have the final SACB decision, it was held at the very climax of the second concurrent attack on the Committee. This took the form of an "investigation" launched by Representative Walter and his House Un-American Activities Committee. Allegedly—but as in so many un-American attacks the "alleged" differed from the actual—the investigation was to concern itself with the operation of the McCarran Internal Security Act and the Walter-McCarran Act. In fact it concentrated on the activities of the ACPFB, with its objective the disruption of the impending Annual Conference, scheduled for Los Angeles on Friday, Saturday, and Sunday, December 7, 8 and 9, 1956.

Congressman Walter began his hearings in Washington on November 12, 1956, when intensive preparations for the conference had just begun. He then took his investigation on tour to Youngstown, Ohio, and Chicago. For two weeks before the Conference subpoenas were distributed wholesale in Los Angeles, where he arrived in time to hold hearings on the Thursday before the Conference, continued it on Friday and held an unprecedented Saturday session. After the Sunday closing of the Conference, Walter continued his tour to San Francisco and Seattle.

At each one of these stops, Walter not only harassed the local area committee, but involved every other committee within the broad region surrounding it, dragging witnesses over long distances to appear before the hearing. He subpoenaed a miscellaneous group, some of whom had had only brief and long-past relations with defense of the rights of foreign-born Americans. There was a rather obvious preference for those who might be expected to lose status or employment because of the subpoena. Bishop Mitchell, who had a long record of cooperation, as well as the three honorary co-chairmen of the ACPFB were ignored. They had no jobs to lose since all were "retired." Little, if any, new information was gained; most witnesses (except those in government pay) availed themselves of their constitutional right to refuse to answer questions.

The climax of Walter's attempt to prove the Committee an adjunct of the Communist Party, engaged in organizing an international conspiracy, came in Los Angeles. The hearing room was packed with visitors. They heard many unproved charges and many insulting insinuations directed against the witnesses—and not against the witnesses only. Attorneys who appeared with client witnesses to protect their rights were labelled communists because of their very presence. The attorney for Mrs. Rose Chernin, executive secretary of the Los Angeles Committee, was ousted from the hearing because of his strong defense of his client, and Mrs. Chernin was told to come back to the Saturday hearing with another attorney. She came, as ordered, with one of the leaders of the California Bar Association, who argued only one point: the right of Mrs. Chernin to an attorney of her own choice. However, unwarranted abuse continued.

The Annual Conference, despite Mr. Walter, was held as scheduled. Abner Green, in his report, announced firmly:

> To Congressman Walter we say: We will not be swerved from our determination to fight for repeal or revision of the hated Walter-McCarran Law and for an end to the harassment and persecution of foreign-born Americans. . . . We join with the late Franklin Delano Roosevelt in repeating his statement of 1940 that "we are fighting for a free America—for a country in which all men and women have equal rights to liberty and justice. . . ."

The Conference was, of course, hampered. Preparations were disrupted by the hearings in various parts of the country. The Los Angeles Committee did such an outstanding job of mobilizing protests and attendance at the hearings, that their participation in the Conference, which took place simultaneously, was of necessity curtailed. And regrettably, some liberals, apparently frightened by the Walter spectacle, cancelled their participation in the Conference. The welcome for those who came was the more enthusiastic. And the regular delegates went on with their business unperturbed. The program of work for 1957 was formulated and voted unanimously.

On August 16, 1957, the Un-American Committee filed its report on the hearings. Its conclusions were as inevitable as the decision of the SACB hearing officer. The report summarizes the activities of the ACPFB and the independent area committees in seeking to win repeal of the Walter-McCarran Law and in defense of victims of the Law.

The report of the investigation does contain numerous quotations from "cooperative" witnesses, including such discredited informers as Matthew Cvetic. And it pronounces all the ACPFB's activities in defense of democratic rights "subversive." The validity of this conclusion can be evaluated from the following example: The group of young people, "The Sons and Daughters of the Foreign Born," who organized to help keep their parents in the United States, is called "one of the most reprehensible" of the Committee's "enterprises." Such judgments are hardly sapient.

But there was a third simultaneous attack against the ACPFB which began in New York State in the summer of 1955. The first hearings before the SACB in Washington had been recessed on July 8. On August 15, Abner Green was served with an order, signed by Justice McGivern, of the New York State Supreme Court, at the request of New York State Attorney General, Jacob Javitz, to appear in court on August 23 (later postponed to September 12) for questioning. He was also ordered to bring the records of the Committee. The order was asked for on the ground that the ACPFB was violating the law applying to charitable organizations. This law was promulgated as a result of a New York State legislative investigation of a veterans' aid organization, which was alleged to have misused the funds it had collected by appropriating 90 per cent of it for administration and only ten percent for the avowed purpose. But, as is customary in the present atmosphere in the country, laws that were originally intended for the prevention of criminal activity could also be applied to democratic organzations concerned with civil rights for the political purpose of gathering names and addresses for the use of the FBI, and of putting the organizations out of business.

Thus the ACPFB found itself under simultaneous attack by the Attorney General of the United States for being a "communist front" (political) organization and by the Attorney General of New York State for being a "charitable organization." In Washington, the ACPFB was accused of taking money from the Communist Party while, in New York State, the Committee was charged with giving money to the Communist Party. To the non-legal mind this might either be confusing or humorous. They might even cancel each other out. But the jest was lost on government officials who were entirely willing to occupy contradictory positions in the hope that if one failed the other might succeed.

Compliance with the order to produce records would at the time have meant that the names of donors would be available to the State. Abner Green had served one prison sentence for refusing to give names. Furthermore, the Committee was a political rather than a charitable organization and therefore did not rightly come under the law. So the order was challenged by court proceedings and, for the next two years, the case continued with appeals, postponements and rulings from various courts. A non-technical but fair summary of these proceedings runs: "You do what you say you do, but even so you are a charitable organization"; through "If you do what you say you do, you are apparently not a charitable organization, but the truth of your statements needs to be proved"; to "You are three-fourths non-charitable and one-fourth charitable, but this makes you a charitable organization and you must so register under the law."

Hearings before an official referee, Denis O'Leary Cohalan,

were held at Foley Square on January 9, 10 and 14, 1957. Among the witnesses for the Committee were Father Kenneth Ripley Forbes, Prof. Louise Pettibone Smith, Mrs. Anna Taffler (a deportee) and Abner Green. Before the opinion was delivered, Mr. Cohalan died, and the record of the hearings were stipulated for consideration by Justice Steuer. On June 3, he upheld the Attorney General on the ground that providing legal defense to foreign-born Americans was "charitable." An appeal was filed and on June 28, a stay was granted until the appeal should be heard in September. Meantime, of course, Mr. Javits, Senator-elect, still with the label of "liberal" in spite of his action against the ACPFB, left Albany for Washington.

The attack against the ACPFB was promptly intensified by Louis Lefkowitz, who succeeded Mr. Javits as Attorney General of New York State. Four days after Justice Steuer's decision, Lefkowitz secured an *ex parte* injunction from the New York Supreme Court restraining the ACPFB from all activities, including both receiving and expending money. In applying for the injunction, the Attorney General accused the Committee not only with failure to register but with fraud in soliciting funds and with gaining sponsors by concealing the character of the organization. (There is a rather obvious relation here with the charges of the Attorney General of the United States.)

Such an injunction was clearly intended to end the existence of the ACPFB. It could hardly have come at a worse time. The Committee had recently been compelled to move to new quarters and the expenses entailed were not all paid. The copy for the usual "summer appeal" to carry the Committee through the vacation months, when regular meetings and contributions were few, was at the printer's. Weekly wages were owing to the Committee staff, and other administrative expenses had to be met. Preparations for an Annual Festival and Picnic were under way, numbers of tickets had already been sold and orders for more were arriving by telephone and in every mail; a deposit for the rental of buses was due. No hearing on the *ex parte* injunction could be held until three days before the Festival.

Labor unions through the years had experienced the tyranny of this kind of injunction, now came the turn of the ACPFB. The worst element of the situation was not the threat of jail for any officer of the Committee who might violate the injunction; but the certainty that any violation would be seized upon as ground for installing a receiver in the Committee's office.

But the Committee did not stop work. Creditors were understanding and willing to wait. Tickets to the picnic were given without payment. Individuals unconnected with the Committee took charge of parts of the Festival preparations. The *National Guardian* gave full and effective publicity to the Committee's predicament. At the hearing before Justice Conlon on June 20, a stipulation was signed, allowing the Committee to pay wages and other administrative expenses, and to hold the picnic as scheduled on the 23rd. The response was gratifying, over a thousand attended.

On June 27, the decision rendered by Justice Conlon declared that there was no evidence that the Committee had been guilty of fraud either in soliciting funds or in relation to its sponsors. No receiver was appointed. But since legal aid was "charitable," the Committee was enjoined from the public solicitation of funds, although it might disburse money and receive voluntary contributions. An enlightening description of the Committee's position appeared in the *Light of Liberty*, a mimeographed Bulletin put out by the independent Minnesota Committee for Protection of Foreign Born.

> A ray of hope began to gleam for thousands of our foreign born with several recent favorable decisions of the U.S. Supreme Court overruling some of the worst features of the Walter-McCarran Act. The way for the changes was blazed by the ACPFB which for a quarter of a century has carried on a vigorous campaign on behalf of the foreign born. . . .
>
> But our joy at these gains was dealt a severe blow by a legal lethal weapon known as *injunction*. Many labor unions engaging in peaceful picketing . . . can tell you of

> the stab in the back they have suffered from . . . temporary and permanent injunctions.
>
> On June 7 without giving the American Committee any notice, Louis Lefkowitz, the Attorney General of New York State, secured a temporary injunction prohibiting the American Committee and its executive secretary from carrying on any activity . . . "purchasing stamps, mimeograph paper, ink or meeting any bills or obligations. . . ."
>
> Attempts to stop the work of the American Committee especially during the period of McCarthyite hysteria following the passage of the McCarran-Walter Law have taken ingenious forms.

Abner Green characterized the action of the State's Attorney General as "completely unwarranted and undemocratic." He called attention to the

> . . . damning coincidence between [his] indecent haste and the fact that in recent weeks the American Committee has scored important victories in United States Supreme Court decisions in defending the right of foreign-born Americans. The American Committee has opposed vigorously and successfully the excesses and violations of law engaged in by United States Attorney General Brownell. Mr. Lefkowitz in his efforts to destroy the American Committee is apparently cooperating with his Washington superiors in the Republican party rather than protecting or serving the interests of the people of New York State.

Later the injunction was modified to allow the Committee to solicit funds for the office expenses and for its own defense; but when the Appellate Court refused to hear the Committee's appeal, the injunction again prohibited all solicitation of funds. The Committee therefore, was wholly dependent in the latter part of 1957 on unsolicited contributions. The number and the amount of such contributions gave eloquent testimony to the regard in which the work of the ACPFB was held. Money came from people who had not before contributed but who recognized the injustice of the injunction technique. The Committee continued to issue regularly both its "legal" and "defense" bulletins. The 25th Anniversary Conference was held in Chicago on December 7 and 8, 1957, as scheduled, although a Souvenir Journal and certain other concommitants which might be interpreted as solicitation of funds had to be omitted.

The charge made by Attorney General Lefkowitz that the many eminent men and women on the sponsor list of the ACPFB did not know what they were sponsoring brought many indignant letters to both the Attorney General and to the executive secretary of the Committee. The Sponsors gave unanimous and convincing testimony that they were kept fully informed of the purpose and the work of the ACPFB. Since the question of the possibility of registration was raised in some of the letters to Abner Green, he prepared a statement to all sponsors clarifying the position taken by the Committee. It read in part:

> 1. The law does not apply. The legal assistance furnished is different from that furnished by a legal aid society. It is provided as a part of our overall purpose of testing discriminatory and unfair laws. The validity or constitutionality of a law can be tested only through test cases. Our "legal aid" is not provided for its own sake nor as a "charity."
>
> One of the main legal questions at stake . . . is unwarranted government interference in or supervision over an organization which threatens the right of privacy of association guaranteed by the First Amendment to the Constitution. If our legal assistance subjects us to registration, similar attacks on organizations such as the NAACP will undoubtedly follow.
>
> 2. There remains the question whether we can in all good conscience register under the law. If we registered . . . the State Attorney General would have free access to all books and records of the organization. Our books and records are in order. They are audited annually and a public report made. But the Attorney General's examination would provide the State with the names and addresses of

> contributors and possibly with other confidential information about individuals.
>
> When the N.Y. State Banking Department in 1951 obtained the names of people who had loaned money to the CRC Bail Fund, names were turned over to the Justice Department. Similarly, the N.Y. State Insurance Department turned over to the Justice Department the membership lists of the International Workers Order and hundreds of non-citizens were hounded both in their homes and in their places of employment by officers of the Immigration Service. From 80 to 85 percent of the contributors to the ACPFB would be immune to harassment; but that does not justify the Committee for reporting their names. Still less can it risk the activity of the Justice Department in dealing with any non-citizens whose names might be found on the list.

That explanation is unfortunately less needed now since the NAACP and even the ACLU are meeting the same difficulty in various states of the Union. The American right of free association becomes a mockery if names can be demanded from any organization which is locally or temporarily unpopular. Much more than the continued existence of any one organization is at stake. Also, the battle of the ACPFB is now, as it always has been, a part of the battle for the Bill of Rights.

The threats to the existence of the Committee inherent in the Walter hearings, the attacks of United States Attorney General Brownell and of New York State Attorney General Javits (later Lefkowitz) were recognized by Abner Green in his annual report to the Los Angeles Conference, but there was no suggestion of slackening the work. His report closed:

> I feel that we will succeed in withstanding Brownell and Javits and Walter in their desire to destroy the American Committee. It is the people who will decide what organizations shall exist and function. . . . No attorney general is going to put us out of business. . . . We will put ourselves out of business—when we have succeeded in

> ending discrimination against foreign-born Americans. . . .
>
> There can be no doubt that in working for the objectives we have set ourselves there will be many problems and there will be many difficulties. . . . There will be those who will seek to prevent us from engaging in what we regard as the legitimate exercise of our rights and duties as Americans. But they will no more succeed in their attacks upon us than when the Alien and Sedition Laws of 1798 were used to try to silence the Jeffersonian forerunners of the program we espouse today.
>
> . . . We seek no personal gain. We seek only to preserve our rights and the liberties of the people of this great country.
>
> Let us not allow the Un-Americans and the witch hunters to divert us for one instant. Let us proceed to give adequate and needed consideration to the many serious problems facing us so that . . . the ACPFB will be armed with the kind of program and perspective it must have to proceed with its work, to further the democratic rights of the foreign born and contribute thereby to the fullest development of American liberties and American freedom, to advance the welfare of the American people and to enhance our democratic institutions.

However, no organization can exist indefinitely on the basis of "voluntary unsolicited contributions." The Committee found it necessary to make a most serious decision. Were there still vital issues to be fought through in defense of the rights of the foreign born? And, if so, which was more vital at the moment, the direct defense of foreign born in the courts, or the general defense in the areas of legislation and public opinion? The Committee decided that, for the time being, the paramount struggles which had to be conducted with the greatest vigor were in the general field of the rights of the foreign born. It was convinced that people, if there was sufficient publicity, would find ways and means apart from the Committee to support individual cases. Accordingly, the Committee took steps to arrange for a *modus vivendi.*

In refusing to hear the appeal of the ACPFB on January 10, 1958, the New York State Court of Appeals had declared that the injunction against the Committee was a temporary order and that only a *final* order from the State Supreme Court could be appealed. The Committee could not wait for a *final* order from the State Supreme Court; rent, taxes, postage, not to mention salaries, required money. The possibility of continuing any work at all was in jeopardy. The Committee therefore decided to discontinue in the future the raising of funds to pay attorneys in deportation and denaturalization cases. Thus the Attorney General of New York State required of the ACPFB action directly opposed to that once advised by the United States Attorney General, Howard McGrath. The Attorney General's office agreed to discontinue all proceedings if the Committee did not oppose the entering of a permanent injunction against this one phase of Committee activity.

At the same time the Attorney General's office warned that if the Committee did not register as a charitable organization, the State Welfare Department would insist on renewing court action against it as soon as it issued any public appeal for funds. The Department held that any organization working in the public interest or general welfare (what an admission about the role of the ACPFB!) was charitable and had to register. On March 11, the Committee registered as a charitable organization under protest and with the stipulation that it would continue its practice of entering in its receipt books only the amount of the contribution and the purpose for which it was given, with no names and addresses included. These books of the Committee would continue to be audited annually by a certified public accountant, and the report made public each year. Under no circumstances would the ACPFB submit the names of any of the organization's contributors to the State Welfare Department or to any other State agency.

And there for the time being, the matter rests. The Committee still could continue its most valuable work. And the American people still could redeem their democratic traditions.

VIII. ...AMERICANS ALL

28. The Atmosphere Improves

In the last five years there has been increasing defense of the American democratic tradition. The essential value of the rights guaranteed in the first ten Amendments to the Constitution, especially in the First and Fifth, has been forcibly and eloquently asserted by such men as Dean Griswold of the Harvard Law School and by other leaders of public opinion. McCarthy has been officially discredited.

But it cannot be said that the United States has wholly recovered its democratic articulateness. The blight of conformity still affects us. Political apathy has yet to be shaken off. Ideological confusion still has not cleared. The ability to differentiate fact from fiction, news from editorials, life from wishful thinking and honesty from hypocrisy has not yet been fully recovered. As a result, there is an exasperating continuation of retrogressive action in spite of the general progressive movement.

But there is truth in the statement of Bruce Catton in his article, "Where the American Tradition Lives," published in the July 6, 1957, issue of *The Saturday Review*. In discussing recent encroachments on civil liberties and democratic rights in the United States, he stated in part:

> We have seen all of this, and we can still see too much of it if we look around carefully. Yet the crest of the wave is passing. It is passing because the American people are responding once more to that deepest and most profound

> of all their instincts—the instinct to defend the tradition of freedom when it comes under attack. It is passing because the courts of America have stood firmly in defense of individual liberties. It is passing because many groups and individuals have stood up for the rights of their fellow Americans. . . .
>
> The secret of the American tradition is freedom—freedom unabridged and unadulterated, freedom that applies to everybody in the land at all times and places, freedom for those with whom we disagree as well as for those with whom we do agree.

It is regrettable that not all courts merit the positive judgment of Mr. Catton. But court decisions have made outstanding contributions to the changing atmosphere of the country and have implemented the growing revulsion of the American people against undemocratic pressures. However, the extent to which reaction still prevails is manifested when, after the courts have spoken their independent judgment, Senators Jenner, Butler and others like them attempt by legislative means to curb the courts, to intimidate them and to make them dependent on Congress rather than allow them to remain an independent part of the government.

Recent important court decisions covered many areas of the civil liberties field; but it is necessary to concentrate here on the important decisions which concern the foreign born. (It is of course obvious that civil liberties decisions interact, set precedents, clarify policies and establish legalities that inevitably go beyond the specific case or issue involved.)

The change in the courts is noted by the ACPFB in an article in *The Lamp* of May-July, 1957, in which it commented on the decisions in the Witkovich and Sentner cases:

> In its decisions . . . the United States Supreme Court in 1957 differed sharply with the 1952 decisions . . . in the Carlson and Harisiades cases, insofar as the democratic rights of non-citizens in the United States are concerned.
>
> The intervening five years have seen important changes

> in the public atmosphere and a lessening of international tensions. The decreased tension and the gradual elimination of hysteria have helped to re-establish public understanding and sanity, a reawakened awareness of basic democratic truths. . . .
>
> The decisions . . . are welcome reaffirmation of our democratic understanding. The democratic goal, unfortunately, is far from achieved. Deportations and denaturalizations continue as a part of what Mr. Catton calls "the latest of these spasms of fear."
>
> The Supreme Court, too, demonstrates still to some extent the fruits of hysteria which followed the close of the Second World War. It must be recorded that in deportation—as distinct from the supervisory parole cases of Witkovich and Sentner—the Supreme Court has not yet announced any changes in its attitude or policy. In a series of decisions in deportation cases this past year, the Supreme Court has continued to ignore the rights and welfare of non-citizens in the United States. . . .
>
> This next term of the Sureme Court may indeed be an historic session in helping to overcome the undemocratic manner in which the rights of foreign-born Americans are treated under the Walter-McCarran Law.

The ACPFB proved to be a good prophet. The first decisive decision on deportation of the Supreme Court was handed down on December 9, 1957.

It seems poetic justice that this decision came in the case of Charles Rowoldt. Rowoldt was fifty-three when he was arrested for deportation on February 5, 1936, after living twenty-two years in this country. He was seventy-four years of age when the decision in his case was finally rendered in December 1957. (The fight was carried on primarily by the Minnesota Committee for Protection of Foreign Born under the inspiring leadership of Alma Foley.) It is gratifying that in his case justice and common sense prevailed. But the final triumph of justice does not cancel the misery inflicted on non-citizens and their families who have to live under the threat of deportation as

Charles Rowoldt did for *twenty-two years.* What did Rowoldt do to merit such punishment? Was there an accidental error in the carrying out of justice, as sometimes occurs, or was there deliberate persecution? What manner of man is this Rowoldt? There is nothing about him that is not typical of a majority of immigrants, and of a great number of the deportees. We have his story in his own words, as it was distributed by the Minnesota Committee for Protection of Foreign Born when the case was appealed to the Federal Circuit Court. It gives a most graphic picture of the impact of our immigration policy on foreign-born Americans.

* * * * *

I was born in now Eastern Germany in 1883 and am now 72 years old. In the year 1914 I came to the U.S. a few months before the outbreak of the first world war. Jenny, my wife, came a few months later.

In New York I went immediately to the evening schools, because I didn't dare ask for work on account of not being able to talk the language. I heard the teacher tell us that in America they have a Constitution like no other country in the world and that this Constitution is considered the highest law of the land. All the courts have to make their judgments according to the Constitution and its amendments. The teacher also told us that Congress is not allowed to make certain laws interfering with the natural rights of man, like *ex post facto*, second jeopardy, restraining laws, etc.

After a few months' school I started working. The first job was in an apple orchard. When Jenny arrived in America from Germany in June we left this farm and went to Chicago. I started working in a margarine factory, but this job didn't last long because one day I came to work and the place had burned down.

Jobs were hard to get. I gave up a job at Wrigley's because Wm. Wrigley, Jr. had made a remark to someone in the office that he was going to throw every Hungarian, Turk and German out of the building. Being a German, I thought I would be fired, so I quit.

So I went across Lake Michigan and landed in some farm out in the wilderness. I pulled and topped twenty acres of beets and after that I hauled them down to the nearest factory. From there I went to Fort Huron, Michigan, and landed a railroad job pulling clinkers out of the incoming engines. Now this job was very interesting because it was the first time I worked on a railroad. Nobody stayed after the first pay day. One day the boss came to me and told me to run the engine.

"I don't know how to run it," I said.

"Sure, you can do anything," he told me. "This is the throttle and this is the brake. Now run it over to the turntable."

So I did, and after that I ran it back and forth in the yards. This job lasted until the fall of 1918.

My son Walter was born in Chicago in 1915. I was offered a job as a butler. Jenny said to take it. She and Walter lived in a room. I worked one winter for Mrs. Green as her butler, and liked it fine too, but in the spring I had to leave because Jenny was sick and I wanted to take care of her and Walter. She had been sick for a long time, but she wasn't one to complain. She was sick for a year and a half before she passed away—on Armistice Day in 1918. She was 28 years old when she died.

After Jenny died I had always to find a homelike place for Walter. I worked on a farm in North Dakota for 7 years from seeding to harvest. Lucy, the farmer's wife, was like a mother to Walter. I lost my boy Walter in 1928. He had a ruptured appendix and died in my arms before the doctor could get there.

In all this I forgot to take out my citizenship papers.

In 1933 I was working in a restaurant in Minneapolis when suddenly the boss told me, "Charlie, I can't pay you anymore."

"Why can't you pay me?"

"Business is no good, Charlie, but I want to keep you all."

I stayed a little longer, and for the third time he told me,

"I can't pay you." Every time he cut my wages. I looked around for another job. So when I lost this job and tried to find another one I found all the jobs closed up. I tried selling, but that was dead too. I looked until I was out of money.

What was now the *logical* thing to do? To commit suicide? Not to my way of thinking. To look around and find how one can get food, clothing and shelter. I asked another hungry looking fellow on Washington Avenue how to get something to eat. He answered, "Go to the Communists. They will help you."

"I never heard of them. Who are they?"

"They are at 212 Hennepin Avenue."

So I went there. I asked them, "Can you help me? Are you the Communists?"

"No," they said. "We are the Unemployed Council."

So they sent a committee along with me to the Court House, and they got me something to eat, some relief work and a place to stay. So it went on, and I got well acquainted with this organization.

So one day they had an election of officers and they elected me Secretary-Treasurer. Now this organization became nationwide and later on united with another unemployed organization in Chicago, and the national organization of these two groups was named Workers Alliance.

Now the national organization as such started demanding security against future depressions, and Congress was forever bombarded with resolutions for laws like our present day Social Security and Unemployment Compensation. Of course I did all I could. I wrote many resolutions to our Congressmen because I thought it was necessary to safeguard the American working people.

We pulled as good as possible through the depression of the thirties. Triumphantly we came out of it with Social Security and Unemployment Compensation. The Workers Alliance was taken into the CIO as an unemployed local, and later when almost everyone could find jobs again, it was disbanded. I went to work in the Dykman Hotel, and have been working ever since. I joined Local 665 of the Hotel Workers, where I stayed a member for as long as I was working in hotels.

For all the good work I did helping the unemployed I was thrown in jail in 1936 because the immigration claimed I was an alien who believed in the overthrow of the government by force and violence. Mr. Arthur LeSueur was picked as a lawyer for me by friends of mine and in the beginning of 1936 I was taken to the Federal Court House for trial. At this trial I got the greatest surprise of my life. Friends of mine, who I had known alright for years but never thought much more of than as a friend will think of friends, turned out to be so beautiful, tears come to my eyes that I even cannot describe the beauty they displayed in speaking for me and about me to the presiding inspector, prosecutor and judge, all in one person. So at this hearing I was sentenced to be deported.

Of course, Mr. LeSueur appealed this sentence, and a few years later my case was dropped.

So, my deportation case dismissed, Adams from the immigration called me and two witnesses in 1945, shortly before Roosevelt's death, in order to get my citizenship papers. I paid a few more dollars for it and was told in a few days I would get the papers.

But as soon as Roosevelt passed away I was never asked again to get my papers. Contrary, in 1948, the immigration started arresting me again [on the basis of statements he had volunteered to the Immigration and Naturalization Service in 1947].

I was able to keep myself out of jail this time because I went with officers to the St. Paul immigration office and told them I was unable to go to jail because I had to go to work. One of the officers let me go on my own word of honor. Of course I had to report to the immigration office every so often.

Later I was working in a hotel when I was arrested again to be immediately deported. One of the officers took me out of jail that morning to take me downtown to change my money into German money, pack my suitcases and see my lawyer. I was told that the next morning I would be shipped to Ellis Island and then to Germany. My lawyer got a *habeas corpus* which stopped this deportation. A hearing was called a few days later again in federal court. Judge Joyce claimed according to the law he could not dismiss my case and returned me to the Immigration, saying he was sorry because he knew I was a better citizen without papers than many walking the streets with papers.

Now my lawyer appealed this decision, and before it was decided the Supreme Court ruled in another case that the hearings were illegal because the Immigration didn't go by the rules of the Administrative Procedure Act. Then all the hearings that had been held were thrown out, and mine was thrown out too.

Meanwhile the McCarran Law came into power stating that anyone who ever has been a member of the Communist Party and isn't a citizen must be deported. Other things are in the law too, such as: after the highest deportation order a deportee has to try to deport himself in 6 months. If he doesn't he can be sent to jail for 10 years. If the Attorney General or the deportee can't find a place to go in 6 months he has to be under supervisory parole.

In 1951 they started holding hearings under the McCarran Law.

Suddenly I was arrested again late one night. This was on March 28, 1952. They wanted $4,000 bail before they would let me go. This time I was in jail for almost three weeks, but nevertheless in jail I could feel the working of friends on the outside. One morning one of the people in jail came running with the morning paper. "Charlie, Charlie, they held a great meeting for you in Minneapolis. They collected $4,000. Now you must have many friends?" they would ask me. "I have no $4,000, so I must have many friends," I replied.

I was soon out on bail. After a few days the Immigration

sent me another letter stating my appeal to the highest Immigration Board had been turned down, and I must try to find a place to be deported to or I might spend 10 years in jail.

So it went along. I tried to deport myself, because by law I had to, writing and talking to representatives of different countries. But I did not get any travel papers for myself, and neither did the Immigration get any for me. So after six months they said I would have to be under supervisory parole. I had to report to the immigration office twice a month in person and once a month in writing.

I had one great victory. When the Immigration tried to put me on supervisory parole and still keep the $4,000 bond money my lawyer [Kenneth Enkel] went to work and asked the court to test the right of the Immigration Department to keep me on parole and bail at the same time. Judge Joyce ruled that the Immigration Department should release the bail. Of course the Immigration Department appealed this judgment to the Circuit Court, but they agreed with Judge Joyce's decision, and the bail money was returned. [This was the first victory on the return of bail won in December 1954 and June 1955. See page 332.]

For over two years it went along this way. I worked in a store, and later painting, and in a filling station. Now I am getting old and like to sleep a little late in the morning, but one morning at 7 o'clock Stoltz from the Immigration came to my room. "Hurry up, Charlie, pack your things. Tomorrow you are going to Germany." [This was on March 22, 1955. There had been no warning, Rowoldt had only $2 in his pocket.]

I didn't know what to do. There were my tools laying all around the room. Even my clothes weren't washed. "Hurry up, are you going to take this?" And he started throwing clothes into my suitcase, clean clothes and dirty clothes all together.

"Well, I have to shave," I started going downstairs because there is no water in my room.

"Don't call anyone," he said.

"Well, I have to call my lawyer."

"You can do that later."

He took me to the Immigration office in St. Paul and from there I telephoned Alma Foley from the Minnesota Committee for Protection of Foreign Born, and she got my attorney, Kenneth Enkel, to get a *habeas corpus* petition (which was granted).

I applied to the Board of Immigration Appeals to reopen my case and let me apply for suspension of the deportation order. But they refused. Judge Nordbye denied the petition for a writ. Now I am appealing his decision to the Circuit Court in St. Louis.

Every real American who is honest and understands American democracy must agree with me that it is a great injustice and an anti-constitution deed to reach with second jeopardy, *ex post facto* and containment laws into the way past to pull honest to goodness people who are by now well up in age to the front for arrest and prosecution.

I ask your help in whatever way you can help.

* * * * *

This is the story of Charles Rowoldt. But there were two more years of tense waiting. In August, 1955, the Court of Appeals in St. Louis granted a stay of deportation while the appeal was pending. When the court made an adverse ruling, it was appealed to the Supreme Court which on March 26, 1956, granted *certiorari*. In announcing that the case would be argued before the Supreme Court, the Minnesota Committee stated:

> We will try to persuade the Court to take a new look at the entire matter of deportation. We will ask the Court to decide whether our nation, built by immigrant labor, has the right to banish a man who has spent more than half his lifetime working here.

At the 1955 Annual Conference of the ACPFB, the legal

panel had discussed at length what measures might be taken to persuade the Supreme Court to consider again the whole question of political deportations, and the necessity for such an effort was presented to the Conference as a whole. The atmosphere had altered since the days of Senator McCarthy, and the attitude of the Supreme Court had changed since the Harisiades decision. Although the Galvan decision still upheld the right of Congress to ignore the Bill of Rights when legislating in regard to non-citizens, the 4 to 4 vote in the cases of David Hyun and Cecil Jay implied the beginning of a recognition of the inconsistency involved. When the Court accepted the Rowoldt case, it had its opportunity.

The ACPFB accordingly prepared for a national campaign centering on the Rowoldt case. The National Lawyers Guild agreed to offer an *amicus* brief. The Committee also undertook the preparation of an appendix to the regular brief which would present evidence covering political deportations as a whole, all defense committees cooperating in gathering the material. (This appendix was prepared under the supervision of Ann Fagan Ginger.) Attorneys Joseph Forer and David Rein of Washington, D. C., prepared the brief and argued the case.

On December 9, 1957, the 5 to 4 decision was delivered by Justice Frankfurter, ordering the deportation proceedings cancelled. It was based, according to the usual Supreme Court procedure, not on broad constitutional grounds but on the specific meaning of Communist Party membership in the McCarran Act of 1950 and its amendments. Justice Frankfurter, in his opinion, stated in part:

> Bearing in mind the solidity of proof that is required for a judgment entailing the consequences of deportation, particularly in the case of an old man who has lived in this country for forty years . . . we cannot say that the unchallenged account given by petitioner of his relations to the Communist Party establishes the kind of meaningful association required. . . .

This was a victory of first-rate importance. But the victory celebration planned by the Minnesota Committee had to be postponed until April because Charles Rowoldt was seriously ill in the hospital.

Charles Rowoldt, who "made friends wherever he went, for (he) gave richly of himself; (who) is a man so gentle that it bothers his conscience to have to kill a pocket gopher that steals his potatoes; (who) spends long hours helping a little boy to learn to read," can remain to live out his days in the country he chose as his own. Hundreds of other foreign born can feel safer because of the fight he and his attorneys put up. But with the information needed for the Appendix to the Rowoldt case, from a group of deported Americans in Europe came a letter with the question "If this case is won, will it mean that we can come home?" On the basis of the Rowoldt decision, these exiles were presumably not legally deportable. But the Justice Department makes no provision for correcting such mistakes.

Charles Rowoldt is the first non-citizen in our history to have his deportation cancelled by the Supreme Court when the charge was membership in the Communist Party. In the past, mere membership in the Communist Party—no matter how innocent or even mistaken—was sufficient ground for the deportation of a non-citizen. The effect of this decision was to be observed immediately in the case of another deportee, Leon Callow, who was arrested for the first time in 1934 at the age of forty and had been fighting deportation for *twenty-four* years.

Leon Callow of Niles, Ohio, a Macedonian who came to this country in 1915, was first arrested for deportation to Bulgaria in November, 1934, an action arising out of his activity as a leader of the Trumbull Unemployed Workers' Union, Trumbull County, Ohio—an area dominated by Republic Steel. He was charged with endeavoring to overthrow the government by force and violence. He is the father of nine children, with one daughter now married and his oldest son serving in the U. S. armed forces. During the years since 1934, his deportation proceedings were constantly being renewed, with the place of deportation shifted from Bulgaria to Greece, and the charge altered to membership in the Communist Party, as the situation changed here and in Europe. The facts are stated much more clearly in the Memorandum Opinion by District Court Judge Jones of Cleveland, of December 16:

> This case long has been delayed because of hearing and rehearing by the Supreme Court of the United States in the case of *Rowoldt v. Perfetto,* which on the facts and the law is analogous to this case. This court has withheld considering and formulating an opinion in this case because of the pendency in the Supreme Court of the Rowoldt case. On December 9, 1957, by a vote of five to four, the Supreme Court decided the Rowoldt case adversely to the Immigration Service in reversing the decision below and, in effect, overriding the order of deportation. . . .
>
> A Macedonian by birth in 1895, the plaintiff lawfully entered the United States in June, 1915, for permanent residence and since that date has resided continuously in the United States. Commencing in June, 1930, he was arrested several times upon rather obscure charges with no definite resulting legal action. On some one or more of these occasions he voluntarily disclosed that he had been a member of the Communist Party from 1927 to 1931. In May, 1935, he was given a hearing by an Immigration Inspector under a warrant of arrest charging him with believing in, advocating and teaching the overthrow by force and violence of the Government of the United States. His response was a denial that he believed in any form of force or violence and had no idea of overthrowing the Government; that since his expulsion from Party membership in 1931, he had tried to meet all the requirements of good American Citizenship. Proceedings have been pending since the initial hearing in May, 1935; deportation action was commenced in 1948 and deportation ordered January 21, 1952. The present action for injunction and declaratory judgment was filed in May, 1955.

The plaintiff is 62 years of age; has been in this country continuously for 42 years; he and his American citizen

> wife are the parents of nine American citizen children ranging from twenty-four to eight years of age. He was an unemployed organizer in New York State, a Trade Union Organizer in the State of Pennsylvania and a Party Organizer in the City of Toledo, Ohio, over the period of January or February 1930 to May of 1931. This latter was the extent of his activities and for the past twenty-six years he has not been identified with the Communist Party.
>
> Reviewing and considering the facts in this case and applying the legal interpretation and conclusion reached by the Supreme Court on the facts in the Rowoldt case, supra, I find no obstacle to as favorable a finding as there made, to the facts and circumstances in the case here. My conclusion is that the order of deportation should be reversed and permanent injunction and judgment for the plaintiff entered as prayed.

The next vital decision of the Supreme Court came on January 6, 1958, in the case of Knut Heikkinen. This case had lasted *only* eight years; but it provided an incontrovertible example of the kind of persecution made possible by the present laws.

In the deportation drive of November-December 1949, Knut Heikkinen, editorial worker for the Finnish-American daily, *Tyomies-Eteenpain,* was among those arrested. Bail, originally set at $10,000, was "voluntarily" reduced by the Justice Department to $5,000 after the ACPFB had appealed to the Federal court. On January 6, 1950, the Finnish-American Freedom Committee held a testimonial dinner to honor Heikkinen on his sixtieth birthday. His picture appeared with those of four other editors of foreign language newspapers in a leaflet, "Attack on the Freedom of the Press," published in 1950 by a Freedom of the Press Committee Against Deportations. And on May 24 of the same year, twenty-three editors of foreign language newspapers issued a joint public statement, declaring, "A new danger to the freedom of the press has arisen in the arrest for deportation because of their political opinions of several editors who have for years been connected with the foreign language press in the United States."

But it was not the issue of freedom of the press which brought Knut Heikkinen's case to the Supreme Court. Heikkinen was rearrested in Superior, Wisconsin, on October 23, 1950, and held in a county jail in Duluth without bail for almost three months. The Federal District Court dismissed an appeal for *habeas corpus* (still the only recourse), but the Court of Appeals in St. Paul agreed to hear the case on May 4, 1951, and granted bail of $2,500. The appeal was lost in April, 1952, and Heikkinen was ordered deported to Finland on the charge of past membership in the Communist Party. He was told both orally and in writing that arrangements for his deportation would be made and that he was to hold himself in readiness. At the request of the Immigration and Naturalization Service, he supplied the data they needed to enable the Service to deport him to Finland.

In February, 1953, he was again interviewed and asked what steps *he* had taken to get the necessary papers. As a matter of fact, because of the continuous harassment, Heikkinen was ready to leave the country voluntarily. But his Canadian citizenship was revoked in 1953, making valueless his passport to Canada to which he wanted to return. Until it was revoked, he could not be admitted to Finland. This complication had delayed the papers. Now negotiations were resumed with the Finnish government, and finally he was given papers permitting him to enter his country of origin, which were good until June 3, 1954. The immigration authorities were informed of these efforts and of the progress being made.

But on October 12, 1953, Heikkinen was suddenly arrested again, charged with wilfully failing to apply for travel documents and to deport himself. The penalty was ten years in prison! Bail was set at $10,000, and when he could not raise it, he was locked up in jail in Duluth. After a trip to the District Court and the Court of Appeals, during which the government argued against a reduction of bail because "he would leave the country" (which was supposedly what the government wanted!) he was released on a reduced bail of $3,000. This is how the situation could be summed up. The government said it wanted to deport Heikkinen. Heikkinen wanted to leave. The government of Finland had given him permission to return. But the Justice Department would not let him go. This was not so much absurdity as persecution. For Brownell wanted to send Heikkinen to prison first for ten years—and then deport him!

On April 12, 1954, Heikkinen found himself in the Federal court on two counts, failing to depart from the country and failing to apply for travel documents. Each carried a five year prison term. In imposing the full sentence, the judge ignored that section of the law which allows suspension of the sentence for various reasons, all of them applicable in this case. Officials of the Justice Department gave the reason, stating openly that their purpose in demanding the full penalty was the effect it would have on hastening the departure of others. The Justice Department needed an "example."

After the Court of Appeals in 1955 found a technical error and returned the case to be retried, the sentence was reaffirmed in the District Court and then was sustained in the Court of Appeals. It was this sentence which finally reached the Supreme Court in 1956. In the decision of January, 1958, the Supreme Court reversed the lower courts, avoiding as usual the constitutional question and basing its judgment on the insufficient evidence offered by the government. The Court found that Heikkinen should not have been indicted or convicted. Heikkinen had been arrested three times and served time in jail twice, had had to go through two trials costing aggravation and money, had been deprived of the right to travel and forced to stay in Superior, Wisconsin, because of the attitude taken by the U.S. Attorney and the Federal District Court. And all this time Heikkinen had been innocent of any wrong-doing!

From the first he had maintained his innocence on the very ground on which the Supreme Court had *unanimously* ordered him freed. Justice Whittaker, in his opinion for the Court, stated that on the first count (willful failure to depart) there was no evidence that, during the six months following the final order of deportation, "any country was willing, in that period to receive petitioner. There can be no willful failure to depart until the country willing to receive the alien is identified." On the second count (willful failure to make timely application for travel documents) Justice Whittaker pointed out that the Service wrote to Heikkinen: "Arrangements to effect your deportation . . . are being made and when completed you will be notified when and where to present yourself for deportation." An immigration inspector secured from Heikkinen all the information for a Passport Data Form. Said Justice Whittaker:

> There can be no willful failure by a deportee . . . in the absence of evidence, or an inference permissible under the statute, of a "bad purpose" of "(non-) justifiable excuse," or the like. . . . In this factual setting, we believe there was not sufficient evidence to support the jury's finding that petitioner acted *willfully* in failing to apply for documents necessary to his departure within the time prescribed.

But the U.S. attorney, the judge and two juries found him guilty of a crime warranting his imprisonment for five years, despite the fact that the record so obviously proved his innocence. The two juries, of course, were guided by the judge who sat in both trials, and, in the main, the error was the judge's as were the harassment and persecution in keeping Heikkinen a virtual prisoner in Superior for more than four years. Some courts certainly do not deserve the praise expressed by Bruce Catton for the courts in general. But the Supreme Court decision, although it leaves the wording of the law unchanged, does far more than exempt Heikkinen from the prison sentence. It proclaims again that the right of due process has meaning in the United States for the non-citizen. It may well prevent similar attempts to use the police-state provision of the Walter-McCarran Law in order to railroad non-citizens to jail.

On June 2, 1958, the Supreme Court rendered another key decision in a case dealing with deportation. Frank Bonetti came to this country from Italy in 1923. Between 1932 and 1936, he was a minor official in the Communist Party. In 1937 Bonetti went to fight in Spain as a member of the Abraham Lincoln Brigade. Returning in 1938, he was legally admitted for permanent residence as a quota immigrant. In 1939 he made a brief trip to Mexico. In 1952 deportation proceedings were begun against him by the Immigration Service under the Internal Security Act because he had been a member of the Communist Party after he first entered the United States.

The questions presented to the Court by Bonetti through his attorneys, Forer and Rein, were the following:

> 1. Whether the statutory provision for deportation of aliens who become members of the Communist Party after "entering" the United States applies to the petitioner, who entered the country for the first time in 1923, was a member of the Communist Party from 1932 to 1936, left the country in 1937 giving up residence and all rights to return, and entered the country again as a new immigrant in 1938, at which time after a hearing in which he acknowledged his past membership in the Communist Party, he was adjudicated admissible and admitted for permanent residence and has not since been a member of the Party.
>
> 2. Whether deportation under the above circumstances and on a record which used against the petitioner the testimony he gave at the hearing at which he was adjudicated admissible, violates due process of law.
>
> 3. Whether the statute providing for the deportation of aliens for past membership in the Communist Party is unconstitutional on its face or as applied to the facts in this case.

The Justice Department insisted that membership in the Communist Party after any entry was ground for deportation, and this contention had been upheld by the lower courts.

The Supreme Court, in a six to three decision, thought that the specific entry did have relevance and barred the deportation order. Justice Whittaker, in delivering the opinion for the majority, held that, in going to Spain in 1937, Bonetti had abandoned all his rights to residence in the United States and that his legal re-entry as a permanent resident in 1938, after a hearing, should be considered as the time from which membership in the Communist Party might be a basis for deportation. Again the Supreme Court bypassed the constitutional question, and relied upon a technical question. But that the ruling was of decisive importance was recognized by Justice Clark, who declared in his dissent that the ruling crippled the effectiveness of the Internal Security Act of 1950 (which should disturb no one but the Tom Clarks).

In the field of denaturalization, the Supreme Court decisions in the cases of Stanley Nowak and Rebecca Maisenberg, handed down on May 26, 1958, were no less decisive. Stanley Nowak was born in Poland in 1903 and came to the United States in 1913. He became extremely active in the labor movement and, in the 1930's, was active in the organization of a number of unions into the newly formed CIO. He became so well-known for his advocacy of the rights of labor and of social justice that, five months after he acquired United States citizenship, he was elected in November, 1938, for his first term in the Michigan State Senate, to which he was returned for an additional four terms, serving a total of ten years and acting as minority leader for two of those years.

On December 11, 1942, after having just been elected for his third term by a majority of nearly 14,000 votes, Nowak was charged with having sworn falsely in his naturalization proceeding in 1937 that he was not opposed to organized government and that he was not a member of any organization "teaching disbelief" in organized government. One hour after the grand jury indictment was returned, Nowak was arrested by FBI agents and held incommunicado over-night. The reasons for attempting "to get" Nowak in Detroit, scene of Black Legion violence, labor massacres and Coughlin rabble-rousing, were quite obvious. A United Press dispatch in the *Detroit News* of December 13, 1942, reported:

> Nowak's record in the legislature has been solidly New Deal. He has backed pro-labor legislation and bitterly fought conservative and reactionary acts. . . .

In April, 1943, after the excitement was over, James C. Hasewell wrote an article for the Detroit *Free Press,* whose Lansing correspondent he was, entitled "An Objective Appraisal of Labor's Senator," in which he said:

> His is the unwelcome voice of the consumer, the employee, the welfare client, the pedestrian. His counsel is the counsel of the Little Man, the fellow about whom all the laws—in the last analysis—are made. . . .
>
> . . . Nowak never has preached revolution or anything approaching revolution in the state senate. He never expressed dissent with the principles of American government. He has preached a gospel of giving the victim a better break.
>
> He has argued for more liberal compensation for injured workmen, larger benefits for the unemployed, more adequate pensions for the aged . . . regulation of working conditions for children and women, and he has argued against using welfare to drive wages down.
>
> . . . He is a labor organizer, he is foreign-born, he's a Democrat, he comes from the big city's working class, he's not a business man, nor a property spokesman.

In fact, the attack on Nowak was so obvious, so raw, that Clarence Reid, then Republican State Senator, later Michigan's Lieutenant Governor, declared:

> You can gauge a man by his actions and deeds. Nowak by his attitude, honesty and sincerity in behalf of the war effort does not deserve . . . such an indictment.

Support for Nowak came from a tremendous number of people, of various political opinions, of many different walks of life. A violent campaign, spearheaded by Gerald L. K. Smith to prevent the seating of Nowak in the State Senate in 1942, was decisively rejected even by the most conservative State Senators. The Justice Department ordered John C. Lehr, U. S. Attorney in Michigan, to dismiss the indictment. Lehr refused to do so, and U.S. Attorney General Francis Biddle was forced to fly a special representative, Henry A. Schweinhaut, to Detroit to quash the proceedings personally. Attorney General Biddle took the unprecedented step of issuing a personal statement saying:

> In this particular case, the Attorney General feels the facts are not such as to warrant a criminal prosecution, and he takes entire responsibility for the error in judgment in seeking a criminal indictment.

Mr. Schweinhaut told the press that not only was this criminal action completely ended, but that no other action, such as a civil suit, was contemplated.

But, ten years later, on December 23, 1952, Christmas Eve, the same Christmas Eve on which the Walter-McCarran Law went into effect, denaturalization proceedings were initiated against Nowak, despite the categorical statement of Attorney General Biddle. Interestingly enough, in an interview with the press on January 4, 1953, Lehr, the recalcitrant U.S. Attorney, then the president of a fraternal insurance company, declared, "I am glad that even at this late date some action is being taken in this matter." The pressure of public opinion, he acknowledged, had brought about the dismissal of the indictment of Nowak in 1942 by an administration which was responsive to the voice of the people. But "a decided change has occurred within the Government within the last year or two. . . ." It most certainly had. And among the changes was the fact that Herbert Brownell with his declared purpose to deport and denaturalize controlled the Justice Department.

The denaturalization trial began on July 13, 1954, before Federal District Court Judge Frank Picard in Detroit. It was a lengthy trial during which the government presented the usual parade of informers and paid witnesses. On July 15, 1955, Judge

Picard ordered Nowak's citizenship cancelled on the ground that he had obtained citizenship on the basis of "illegal procurement" and "fraud." Actually the citizenship was cancelled eighteen years after Nowak had become a citizen on the basis of "testimony" available to the government in 1942, if not at the time he had become a citizen, which the government had then considered insufficient. On November 26, 1956, the Federal Court of Appeals sustained the cancellation of citizenship.

In the meantime, another case was going through the legal mill. Mrs. Rebecca Maisenberg was born in Russia in 1901. She entered the United States in 1912 and lived in New York City. In 1917 she married and, in 1926, she and her husband, a naturalized citizen, moved to Detroit, where they have lived ever since. Mrs. Maisenberg was naturalized in Detroit in January, 1938. She is the mother of one daughter and has two grandchildren. The denaturalization proceedings were initiated in March, 1953. On August 11, 1955, Judge Picard ordered Mrs. Maisenberg's citizenship cancelled on the ground that she had obtained it by misrepresentation and concealment of a material fact. On November 26, 1956, the Court of Appeals sustained the cancellation.

The cases were appealed to the U.S. Supreme Court. The ACPFB had recognized from the beginning the importance of these cases. In a Campaign Bulletin issued on June 6, 1957, it declared that these

> cases must be viewed as *national test cases* since they may determine the outcome of forty other political denaturalization cases now pending and what happens in the 10,000 denaturalization proceedings the Attorney General announced the Justice Department is prepared to initiate. The Nowak case tests the provisions of the 1906 denaturalization law as amended by the 1940 law. The Maisenberg case tests the denaturalization provisions of the 1952 Walter-McCarran Law.
>
> The issues are clear—the rights of naturalized American citizens, and the Justice Department's attempt to over-

> throw the 1943 decision by the Supreme Court in the case of William Schneiderman, which was argued by Wendell Willkie.

The ACPFB called for support for an *amicus brief* that was being prepared by Frank Donner, a New York attorney.

The government based its case, among other things, on the requirement that the applicant for citizenship shall have been "attached to the principles of the Constitution" for five years prior to naturalization and that membership in the Communist Party was proof of lack of attachment. It also argued that Nowak had given a false negative answer when he denied that he believed in anarchy or belonged to an organization advocating anarchy or the overthrow of the government.

The court ruled, 6 to 3, that the affidavit of good cause served in the Nowak case was sufficient. As to the false statement, the court held that it was not proved because the question was not sufficiently clear or unambiguous. With regard to lack of attachment to the Constitution, Justice John M. Harlan, in delivering the opinion for the majority, reserved decision as to whether membership in a party advocating the government's overthrow was necessarily proof of lack of attachment to the Constitution. In any case, he said, the government had to prove "that Nowak knew of the party's illegal advocacy." This the government failed to establish. The fact that Nowak was an active member and functionary in the (Communist) Party does not of itself suffice to establish this vital link in the Government's chain of proof. . . . At no point does the record show that Nowak himself ever advocated action for violent overthrow, or that he understood that the Party advocated action to that end." The Court therefore reversed the cancellation of citizenship in the case of Nowak. It acted on the same basic in the case of Mrs. Maisenberg.

Again the constitutional questions remained essentially unanswered. But the decision placed still another restraint on the outrageous use of the Walter-McCarran Act and marked another milestone on the return to democratic sanity.

29. The Bitter-Enders

Such a series of court decisions gives convincing evidence of the need to repeal or amend our immigration and naturalization law. Two reasons for the delay in so doing are obvious. The first is the failure of the Supreme Court to deal with the constitutional questions involved. So long as decisions are based on technical grounds, there is always the hope that they can be circumvented by legal ingenuity so that the policy of the Immigration and Naturalization Service may remain unaltered. The second reason is the power of reactionary (or as they prefer to call themselves, "conservative") forces, both inside and outside of government—especially in the Department of Justice, including the Immigration and Naturalization Service itself. And too, in Congress, where positions of power are held often through the combination of the restricted suffrage in the one-party Southern States, the seniority rule, and the strategy of political party leaders, rather than by the will of the people.

The lack of respect for law as well as for justice, which so often characterizes the forces of undemocratic reaction, was unintentionally advertised throughout the nation by the procedure of the Immigration Service in the case of William Heikkila. The verdict against that procedure was pronounced not by the Supreme Court but by the indignant condemnation of an aroused public opinion. The story of the case is as fantastic as any popular mystery or adventure tale.

William Heikkila's parents came to the United States in the 1890's and settled in the State of Minnesota. In November, 1905, they went to Finland for a Christmas visit, but had to extend their visit because of the birth of William on March 14, 1906. When he was three months old, William Heikkila's parents returned with him to the United States. Heikkila has lived in the United States ever since, in Minnesota, Nebraska, Oregon and California. Married in 1953 to an American citizen, he now works as a structural draftsman in San Francisco. Twice he had tried to become an American citizen but failed each time because of circumstances over which he had no control.

In December, 1947, the Justice Department arrested Heikkila for deportation. But the hearings were not held until 1951, prolonging the misery of insecurity. The only evidence against him was his own statement as to his former membership in the Communist Party, made when he applied for citizenship during the early 1940's. A final deportation order was entered in February, 1952, and Heikkila immediately challenged the deportation order in the Federal courts. In March, 1953, the U.S. Supreme Court held that the wrong legal procedure had been used in the appeal and the case was returned to the lower courts. The Heikkila appeal was taken to the Supreme Court for a second time in 1955 but, again it was sent back on a technicality. Thus, although the Heikkila case has been before the Supreme Court twice, the Court has failed to consider the facts in the case or to rule on his deportability.

The third challenge was started *after* the Supreme Court had given the Rowoldt decision, holding that non-citizens could not be deported for past membership in the Communist Party unless there had been a "meaningful association." This dating is important since it explains the behavior of the Immigration officials, and added to the sense of outrage of the American people. What happened was obviously an attempt by the Immigration Service to circumvent the Supreme Court decision.

In March, 1958, Federal District Court Judge Edward P. Murphy, in San Francisco, ruled against Heikkila in the court proceedings, sustaining his deportation. When counsel for Heikkila and the government could not agree on the wording of the court order, Judge Murphy set May 2 for a hearing to decide on the wording of the order to be entered in the Heikkila case. Once the Judge's order was signed and entered, Heikkila could appeal his decision to the Appeals Court and then, if necessary, to the Supreme Court.

Up to this point the case was "routine"—just a man's ten year fight against deportation, from the land where he had lived all his life, to Finland, a country of which he had no knowledge, where he had neither relatives nor friends; against forcing on his wife the hard choice between exile from her country or separation from her husband. Suddenly the routine was interrupted.

On Friday afternoon, April 18, at 5:00 P.M., as he emerged from the building in which he worked, Heikkila was stopped by two immigration agents who hurried him into a waiting automobile and whisked him away. Fortunately, he had a chance to call to a fellow-worker who had come out with him to telephone his wife that he had been taken by immigration agents. Heikkila was taken by car directly to the San Francisco airport and within twenty-five minutes after his arrest, he was on board a plane for Vancouver, British Columbia, Canada. In Vancouver, B.C., he was held in a jail incommunicado, registered under a false name, from 11:30 P.M. Friday until 1:50 P.M. Sunday, when he was put aboard a Canadian commercial plane for Amsterdam, where he was to get a plane for Helsinki. He arrived in Helsinki on Tuesday, April 22. When he was arrested in San Francisco the temperature was 70 degrees. He arrived in Helsinki in a sleet storm with the temperature below freezing. Heikkila wore the suit in which he had been arrested. He had thirty cents in his pockets and no overcoat. After fifty-two years of living in the United States, Heikkila returned to his "homeland" without sufficient clothing, without any money, without any friends.

In the meantime, Heikkila's fellow-worker called Phyllis Heikkila and informed her that her husband had been taken into custody. Mrs. Heikkila tried to find out what had happened to him. But Bruce Barber, District Director of the Immigration Service in San Francisco, made himself unavailable. At midnight, immigration officials finally informed Mrs. Heikkila that her husband was out of the country but refused to tell her where he was. (At the time he was being held in a Vancouver, B.C. jail under a false name.)

The following morning, Saturday, Heikkila's lawyer, Lloyd McMurray, obtained a writ of *habeas corpus* signed by Federal District Court Judge George Harris, which ordered Heikkila's immediate release. Judge Harris' order was directed to Barber "and all persons acting in concert with him." Barber stated that "Heikkila is not with us. He is en route to Finland." This was factually untrue since at that moment, as Barber well knew, Heikkila was in a Vancouver, B. C. jail, where he was being guarded by a United States immigration agent, a representative of Barber, who stayed with him until he was put on a plane for Amsterdam at 1:50 P.M. on Sunday, the following day. (This procedure, when it was discovered, raised a storm of protest in Canada.)

On Monday, April 21, Judge Murphy stated that "this proceeding smacks of the Gestapo and the rack and the thumbscrew." He went on further to declare: "This man was entitled to an appeal. I shall do all in my power to get him back here so he may have his day in court." Judge Murphy ordered Barber to appear before him and it looked as if Barber might be held in contempt for ignoring Judge Harris' order on Saturday to release Heikkila. Meanwhile, over the weekend, the press in the United States, as well as in Europe, made the Heikkila kidnapping front page news. The same was true of radio and television newscasts. The storm of protest broke.

Barber took the position that no one could complain of

Heikkila's treatment since he had admitted that he had been a member of the Communist Party from 1929 to 1939 (this, after the Supreme Court decision in Rowoldt!). Merrill R. O'Toole, regional director of the Immigration Service in San Pedro, California, stated: "In this case and in similar ones involving Communists and fellow travelers, we have to act fast. With these people, delay is common and, when we aren't legally restrained, we move before they can get ready. That's why we didn't consult his wife or his lawyer."

But protests against Heikkila's treatment mounted in force and volume. Newspapers across the country voiced editorial condemnation of the Justice Department's behavior. Said the *San Francisco Chronicle* on April 22:

> The United States Immigration Service, which frequently behaves like a terror agency of a police state, has outdone itself in the case of William Heikkila, ex-Communist, and has given a performance that outrages simple decency and the people whose servant it ought to be.

The Portland *Oregonian* stated on April 23:

> It is abominable that this arbitrary action should have been taken in the name of the people of the United States. . . . The treatment of Heikkila has gone far beyond harassment. He was seized and spirited to Europe in true gestapo style. Here is a clear case of bureaucratic usurpation. Call it zeal. It has no place in America. Those responsible should be called to book.

The Portland (Oregon) *Journal* of April 24, went further:

> We might examine this whole business of deportation. . . . Judge Gus Solomon of the local federal district court, said the Walter-McCarran Immigration Act is "a terrible law." It appears that we should re-examine not only immigration department policies, which allow the use of gestapo tactics, but the immigration and deportation laws as well.

U.S. Senator Thomas Hennings, of Missouri, announced that he was asking for a full explanation of the Heikkila deportation and might even ask for a Senate investigation of other deportation practices by the Immigration Service. The protest was too loud to be ignored. As the *New York Times* reported on April 23, "The Justice Department had made it plain it was embarrassed by unfavorable publicity over the hasty deportation." In addition to the statements of Judge Murphy and others, there was the threat to hold Barber in contempt of court. Late in the day of April 22, Lieut. Gen. Joseph M. Swing, Commissioner of Immigration, announced the decision to bring Heikkila back.

> I have come to the conclusion that an error in judgment was made in not returning Heikkila from Vancouver, B.C. last Sunday.
>
> I am confident that those concerned acted in good faith. Nevertheless, I am directing that Mr. Heikkila be permitted to return to the United States forthwith to await further action by the court.

If General Swing thought this would silence the anger, he was greatly mistaken. Said the Milwaukee *Journal* on April 24:

> The Justice Department (of which the Immigration Service is a part) must repudiate the whole affair, kidnapping and all, and give assurance—shocking as it is to find the need for it in America—that it will not countenance terrorism in its ranks.

And the Milwaukee *Sentinel* stated on the same day:

> The only good thing in this deplorable matter is that the Immigration Service was quick to reverse itself and was big enough to do so. But the country is still interested in knowing how and why such a stupid thing was done in the first place and a congressional investigation into the whole affair is strongly indicated.

The Madison (Wisconsin) *Capital Times* said on April 24:

> It matters not that the Immigration Service has admitted its error and that Heikkila will be brought back to San Francisco. That such a thing could happen in the land of the free is horrifying.

The New York *World Telegram and Sun* declared on the same day:

> More care should be exercised in the selection of officials. The agent responsible for this case should be relieved of his authority. It also should be asked who gave him the legal advice or orders upon which he acted. A close look should be taken at the whole immigration law enforcement organization in San Francisco.

And on the following day, the Minneapolis *Tribune* stated:

> Lt. Gen. Joseph Swing, Commissioner of Immigration admits that "an error of judgment" was made in handling this case. This strikes us as being a classic understatement. It would be more to the point if Swing admitted that a shocking lapse from American standards of fair play and justice had occurred within the Service. . . . Now let it move to root out the kind of officious thinking that lay behind that blunder.

But various statements reported from General Swing do not indicate much probability that he will do any "rooting out." "How are we going to get rid of these deportable aliens who keep going back to court?" the *New York Times* quoted him on April 25. (Is the answer kidnapping in order to prevent them from asking legal protection?) "What we are dealing with is human beings. You can't write a law that covers every case, and so you've got to leave discretion to the fellow implementing it." Which appears to be the reason why, as the *New York Times* put it on April 25, "Our immigration laws are being enforced in an inexcusable spirit of inhumanity." General Swing is reported to have declared further that people like Heikkila were "nogoodniks who can't be gotten out any other way." And he gave this demonstration of his "approach as that of a soldier 'with a big heart,'" as the *New York Times* biographer portrayed him on the same day, when Swing said, "This man is just as much an enemy as the Japs I fought in the Pacific. When a Jap was captured, did we say 'Go on home and kiss your wife goodby?'" And finally General Swing vowed that he would deport Heikkila "if it takes from now until I get kicked out."

To this, the Washington, D. C., *Post & Times-Herald* commented on April 24:

> It would be well at this juncture to reflect on the idiocy of an immigration law which makes a man deportable in 1958 for having been a member of the Communist Party from 1929 to 1939, when membership was entirely legal. "We'll deport Heikkila," said Commissioner Swing, presumably between clenched teeth, "if it takes another eleven years." The Commissioner's energy might better be devoted to some worthier cause.

Even as late as June 4, 1958, General Swing could not grasp what was involved in the Heikkila situation. Robert G. Spivak, Washington correspondent of the *New York Post* reported on that date:

> U.S. Immigration Commissioner Swing is not giving up in his efforts to deport Finnish-born William Heikkila. . . . Swing is said to be so angry at the criticism of the way his men handled the case that he would regard any attempt to drop the proceedings as a personal affront.

And Mr. Spivak went on to say that influential forces in Washington fear "that if Heikkila is not sent out of the country, Swing will make good his threat to resign." This anger at criticism sounds like a General reacting to insubordination in the army; it is certainly a most inappropriate attitude for an official of the Department of Justice. The resignation might be a step toward needed changes in the Immigration and Naturalization Service.

What has been the Commisisoner's record in office hitherto? In the *Cleveland Union Leader* August 3, 1956, appeared an editorial entitled, "What About This Mess?" It is reproduced in full:

> President Eisenhower, who promised to "clean up the mess in Washington," has been confronted with a good deal of a mess in his own administration, and has eased out several high officials after they became involved in unsavory scandals. Along that line, Ike might well take a look at his old West Point classmate, General Joseph M. Swing.
>
> After Eisenhower made Swing Commissioner of Immigration, things began to pop. First, some members of Congress, of both parties, charged that Swing, who seems to be an arrogant military character, was going around insulting career immigration officials as contemptuously as though they were army recruits.
>
> Then Senator Lyndon B. Johnson (Dem. Texas) aired the incident in which Swing used Immigration Service employees to obtain for his Washington home a low-wage maid from Mexico. Also, columnist Drew Pearson reported that Swing gave his daughter a fat government job in his Immigration office.
>
> Next, a House Committee scorchingly criticized Swing for using government airplanes, cars, trailers on hunting trips to Mexico and Canada, at the taxpayers' expense. Swing said these were "goodwill" trips and the hunting was "incidental." That claim was called ridiculous by Congressman Robert H. Mollohan (Dem. W. Va.), who has been keeping his eye on the General's strange activities.
>
> This week the Scripps-Howard papers reported that Swing has "promoted the pilot of his personal government plane to a newly-created $10,320 post as District Immigration Director."
>
> That may be all right, but Swing's record as a whole suggests Ike should take a hand and see whether his old

> classmate isn't too reckless with the public money and the public interest.

And on May 9, 1958, Drew Pearson wrote a column entitled "Swing Deports Many Hurriedly," in the Washington *Post & Times-Herald*:

> There is more than meets the eye behind the abrupt deportation of William Heikkila from San Francisco to Finland. New Attorney General William Rogers, who is breathing fresh life into the Justice Department, promptly reversed Gen. Joseph Swing, the swaggering Commissioner of Immigration, and ordered Heikkila back to the United States to have a chance to say goodbye to his wife and family and exhaust his due process under the law. Rogers' Commissioner of Immigration, however, remained completely unrepentant. He even bragged that about 97 to 98 per cent of the deportations from the United States were handled the same way.
>
> The *New York Times*, which simultaneously carried a biographical sketch of the Commissioner picturing him as a "soldier with a big heart," soft-pedalled Swing's statement. The *Times* quoted Swing as saying: "About 97 percent of the deportable aliens go without protest and are given ample time to wind up their affairs."
>
> But what the West Point Commissioner of Immigration actually said in testimony before the House Judiciary Committee was: "About 97 to 98 percent of our people are handled this way. We give them about 72 hours or a week or 10 days or a month if they have business to settle. There is about three percent of these nogoodnicks and the only way to handle them is—they know they're deportable and they know that if we get our hands on them, they will be summarily deported." (The grammar is the General's.) "Last year," he said, "we physically deported 6,700 odd aliens and the year before over 7,000. It has averaged about 7,000 a year."
>
> The real inside record on General Swing shows him to be anything but the *New York Times*' soldier "with a big

> heart," except possibly in putting his daughter, Mary N. Swing Mitchell, on the Government payroll at $4,500 a year. He was also big-hearted about supplying a Government immigration plane to Attorney General Brownell for a purely political trip to confer with Governor Shivers of Texas.
>
> General Swing, a 1915 West Point classmate of Eisenhower's is the first military man ever to become Commissioner of Immigration. He promptly appointed two other military men, Gens. Frank H. Partridge and Edwin B. Howard, to be his assistants, thus pretty well militarizing this civilian branch of government.
>
> General Swing also exhibited his big-hearted proclivities when he instructed the U.S. Immigration officer in El Paso to obtain a Mexican maid for his home in Washington at much less salary than that paid in Washington. . . . On June 30, 1957 this column further reported on General Swing's big-hearted activities, especially his use of a Government DC-3 to fly to Mexico for week-ends where he was met by a Government-owned house trailer and relaxed on delightful hunting trips. General Swing even charged the Government for his personal expenses on these hunting trips and was forced to return $73.85. In contrast, a Florida employee of the Immigration Service overcharged the Government for a local taxi fare and he was fired.

However, what is more disturbing than the character of General Swing is the fact that, as reported by Spivak in the article previously quoted,

> Although Swing does not enjoy the prestige on Capitol Hill of FBI Director Hoover, he does have a number of Congressional supporters who would go to bat for him and make things hot for the Attorney General if the Justice Department reversed its decision.

The fact is that, despite the improved political atmosphere in the country, suppression of dissent, guilt by association are still with us. There are still too many men in authority who are trying to turn the clock backwards. The comment of Rep. Walter, co-author of the Walter-McCarran Law, on the Heikkila case was (*New York Times*, April 25):

> Where you fellows made a mistake is in not realizing who you were dealing with—a bunch of tough, hard-boiled Commies who would stop at nothing to discredit the Government. You should have issued him an engraved invitation.

After this inept attempt at humor, Rep. Walter "asserted that General Swing had provided 'a field day' for critics of the McCarran-Walter Immigration Act. . . ."

Or consider the report of Rep. Hillings, Republican from California, (according to Spivak of the *New York Post*, a close personal friend and political associate of Vice-President Nixon), who is one of those pushing hardest for Heikkila's deportation. Assigned by Rep. Walter to "investigate" the case, Rep. Hillings made an "exhaustive" one-hour study by talking only to Barber, according to the *Post* of May 6. Asked why he had not interviewed Heikkila or his lawyer, Lloyd McMurray, he answered, "I have all the information I need." And this information, except for some sensational disclosures which he promised but has not yet produced, consisted of his claim that "Heikkila's legal fees in his 11-year fight against deportation had been paid by the Northern California Committee for Protection of the Foreign Born," and that this Committee was "a subsidiary of the American Committee for the Protection of the Foreign Born, which is on the Attorney General's subversive list."* Presumably it was for this reason that he came to the absurd conclusion that "the action in the Heikkila case was 'fully legal and justified.'" Apparently, to insist on "due process of law" is to be unfair to the Justice Department.

* The Northern California CPFB, under the leadership of Grace Partridge, is an independent organization which has cooperated with the ACPFB and also with the independent Heikkila Defense Committee.

And finally, what is the position of the present Attorney General, William P. Rogers? As we understand it, it is the duty of the Justice Department not only to prosecute actual or alleged lawbreakers, but to make justice available to all Americans. Much dissatisfaction has been expressed at the Department's failure to check instances of force and violence committed by white Americans in connection with the desegregation of the schools and the refusal of voting rights to Negroes. And how can this duty to safeguard justice be reconciled with a *Times* dispatch from Washington dated April 24, 1958:

> At a news conference later today, Attorney General William P. Rogers urged approval of an Administration proposal to confine aliens to one round of appeals on deportation orders. He said some steps had to be taken to prevent repetitious appeals.

Surely it is the duty of the Attorney General to see to it that the full measure of "due process" is available to all; not to try to curtail it for some.

William Heikkila stood closer to the tradition of those who signed our Declaration of Independence when, arriving with no overcoat in a Finnish sleet storm, he told reporters that he would "fight for the right to return to the United States. . . . I regard it as my home country"; when, on his return, he told his wife Phyllis simply "It's good to be back" and told reporters that he "was not bitter."

William Heikkila will have to fight hard to win his right to remain in his own country. But the American people will have to fight equally hard to re-establish the true democratic principles on which this country was founded, to make it possible not only for a Heikkila to remain here, but for all Americans to live here in freedom and in mutual respect.

30. "Stepchildren of a Nation"

ONE group of foreign born in the United States requires separate consideration, both because of its numbers and because of the special circumstances which have contributed to its special difficulties. The position of Americans of Mexican origin is partly the product of past history which set a pattern for exploitation. The relation between Mexico and the United States presents one of the more unhappy aspects of American history, culminating in a war of dubious validity, followed by the seizure of extensive Mexican territory.

The continued mistreatment of Mexican nationals and of American citizens of Mexican descent has kept alive the bitter memories. It is not simply geography that has made the difference between our relationship toward our neighbor to the South and its people and that towards our northern neighbor. Racial prejudice plays its part.

The economic importance of Mexican migratory labor in various parts of the country, especially in the Southwest and California, is also an important, perhaps the most important factor in the present situation.

There are today approximately 5,000,000 people of Mexican descent, of whom 1,500,000 are non-citizens, in the United States—the single largest bloc in the country, with the special characteristic of a subjugated people. Louisa Moreno, of the Spanish-Speaking People's Congress, spoke on the general situation of the Mexican-Americans at the ACPFB 1940 Annual Conference. She stressed the long-continued discrimination against Spanish-speaking citizens and non-citizens alike; told of the miserable wages, the inadequate shacks in which the workers were housed, and the difficulties in the way of naturalization. She pointed out that only an average of 100 out of 1,000,000 became citizens in a year because, among other things, a Mexican-American family on hunger wages would have to stop eating entirely for two and a half months to pay for the citizenship papers for one member. Yet 1,400,000 people could not be "repatriated" without recourse to the treatment accorded the Jews in Germany. And if they were all sent back to Mexico, who would harvest the cotton in Texas, or the fruit in California, or who would cultivate the sugar beets?

During the war, Mexican labor was much in demand and conditions were somewhat improved, but the anti-immigrant prejudices of the post-war years included the Mexican-Americans who were especially vulnerable. From the ACPFB Conference in 1947 came a much fuller discussion of the whole problem: *Step-Children of a Nation,* by Isabel Gonzales, of Denver, Colorado. This pamphlet traced the "inferior status" of Mexican-Americans from the beginnings in 1848, when the Mexican population lost political control of their native Southwest; their titles to farm land and mines were invalidated; English replaced Spanish as the official language; and equal civil rights were practically abolished. Then came the demand for cheap labor in the Imperial Valley in California, the sugar beet fields of Colorado, the cotton fields of Arizona and Texas; the forcible repatriation of the depression years; the war-time emergency program of 1942.

The author stressed especially the threat of deportation, "which has served as a very effective weapon to keep the Mexican people as a whole in bondage." For, since accurate records of entry were never kept, proof of legal entry was always difficult and expensive and often impossible to obtain. "As soon as a leader arises among them, deportation proceedings are immediately used to remove him from leadership." Large numbers who remain unnaturalized although they speak fluent English and have lived in the United States most of their lives "frankly admit . . . that they have neither the finances nor the courage to tackle the job of proving they entered legally."

On the last page of the pamphlet, the ACPFB cited as illustrations of the author's charges the cases of Humberto Silex (born in Nicaragua, a leader among the Mexican-Americans and a former officer of Mine, Mill and Smelter Workers Union) and Refugio Roman Martinez, Mexican born, a member of the staff of the United Packinghouse Workers, CIO.

The year 1949 saw a concerted drive on the part of the government with the declared aim to deport 250,000 Mexicans "illegally" in the country. The issues of *The Lamp* for that summer carry protests against violations of law by government agents: "systematic forays into Mexican-American neighborhoods and private homes without proper warrant or regard for constitutional guarantees" and the deportation as well of American citizens, both naturalized and native born.

Since the early work of the ACPFB was centered in New York City, the Committee's interest in the first years was limited to the infringements of the rights of individual Mexicans for whom it made appeals. But by 1939, its interest in the Mexican-Americans began to broaden, as reflected in reports to the Annual Conferences. In November, 1949, efforts were begun to establish a Committee for the Protection of Foreign Born in Los Angeles. The Committee was formally organized in September, 1950. This Committee was of course confronted directly with the mass deportations of Mexicans from Los Angeles itself. And in 1953, the Los Angeles Committee opened a branch office in the center of the Mexican community. The existence of a Committee especially close to the Mexican problem did not mean that the ACPFB ceased to feel its own responsibility. On the contrary, accounts of the situation by an independent group brought a still clearer recognition of that responsibility.

The treatment of individual Mexican-Americans continued

to be reported in *The Lamp*. There was, for instance, the deportation of Eusebio Mejia, a resident of the United States for thirty-six years, on the ground of a "felony" committed in Mexico; or the kidnapping by government officials of Jose Estrada, of Dallas, Texas, which left his American-citizen wife and ten children—one a recipient of the purple heart—without support in the United States. But in addition to this concern with specific cases, the necessity of action to alter the whole situation was recognized and conferences passed resolutions with that intent. At the 1951 conference, Ralph Cuaron made an eloquent plea in behalf of all Spanish-speaking Americans. At a New York Conference of Defense Committees in 1952, major emphasis was on the persecution of Mexican-Americans, on creating facilities to meet their needs and on the necessity for much wider publicity on the treatment of Mexican-Americans in this country.

The passage of the Walter-McCarran Law made the situation even worse. The first to be deported under the law was the Mexican Jose Estrada, a legal resident for forty-five years. In the first six months of 1953, 480,000 were deported, double the whole number for 1950. Senator McCarran was himself in Los Angeles in 1953 and when questioned about the hundreds of families divided by the deportations, he replied calmly and with complete serenity, "That's just their tough luck."

The nature of the Walter-McCarran Law drive is illustrated by a March 3 news report by the Associated Press from Fresno, California, and recorded by Abner Green in the March-April issue of *The Lamp*, under the heading "Treatment of Persons of Mexican Birth or Descent under the Walter-McCarran Law."

> Three hundred and twenty-five Mexican immigrants—including sixteen women and seven children—were rounded up in a search in which "mounted riders and an airplane were used." These 325 people—hunted down like animals by an airplane and horseback riders—were arrested without warrants, put on a chartered bus and immediately

> deported to Mexico without any hearings or any semblance of legal procedure.

This proved to be only a practice exercise for the real thing that was to come.

On June 14, 1954, Attorney General Brownell announced "the government's biggest offensive against Mexican 'illegals' in history." "Operation Terror," which began at 12:01 A.M. on June 17, was under the direct command of that soldier "with a big heart," General Swing. Flying squadrons of U.S. deputies swept through the Mexican-American communities to ferret out and capture the victims in order to herd them over the Mexican border. Airplanes located workers in the fields. Places of business and private homes were searched without warrant. The May-June issue of *The Lamp* describes the events as follows:

> In one of the most vicious deportation drives in the history of the United States, the Justice Department has unleashed a Walter-McCarran Law reign of terror against Mexican communities in the Southwest and Northern California. The drive was centered in Los Angeles where 750 immigration agents from all over the country were concentrated. Elysian Park, located in the heart of the Mexican community in Los Angeles, was converted into a concentration camp, where Mexican immigrants arrested in the roundup were held. As dawn broke on the morning of June 17, immigration agents swept down on the Mexican community in Los Angeles. Private homes were broken into, doors forced, and persons taken from their beds. Others were run down and captured by agents in fast automobiles on the public streets. Later that morning, immigration agents raided factories employing Mexican immigrants and large numbers of workers were taken off their jobs. Similar raids were carried out in San Diego, San Francisco and elsewhere. Thousands of Mexican immigrants and their American citizen families—as well as many native born American citizens of Mexican descent—were deported without any hearings and without any

opportunity to consult counsel or, in many cases, without any opportunity to secure wages owed to them by employers or gather what belongings they possessed. This disgraceful conduct by the Immigration and Naturalization Service was condemned by organizations and individuals throughout the country.

In the July-August issue, the protest actions of the Los Angeles Committee were reported: a picket line at Elysian Park, delegations from trade union and civic groups to the District Director of the Immigration Service, a protest mass meeting, distribution of 35,000 leaflets and of a folder, "Know Your Rights," in both Spanish and English. The September-October issue reported a protest by the Mexican Chamber of Commerce of Harlington, Texas, which charged that the United States Border Patrol was guilty of "brutality" toward Mexican nationals caught in the deportation dragnet in the Rio Grande Valley. The charges were fully substantiated in a memorandum of protest submitted to Commissioner Swing. The Chamber of Commerce reported that thousands deported from California were stranded and starving in Mexicali, Mexico. And the August convention of the Mexican Chamber of Commerce in Los Angeles was the first to describe the action as "Gestapo methods." But Gen. Swing proceeded to establish a Chicago-to-Mexico airlift to facilitate the deportation drive against some 20,000 to 35,000 persons in the Midwest area.

The Los Angeles Committee in September published a pamphlet, *Shame of a Nation,* which began with an account of the June 17 "Operation Terror" and went on to summarize the history of Mexicans in the United States. It also prepared and printed "A Bill in Search of Legislative Sponsors," which was designed to secure justice for Mexican-Americans. The report of Harriet Barron at the legislative conference in Washington in March, 1955, gave the number deported under the Walter-McCarran Law as a million and a half "with no due process, no right to counsel, no human or civilized decency." Abner Green's Annual Report for 1956 declared:

> Perhaps the most serious disregard of human beings and human rights [under the Walter-McCarran Law] is to be observed . . . in the Mexican-American communities in the United States. The treatment of Mexican immigrants —as well as of native-born Americans of Mexican descent (more than one million were deported in 1954)—is a shocking record of inhumanity.

He cited as one of the most shocking episodes the use of the S.S. *Mercurio* to transport the deportees in lots of 500, although the boat did not meet the minimum standards of an 1882 law for bringing steerage passengers from Europe. It had inadequate toilets, berths, kitchens. It had leaky lifeboats and too few of them. It had corroded boilers. A House Investigating Committee had called it "a hell ship." But in August, 1956, William P. Rogers, then still Deputy Attorney General and still seeking promotion, referred to deportation by the *Mercurio* as a "delightful Caribbean cruise."

Nor did the situation improve with the years. When, after twelve years of operation, the United States and Mexican governments' contract, which determined the conditions under which Mexican farm laborers were to be recruited and employed in the United States, came up for renewal on January 15, 1954, the Mexican government refused to accept certain changes proposed by the United States government. Some of the issues involved were revealed in a letter by Assistant Attorney General J. Lee Rankin on November 20, 1953, to U.S. Sen. Paul H. Douglas. He wrote:

> We have advised the Mexican government that we expect to obtain substantial modification in the present agreement in articles dealing with wages, subsistence, insurance coverage, blacklisting of employers, and workers' obligations. We have also asked for . . . a provision to permit the withholding of a portion of the worker's salary to guarantee faithful fulfillment of his contract obligations. In the past "skips" have been a serious problem, because

> there was no incentive for a worker to remain on the job if more attractive employment was offered elsewhere.

Special pressures were brought to bear by the United States government, including special legislation, and on March 10, 1954, the State Department announced that it had reached an agreement with Mexico to be in effect until December 31, 1955, the terms of which were not made public.

But that the Justice Department imposed onerous conditions on Mexican agricultural laborers, leaving them at the mercy of unscrupulous employers paying starvation wages, was revealed as late as June 13, 1958, when the *New York Times* reported that "at a hearing of a House Agriculture subcommittee on proposed legislation to continue a long-standing Government program of recruiting Mexicans to work on American farms," Rev. James L. Vizzard, on behalf of the National Catholic Rural Life Conference, "testified that the program had produced illegal bribery and profit-making and exploitation that 'would make the corruption found in the teamsters union seem only like petit larceny,'" that "imported Mexicans were being exploited as 'slave labor' by big farmers in the West and Southwest."

Father Vizzard "said that the 'prevailing wage' was set by employers who 'simply decide unilaterally what might be the absolute minimum they can get away with' . . . that employers hired Mexicans because they were willing 'to accept wages, living and working conditions that are intolerable to United States citizens.'" The priest said that the fewer than "5,000 corporate farms" that employ most of the Mexicans "have 'the equivalent of a slave-labor force provided to them at the cost of tens of millions of dollars to the American taxpayer.'" He "said that the program of recruiting Mexicans had produced economic, social and spiritual evils," and he "urged Congress to make an 'irrevocable commitment' to terminate it in a reasonable time." In this, Msgr. George C. Higgins, director of the Social Action Department of the National Catholic Welfare Conference, concurred.

31. Issues and Policy

THE change in the political atmosphere in the United States has come about through no accident. If this change is to develop further and full rights under the Constitution are to be secure for the American people, the people themselves must have an understanding of why and how these rights have been attacked and of why and how they must be defended. A valuable contribution toward such understanding was made at the Annual Conference of the ACPFB in Los Angeles in 1956. The speaker was Blanch Freedman, former law partner of the late Carol King, who since the death of Mrs. King has carried a large burden of the cases involving the rights of the foreign born. Her analysis offers a starting point for examining the present situation, and we give it here in full.

* * * * *

We, the people of the United States, are slowly but surely being transformed into a people alike as the traditional "peas in a pod." The impact of McCarthyism and reaction in this country over the past ten years had been far more insidious, penetrating and corrosive than we are wont to acknowledge, or perhaps realize. Where once an embattled people stood ready to speak out their differences and be heard "round the world," now sits a public acquiescent and obsequious, complacent, tranquilized. We have had in the past our infamous periods of pillory; and of witch burning and of midnight raids, wherein the articulate dissenters were exorcised and the citizenry silenced. Silenced—but never convinced! Silenced—but not subdued! What has been developed today, and what we are now experiencing, is of an entirely different character. We are a people as characterized by Professor Nevins, of Columbia University, rendered "comfortably inert." We have become what another writer calls "the Consensus American."

Over the past years the combined political, social and economic pressures have been exerted to invidiously inculcate a sameness and alikeness in our thinking, in our habits, in our culture. Differences are taboo! Differences, that heretofore were welcomed and encouraged because they enriched our national life and strengthened the individual, are today the hallmarks of that which is bad, that which is destructive. To be different is to be shunned.

Time doesn't permit any extended analysis of the processes that have brought about this mesmerization of the American people. Briefly, we can point to the general intimidation precipitated by the frenzy of investigating committees, the fantastic loyalty and security programs that were put into operation, the creation by the Attorney General of lists that decreed what associations were improper. Employers and unions, in very short shrift, accommodated themselves to these governmental actions. Professional organizations hastened to follow suit. Educational institutions quickly frowned upon controversial discussions. And men and women from all strata adapted themselves to, or were pressed into, a mold of respectability—the pattern of conformity.

Suffice it to say that conformity is the god of our times. And so it is quite understandable how anything that is foreign, anything that is strange, different, offends the worship of conformity.

In this environment nothing is more tangibly non-conformist than the foreign born, for they stand as physical, objective examples of something different. Their foreign background, accent, customs, habits and culture make them an inevitable target of the disciples of conformity. The peculiar feature of our non-citizen population was tersely illuminated by Prof. Henry Armour of Scripps College, in his satirical account of European History: "People," says Prof. Armour, "who live in Europe are Europeans—but when they come to America they . . . become transformed into . . . foreigners."

It is in this light that we should view the attacks upon the foreign born, legislative and otherwise. Essentially it is striking out at this element in the population because of its inherent differences.

It is not an accident, but also an historical imperative, that the author of the Walter-McCarran Act should be chairman of the House Committee on Un-American Activities, the agency that has had the greatest influence in foisting the dogma of conformity upon this nation.

I suppose we would all agree that there are evidences today of some turning of the tide, a lessening, perhaps of the binding pressures. Here and there voices are beginning to be heard in resentment against the self-imposed restrictions which conformity demands.

The time is approaching—if not already here—when an all out effort must be made to destroy the fetish of conformity, and to restore to the people the freedoms which originally were its appeal to mankind the world over, and which in large measure, was the parent of its great creations and inventions. I would say, that to President Roosevelt's four freedoms there must be added a fifth: the freedom to be different, the freedom of diversity, the freedom of multi-expressions.

In our nation's life unity is not uniformity. We have grown and thrived by the very multiplicity of the varied national strains and cultures that constitute our American population. Our history is the most powerful proof that heterogeneous origins can, and do, produce a homogeneous society.

Our action, our work to free the foreign born from legal strictures and social discriminations is an integral part of any movement against conformity, for they are its direct victims.

The campaign on behalf of the foreign born is—and must be—more than to abolish discriminations against them, it must be to establish affirmatively the right to be accepted though different, the right to be free and to live in a cultural pattern of their own choice without ostracism.

I am always reminded of the wisdom and humanity of the late Carol King, for many years the General Counsel for the American Committee, whose untimely death continues to be an unremitting hurt to me personally, to the American Committee specifically and the country generally. Years ago, Carol King, with her foresightedness and ingenuity, all of which stemmed from her highly individual and iconoclastic character, laid down this thesis: said she, "There are no aliens here—there are only Americans, some native born, some foreign born, but all Americans." Carol loved this land of hers and ours with deep-rooted feelings of patriotism and she labored throughout her adult life to keep it brave and free, as Abner Green and the American Committee are doing and as I, too, would like to emulate. Not, however, in the arrogant, nationalistic spirit of a James Monroe: "My country, right or wrong, my country," but rather in the universal brotherhood spirit of a Carl Schurz: "My country—please God, may she always be in the right—and while right kept right—and when wrong made right."

* * * * *

We have gone further on the path toward recovery of democratic freedom since the day Mrs. Freedman spoke. But the all-out effort which she anticipated has not yet been made. And yet without such an all-out effort we shall continue to acquiesce in the shameful treatment of the Negro people, acts of anti-Semitism, the continued harassment of the foreign born, the persistent forcing of the American people into the straitjacket of conformity.

How can we explain that a movement of such breadth and weight as the movement against the Walter-McCarran Law, reflected in the Report of the President's Commission was so singularly futile in repealing or revising the Act? Is it true that Congress is always slow to reverse itself; that the blockade set up by Senator Eastland and Representative Walter is formidable? Repeal of a law is possible—witness the prohibition amendment, a statute which certainly did not fall into the same weighty social category as the welfare of the foreign born. And yet a frontal attack on the Walter-McCarran Act of such formidable proportions has not succeeded.

Analogies are always dangerous, and in this instance it seems almost ludicrous to equate in any way the right to have a drink with the tragedy of shattered hopes, broken homes and uprooted lives. And yet there is perhaps a clue here. President Roosevelt thought he saw a connection between the ban on the sale of liquor and the economic crisis, and he fought to repeal prohibition as he fought for his other policies to get the country out of economic chaos. But President Eisenhower, whatever his understanding of the inter-relationship between the rights of the foreign born and the true security of the nation, never thought it necessary to fight for the revision of the Walter-McCarran Law promised in his campaign speeches, as he fights for, say, the reorganization of the Pentagon. Such a blind spot adds to the difficulty of recognizing in the immigration and naturalization law one reason why the international prestige of the United States continues to dip so disastrously. What the people of the world seem to gather from United States policy with regard to the foreign born, and to civil liberties in general, is that the United States is not so much "exporting" democracy with its economic and military aid as attempting to exile it. And, without its democracy, America appears to the world as only another form of the old imperialism and colonialism.

In examining the failure to date of the movement to repeal or revise the Walter-McCarran Act, many factors must be taken into account. If there is merit to the contention that basic causes for immigrant-baiting are domestic and international political or economic crises, then the continuation of world tensions are a serious barrier to the elimination of anti-foreign born legislation and action. Therefore without the lessening of world tensions, any movement in defense of the foreign born must face especial difficulties.

Another factor that must be noted is that, so long as aspects of McCarthyism, the reflection of the domestic political crisis, continue to exert influence in the administration, in the legislature and in the life of America, so long will the struggle for justice for the foreign born find an irreconcilable enemy with power to implement its recalcitrance. In fact, one of the major weaknesses of the Report of the President's Commission was its acceptance as fact of some of the arbitrary definitions and findings written into the McCarran Internal Security Act of 1950.

There were already on the statute books laws to prevent or punish conspiracy, espionage or subversion which can be proved in court. But such men as McCarthy, McCarran, Walter and Eastland were apparently unwilling to permit their own peculiar concepts of conspiracy and subversion to be limited by the courts. Hence, they found it necessary to establish them through legislative fiat and support them with special criminal statutes. Acceptance of these unproved legislative pronouncements as fact serves as the very base and justifies the existence of the Walter-McCarran Act, which simply echoes in a particular field the generalities of the Internal Security Act. Furthermore, these laws give such men and their supporters the "legal" weapons to strike down the opponents of anti-foreign born laws.

Nevertheless, despite the difficulties, a fight against the Walter-McCarran Act is essential. What is more, it can be won! It would be totally incorrect to think or imply that world tensions must be lessened and McCarthyism must be wholly eliminated before the plight of the foreign born can be alleviated. On the contrary, the very fight to repeal or fundamentally revise the Walter-McCarran Act and the victory of such a campaign will help rout the McCarthyites and will strengthen the forces inclined toward lessening world tensions. But for this kind of victory to be achieved, the all-out effort, of which Mrs. Freedman spoke at the ACPFB Conference, is a prerequisite. It was put another way by Representative Celler before the Association of Immigration and Nationality lawyers on May 2, 1958.

> Let's make no mistake. . . . Too many of us get weary of the old subjects, tired of the old tune, not realizing, of course, that we must go on talking, must go on agitating, must go on sponsoring, because the remedy—the just and right remedy—has not yet been supplied. This is precisely what has happened in the whole area of refugee relief.

What happened to the work of the President's Commission and the movement of support that sprang up around it should serve as an object lesson. The fact is that neither the Commission nor the movement around it conducted a sustained drive to implement its generally outstanding report. Certainly there were difficulties. The welcome campaign for the admission of refugees that emerged at the time was used by the Walters as a diversionary move and confused the people, even critics of the Walter-McCarran Act. In breaking through on the question of the admission of refugees, they felt that the problem in general was solved.

What is essential is a *united* and persistent campaign based on a commonly accepted *minimum* program. The elements of such a program, it appears, are in existence and generally accepted today. They include the following:

1. Revision of the Walter-McCarran Law. Appropriate bills have repeatedly been introduced in Congress. In 1957, a bill introduced by Representative Celler was co-sponsored by thirty-two other Representatives. The revision should eliminate the discriminatory features of the present law by ending the quota system based on national origin or race. It should remove all provisions for retroactive application of deportation proceedings, and establish a statute of limitations after which a person may not be deported on any ground at all. All administrative decisions made in all immigration and naturalization processes, including deportation and entry, must be subject to full and unlimited judicial review, with the right to bail guaranteed. The

Attorney General must be prevented from ever arrogating to himself the right to detain for life—concentration camp imprisonment—non-citizens whether in the course of deportation proceedings or after deportation is ordered, or to control the political thoughts and associations of non-citizens. The law should establish full rights under the Constitution and the Bill of Rights for all long-time residents and for relatively recent refugees as well and should eliminate all elements of police-state surveillance or investigation of their thinking, activities or associations. It should set a minimum period of legal residence after which the non-citizen might achieve speedy naturalization without technical and arbitrary obstacles and barriers; and set a similar period after which naturalized citizens may not have their citizenship revoked on any ground at all. It should wholly remove the concept of two classes of United States citizens, native born and naturalized, and do away with any grounds for the loss of citizenship by naturalized citizens other than those that apply to native born citizens.

2. Because of the special situation with regard to Mexican-Americans, special steps should be taken to win for those of Mexican descent the right to adjust their status to permanent residence after living here for two years, and to facilitate their naturalization; to win for Mexican immigrants due process in deportation proceedings, especially the right to counsel, the right to qualified interpreters, the right to hearings; to prohibit deportation raids in Mexican-American communities; and to guarantee strict observance of the rights of United States citizens of Mexican origin.

3. Because of the very nature of the origin of the United States it seems most appropriate to establish the observance of an annual national foreign born day on October 28, the anniversary of the dedication of the Statue of Liberty. In this connection there should be conducted educational campaigns on naturalization, on the rights of non-citizens and of naturalized citizens, and to develop understanding of the contributions made by the immigrant to the building and development of the

United States, as well as to commemorate and honor the various national cultures that have contributed to the development of American culture.

Shades of emphasis, differences in details, notwithstanding, there is nothing in this program that should be seriously controversial or divisive to men of good will. Indeed, getting together on this issue, which could only redound to America's honor, would contribute to cementing national unity with a forward look.

The ACPFB at its 25th Anniversary National Conference, adopted a program of action which reflects this policy and was summarized in the following eight points:

1. Win public hearings on the Celler bill.
2. A national campaign for a statute of limitations in the deportation and denaturalization laws.
3. Educational campaigns in naturalization, the rights of non-citizens and the rights of naturalized citizens.
4. An educational campaign to inform the American people of the immigration, naturalization, deportation and denaturalization provisions of the Walter-McCarran law.
5. Develop public understanding of the contributions made by immigrants to the building and development of the United States.
6. Promote the nationwide observance of October 28th as "Statue of Liberty Day."
7. A nation-wide fight for the rights of Mexican-Americans.
8. Defense of the American Committee for Protection of Foreign Born.

At its 26th Annual Conference, the ACPFB adopted the following 11-point Program of Action for 1959:

1. A campaign to win repeal or revision of the Walter-McCarran Law in the 86th Congress convening in January, 1959.
2. A campaign for a statute of limitations in the de-

portation and denaturalization laws.

3. Secure public attention to the challenge in the Federal courts of the Justice Department's attempt to impose travel restrictions in Supervisory Parole orders.

4. Present a Special Petition to the Human Rights Commission of the United Nations on the treatment of the Mexican immigrant in the United States.

5. Establish a basis for a constitutional challenge in the Federal courts of the government's right to deport legal residents or long-time residents of the United States.

6. Develop public understanding of the contributions made by the immigrant to the building and development of the United States.

7. Promote the nation-wide observance of October 28th as "Appreciation of Foreign Born" Day.

8. Bring to public attention the facts and issues involved in the cases of persons threatened with deportation and denaturalization or with frame-up proceedings under the Walter-McCarran Law.

9. Develop an educational campaign to inform the American people of the immigration, naturalization, deportation and denaturalization provisions of the Walter-McCarran Law.

10. Initiate a challenge in the Federal courts of the Attorney General's listing of the American Committee for Protection of Foreign Born as a "subversive" organization.

11. Defend the American Committee for Protection of Foreign Born in proceedings pending before the Subversive Activities Control Board.

32. One Country — One Freedom

TWENTY-FIVE years have gone by since the ACPFB was first organized in 1933. But laws which make secure the rights of the foreign born and fair administration of the laws have not been won. Victories in individual cases, such as that of Charles Rowoldt, can alter for the better the interpretation of the Walter-McCarran Law, but the Law remains on the statute books, a threat to others. An arbitrary administrative procedure, like the kidnapping of William Heikkila, can be reversed as an "error," but similar "errors" remain and continue to be made.

The efforts of the foreign born alone cannot reform our immigration laws nor modify essentially the attitude of the Immigration and Naturalization Service and of the Department of Justice. Reform will come only when the native born recognize that these laws and procedures also injure us. It is of course true that resolutions condemning the Walter-McCarran Act have been passed by countless representative bodies of churches, labor unions and even of the major political parties. But members of Congress are not elected by resolutions, nor by the relatively few men and women present at Conferences and Conventions. The "man in the pew," the "rank and file" union member, the "average voter" must understand how injustice to the foreign born works to his own disadvantage. He must recognize that:

One of the things we have learned in this country is

> that freedom has to be indivisible. Anything that limits any part of it for anyone is a menace to all of us, a threat to the tradition by which we live.
>
> [Bruce Catton, *Saturday Review,* July 6, 1957]

Injustice to the foreign born injures not only the foreign born but the native born also, and in many ways.

The harm done to the American-citizen members of a family by FBI investigation preceding deportation, not to mention the deportation of a husband or wife; to American-born children by deportation of a father or mother is obvious. And the atmosphere of tension and anxiety produced in a home by a deportation warrant which may bring arrest any day is equally obvious. Children born in "free America" ought not to have to live in that kind of insecurity.

It is obvious also, that the kind of investigations carried on by the Justice Department, whether by agents of the Immigration and Naturalization Service or the FBI, especially in connection with "political" deportation warrants where threats of loss of employment or of further deportation warrants for the "disloyalty" of refusing to cooperate in the accusation of neighbors are freely used, can often frighten a whole community into the repudiation of any kind of civic responsibility. Who knows that a petition for adequate schools or even for a sewage disposal plant might not be labelled "subversive" or "creeping socialism" and therefore Communistic by influential taxpayers?

Of course it is not only the foreign born with their children who can thus be intimidated. Questions can be asked of the native-born neighbors also. Fear is contagious. If dissent is penalized as potential treason in one group, dissent becomes precarious for us all. We, too, can be dismissed from our jobs. History has shown too often that repression begins always with an unpopular minority, but extends quickly to ever wider circles in the body politic. Witness Pastor Niemoeller's often quoted:

> They imprisoned Communists and we weren't Communists; they imprisoned Jews and we weren't Jews; they imprisoned trade-unionists and we weren't trade-unionists. When they imprisoned me, it was too late to do anything.

We must begin the defense of freedom where freedom is first attacked, if we would preserve our own freedom.

Of concern also to native born is the damage done to the reputation of the United States in the outside world. There are many testimonies to the resentment aroused everywhere by the racial implications of the authorized quotas for immigration and by the difficulties in obtaining visas even for distinguished visitors. The difference between our claim to be a "leader of the free world" and the actual practice of our representatives abroad, has been effectively publicized. The same kind of difference is evidenced of course, when long-time residents of the United States are returned to their "country of origin." As Giacomo Quattrone asked sadly: "What shall I say in Italy when they ask me about freedom in the United States?" Or as a Norwegian newspaper put it:

> If this deportation is carried out . . . it will . . . greatly tax many Norwegians' friendship for our mighty Western neighbor. . . . What registers with us is the political hysteria in 1956 expressing itself so crassly in the very country that pledges allegiance to the fundamental principles of Lincoln and Roosevelt.

But this kind of discrepancy between profession and practice has an effect within the United States which is still more serious. Whenever the gap between legality and justice widens, the general respect for law and the general sense of justice inevitably decrease. Such a gap, when coupled with public praise of justice, seems to give incontrovertible evidence of hypocrisy. No one can say how much of the increasing juvenile delinquency and the widespread contempt for law is the result of such a gap and of the cynicism and distrust which it produces; it is certainly a contributing factor. We teach the children one thing in the salute to the flag and in the refrain of our national anthem. But we put and keep on the statute books and we appropriate millions of dollars to administer laws which negate "justice for all" and make freedom a mockery for many.

Harm of quite a different kind is also done to the welfare of all of us by laws like the Walter-McCarran Law. By it this country of ours is being robbed of a very large proportion of the contributions which those of us who are Americans by choice, might give. The fitting metaphor for this country is not a melting pot in which all the varied national characteristics become indistinguishable but a symphony orchestra in which all the differing instruments work together to produce harmony. If certain instruments are silenced, the music can no longer be rightly heard.

Furthermore, it is precisely those whom we try to deport or silence who can give us the kind of help we most need. Abuses and stupidities exist in all human societies. Those of independent mind who come to us from other lands are precisely those whose criticism can point out to us what most requires correction in conditions which we, through long use, have come to take for granted. Even when their judgments are at times hasty and superficial, they still indicate to us the situations where all is not right. The native born harm themselves most when they allow such criticism to be penalized as disloyal.

In closing this history of twenty-five years of struggle, I may be pardoned a personal word. My own ancestors have been "native born" since colonial days; and for all the reasons just set forth, I should have recognized, at least fifty years ago, my responsibility to cooperate in all efforts to give to newer Americans their share of the rights and responsibilities affirmed in the Constitution. Yet even my connection with the ACPFB did not begin until 1950, and it began for none of the reasons I have listed.

In the summer of 1936, I had seen something of the effect of

Hitler's methods of thought control in Germany, especially in University circles. Suddenly in the early years of the Cold War, I discovered from the casual remark of a younger colleague that the same kind of force was beginning to operate in the College and University faculties in the United States. Some kind of active participation in the defense of American civil rights and liberties became imperative for me. I signed a few petitions; I attended a few conferences, I joined an organization or two, and made a few speeches, chiefly on academic freedom.

When I was asked to become a Sponsor of the American Committee for Protection of Foreign Born, only one answer was possible. For more than thirty years I had been a teacher of the Bible. Each year I had pointed out to classes of college Sophomores that one of the glories of the Old Testament was that there, for the first time in human history, the principle was formulated: "You shall have one law for the home-born and for the stranger that sojourns with you (the resident alien)." (Lev. 24:22 et al.) I became a Sponsor of the Committee and in the next year, after the Rev. John Darr's departure for Europe, I became co-chairman with Mr. George B. Murphy, Jr.

The extent of the need for the work of the Committee and its far-reaching implications I have learned in the past eight years from those who have been working to defend the rights of the foreign born far longer and with far greater understanding. There is not room here to mention individuals. Even a list of those who have taught me so much and who have had so much patience and tolerance for my prejudices and my ignorance would take too much space. There was George B. Murphy, Jr. who guided me through the mazes of the first conference at which we presided together. There were Harriet Barron and Alec Jones who kept the Committee functioning those months when the executive secretary was in prison and who carried heavy administrative loads thereafter. There were Grace Johnson, Helen Morgan and Charles Musil in the Committee office in New York. There were friendly folk across the country, connected with the independent area committees. From them all

I have gained a fuller understanding of the meaning of "liberty and justice for all." There were the "deportees" themselves, who have given me such vital lessons in true patriotism, in loyalty to country and devotion to freedom.

The greatest debt is owed by me, as by many others, to Abner Green without whose leadership there would have been no continuing ACPFB. On April 14, 1954, when the Committee was under special attack from the Attorney General, a testimonial dinner was given in New York to celebrate Abner Green's fortieth birthday and simultaneously his twenty years of work with the ACPFB. (A very slight juggling of dates brought the neat coincidence.) The announcement of the dinner was signed by the Honorary Co-Chairmen, Bishop Moulton and myself, and by the Co-Chairmen, Father Forbes and Mr. Murphy. We paid our own tribute in the words:

> To us who have worked closely with Abner Green, his untiring efforts and his deep sincerity have been an inspiration. We feel that his work and the work of the American Committee stand out in this period of repression as a defense of American liberty and justice, not only for the foreign born among us but for all the American people.

From the folder of greetings sent to that dinner, only a few quotations can be given. There are many telegrams. There are letters, long and short, some signed by names known the country over; others from those associated with the Committee's work.

From C. H. Fisher, president of the Washington Pension Union:

> It is a real pleasure . . . to congratulate you on your birthday and your twenty years of service to the foreign-born Americans in working for the defense of liberty and justice to the foreign born. May you and your organization survive present attacks for continued service. . . .

From Dr. W. E. B. Du Bois:

> Let me congratulate you on your birthday and your years of devoted service. . . . Count me as one of your admirers and co-workers.

From Bishop Edward Parsons of San Francisco:

> . . . this note . . . brings you my warm congratulations for both anniversaries, and the assurance of my appreciation of the self-sacrificing work which you have done during all these last twenty years. The task does not become easier in these days. Indeed every day not only brings troubles for the foreign born but our own liberties seem to be more and more imperiled. All we can do is to keep going with the faith that the right will triumph in the end.

From William Harrison, Associate Editor of the *Boston Chronicle*:

> For any man . . . to have spent half of his . . . life as Abner Green has done . . . in the service of a cause of such importance as the well-being of our foreign-born fellow citizens and residents is a cogent and persuasive argument that he is unusual and therefore to be cherished. I agree that the best gift which we can bestow upon him is the assurance of our unrelenting persistence in guaranteeing perpetuation of the Committee's necessary tasks in championing the foreign born, especially today when so many of the best of those contributors to the defense of American freedom have been imprisoned and deported. Long may Abner Green live to enrich our national heritage bequeathed to us in the Declaration of Independence and the Bill of Rights. Happy birthday to a leader whose constant endeavor is to remind us that the bedrock of American democratic freedom is defense of the rights of all Americans, Negro and white, Catholic and Protestant, Jewish and Gentile, native and foreign born!

There are tributes from officials of labor unions, too many and too long to be given in full. Only two are quoted in part.

From Russ Nixon, Washington representative of UE:

> Yours is an unusually consistent and devoted record of 20 years of service to people who especially have required protection in our country. Certainly there have been many trials and probably some disappointments along the way and there will be more in the future, but you can have a tremendous feeling of pride about your work during half of your life time. Every one else is proud of you, too.

And from Hawaii, from Newton Miyagi, Secretary-Treasurer of Local 142, ILWU:

> We would like to take this means of extending our "Aloha" . . . to you on your 40th birthday. We salute you for the role you have played in defense of civil liberties—a service of twenty years especially beneficial to the foreign born in the United States.
>
> We in Hawaii have also benefited by the work carried on by your committee . . . the aid given . . . a longshoreman in our union who was indicted under the McCarran Act in 1951.

And to close the file, a letter given in full from Giacomo Quattrone, written from the Immigration Detention Center in East Boston:

> Inspired [in spite] of the Walter-McCarran Act and the McCarthy fascist Fear, I wish to you a Happy Birthday.
>
> Long live the American Committee for Protection of Foreign Born.

This book is dedicated to the memory of those no longer living who shared in the fight for the defense of the foreign born. But in a very real sense it belongs to those who are still carrying on that fight. To all of them, individually, the author offers it as a token of her gratitude to them.

Index of Topics

Administrative Procedure Act, 221, 258, 288
Alien and Sedition Act, 15, 17, 201
Alien Registration Act, 79-85, 187
American Civil Liberties Union, 32, 44f, 46, 49, 72, 99, 106, 204, 341
American Federation of Labor, 38, 43, 79, 149, 231, 312, 324, 326
"Americans All Week," 129f
American Slav Congress, 143, 178
Anarchists, 26, 27
Annual Conferences, American Committee for Protection of Foreign Born, *(1938)* 101; *(1939)* 59; *(1940)* 33f, 72, 73, 74, 80, 101, 115-127, 417f; *(1941)* 74, 95, 164, 172; *(1942)* 147-149, 155, 161f; *(1943)* 141-145, 157, 165f, 174; *(1945)* 223-231; *(1947)* 234, 418; *(1948)* 215-217, 234; *(1949)* 234-239; *(1950)* 260, 269-271; *(1951)* 283, 284-291, 420; *(1953)* 309, 322-324, 344, 345-348; *(1954)* 345, 348; *(1955)* 345, 348f, 365f; *(1956)* 346, 349, 370-372, 378f, 422f; *(1957)* 377, 433; *(1958)* 433f
Arrest without warrant, 38, 42, 266
Asylum, right of, 14, 16, 22, 24, 26, 56-68, 126, 180, 212f, 231

Bail, return of, 332, 389
Bail, right of, 48, 199f, 213, 216, 219f, 256f, 263f, 266, 276, 278, 289, 292, 296f, 324, 335f, 338f, 341, 431
Bill of Rights, 15, 51, 75-77, 84f, 195, 207, 221, 234, 238, 250, 260, 268, 270f, 273, 275, 277, 292, 298, 299, 305, 310, 319, 338, 344, 361, 362, 378, 432
Boston Chronicle, 441

Cannery Workers Union, 328f
Celler bills, 57-59, 433; *see* Lehman-Celler Bill
Charitable organization registration, *see* New York State *vs.* ACPFB
Chinese, exclusion of, 23, 158
Chinese seamen, 157f
Commonweal, 252
Communism, 49f, 64f, 127, 139, 171f, 174, 204, 207, 216f, 236f, 246, 248, 253, 259, 266, 337f, 373, 386
"Communist Action," 259
"Communist Front," 259, 359
Concentration camps, *see* Hobbs Bill
Congregational-Christian Church, Social Action, 128, 129
Congress of Industrial Organizations, 94, 123, 150, 226, 312, 318, 324, 347
Contract labor, 158, 187, 208, 423f
County jails, 340f

Defense Committees, 10f, 275-277, 289f
Denaturalization, 37f, 171-174, 209, 216, 260, 267, 271, 277, 284, 315, 317, 319, 323f, 333-335, 359, 399-403
Deportation, 24, 26f, 32, 36, 38-42, 47-51, 59-68, 71, 169, 187, 196, 210, 212-216, 231, 234-244, 260-262, 266f, 271, 273, 281, 284, 287-289, 291, 316, 318, 352-356, 369, 387f, 389f, 418f, 431f, 436, 437
Discrimination, employment, 37, 52, 71, 87f, 90-95, 105, 153-155, 156, 181, 186, 231, 233; racial, 14, 23, 26-29, 37, 184, 229f, 267f, 316, 431; relief, 37, 88-90, 92-94

Exclusion, 23f, 28f; quotas, 267f, 316, 320, 328f; refugees, 212f

Fair Employment Practices Commission, 149, 156
Farrell, town of, 209f
F.B.I., 194, 256, 268, 311, 357, 436
Filipino-Americans, 101, 126f, 150, 226f, 232, 327f
Fish amendment, 88-90

German-Americans, 11, 141, 150
"Guilt by association," 196, 233, 294, 305

Hawaii, 442
Hobbs Bill, 74-79, 221, 257
Hunger Strikers, 217-220, 222, 339

Immigration and Naturalization Service, procedures of, 22, 36, 42, 44, 45f, 50, 67, 78, 125, 236, 261, 268, 274f, 311, 409-414, 421f, 436
Informers, 215, 250f, 336, 339, 342, 346f, 372
Injunctions (ACPFB), 374-377, 380
International Juridical Association Bulletin, 308f
International Labor Defense, 44f, 46, 49, 106, 365
International Workers Order, 107f, 170, 329f
Italian Americans, 63, 140f, 150, 232

Jamaicans, 158, 218, 268
Japanese-Americans, 150, 159-163, 164, 178f
Justice, Department of, 157, 198, 206, 215f, 219, 228, 234, 238f, 268, 274f, 293, 329, 350f, 396, 436

"Know Nothing" Party, 20

Labor, organized, 41, 42, 44, 114f, 149, 212, 215-220, 224f, 231, 236, 242, 312, 324, 326

Law journals, 9, 304, 312
Legal defense, 53f, 278, 379f
Legislative activity (ACPFB), 52f, 58, 71-84, 166f, 185f, 232f, 242f
Legislative conferences, 242f, 422
Lehman-Celler Bill, 321f
Literacy test, 25f, 96f, 184
Los Angeles Committee PFB, 278, 283, 296f, 371, 419, 422

McCarran Security Act, 249-251, 256-263, 270, 273, 279, 358, 430
McCarran-Walter Act, *see* Walter-McCarran Act
Methodist Federation for Social Action, 324f
Mexican-Americans, 268, 287, 347, 417-424, 432, 433, 434
Michigan Committee PFB, 276f, 283
Midwest Committee PFB, 242, 275, 276, 283
Migratory labor, *see* contract labor
Minnesota Committee PFB, 375, 384, 390

Nation, The, 358
National Catholic Rural Life Conference, 424
National Guardian, 297, 336f, 338, 375
National Lawyers Guild, 78, 391
Native born obligation, 435-438
Naturalization, 37f, 52, 93, 96-103, 150, 167-170, 180, 181, 184f, 207-209, 231, 233, 269, 271, 319, 354, 418, 419, 432
Naturalization Aid Service, 101f, 167-170, 184f, 187
New York *Herald Tribune,* 212, 245
New York *Post,* 98f
New York State *vs.* ACPFB, 372-380
New York Times, 116, 211, 322, 325, 339, 340f, 410f, 424
New York *World-Telegram and Sun,* 116, 410

Northern California Committee PFB, 415
North West Committee PFB, *see* Washington State Committee PFB

October 28th, *see* Statue of Liberty

Palmer Raids, 35, 43f, 221, 228, 229, 241, 254, 301, 304
Peace, 176-182
Political activity (ACPFB), 174f
President's Commission on Immigration and Naturalization, 312-320, 350, 429, 431
Press, freedom of, 337-339, 394
Publications (ACPFB), 50, 52f, 57, 62, 63, 65f, 72-74, 75, 77, 82, 84, 87f, 90, 91f, 99f, 102f, 120f, 146f, 150, 151, 153, 154, 156, 157, 158, 166, 176, 181, 211f, 231, 242, 260, 264-268, 272, 281, 294, 297, 329, 350, 351, 359-361

Re-entry, 217, 268, 328f
Registration (ACPFB), 372f, 377, 380
Registration of aliens, 29, 79-85, 187, 260, 308, 316, 331

S.A.C.B., 249f, 259, 358f, 362f, 369, 372, 434
S.A.C.B. hearings (ACPFB), 361, 363-369, 372
St. Louis *Post-Dispatch,* 92
Schneiderman decision, 173f, 277, 403
Seamen, 77, 150, 157, 169, 187, 208, 210-212, 218f
Smith Act, *see* Alien Registration Act
Southern attitude in Congress, 33f, 70f, 227
Spain, Loyalist veterans, 65-68, 128, 214
Statue of Liberty, 13, 62, 128, 151, 232, 237, 280, 283, 432, 433
Statute of Limitations, 267, 431, 433, 434
Subversive Activities Control Board, *see* S.A.C.B.
"Subversive List," Attorney General's, 221, 280, 426, 434
Supervisory Parole, 267, 331-333, 368f, 389, 434
Supreme Court, appeals and decisions, Bonnetti, 397-399; Bridges, 188-200; Carlson, 335; Chew, 327; Galvan, 355; Gonzales, 328; Harisiades, 292, 296f; Heikkinen, 394-397; Hyun, 391; Jay, 356; Maisenberg, 402; Mangaoang, 327f; Nowak, 399-402; Pedriero, 341; Quattrone, 355; Rowoldt, 352, 383-392; Schneiderman, 171-174; Strecker, 64f; Supervisory Parole, 332f, 382f; "Terminal Island," 297f; Zucca, 334

Ukrainian-Americans, 290
Un-American Activities Committee, 370f
United Auto Workers, 31, 225, 235-237, 287
"United Nations in America" dinner, 150f
Unity Conferences, 170-182

Voting rights, 185f

Walter-McCarran Act, 51, 264-268, 292, 312-326, 344-350, 359, 362, 388, 401, 420f, 423, 428-434, 437f
"War effort" (ACPFB), 146-150, 154f, 165f, 175f
Washington delegations, 272-274, 275
Washington "Mobilization," 243f, 369
Washington State Committee PFB, 275, 328
Western Pennsylvania Committee PFB, 342
Wickersham Commission Report, 60

Yugoslav-Americans, 142-144, 209

Index of Persons

Abbott, Edith, 16, 18, 19f, 21
Adamic, Louis, 142-144, 224
Addes, George F., 31, 144f, 157
Alcantra, Alec, 328f
Alvarez, Anita, 244
Athenagoras, Archbishop, 118

Baehr, Karl, 240f
Baldwin, Roger, 45, 57, 106, 113f
Barron, Harriet, 270, 287-290, 422, 439
Belfrage, Cedric, 336-339
Biddle, Francis, 153f, 157, 193f, 401
Black, Justice Hugo, 298, 328, 362
Bonnetti, Frank, 67, 397-399
Bridges, Harry, 188-200
Brownell, Herbert, 335, 357, 359, 421
Buck, Pearl, 340

Cain, Harry, 358f, 362, 369
Callow, Leon, 243, 369, 392-394
Carlson, Anton J., 323f, 367f
Carusi, Ugo, 187, 207, 209f, 211
Catton, Bruce, 381f, 435f
Celler, Emanuel, 57-59, 60, 75, 93, 95f, 97, 101, 228, 257, 431
Chafee, Zechariah, Jr., 247-251, 253f, 255
Chandra, Krishna, 329f
Chernin, Rose, 278, 335, 371
Clark, Tom, 206f, 212, 215, 216, 219, 221, 257, 280, 339
Cooper, Rt. Rev. John Montgomery, 73
Corsi, Edward, 63, 325
Cronbach, Dr. Abraham, 240
Cushing, Archbishop, 314

Darr, John, Jr., 235, 243, 274, 284
De Lacey, Hugh, 146, 148, 156, 164f, 212
Dies, Martin, 38, 53, 70, 137, 139, 179
Doak, William, 36
Douglas, Justice William O., 197, 286f, 297
DuBois, Dr. W. E. B., 284, 440f
Dulles, John Foster, 133
Dwight, Timothy, 17f

Eisenhower, Dwight D., 151, 183, 210, 321
Emerson, Thomas, 304-309
Englander, Isidore, 165, 294
Enkel, Kenneth, 389, 390
Estrada, Jose, 420
Evans, Rev. Joseph, 322f

Finucane, Thomas G., 225, 235, 313
Foley, Alma, 383, 390
Forer, Joseph, 366, 391, 398
Fox, Ernest, 187f
France, Clemens, 272-274
Frankfurter, Justice Felix, 297, 333
Franklin, Benjamin, 15f
Frantz, Laurent B., 358
Freedman, Blanch, 299, 425-428

Ganley, Ann, 237f
Garis, Roy L., 25, 29
Gates, Mike, 331
Geyer, Lee E., 33f, 74, 124
Ginger, Anne Fagan, 352, 391
Goepel, Hans, 57
Gollobin, Ira, 226, 327
Gonzales, Isabel, 418
Green, Abner, 61f, 74, 115, 150, 155, 158f, 165, 175, 216f, 227, 231, 242, 260-263, 265-268, 269f, 278f, 281-283, 286, 287, 291, 346-348, 349, 351, 359, 364-366, 369, 378f, 420, 440-442

Hale, Edward Everett, 20f
Handlin, Oscar, 265, 331
Harisiades, Peter, 291, 292-296
Harrison, Earl G., 148f, 151, 155f, 167f, 169, 170, 180, 206, 226, 313, 329
Harrison, William, 441
Hart, Pearl, 115, 164, 240, 242 286
Heikkila, William, 311, 404-416
Heikkinen, Knut, 394-397
Hemingway, Ernest, 122
Higgins, Msgr. George C., 424
Higham, John, 23, 25, 28
Hillis, Newell Dwight, 28
Hillman, Sidney, 79, 234
Hoover, J. Edgar, 35f, *and see* F.B.I.
Houston, Charles H., 126
Hurst, Fannie, 232f
Hyun, David, 336, 391

Javits, Jacob, 372, 374
Jefferson, Thomas, 14f, 17, 272
Johnson, Grace, 439
Jones, Alec, 439

Keller, James, 276, 332
Kettunen, Paul, 41, 48f, 53
Kilgore, Harley, 325f, 348f
King, Carol, 128, 165, 173, 188, 189f, 215f, 232, 270, 294, 295, 299-310, 343, 428
Kinney, Marian, 328

La Guardia, Fiorello, 154
Lazarus, Emma, 13
Lefkowitz, Louis, 374-377
Lehman, Herbert, 9, 79, 267, 321
Lerich, Anton, 169f
Le Sueur, Arthur, 241f, 387
Lewis, John L., 72
Link, Arthur S., 84, 116, 132, 204
Liu Liang Mo, 157f

MacCormack, Daniel W., 36, 42
MacKay, James, 243, 276
MacLeish, Archibald, 123
McCarran, Pat, 257, 285, 420
McGrath, Howard, 235, 272, 380
McWilliams, Carey, 82f, 95, 115, 159-163
Maisenberg, Rebecca, 402
Mann, Thomas, 233, 270
Mannisto, Oscar, 40f, 48f, 53
Marcantonio, Vito, 59, 60, 63, 82f, 100f, 107, 127, 128, 150f
Martinez, Refugio, 347, 419
Maslow, Will, 9f
Meldahl, Horace, 367, 369
Miller, Alfred, 60-62
Morena, Louisa, 416f
Morgan, Dwight, 14, 27, 32, 37, 45, 46, 48, 52-54, 60, 89, 104-113, 127
Morgan, Helen, 439
Moulton, Bishop Arthur W., 243f, 270, 291, 360
Murphy, Justice Frank, 12, 189-191, 195-197, 239, 296
Murphy, George B. Jr., 285, 291, 439
Murray, Philip, 94, 150, 226, 318
Musil, Charles, 439

Nielson, William Allan, 122f
Niemoeller, Pastor Martin, 436f
Novick, Irving, 110, 115, 165
Nowak, Stanley, 72, 124, 178, 240, 277, 335, 399-403

Panunzio, Constantine, 21f, 22, 23, 26, 27, 29
Partridge, Grace, 415
Pepper, Claude, 123, 210, 212
Perkins, Frances, 42, 50, 53, 84, 119f
Petioni, Charles, 158
Petrosky, Stella, 39f, 49f
Popoff, Christ, 53, 98

Quattrone, Giacomo, 355, 437, 442
Quill, Michael J., 224f

Rautenstrauch, Walter, 164

Reining, Heinrich, 57
Reissig, Rev. Herman F., 55, 73, 108f, 113, 115, 127
Richter, Otto, 62f
Rogers, William P., 357, 416, 423
Roosevelt, Franklin D., 122, 147f, 154, 174, 180, 183, 201, 360, 371
Roosevelt, Theodore, 25
Rowoldt, Charles, 332, 383-392

Sabath, Adolph, 212, 224
Saltzman, Sadie, 367-369
Scarpone, Thomas, 63, 208
Schneiderman, William, 171-174
Schwellenbach, Lewis B., 71f, 75, 226
Seldes, George, 65f
Sentner, Antonia, 332
Sentner, William, 272
Shorr, Isaac, 207, 228f
Silex, Umberto, 208, 419
Smith, Alfred E., 70, 79f
Smith, Louise Pettibone, 291, 438f
Soldo, Charles, 342, 367
Stewart, Donald Ogden, 150f, 300
Strecker, Joseph, 64f
Swinburn, Curt, 77, 95, 115, 164f
Swing, Gen. Joseph M., 409-414, 421, 422

Takagi, Yoshitaka, 178f
Tandaric, Steve, 214f
Taylor, Bayard, 23
Tenerowicz, Rudolph G., 31f, 81
Thomas, Norman, 57
Truman, Harry S., 258f, 273
Tyler, President John, 21

Uhl, Byron, 50

Van Kirk, Rev. Walter, 314f
Vendemmia, Henrietta, 41f, 52
Villard, Marquita, 60, 109

Wagner, Robert F., 60
Wallace, Henry A., 225, 301
Walter, Francis, 370f, 427
Washington, George, 16, 59
Wasserman, Jack, 229f, 231
Weber, Joe, 276
Willkie, Wendell, 173
Wilson, Woodrow, 26
Witkovich, George, 332f
Wright, Bishop R. R., 241

Yergan, Max, 115, 164
Young, Martin, 335